Conversations
with Hyaluronan Scientists

Selection from other books by Magdolna Hargittai and István Hargittai

IH, *Judging Edward Teller: A Closer Look at One of the Most Influential Scientists of the Twentieth Century.* Prometheus, 2010.

MH, IH, *Symmetry through the Eyes of a Chemist.* Third Edition. Springer, 2009 (Softcover edition 2010; Russian translation of first edition, MIR, 1989).

MH, IH, *Visual Symmetry.* World Scientific, 2009.

IH, *The Martians of Science: Five Physicists Who Changed the Twentieth Century.* Oxford University Press, 2006; 2008.

IH, *The DNA Doctor: Candid Conversations with James D. Watson.* World Scientific, 2007 (Chinese translation, Shanghai Scientific, 2009).

IH, *The Road to Stockholm: Nobel Prizes, Science, and Scientists*, Oxford University Press, 2002; 2003 (Japanese translation, Morikita, 2007; Chinese translation, Shanghai Scientific, 2007).

IH, MH, B. Hargittai, *Candid Science I–VI.* Imperial College Press, 2000–2006 (Russian translation of Volumes I; II, URSS, 2003; 2005).

IH, *Our Lives: Encounters of a Scientist,* Akadémiai Kiadó, 2004 (German translation, Lj-Verlag, 2006).

IH, MH, *In Our Own Image: Personal Symmetry in Discovery.* Kluwer/Plenum, 2000.

IH, MH, *Symmetry: A Unifying Concept.* Shelter Publications, 1994; Random House, 1996 (German translation, Rowohlt, 1998).

R. J. Gillespie, IH, *The VSEPR Model of Molecular Geometry.* Allyn & Bacon, 1991 (Russian translation, MIR, 1992; Italian translation, Zanichelli, 1994).

Edited books

Strength from Weakness: Structural Consequences of Weak Interactions in Molecules, Supermolecules, and Crystals (A. Domenicano, IH, eds.), Kluwer, 2002.

Symmetry 2000 (in two volumes, IH, T. C. Laurent, eds.), Portland Press, 2002.

Advances in Molecular Structure Research, Vols. 1–6 (MH, IH, eds.), JAI Press, 1995-2000.

Spiral Symmetry (IH, C. A. Pickover, eds.), World Scientific, 1992.

Fivefold Symmetry (IH, ed.), World Scientific, 1992.

Accurate Molecular Structures (A. Domenicano, IH, eds.), Oxford University Press, 1992 (Russian translation, MIR, 1997).

Quasicrystals, Networks, and Molecules of Fivefold Symmetry (I. Hargittai, ed.), VCH Publishers, 1990.

Crystal Symmetries, Shubnikov Centennial Papers (IH, B. K. Vainshtein, eds.). Pergamon Press, 1988.

Stereochemical Applications of Gas-Phase Electron Diffraction (IH, MH, eds.), Vol. A: *The Electron Diffraction Technique.* Vol. B: *Structural Information for Selected Classes of Compounds.* VCH Publishers, 1988.

Symmetry: Unifying Human Understanding, Volumes 1 and 2 (IH, ed.), Pergamon Press, 1986 and 1989.

Hyaluronan

From Basic Science to Clinical Applications

Endre A. Balazs, General Editor

Volume 1

Conversations
with Hyaluronan Scientists

Magdolna Hargittai and István Hargittai

PubMatrix

Edgewater, New Jersey, 2011

Published by

PubMatrix, Inc.
725 River Road, Suite 205
Edgewater, New Jersey 07020
U.S.A.

Magdolna Hargittai and István Hargittai
Budapest University of Technology and Economics
and Hungarian Academy of Sciences
P. O. Box 91
1521 Budapest
Hungary

First edition, 2009 (pbk) ISBN 978-0-9820350-0-9
Second edition, 2011

Library of Congress Cataloging in Publishing Data
Conversations with Hyaluronan Scientists
By Magdolna Hargittai and István Hargittai
Volume 1 in: Hyaluronan: From Basic Science to Clinical Applications
General Editor: Endre A. Balazs
ISBN: 978-0-9820350-3-0

Printed in the United States by Worzalla Publishing Company

Front cover: the three-dimensional image (by Zoltán Varga, Budapest) depicts a
portion of the hyaluronan molecule.

Foreword

In September 2002 and June 2003, two meetings were held in St. Tropez, France, in the same city on the northern coast of the Mediterranean Sea where the first international conference on hyaluronan was held in 1985. The meetings in the early 2000s were called "Conversations on Hyaluronan". A few scientists concerned with the future development of hyaluronan sciences discussed plans to support and encourage basic research and the biomedical development of this molecule. The first direct result of these conversations was the founding of the International Society for Hyaluronan Sciences (ISHAS) in 2005. This book is the second accomplishment originating from these meetings in St. Tropez.

Hyaluronan is directly connected with the biology of the intercellular matrix. This molecule is a key component of the highly organized, complex structure filling and maintaining the space between the cells. Some of us believe that its importance as the sole macromolecular polysaccharide in the intercellular matrix is comparable to that of the nucleic acids in the cell.

This book, as the beginning of a series, initiates a major effort to review in an encyclopedic style our knowledge of this molecule in all aspects of scientific and technological developments. This first volume introduces some of the key players in this field; a further one will follow introducing others. After all, the success of hyaluronan science depends on the work of these people and their students and associates.

To create this book I invited two structural chemists who had demonstrated their skill in bringing out the human stories behind scientific achievements without neglecting the science itself. Their critically acclaimed six-volume *Candid Science* series of interviews with famous scientists served as example of what we wanted to emulate on a smaller scale. István and Magdolna Hargittai approached their subjects as outsiders turned insiders in the hyaluronan field, but they have been insiders in scientific research and science history all along.

It is important to note that this volume presents not only the interviews, but also a brief summary of the progress made in this field by these scientists and their coworkers. If the information presented here helps to understand how scientists work and what drives us to success in scientific endeavors, then our objectives are accomplished.

Edgewater, New Jersey, September 2008   Endre A. Balazs

Preface

This volume of interviews, together with the subsequent volume, inaugurate Endre A. Balazs's—Bandi's, as popularly known to everyone around the world—new series of books, *Hyaluronan: From Basic Science to Clinical Applications*. Six years ago, when he invited us to conduct some interviews with researchers in the hyaluronan field, we understood that the reason he asked us to participate in this project was that he liked our volumes of interviews with famous scientists (*Candid Science Vols. I–VI,* Imperial College Press, London, 2000–2006).

For us, this was a new challenge. Previously, in our *Candid Science* project, we interviewed world renowned scientists about whom we had known a great deal from the literature. More than half of them were Nobel laureates, and they worked in the most diverse fields from the biomedical sciences to chemistry, physics, mathematics, and materials science. In the undertaking Bandi proposed to us, the majority of the potential interviewees worked within a relatively narrow area, all around various aspects of a particular molecule, hyaluronic acid. Initially, we even found it difficult to pronounce this name— hyaluronic acid or, using its modern term, hyaluronan. Our decades' long experience of being chemists did not help us much as we had hardly heard about this substance.

There was, however, a link between the two interview projects in the persons of Endre Balazs and Torvard Laurent, both significant figures for their oeuvres, who had been interviewed by us for the *Candid Science* project. There was another fortunate circumstance; the topic of the hyaluronan workshop in 2002 in St. Tropez—the first venue for our interviews—was about the structure of hyaluronan. This topic helped to bridge the possible professional gap between our interviewees and ourselves as we have been structural chemists for all our respective careers.

Science must be brought in human proximity if we would like to alleviate the alienation of the general public from hard science. We also see in these interviews an opportunity to bring out aspects of scientific research that never find their way into published research papers, even reviews, partly because of the scarcity of journal space and partly because people shy away from exposing personal experiences in scientific research. In addition, we considered it our mission to make the hyaluronan field better known and better recognized.

Hyaluronan has become a major component in modern medicine, especially in ophthalmologic surgery and in the treatment of osteoarthritis, and it is also receiving a lot of attention in skin care. It is a simple polymeric sugar and many still view it as a mere mechanical device in the human organism; it is certainly a major component in the intercellular matrix. Recent studies have pointed to the possibility that this substance might have pivotal regulatory and controlling roles for processes inside the cell as well. Yet this is the research direction that is hard to popularize because of the apparent simplicity of the hyaluronan molecule. However, we remember that almost until the middle of the twentieth century, DNA also was considered a dull molecule. Recently an application for support of research into the role of hyaluronan in cellular events was turned down by a major funding agency because the reviewers just could not imagine a more sophisticated role for hyaluronan than being an inert space-filler. Our hope with introducing the scientists in this volume, and in the next, is to spread the word about the potentials and promises of this emerging field and contribute to its recognition.

At the completion of the first volume, we consider it our most pleasant duty to express some acknowledgements. First and foremost we appreciate Bandi's and Dr. Janet Denlinger's—Jenti's—initiative in getting this project started. Their encouragement and hospitality, their attention and multi-level assistance were crucial in steering our work to the finish line. We enjoyed the cooperation of our interviewees. We are grateful to all members of the Matrix Biology Institute in Edgewater, New Jersey, and the staff at villas Nifnaha and Hylan in St. Tropez,

France, for their help and kindnesses. We thank the Matrix Biology Institute for a travel fellowship during the spring semesters of 2007 and 2008 when much of the work for these volumes was carried out. We also appreciate the Budapest University of Technology and Economics and the Hungarian Academy of Sciences for granting us the necessary leaves to complete this work and their continuous support of our research activities. Special thanks are due to Joanne Caha (Edgewater) and Judit Szücs (Budapest) for their valuable technical assistance

Matrix Biology Institute, Edgewater, New Jersey
Budapest University of Technology and Economics

July 2008   Magdolna Hargittai and István Hargittai

About the Authors

Magdolna Hargittai is Research Professor of the Hungarian Academy of Sciences (HAS) at Budapest University of Technology and Economics (BME). She is a member of the HAS and the Academia Europaea, London (AE). She holds a Ph.D. degree from Eötvös University (EU), D.Sc. degree from the HAS, and a Dr.h.c. degree from the University of North Carolina (UNC).

István Hargittai is Professor of Chemistry and head of the George A. Olah Ph.D. School at BME. He is a member of the HAS and the AE, and foreign member of the Norwegian Academy of Science and Letters. He holds a Ph.D. degree from EU, D.Sc. degree from the HAS, and Dr.h.c. degrees from Moscow State University, the UNC, and the Russian Academy of Sciences. He is Editor-in-Chief of *Structural Chemistry* (Springer-Verlag).

Contents

Anthony J. Day, 2007 (photograph courtesy of A. Day)

Anthony J. Day

Anthony John Day (b. 1962, Kirby Muxloe, Leicestershire, UK) received his B.A. degree in Chemistry (1985) and M.A. degree (1989) at Exeter College, Oxford, and his D.Phil. from Wolfson College, Oxford (1988). He was a postdoctoral fellow at the Medical Research Council (MRC) Immunochemistry Unit, University of Oxford (1988-91) and worked as an Arthritis Research Campaign (ARC) research fellow at the Department of Biochemistry, University of Oxford (1991-98). In 1998 he took up a Senior Scientist position at the MRC Immunochemistry Unit, University of Oxford, where he remained until 2005 when he was appointed as a Professor of Biochemistry at the Wellcome Trust Centre for Cell-Matrix Research, Faculty of Life Sciences, University of Manchester. He is a member of several scientific societies, including being a founding member of the International Society for Hyaluronan Sciences (ISHAS).

Interview*

You are by far the youngest person at this meeting; how do you view this area of research?

Hyaluronan is my main area of research. There are two main topics that I am working on in my lab; one of them is the structural basis of hyaluronan-protein interactions. Obviously, this is focused completely on hyaluronan and more importantly on trying to understand how proteins and hyaluronan associate together and how such interactions underpin the biology of this fascinating polysaccharide. The other topic is the function of a particular hyaluronan-binding protein called TSG-6. Of course, TSG-6 does a lot of other things in addition to interacting with hyaluronan, so we're going wherever the TSG-6 protein takes us, even if the particular question is not necessarily related to hyaluronan.

[TSG-6 has been demonstrated as having a critical role in female fertility (in the mouse, at least) being involved in the formation of a hyaluronan-rich matrix, which is assembled around the oocyte and is necessary for successful ovulation and fertilization *in vivo*. TSG-6 is also produced during inflammation, where it has been implicated as having a protective and anti-inflammatory role, for example, reducing joint destruction during arthritis. These activities involve other ligands in addition to hyaluronan. Recent work in conjunction with Dr. Caroline Milner (my much better half!) and Dr. Afsie Sabokbar (in Oxford) has revealed that TSG-6 is

---

* This interview was recorded during the first meeting "Conversations on Hyaluronan" in St. Tropez, September 2002. The text was augmented by Anthony Day in April 2008. Footnotes and additional information in square brackets were also added to provide clarifications and extend some points.

likely to be a potent inhibitor of bone breakdown[1]—the chondroprotective and anti-resorptive activities of TSG-6 are a major focus of our current research.]

Hyaluronan is such an amazing subject – one wonders how anyone can work on anything else! It touches so many areas of biology, and the diversity of the biology is remarkable, considering the simplicity of the hyaluronan molecule. It is a very dynamic research area. I think that hyaluronan research has gone through quite a number of cycles and we're going into a new phase with lots of new people coming into the field—it's certainly a very vibrant time for hyaluronan studies. There are several big questions to answer that will tell us more than just about hyaluronan; for example, they'll teach us a lot about proteins and protein interactions, particularly with sugars. Also it is a very friendly field if I might say so; there's a very nice crowd of people, with very few—if any! —big egos and it is possible for new people to come into it quite easily and be accepted, and that makes it very special, compared to some other fields.

You work at an MRC (Medical Research Council) unit in England. MRC is roughly the equivalent to NIH in the US even if on a much smaller scale. Interestingly, NIH doesn't seem to be too eager to support this area, whereas according to your impression MRC is very supportive of it.

Well, I don't think MRC head office completely understands what I do, to be quite honest with you. The MRC does not have any particularly strong interest in supporting research into hyaluronan *per se*, but the systems we are studying (i.e., the role of hyaluronan-protein interactions in the context of inflammatory processes) are clearly in-line with MRC strategy and funding priorities. When talking to the MRC I have to wear my "immunologist's hat" because I am part of a structural immunology unit, the MRC Immunochemistry Unit, and package what I do on the basis of its relevance to immunology. This is partly why I've focused in the last few years on hyaluronan's involvement in leukocyte migration. That said, since starting to do scientific research I have always been interested in immunology, and our work on hyaluronan in inflammatory processes fits comfortably into the

Immunochemistry Unit's program of research. Innate immunity and inflammation are unifying themes throughout my career to date. In addition to MRC funding, we have been very fortunate that we have had a considerable amount of research support from the Arthritis Research Campaign. At one point, when I was an ARC research fellow, effectively all of my funding came from this UK charity and now they support about half of my lab. [a]

There are relatively few people in the UK who work on hyaluronan,[b] so I don't think it is true to say that there is more funding in the UK for hyaluronan research, but, on the other hand, it is clearly possible to obtain funding for it if one can justify its importance in the context of relevant biological systems or disease processes.

> [The MRC Immunochemistry Unit (Oxford) is closing in September 2008 on the retirement of Professor Ken Reid. It was the decision to close the Immunochemistry Unit that lead to my relocation to Manchester (to be part of the Wellcome Trust Centre for Cell-Matrix Research), where this move was assisted and generously supported by the MRC.]

What made you interested in science originally?

This is a bit of a long story! First of all, I'm dyslexic, so I learned to read and write rather late; I didn't start reading until I was 7 or 8, my mother taught me to read. Even now I read very slowly, and that's a problem; it means I need to take a long time to read scientific papers and review manuscripts and grant applications, but writing has become easier, especially with spelling and grammar checks on computers. When I went to primary school in Kirby Muxloe at five years of age, I found it a real struggle and was not doing well. I just sat in the corner and was largely left alone! When I was about 10 years old, although my parents were not particularly in favor of private education, they sent me

---

[a] [The ARC are still major funders of the Day/Milner group, for which we are greatly appreciative!]
[b] [This was certainly the case in 2002 and sadly there hasn't been an explosion in interest in HA in the UK in recent years!]

to Stoneygate Preparatory School, in Leicester, because they were so worried about my lack of progress.

In fact, I failed the entrance exam (not surprisingly) – but my grandfather knew the headmaster of the school and they agreed to take me. I have often wondered what I would have achieved had I not gone to this school. I am very grateful to my parents for sending me to this, and subsequent, schools, and for all their support and encouragement through the years.

Of course, I had a terrible time initially at Stoneygate school because I could still hardly read and write. And in addition to this, I had to learn Latin and French as well! For the first 6 months I was really very miserable. However, it was during this time that I fell in love with science – I had an amazingly charismatic teacher called Mr. Greenhaugh, who taught all the sciences and he was just brilliant. So, finally I found something that interested me and that I could do – I was very soon top of my class in science! While I still wasn't any good at much else, I started to work really very hard to try and catch up in the other subjects. When I left the school at age 13, I was presented the Page cup, which was given each year to the boy who had made the most progress throughout his time at the school – it is the only prize I have ever won! I continued to work extremely hard at Wellingborough School, Northamptonshire, and King Edward's School in Bath, and finally managed, quite remarkably, to get accepted to Exeter College, Oxford, to do a degree in chemistry – there was clearly a poor choice of candidates that year! Before starting my chemistry course, I worked for six months as a lab technician for two lecturers from Bath University; their laboratories were situated at the Royal United Hospital (RUH) – I did a lot of immuno-histo-chemistry on tissue sections from inflammatory bowel disease patients and also preparation/culturing of human lymphocytes. This gave me my first taste of scientific research and was a really wonderful experience. On going to Oxford, I must admit that I really struggled because I found chemistry a very hard and "dry" subject at the university level. Fortunately, the entire 4th year of the degree was a research project, and I was allowed to move out of chemistry and do my research at the MRC Immunochemistry Unit, based in the Department of Biochemistry, Oxford. This was a perfect match for me, given my previous experience at the RUH in Bath. I also did my Ph.D. (in Oxford this is called a D.Phil.) in the Immunochemistry Unit working on the complement system, which is a part of the humoral immune system.

Coming back to the hyaluronan work...

I got into that more or less by an accident. After my Ph.D., I worked on the hormone amylin for a few of years (1988–1991) but I was keen to get back into research on the structure of protein modules, which is something I had developed an interest in during my doctoral studies. In late 1991 I began an ARC 5-year research fellowship, with Professor Iain D. Campbell as my sponsor, to investigate the structure of the sugar-binding domain of L-selectin – a cell-surface receptor that is involved in leukocyte migration. One day in early 1992 my former Ph.D. supervisor, Bob Sim (Dr. Robert B. Sim), passed me a paper that had just come out on a protein called TSG-6 saying that this might be of interest to me. The reason for this was that TSG-6 contained a CUB module, which is a type of protein domain found in some of the complement system proteins, for which at the time there was no tertiary structural information. I also thought that this might be interesting especially given that TSG-6 appeared to be an inflammation-associated protein and therefore of potential relevance to arthritis, and so I started working on TSG-6; this was as a "side-line" to my studies on L-selectin. TSG-6, in addition to having a CUB module also contained a Link module domain. There was no structural information available for this type of domain either. So, I attempted to express both the Link and CUB modules to allow structural determination to be carried out. Eventually and after significant difficulties, we managed to get the structure of the Link module, a domain that is responsible for mediating hyaluronan binding in many proteins. So this is how I got into this field.

[The Link module structure was published in the journal *Cell* [2] and it would be true to say that this paper had a huge impact on my career – allowing me to obtain renewal of my ARC Fellowship and securing my post with the MRC in 1998 as well as getting me invited to speak at conferences on hyaluronan and proteoglycans. Interestingly, I didn't really make much progress on my research on L-selectin (although, quite unexpectedly, we discovered that the fold of the Link module is related to that of the C-type lectin domain found, for example, in L-selectin!) and I didn't manage to make recombinant CUB module suitable for structural studies. Therefore, it is really fortunate that the work on the TSG-6 Link module panned out and forced me to focus on its hyaluronan-binding properties, thus determining my future career direction. However, I didn't give up on the TSG-6 CUB module, and last year we obtained its X-ray crystal structure, which we are currently in the process of writing up for publication.]

The three-dimensional structure we determined for the Link module defined the fold for this type of domain. We used NMR spectroscopy, so we could not get the same resolution as you would with X-ray crystallography, but, of course, working in solution rather then in the solid phase, you get more idea about the dynamic ensemble that is there – so it's probably a more accurate reflection of a structure in many ways than a rather static view of a structure that you get from X-ray crystallography.

Has the X-ray structure been done?

It hasn't as of yet.

It would be interesting to see the difference.

Yes, absolutely. We hope to crystallize the Link module eventually.[c] Our original paper was published back in 1996, but we've been working on the structure ever since. In fact, we've just done a refined structure by NMR, which was possible through the use of better

---

[c] [We have recently achieved this – the X-ray crystal structure of the Link module from human TSG-6 was published last year[3]]

techniques, including isotopic labeling of the protein with ^{13}C and ^{15}N that allowed us to get a much more highly defined structure.[4] We now also have a structure of the protein when it's bound to hyaluronan, published in the same paper. We don't have the hyaluronan conformation yet, but having defined the structure of the protein in its ligand-bound form, we can model in the hyaluronan.[5] We're working towards getting the structure of the hyaluronan in its bound state.[d]

But going back to your question about the possible comparison with X-ray studies, we have just finished the structure of another Link module-containing protein, called CD44. This is the major hyaluronan receptor – it's found on most cells. The hyaluronan-binding domain of CD44 is not only composed of a Link module but it also has N-terminal and C-terminal extensions, which come together in space to form an extra lobe of structure in intimate contact with the Link module – in other words, this is a form of extended Link module. We've just finished the NMR structure of the CD44 hyaluronan-binding domain after working on it for more than 5 years. We collaborated on this with another group, Professor David Jackson, based at the MRC Human Immunology Unit in Oxford, and they have also worked out the crystal structure, in collaboration with Prof. Martin Noble, Department of Biochemistry, Oxford. Interestingly, it is almost identical to the NMR structure, so it shows that you can get to the same answer by these two different techniques.[6] There are, of course, cases when NMR and X-ray structures are somewhat different. For the TSG-6 Link module, the refined solution structure and that derived from X-ray crystallography do turn out to be very similar; however, there are some interesting differences (see ref. 3). But I tend to prefer NMR because the solution structure is more dynamic and flexible and, I think, there are cases where the NMR can tell you things that the crystal structure can't.[3] This is why we're using NMR because we think that when you're dealing with a dynamic molecule like hyaluronan, it's important to be working in a solution phase. Undoubtedly, it is a challenging project, trying to determine the structure of sugars by NMR in their complexes with proteins; not too many such structures have been determined yet.

---

[d] [this is something we have still not achieved for the TSG-6 Link module]

Day's group in Oxford (2005). From left to right, front: Nai Tongsoongnoen, Vicky Higman, Caroline Milner; middle: Andy Almond, Joe Tongsoongnoen, Anthony Day, Marilyn Rugg, Dave Mahoney; back: Julian Heuberger, Simon Clark, Charlie Blundell, Helen Fielder (photograph courtesy of A. Day)

Part of the group of A. Day in Manchester (2007). From left to right: Dave Briggs, Simon Clark, Antonio Inforzato, Tariq Ali (with Pythagoras Parrott), Andy Marson, Lisa Collinson, and Caroline Milner (photograph courtesy of A. Day)

Comparing the HA-binding domains of TSG-6 and CD44

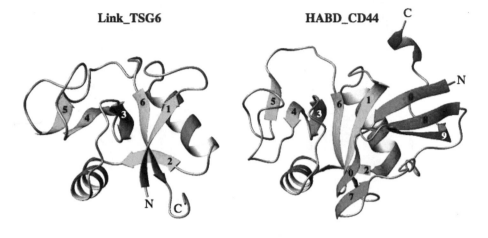

β-sheet I: strands 1, 2 & 6   β-sheet I: strands 0, 1, 2, 6, 7, 8 & 9
β-sheet II: strands 3, 4 & 5   β-sheet II: strands 3, 4 & 5

A comparison of the NMR structures of the Link module
from human TSG-6with the HA-binding domain from human CD44
(see, refs. 4 and 6)

[While we have made some progress towards determining the
structure of the TSG-6 Link module in complex with
hyaluronan, which has been aided by isotopic labeling of
hyaluronan (through a collaboration with Prof. Paul
DeAngelis, Oklahoma, USA[5]), this turns out to be a very
difficult problem. Currently we are focusing our efforts on
trying to obtain protein/hyaluronan co-crystals for X-ray
crystallography. This change in approach was influenced in
part by the success of obtaining the structure of the murine
CD44 hyaluronan-binding domain in complex with a defined
hyaluronan oligosaccharide by X-ray crystallography, which
was done in collaboration with David Jackson and Martin
Noble[7]]

Are these complexes held together by weak linkages?

Yes, they are partly electrostatic and partly hydrogen bonds. Our calorimetric studies on the TSG-6 Link module indicate that about 25% of the binding energy comes from electrostatic interactions – salt bridges – and the rest is probably hydrogen bonds. These are, of course, very important questions. Hyaluronan is a negatively charged sugar; therefore, many people have suggested binding mechanisms based purely on electrostatics – basic residues binding to the carboxylate groups of HA – but the real situation is likely to be a lot more complicated than that. There are many other factors involved.

[For example, in the TSG-6 Link module we have proposed that two tyrosine residues could make aromatic stacking interactions with sequential sugar rings of the hyaluronan and that this mechanism might be conserved in some other members of the Link module superfamily.[5] Interestingly, the hyaluronan-binding domain in CD44 does not have any such tyrosines. Also, in the case of CD44, for which we now have a high-resolution structure of this protein in complex with hyaluronan,[7] there are no salt-bridges and the interaction is completely mediated via hydrogen bonds. Even the interaction of the critical basic amino acid (R45 in the mouse that is equivalent to R41 in human) with hyaluronan is via a water-mediated hydrogen bond].

In fact, our recent work indicates that each individual hyaluronan-binding protein is likely to bind to hyaluronan in a slightly different way. This is one of the issues that I find very exciting in this research. Hyaluronan is particularly interesting because it is a simple molecule, a repeating disaccharide with no modifications, made up of this ABAB repeat, so how can it be that such a simple molecule can be so crucial in development, so crucial in fertilization and ovulation, so crucial in the immune system, and so crucial in tissue structure? Where does that diversity come from? In other sugar systems, such as heparan sulfate, the answer is more obvious; it comes from the sequence of the sugars resulting from variable sulfation and epimerization of the sugar rings, and you can easily imagine how various bioactive sequences of the sugar can give specificity through mediating the binding to specific proteins. In hyaluronan there is no such structural heterogeneity, so the biological diversity has to come about from the proteins that interact with it rather than from any sequence information in the hyaluronan itself. And that was a realization that came about through the work we were doing on mapping the hyaluronan-binding site on the TSG-6 Link module and comparing this with other members of the Link module superfamily.[8] At the start of the work we were expecting to be able to determine the structure of one hyaluronan-binding protein – and then infer the mode of binding to all others. Given that the Link module is found in lots of different hyaluronan-binding proteins, and that the same face is probably used for hyaluronan binding in all cases, it seemed likely that they would all interact with hyaluronan in a similar way. What we found was, in fact, that there are likely to be subtle differences (and sometimes not so subtle differences) in the way particular hyaluronan-binding proteins bind to hyaluronan. We didn't understand at first how this was possible. Then we realized that the combinations of the amino acids that are used to mediate hyaluronan binding are likely to be different, such that the interaction network is going to be distinct in, say TSG-6, compared to CD44.[e]

The big question is: how can this be so? From my discussions with John Sheehan at the HA2000 meeting I learned that hyaluronan can take up many different conformations in solution – and then came the realization that maybe different hyaluronan-binding proteins could capture and stabilize distinct conformations of the polysaccharide. This could lead to the formation of different fibular structures, because the repeating nature of hyaluronan makes it a plastic molecule, which is perfect for setting up fibers.[9] In fact, in my opinion, it is this plasticity combined with the different binding properties of the hyaluronan-binding proteins that generates the diversity of different "architectures" of hyaluronan/protein complexes that underpins the biology of hyaluronan. The solution properties of hyaluronan come largely from its size and its dynamics – one might predict that a low level of modification, such as the addition of the odd sulfate group – which of

---

[e] [this has been born out by our recent structural studies[5,7]]

course does not happen! –, would have little effect on these. However, such modifications would have a dramatic and deleterious effect on the formation of periodic hyaluronan/protein complexes and would act as periodicity breakers – this would really mess up the formation of fibrillar structures that rely on the repetitive nature of hyaluronan. Presumably, this is why no such modifications occur – to protect the protein binding function of hyaluronan.

> [See refs 9 & 10 for further discussion of this]. [Interestingly, a lot of recent research has focused on the covalent attachment of heavy chains, derived from the proteoglycan inter-α-inhibitor, on to hyaluronan.[10,11] As well as potentially leading to the cross-linking of hyaluronan chains, these will serve as periodicity breakers and thus disfavour the formation of regular, fibrillar hyaluronan/protein complexes.]

The fibril-forming properties of hyaluronan and its ability to form complexes with different architectures is something that gets me excited. This is one of the questions we are trying to understand: to see if different hyaluronan-binding proteins do indeed induce hyaluronan to form different types of fibrils and whether the different fibrillar structures do have different biological activities.

You mentioned earlier that hyaluronan research has gone in cycles, would you care to elaborate on that a little?

I don't know a huge amount about the history of hyaluronan but there was clearly a resurgence of interest in it in the early 1970s when people like Tim Hardingham working with Helen Muir and Vince Hascall with Dick Heinegård started to characterize proteins from cartilage that interacted with hyaluronan. From my perspective that was a really golden age for hyaluronan research. Of course I know about its beginnings, its discovery in 1934 by Karl Meyer* and then his working out the chemical structure published in 1954. Also I know that there was a lot of interest during that early period regarding its solution

---

*Editor's note: Karl Meyer confirmed that "hyalomucoid" contained no sulfate, and renamed it "hyaluronic acid".

and rheological properties – in particular Bandi's (Endre Balazs') and Torvard's (Torvard Laurent's) work in the 1950s and 1960s – but I think that there was a new resurgence of interest when people started to realize that there were specific hyaluronan-binding proteins, and that's the time point at which I really started to go back to read the scientific literature. I came into this field in about 1992, when I started working on Link modules, but I suppose it wasn't until 1994-1995, when we started getting close to having a structure of the TSG-6 Link module that I got really excited about reading the old literature. It was Tim's papers with Helen Muir and Vince's papers with Dick Heinegård, in particular, that I enjoyed reading – they became heroes of mine. Their work was superb and we're still investigating ideas that they put forward originally. So in my opinion that was a golden age. Another important milestone was the characterization of CD44 the sequence of which was published in 1989 – the realization that there were specific cell surface receptors for hyaluronan was a major breakthrough and turning point in the history of hyaluronan research. This promoted a new interest in hyaluronan. Then, in the 1990s, when all the hyaluronan synthases were being characterized and we started to understand about the biosynthesis of hyaluronan that again was an exciting time. In the last 5 to 10 years there has been an explosion of interest, with so many people working on different aspects of hyaluronan. We're entering into a new era in hyaluronan research; the number of people who are now working on it is incredible, and a lot of new researchers have come in to this field recently and that is good and very exciting.

How does it feel to work as a relative newcomer and see Bandi who has been a major player in it for about six decades?

It's embarrassing to say that I don't know a great deal about Bandi's research because my reading when I got interested in this area really started around 1972. It was only when I went back to some earlier papers in the process of preparing for this conference that I got a greater appreciation for what was done before. Of course, I learned all about Bandi at the first conference I went to on hyaluronan – that conference was held in Bandi's honor. Before this meeting I didn't know anything about him. This was the Wenner-Gren Foundation Symposium in 1996 in Stockholm, organized by Torvard Laurent. It was my first HA meeting. The only person I "knew" at this meeting was Professor Dick Heinegård, who I had met once before – which was that summer at a meeting in Cardiff on the Synovial Joint, where I had a poster on our Link module structure. I think it was Dick who suggested me as a speaker for the meeting in Sweden. Obviously, I realized that Bandi was very highly regarded, because everybody was saying nice things about him, and, of course, I now know he pioneered the medical use of hyaluronan in eye surgery and joint viscosupplementation. Unfortunately, I can't say I've gone back to the early literature and worked out in detail what various people have done previously.

This meeting is about forming a general overview of the field.

I can understand that Bandi wants to leave a legacy of knowledge to the hyaluronan field. This will provide an introduction to those starting out in the field or potentially even provide a new perspective to more experienced researchers. That's a very laudable aim and I think it is achievable. On a personal level, I think having the opportunity to look back at some of the old literature is very valuable and having this resource of all these papers is terrific. I believe we can come to a conclusion of what is known and what the open questions are. I think the aims are possible but that they're not achievable in the time scale that Bandi has set; it will take a lot longer to do this, because we're all very busy and to find time to write things of this sort is difficult when you have to write grant applications and write papers etc. Especially for me, I think, as the youngest here – I'm still on very much of a steep curve trying to get papers out and trying to get grants, and build a group and establish myself in the field. I have got a permanent post: I'm a MRC Senior Scientist, which is a career appointment, but there are a few caveats in that we have a 5 year review system, and if you don't get the highest rating then your career status could be removed.[f]

Being the youngest person at this gathering, there must have been a reason to be singled out.

Yes, maybe that's because of the close collaboration I've had with Vince Hascall. I think it is true to say that Vince has acted as an important mentor to me (as he has to countless others in the hyaluronan field) – his support and input is greatly appreciated. I am sure there are other people who could have been invited instead of me who would have brought important insights into hyaluronan research. One thing that worries me is that my work is not very well known given that I have only been publishing in this field since 1996. So in some ways I have asked the question "why I am here?," which is a good philosophical question anytime! Perhaps I could be the young researcher at whom this hyaluronan overview is aimed …

References

1. Mahoney, D.J., Mikecz, K., Ali, T., Mabilleau, G., Benayahu, D., Plaas, A., Milner, C.M., Day, A.J. and Sabokbar, A. TSG-6 regulates bone remodeling through inhibition of osteoblastogenesis and osteoclast activation. Manuscript submitted.

2. Kohda, D., Morton, C.J., Parkar, A.A., Hatanaka, H., Inagakai, F.M., Campbell, I.D. and Day, A.J. (1996). Solution structure of the Link module: a hyaluronan-binding domain involved in extracellular matrix stability and cell migration. Cell 86, 767-775.

3. Higman, V.A., Blundell, C.D., Mahoney, D.J., Redfield, C., Noble, M.E.M. and Day, A.J. (2007). Plasticity of TSG-6 HA-binding loop and mobility in TSG-6-HA complex revealed by NMR and X-ray crystallography. J Mol Biol 371, 669-684.

---

[f] [Or as it turned out the MRC could decide to close the Unit, forcing a move into an academic position at a University, with other duties in addition to those of research.]

4. Blundell, C.D., Mahoney, D.J., Almond, A., DeAngelis, P.L., Kahmann, J.D., Teriete, P., Pickford, A.R., Campbell, I.D. and Day, A.J. (2003). The Link module from ovulation- and inflammation-associated protein TSG-6 changes conformation on hyaluronan binding. J Biol Chem 278, 49261-49270.

5. Blundell, C.D., Almond, A., Mahoney, D.J., DeAngelis, P.L., Campbell, I.D. and Day, A.J. (2005). Towards a structure for a hyaluronan-TSG-6 complex by modeling and NMR spectroscopy: insights into other members of the Link module superfamily. J Biol Chem 280, 18189-18201.

6. Teriete, P., Banerji, S., Noble, M., Blundell, C.D., Wright, A.J., Pickford A.R., Lowe, E., Mahoney, D.J., Tammi, M.I., Kahmann, J.D., Campbell, I.D., Day, A.J. and Jackson, D.G. (2004). Structure of the regulatory hyaluronan-binding domain in the inflammatory leukocyte homing receptor CD44. Molecular Cell 13, 483-496.

7. Banerji, S., Wright, A.J., Noble, M., Mahoney, D.J., Campbell, I.D., Day, A.J. and Jackson, D.G. (2007). Structures of the CD44-hyaluronan complex and new insight into a fundamental carbohydrate-protein interaction. Nat Struct Mol Biol 14, 234-239.

8. Mahoney, D.J., Blundell, C.D. and Day, A.J. (2001). Mapping the hyaluronan-binding site on the Link module from human TSG-6 by site-directed mutagenesis. J Biol Chem 276, 22764-22771.

9. Day, A.J. and Sheehan, J.K. (2001). Haluronan: polysaccharide chaos to protein organisation. Curr Opin Struct Biol 11, 617-622.

10. Day, A.J. and de la Motte, C.A. (2005). Hyaluronan cross-linking: a protective mechanism in inflammation? Trends Immunol 26, 637-643.

11. Rugg, M.S., Willis, A.C., Mukohpadhyay, D., Hascall, V.C., Fries, E., Fülöp, C., Milner, C.M. and Day, A.J. (2005). Characterization of complexes formed between TSG-6 and inter-α-inhibitor that act as intermediates in the covalent transfer of heavy chains onto hyaluronan. J Biol Chem 280, 25674-25686.

Bibliography*

Hyaluronan-Related Publications

1. Day, A.J., Aplin, R.T., and Willis, A.C. (1996). Overexpression, purification, and refolding of Link module from human TSG-6 in Escherichia coli: Effect of temperature, media and mutagenesis on lysine misincorporation at arginine AGA codons. Protein Exp Purif 8, 1-16.

2. Kohda, D., Morton, C. J., Parkar, A. A., Hatanaka, H., Inagaki, F. M., Campbell, I. D., and Day, A.J. (1996). Solution structure of the Link module: A hyaluronan-binding domain involved in extracellular matrix stability and cell migration. Cell 86, 767-775.

3. Kahmann, J.D., Koruth, R., and Day, A.J. (1997). Method for quantitative refolding of the Link module from human TSG-6. Protein Expr Purif 9, 315-318.

4. Parkar, A.A., and Day, A.J. (1997). Overlapping sites on the Link module of human TSG-6 mediate binding to hyaluronan and chondroitin-4-sulphate. FEBS Letters 410, 413-417.

5. Bajorath, J., Greenfield, B., Munro, S.B., Day, A.J., and Aruffo, A. (1998). Identification of CD44 residues important for hyaluronan binding and delineation of the binding site. J Biol Chem 273, 338-343.

6. Banerji, S., Day, A.J., Kahmann, J.D., and Jackson, D.G. (1998). Characterization of a functional hyaluronan-binding domain from the human CD44 Molecule expressed in Escherichia coli. Protein Exp Purif 14, 371-381.

7. Day, A.J., and Parkar, A.A. (1998). The structure of the Link module: a hyaluronan-binding domain. In *The Chemistry, Biology and Medical Applications of Hyaluronan and its Derivatives Proceedings of the Wenner-Gren Foundation International Symposium held in honor of Endre A Balazs, Stockholm, Sweden, September 18-21, 1996* (Ed. Laurent, T. C.), Portland Press Ltd., London (UK), 141-147.

---

* Provided by the interviewee.

8. Parkar, A.A., Kahmann, J.D., Howat, S.L.T., Bayliss, M.T., and Day, A.J. (1998). TSG-6 interacts with hyaluronan and aggrecan in a pH-dependent manner via a common functional element: Implications for its regulation in inflamed cartilage. FEBS Letters 428, 171-176.

9. Day, A.J. (1999). The structure and regulation of hyaluronan-binding proteins. Biochem Soc Trans 27, 115-121.

10. Day, A.J. (2000). Understanding hyaluronan-protein interactions. In *The Science of Hyaluronan Today* (Seikagaku Corporation Glycoforum) (Accessed at www.glycoforum.gr.jp/science/hyaluronan/HA16/HA16Ehtml) (Eds. Hascall, V.C., and Yanagishita, M.), Tokyo (JP).

11. Kahmann, J.D., O'Brien, R., Werner, J.M, Heinegård, D., Ladbury, J.E., Campbell, I.D., and Day, A.J. (2000). Localization and characterization of the hyaluronan-binding site on the Link module from human TSG-6. Structure 8, 763-774.

12. Bayliss, M.T., Howat, S.L.T., Dudhia, J., Murphy, J.M., Barry, F.P., Edwards, J.C.W., and Day, A.J. (2001). Up-regulation and differential expression of the hyaluronan-binding protein TSG-6 in cartilage and synovium in rheumatoid arthritis and osteoarthritis. Osteoarth Cartilage 9, 42-48.

13. Carrette, O., Nemade, R.V., Day, A.J., Brickner, A., and Larsen, W.J. (2001). TSG-6 is concentrated in the extracellular matrix of mouse cumulus oocyte complexes through hyaluronan and inter-alpha-inhibitor binding. Biol Reprod 65, 301-308.

14. Day, A.J., and Sheehan, J.K. (2001). Hyaluronan: polysaccharide chaos to protein organisation. Curr Opin Structural Biol 11, 617-622.

15. Mahoney, D.J., Aplin, R.T., Calabro, A., Hascall, V.C., and Day, A.J. (2001). Novel methods for the preparation and characterization of hyaluronan oligosaccharides of defined length. Glycobiology 11, 1025-1033.

16. Mahoney, D.J., Blundell, C. D., and Day, A.J. (2001). Mapping the hyaluronan-binding site on the Link module from human tumor necrosis factor-stimulated gene-6 by site-direct mutagenesis. J Biol Chem 276, 22764-22771.

17. Mukhopadhyay, D., Hascall, V.C., Day, A.J., Salustri, A., and Fülöp, C. (2001). Two distinct populations of tumor necrosis factor-stimulated gene-6 protein in the extracellular matrix of expanded mouse cumulus cell-oocyte complexes. Arch Biochem Biophys 394, 173-181.

18. Blundell, C.D., Kahmann, J.D., Perczel, A., Mahoney, D.J., Cordell, M.R., Teriete, P., Campbell, I.D., and Day, A.J. (2002). Getting to grips with HA-protein interactions. In *Hyaluronan Volume 1 Chemical, Biochemical and Biological*

Aspects (Eds. Kennedy, J. F., Phillips, G.O., Williams, P.A., and Hascall, V.C.), Woodhead, Cambridge, UK, 161-172.

19. Day, A.J., and Prestwich, G.D. (2002). Hyaluronan-binding proteins: tying up the giant. J Biol Chem 277, 4585-4588.

20. Fujimoto, T., Savani, R.C., Watari, M., Day, A.J., and Strauss, J.F., 3rd (2002). Induction of the hyaluronic acid-binding protein, tumor necrosis factor-stimulated gene-6, in cervical smooth muscle cells by tumor necrosis factor-alpha and prostaglandin E_2. Am J Pathol 160, 1495-1502.

21. Getting, S.J., Mahoney, D.J., Cao, T., Rugg, M.S., Fries, E., Milner, C.M., Perretti, M., and Day, A.J. (2002). The Link module from human TSG-6 inhibits neutrophil migration in a hyaluronan- and inter-□-inhibitor-independent manner. J Biol Chem 277, 51068-51076.

22. Lesley, J., English, N.M., Gál, I., Mikecz, K., Day, A.J., and Hyman, R. (2002). Hyaluronan binding properties of a CD44 chimera containing the Link module of TSG-6. J Biol Chem 277, 26600-26608.

23. Nentwich, H.A., Mustafa, Z., Rugg, M.S., Marsden, B.D., Cordell, M.R., Mahoney, D.J., Jenkins, S.C., Dowling, B., Fries, E., Milner, C.M., Loughlin, J., and Day, A.J. (2002). A novel allelic variant of the human TSG-6 gene encoding an amino acid difference in the CUB module. J Biol Chem 277, 15354-15362.

24. Tammi, M.I., Day, A.J., and Turley, E.A. (2002). Hyaluronan and homeostatis: a balancing act. J Biol Chem 277, 4581-4584.

25. Blundell, C.D., Mahoney, D.J., Almond, A., DeAngelis, P.L., Kahmann, J.D., Teriete, P., Pickford, A.R., Campbell, I. D., and Day, A.J. (2003). The Link module from ovulation- and inflammation-associated protein TSG-6 changes conformation on hyaluronan binding. J Biol Chem 278, 49261-49270.

26. Fülöp, C., Szántó, S., Mukhopadhyay, D., Bárdos, T., Kamath, R. V., Rugg, M.S., Day, A.J., Salustri, A., Hascall, V.C., Glant, T.T., and Mikecz, K. (2003). Impaired cumulus mucification and female sterility in tumor necrosis factor-induced protein-6 deficient mice. Development 130, 2253-2261.

27. Milner, C.M., and Day, A.J. (2003). TSG-6: a multifunctional protein associated with inflammation. J Cell Sci 116, 1-11.

28. Nadesalingam, J., Bernal, A.L., Dodds, A.W., Willis, A.C., Mahoney, D.J., Day, A.J., Reid, K.B., and Palaniyar, N. (2003). Identification and characterization of a novel interaction between pulmonary surfactant protein D and decorin. J Biol Chem 278, 25678-25687.

29. Ochsner, S.A., Day, A.J., Rugg, M.S., Breyer, R.M., Gomer, R.H., and Richards, J.S. (2003). Disrupted function of tumor necrosis factor-alpha-

stimulated gene 6 blocks cumulus cell-oocyte complex expansion. Endocrinology 144, 4376-4384.

30. Ochsner, S.A., Russell, D.L., Day, A.J., Breyer, R.M., and Richards, J.S. (2003). Decreased expression of tumor necrosis factor-☐ -stimulated gene 6 in cumulus cells of the cyclooxygenase-2 and EP2 null mice. Endocrinology 144, 1008-1019.

31. Vankemmelbeke, M.N., Jones, G.C., Fowles, C., Ilic, M.Z., Handley, C.J., Day, A.J., Knight, C.G., Mort, J.S., and Buttle, D.J. (2003). Selective inhibition of ADAMTS-1, -4 and -5 by catechin gallate esters. Eur J Biochem 270, 2394-2403.

32. Blundell, C.D., DeAngelis, P.L., Day, A.J., and Almond, A. (2004). Use of 15N-NMR to resolve molecular details in isotopically-enriched carbohydrates: sequence-specific observations in hyaluronan oligomers up to decasaccharides. Glycobiology 14, 999-1009.

33. Blundell, C.D., Seyfried, N.T., and Day, A.J. (2004). Structural and functional diversity of hyaluronan-binding proteins. In *Chemistry and Biology of Hyaluronan* (Eds. Garg, H. G. , and Hales, C. A.), Elsevier, Ltd., Amsterdam, 189-204.

34. Cao, T.V., La, M., Getting, S.J., Day, A.J., and Perretti, M. (2004). Inhibitory effects of TSG-6 Link module on leukocyte-endothelial cell interactions in vitro and in vivo. Microcirculation 11, 615-624.

35. Lesley, J., Gal, I., Mahoney, D. J., Cordell, M.R., Rugg, M.S., Hyman, R., Day, A.J., and Mikecz, K. (2004). TSG-6 modulates the interaction between hyaluronan and cell surface CD44. J Biol Chem 279, 25745-25754.

36. Mahoney, D.J., Whittle, J.D., Milner, C.M., Clark, S.J., Mulloy, B., Buttle, D.J., Jones, G.C., J., Day, A.J., and Short, R.D. (2004). A method for the non-covalent immobilization of heparin to surfaces. Anal Biochem 330, 123-129.

37. Mukhopadhyay, D., Asari, A., Rugg, M.S., Day, A.J., and Fulop, C. (2004). Specificity of the tumor necrosis factor-induced protein 6-mediated heavy chain transfer from inter-alpha-trypsin inhibitor to hyaluronan: implications for the assembly of the cumulus extracellular matrix. J Biol Chem 279, 11119-11128.

38. Salustri, A., Garlanda, C., Hirsch, E., De Acetis, M., Maccagno, A., Bottazzi, B., Doni, A., Bastone, A., Mantovani, G., Beck Peccoz, P., Salvatori, G., Mahoney, D.J., Day, A.J., Siracusa, G., Romani, L., and Mantovani, A. (2004). PTX3 plays a key role in the organization of the cumulus oophorus extracellular matrix and in in vivo fertilization. Development 131, 1577-1586.

39. Teriete, P., Banerji, S., Noble, M., Blundell, C.D., Wright, A.J., Pickford, A.R., Lowe, E., Mahoney, D.J., Tammi, M.I., Kahmann, J.D., Campbell, I.D., Day, A.J., and Jackson, D.G. (2004). Structure of the regulatory hyaluronan binding domain in the inflammatory leukocyte homing receptor CD44. Mol Cell 13, 483-496.

40. Almond, A., Colebrooke, S.A., DeAngelis, P.L., Mahoney, D.J., Day, A.J., and Blundell, C.D. (2005). Dynamic conformational predictions for hyaluronan: using NMR to confirm aqueous simulations. In *Hyaluronan Structure, Metabolism, Biological Activities, Therapeutic Applications Volume I* (Eds. Balazs, E. A. , and Hascall, V. C.), Matrix Biology Institute, Edgewater, NJ 07020 (USA), 3-6.

41. Banerji, S., Noble, M., Teriete, P., Wright, A.J., Blundell, C.D., Campbell, I.D., Day, A.J., and Jackson, D.G. (2005). Structure of the CD44 hyaluornan-binding domain and insight into its regulation by N-glycosylation. In *Hyaluronan: Structure, Metabolism, Biological Activities, Therapeutic Applications Volume II* (Eds. Balazs, E.A., and Hascall, V.C.), Matrix Biology Institute, Edgewater, NJ (USA), 625-630.

42. Blundell, C.D., Almond, A., Mahoney, D.J., DeAngelis, P.L., Campbell, I.D., and Day, A.J. (2005). Towards a structure for a TSG-6-hyaluronan complex by modeling and NMR spectroscopy: insights into other members of the link module superfamily. J Biol Chem 280, 18189-18201.

43. Day, A.J., and de la Motte, C. A. (2005). Hyaluronan cross-linking: a protective mechanism in inflammation? Trends Immunol 26, 637-643.

44. Day, A.J., M.S., R., Mahoney, D.J., and Milner, C. M. (2005). The role of hyaluronan-binding proteins in ovulation. In *Hyaluronan: Structure, Metabolism, Biological Activities, Therapeutic Applications Volume II* (Eds. Balazs, E.A., and Hascall, V.C.), Matrix Biology Institute, Edgewater, NJ (USA), 675-686.

45. Kuznetsova, S.A., Day, A.J., Mahoney, D.J., Rugg, M.S., Mosher, D.F., and Roberts, D.D. (2005). The N-terminal module of thrombospondin-1 interacts with the Link domain of TSG-6 and enhances its covalent association with the heavy chains of inter-alpha-trypsin inhibitor. J Biol Chem 280, 30899-30908.

46. Mahoney, D.J., Mulloy, B., Forster, M.J., Blundell, C.D., Fries, E., Milner, C.M., and Day, A.J. (2005). Characterization of the interaction between tumor necrosis factor-stimulated gene-6 and heparin: implications for the inhibition of plasmin in extracellular matrix microenvironments. J Biol Chem 280, 27044-27055.

47. Mukhopadhyay, D., Asari, A., Day, A.J., and Fülöp, C. (2005). Inhibition of the heavy chaing transfer from inter-alpha-trypsin inhibitor to hyaluronan by exogenous oligosaccharides during cumulus matrix formation *in vitro*. In *Hyaluronan: Structure, Metabolism, Biological Activities, Therapeutic Applications Volume II* (Eds. Balazs, E.A., and Hascall, V.C.), Matrix Biology Institute, Edgewater, NJ (USA), 687-691.

48. Roberts, S., Evans, H., Menage, J., Urban, J.P., Bayliss, M.T., Eisenstein, S.M., Rugg, M.S., Milner, C.M., Griffin, S., and Day, A.J. (2005). TNFalpha-stimulated gene product (TSG-6) and its binding protein, IalphaI, in the human intervertebral disc: new molecules for the disc. Eur Spine J 14, 36-42.

49. Rugg, M.S., Willis, A.C., Mukhopadhyay, D., Hascall, V.C., Fries, E., Fülöp, C., Milner, C.M., and Day, A.J. (2005). Characterization of complexes formed between TSG-6 and inter-alpha-inhibitor that act as intermediates in the covalent transfer of heavy chains onto hyaluronan. J Biol Chem 280, 25674-25686.

50. Salustri, A., Garlanda, C., Hirsch, E., De Acetis, M., Maccagno, A., Bottazzi, B., Mahoney, D.J., Day, A.J., Siracusa, G., and Mantovani, A. (2005). Role of pentraxin 3 in female fertility. In *Hyaluronan: Structure, Metabolism, Biological Activities, Therapeutic Applications Volume II* (Eds. Balazs, E.A., and Hascall, V.C.), Matrix Biology Institute, Edgewater, NJ (USA), 719-724.

51. Seyfried, N.T., Blundell, C.D., Day, A.J., and Almond, A. (2005). Preparation and application of biologically active fluorescent hyaluronan oligosaccharides. Glycobiology 15, 303-312.

52. Seyfried, N.T., McVey, G.F., Almond, A., Mahoney, D.J., Dudhia, J., and Day, A.J. (2005). Expression and purification of functionally active hyaluronan-binding domains from human cartilage link protein, aggrecan and versican: formation of ternary complexes with defined hyaluronan oligosaccharides. J Biol Chem 280, 5435-5448.

53. Wright, A.J., and Day, A.J. (2005). Hyaluronan in immune processes. Adv Exp Med Biol 564, 57-69.

54. Kuznetsova, S.A., Issa, P., Perruccio, E.M., Zeng, B., Sipes, J.M., Ward, Y., Seyfried, N.T., Fielder, H. L., Day, A.J., Wight, T. N., and Roberts, D. D. (2006). Versican-thrombospondin-1 binding in vitro and colocalization in microfibrils induced by inflammation on vascular smooth muscle cells. J Cell Sci 119, 4499-4509.

55. Milner, C.M., Higman, V.A., and Day, A.J. (2006). TSG-6: a pluripotent inflammatory mediator? Biochem Soc Trans 34, 446-450.

56. Selbi, W., Day, A.J., Rugg, M.S., Fulop, C., de la Motte, C.A., Bowen, T., Hascall, V.C., and Phillips, A.O. (2006). Overexpression of hyaluronan

synthase 2 alters hyaluronan distribution and function in proximal tubular epithelial cells. J Am Soc Nephrol 17, 1553-1567.

57. Selbi, W., de la Motte, C.A., Hascall, V.C., Day, A.J., Bowen, T., and Phillips, A.O. (2006). Characterization of hyaluronan cable structure and function in renal proximal tubular epithelial cells. Kidney Int 70, 1287-1295.

58. Seyfried, N.T., Day, A.J., and Almond, A. (2006). Experimental evidence for all-or-none cooperative interactions between the G1-domain of versican and multivalent hyaluronan oligosaccharides. Matrix Biol 25, 14-19.

59. Almond, A., Blundell, C.D., Higman, V.A., MacKerell, D.A., and Day, A.J. (2007). Using molecular dynamics simulations to provide new insights into protein structure on the nanosecond timescale: comparison with experimentla data and bilogicalinferences for the hyaluronan-binding Link module of TSG-6. J Chem Theory Comp 3, 1-16.

60. Banerji, S., Wright, A.J., Noble, M., Mahoney, D.J., Campbell, I.D., Day, A.J., and Jackson, D.G. (2007). Structures of the Cd44-hyaluronan complex provide insight into a fundamental carbohydrate-protein interaction. Nat Struct Mol Biol 14, 234-239.

61. Blundell, C.D., Mahoney, D.J., Cordell, M.R., Almond, A., Kahmann, J.D., Perczel, A., Taylor, J.D., Campbell, I. D., and Day, A.J. (2007). Determining the molecular basis for the pH-dependent interaction between the link module of human TSG-6 and hyaluronan. J Biol Chem 282, 12976-12988.

62. Forteza, R., Casalino-Matsuda, S.M., Monzon, M.E., Fries, E., Rugg, M.S., Milner, C.M., and Day, A.J. (2007). TSG-6 potentiates the antitissue kallikrein activity of inter-alpha-inhibitor through bikunin release. Am J Respir Cell Mol Biol 36, 20-31.

63. Higman, V.A., Blundell, C.D., Mahoney, D.J., Redfield, C., Noble, M.E., and Day, A.J. (2007). Plasticity of the TSG-6 HA-binding loop and mobility in the TSG-6-HA complex revealed by NMR and X-ray crystallography. J Mol Biol 371, 669-684.

64. Milner, C.M., Tongsoongnoen, W., Rugg, M.S., and Day, A.J. (2007). The molecular basis of inter-alpha-inhibitor heavy chain transfer on to hyaluronan. Biochem Soc Trans 35, 672-676.

65. Seyfried, N.T., Atwood, J.A. 3rd, Yongye, A., Almond, A., Day, A.J., Orlando, R., and Woods, R.J. (2007). Fourier transform mass spectrometry to monitor hyaluronan-protein interactions: use of hydrogen/deuterium amide exchange. Rapid Commun Mass Spectrom 21, 121-131.

66. Day, A.J., Blundell, C.D., Mahoney, D.J., Rugg, M.S., and Milner, C.M. (2008). Hyaluronan-binding proteins in inflammation (in press). In *Molecular*

Aspects of Innate and Adaptive Immunity (Eds. Reid, K.B.M., and Sim, R.B.), Royal Society of Chemistry (RSC), London (UK).

67. Inforzato, A., Rivieccio, V., Morreale, A.P., Bastone, A., Salustri, A., Scarchilli, L., Verdoliva, A., Vincenti, S., Gallo, G., Chiapparino, C., Pacello, L., Nucera, E., Serlupi-Crescenzi, O., Day, A.J., Bottazzi, B., Mantovani, A., De Santis, R., and Salvatori, G. (2008). Structural characterization of PTX3 disulphide bond network and its multimeric status in cumulus matrix organization. J Biol Chem 283, 10147-10161.

68. Kuznetsova, S.A., Mahoney, D.J., Martin-Manso, G., Ali, T., Nentwich, H.A., Sipes, J.M., Zeng, B., Vogel, T., Day, A.J., and Roberts, D.D. (2008). TSG-6 binds via its CUB_C domain to the cell-binding domain of fibronectin and increases fibronectin matrix assembly. Matrix Biol 27, 201-210.

69. Nagyova, E., Camaioni, A., Prochazka, R., Day, A.J., and Salustri, A. (2008). Synthesis of tumor necrosis factor alpha-induced protein 6 in porcine preovulatory follicles: a study with A38 antibody. Biol Reprod 78, 903-909.

70. Yoshihara, Y., Plaas, A., Osborn, B., Margulis, A., Nelson, F., Rugg, M.S., Milner, C.M., Day, A.J., Nemoto, K., and Sandy, J.D. (2008). Human articular cartilages contain bikunin proteoglycan and novel truncated forms of inter-alpha-trypsin inhibitor heavy chains. Osteoarthr. Cartilage (in press).

Paul L. DeAngelis, 2007
(photograph courtesy of the University of Oklahoma)

Paul L. DeAngelis

Paul DeAngelis (b. 1962, Ranson, West Virginia) is Professor of Biochemistry and Molecular Biology at the Department of Biochemistry and Molecular Biology of the University of Oklahoma Health Sciences Center. He received his BA degree at Harvard University (1984), his Ph.D. at the University of California at Irvine (1990), and spent his postdoctoral years at the University of Texas, Medical Branch at Galveston (1990-1993). He moved to the University of Oklahoma in 1994.

Dr. DeAngelis received the "Rooster Award" in 2007 from the International Society for Hyaluronan Sciences (ISHAS) for his achievements in hyaluronan-related research. He is on the Editorial Board of the following scientific journals: *Analytical Biochemistry*, *Journal of Biological Chemistry*, and *Glycobiology*.

Interview*

Please, tell us something about yourself.

I grew up on the east coast of the United States and have been wandering around California, Texas, and now, Oklahoma, pursuing science. Glycobiology has been my focus since college days but I've always been a scientist, even when I was a little kid. I was always trying to figure out how things worked. I would follow how a plant grew, watch animals, bust open rocks, do chemical reactions that sometimes smelled up the house, and cannibalized and rebuilt electronics. So, basically I have always been a scientist; glycobiology just caught my eye because it is a frontier that is new and there is plenty of room to grow.

Yes, plenty of room because usually nucleic acids and proteins are the two main directions...

Yes, that is right. Well, maybe carbohydrates are not that fashionable. Usually when people have a protein with sugar on it they try to get rid of the sugar first in order to study the protein—they simply also forget that DNA and RNA are actually sugar chains themselves. Glycobiology is underlying all of it. Perhaps the problem was that the tools were not available to study sugars. With proteins, you have proteases to cut them; with DNA you have restriction enzymes to cut them; and then you can paste them together with ligases. But this is not so easy or impossible with most sugars. I figure that it is all because of the lack of tools and the lack of defined molecules. I think that if you can get the right tools and get the right defined molecules, it will be shown that sugars will be responsible for keeping life going almost as much as anything else.

---

* This interview was recorded during the Hyaluronan Meeting in Charleston, South Carolina, April 2007.

Do funding agencies feel the same?

They are starting to realize this. Actually, the NIH in the last five to eight years has been recognizing more and more that glycobiology underpins a lot of things and they even have had some extra initiatives. The *MIT Technology Review* counted glycobiology one of the top 10 new areas of science. And more and more people are finding out that simple and complex sugars are all really important; they are not just sugar in your coffee.

That brings us to popular perceptions about chemicals. What is the popular perception concerning sugars? For example, magnetic resonance imaging had to drop the word "nuclear" because people were afraid of that. So when you say "sugar," people may think of getting fat.

Yes, you are absolutely right. And you can't get around it by being more technical either and say "carbohydrate" because people already talk about carbohydrates. Then you call it "glycomics," when you look at all the sugars in a cell and their roles, and perhaps that sounds a little more high-tech. I think that people have to realize that they have been using sugar drugs for quite a while. Just think about heparin that is the biggest sugar-drug used in hospitals at a cost of about 6 billion dollars a year! That is nothing else but a polysaccharide chain. It is used in almost every surgery as an anticoagulant. It turns out that most of the proteins people are using as therapeutics are actually glycoproteins— including antibodies that are actually used in a glycosylated form.

Do the sugars have any function?

Yes. One example of a functional sugar is the blockbuster drug by Amgen --Epogen -- for people who have low blood counts due to chemotherapy or kidney dialysis, for example. After an Epogen injection the red blood cell count goes up, they have more oxygen-carrying capacity and the patient does a lot better. When they made Aranesp, the next generation Epogen with a better sugar chain, it lasted longer in the blood stream; so instead of having to inject it multiple times per week, this new version requires fewer injections, and it is mostly due to the nature of the sugar chains.

What is your main area of research?

A special family of sugar chains called glycosaminoglycans; hyaluronic acid, heparin and chondroitin all belong to this group. These polysaccharides have a characteristic structure with repeating disaccharides that have an amino group; that is why they are called glycosaminoglycans. I got into this field because we were one of the first groups to figure out how glycosaminoglycans are made, and we found the enzyme catalyst that actually polymerizes those chains. As a postdoctoral fellow in Paul Weigel's group, I identified the very first hyaluronic acid synthase and it spawned a lot of the field; there is sequence similarity to other members of this class of enzymes. Then later as an independent researcher, I found a few other enzymes that do this as well and some of them have good biotech capabilities so basically you can build sugar chains. Being able to build a defined sugar allows you to answer one question at a time and that has a lot of advantages. If you take a crude mixture you might have some good molecules and bad molecules or sometimes cross-inhibitory ones, so by being able to synthesize defined molecules makes it very valuable for other scientists who then work with them further and can figure out many other things. We found the first chondroitin synthase from any source, that was the enzyme that makes the second family of glycosaminoglycans, and finally, enzymes that make the backbone of heparin. Other groups also found some other enzymes, but it turns out that we were lucky to find some of the most robust practical catalysts; the other enzymes are so dainty and delicate you can just barely characterize them. So basically we have an enzymology lab studying interesting sugar building enzymes.

Building from what?

Basically glycosaminoglycans are long sugar polymers, so we string together sugar monomers. In this case, the precursors are activated UDP (uridine diphospho) sugars; they have a uridine handle so the enzyme can grab onto the sugar and then the enzyme uses the phosphate's energy to couple sugar units together.

Does this mean that you are now building hyaluronan molecules rather than extracting them from, say, the rooster comb or bacterial fermentation?

Yes. Extraction is a fine thing, too, it just depends on what you're going to use the hyaluronan for application-wise. Researchers are finding out these days that the bulk hyaluronic acid that you extract from a tissue, like rooster comb, or streptococcal bacteria is satisfactory for many things but not for everything. It turns out that in this age of finely focused biological experimentation there are differences between big polymer chains and small polymer chains—various cells respond to the HA polymers differently. The cells can distinguish between a big one and a little one so if you take an extracted HA material, it can be a mixture of all different sizes, or could even be slightly cross-contaminated with other molecules and that could be a bad thing. But if you can synthesize a chain and you know exactly how large it is…

So you are saying that you can produce a well-defined molecular weight?

Very, very, very well defined.

Is it more expensive than using the traditional method?

Yes, for now it is, but in part it is because the demand for the precursor is low in the global scheme of things. But there is no reason for the price not to come down. In analogy, back when people were first making synthetic DNA, those precursors were really expensive and these reagents just kept getting cheaper and cheaper with time so it is widely used around the globe now.

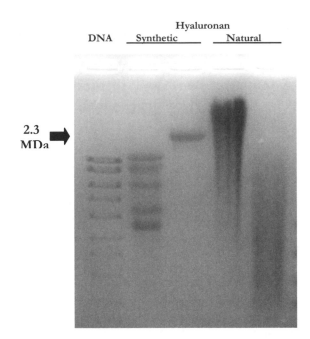

Agarose gel electrophoresis shows the defined size of synthetic HA in comparison to natural HA extracted from rooster or *Streptococcus*. The bands are almost as narrow as DNA fragments which are truly monodisperse.

Do you buy the precursors?

Yes. Well, we buy some of them. Some of the other precursors are custom-made. In these latter cases, instead of making the natural HA polymer, we can make unnatural polymers that have extra handles on them. These handles can be a chemical group for a second chemical reagent to go on or maybe modify the biological effect of HA. So basically we are breaking into this area together with some chemist colleagues and we are trying to make designer hyaluronan that will have new functions. This means that, instead of having to do chemical crosslinking to make the hyaluronic acid gel, for example, maybe we can build stuff that auto-assembles or has good chemistry that allows it to happen a lot quicker or can happen in situ in the body during an operation. That is one realm that we are involved with.

There is also another realm: try to imagine that there are all these hyaluronan sensing systems in your body; different proteins bind hyaluronan, but if they all bind the same HA polymer, how are you going to stop one protein system without hurting all the rest? The idea of selectivity is an important one in medicine. Think about aspirin; it is a good drug to inhibit cyclooxygenases but you do not want to inhibit all the cyclooxygenases—just the ones that are making prostaglandins that give you a headache, or the enzymes that make the signals that activate the platelets. What we are thinking is that if we can make HA, for example, with mostly natural structure and a few key unnatural structures, then maybe we can enhance binding of certain proteins and inhibit binding of other ones.

This utilization of selectivity, is this very recent?

Drug companies always wanted to do it but the sugar world is a little tough because they couldn't build everything they wanted, I mean assemble everything from scratch by organic chemistry. If you could assemble it as easy as you could draw it, that would be good – but it is not so easy with sugars. Making a sugar chain, 3 to 7 units long can be a Ph.D. thesis.

When you synthesize a peptide using Merrifield's method, you add amino acids one by one, is this the way you do it?

We can do it that way for short sugar chains. We have tamed these synthase enzymes, which are normally very fast elongators, adding hundreds of sugars in minutes easily; thus you could never really control them by changing the reaction time. We figured out a way to make them work one step at a time. What we do is basically split the catalyst into two working units, and if you only use one catalytic part at a time then you only add one sugar at a time. So you can actually build chains sugar by sugar.

We make a pair of immobilized mutant enzymes (one adds sugar A and the other adds sugar B). Then you take your starting sugar chain and the next A precursor to go on, and mix them together in the presence of one immobilized enzyme reactor. When this step is done, go to the next step with the other enzyme that is needed and the next B precursor. You then repeat as desired to make polymers like ABABAB and so on; this is one way of building small defined molecules. These molecules are very small, about 5 to 25 sugars.

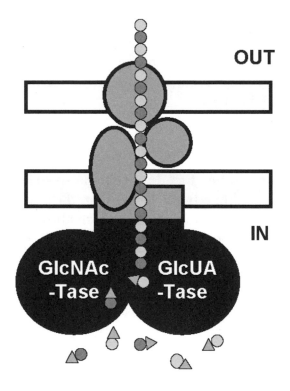

Schematic Model of *Pasteurella* HA Synthase, a Class II HA Synthase.

GlcNAc and GlcUA (*red* or *blue spheres*, respectively) from the UDP-sugars (UDP, *orange triangles*) inside the cell are polymerized by the HAS, a dual-action or bifunctional glycosyltransferase, into long polymer chains. HA is transported out of the cell to form the extracellular coat or capsule in bacteria. The Class II PmHAS (*black*) catalyzes the sugar addition reactions and docks with a polysaccharide transport apparatus composed of multiple proteins (*green shapes*) to translocate the HA across the two membranes of Gram-negative bacteria. The enzyme is a fusion of two glycosyltransferases (*Tase*) that add GlcNAc and GlcUA at the non-reducing end of the HA chain.

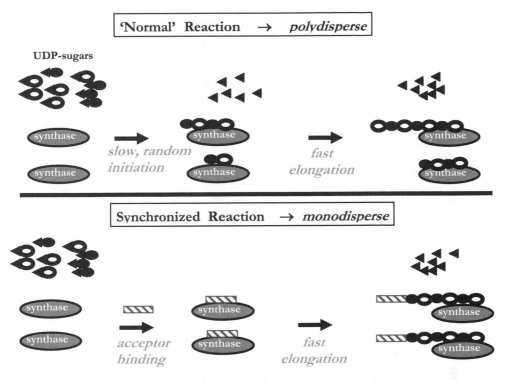

Schematic model for acceptor-mediated synchronization of HA synthesis.

In "normal" reactions *in vitro*, UDP-sugars (*black triangle* UDP; *small black* or *white ovals*, monosaccharides) are bound by the PmHAS (*red HAS*) and the first glycosidic linkages are formed over a lag period due to this rate-limiting step (*slow initiation*). Once the initial HA chain is started, then subsequent sugars are added rapidly to the nascent polymer (*fast elongation*) by the enzyme. Some chains are initiated before other chains thus asynchronous polymerization occurs resulting in a population of HA product molecules with a broad size distribution called polydisperse. In synchronized reactions, the acceptor sugar (*striped bar*) bypasses the slow initiation step. Thus all chains are elongated by the nonprocessive PmHAS in a parallel, synchronous fashion resulting in a uniform HA product with a narrow size distribution called monodisperse. In addition, it is possible to adjust the molar ratio of acceptor to UDP-sugars to control the ultimate polymer molecular mass (*not shown*).

However, we have developed a second technology platform where we actually found out ways to make polymers that are a million molecular weight or so (thousands of sugars) and still, the final polymers are very, very well defined. We achieved this by taking advantage of some basic characteristics of the enzyme. When there are two phases of the reaction, we figured out a way to bypass one, so instead of having a polymer with random molecular weight or a wide size distribution, we make the chains all elongate at the same time so they will be made the same length and, therefore, very well defined.

Could you explain hyaluronic acid to a layman? How do you explain that you are using the same name for, say, 10 units or a million units?

Well, the nomenclature should be better, but basically we could define the hyaluronan (HA) typically by the length of its sugar chains; so if it is two sugars long, you might say it is the hyaluronan disaccharide or "HA2", if it had four sugars, it is "HA4", if it had 100 sugars, it would be "HA100". But you have to watch out because some people will say that the disaccharide repeat is one; so it is, indeed, confusing. Also, some people say "low-molecular-weight hyaluronan" and they may mean 100,000 molecular weight or 500 sugars versus something that is just ten or twenty sugars, so definitely, there has to be a unification. Actually, that is something that is up in the air for the International Society of Hyaluronan Sciences. But to the layman what is hyaluronan? It is the "wonder sugar".

Right. I think, it is increasingly important to talk to the layman.

Yes. I think, people have to realize that cells have software that is the DNA and they have hardware that is the protein and sugars. The protein may be doing more the active functions, it is the sensor or recognizing things but the sugars often tell the proteins what to do. They are the signposts that say: Should I keep growing? Should I die? Should I move over here? Or should I make an arm? Or should I just sit here and wait?

How do they do that?

Well, via cell signaling. Typically proteins tell other proteins a message and you might have heard of phosphorylation or other similar things. Sugars can send signals, too.

Concerning your research direction; did you learn it from somebody or did you start it yourself?

Basically if you find a new protein that is the first of a class, then you do not have any real guidelines—but there were already several basic models. There is some general knowledge on glycosyltransferase enzymes that transfer sugars or make sugar chains but with our class of enzymes there was no specific prototype; so we pretty much had to learn from scratch. As it turns out, especially for the hyaluronic acid-producing enzymes, that there are two very different types. Therefore, you could not have predicted that the paradigm was going to be one way or the other.

What I am trying to ask is whether this work is a continuation of your graduate work?

No. When I was doing graduate work, we were binding sugars to different things—not even hyaluronic acid—they were extracellular matrix sugars that we were binding to proteins. I started this HA enzymology line of work when I was a post doc with Paul Weigel at the University of Texas Medical Branch at Galveston. Weigel had initiated this project, but they did not have any identified candidates; the classical biochemistry approach wasn't working. His team started using molecular biology to find the unknown synthase gene by expression cloning, but did not have luck. Therefore I started using transposon insertional mutagenesis, a method with which you cast out your net widely and you look for the right mutant caused by the transposon jumping in the target gene; then when you have that lead, you follow the transposon. The next step was somewhat like doing genetic repair on the mutant bacterium missing the ability to make HA; I fixed the mutant and then asking what DNA fixed the mutant. It was a two-part scheme and there was a lot of trouble with it; I almost gave the project up a few times because this new HA synthase DNA is unstable. Therefore, when you think that you have the correct DNA, and you are just moving it around to a better system for analysis, in the meantime, the target DNA breaks down into smaller pieces with deletions. Basically I had to develop several different techniques to make this overall process work.

The initial step was similar to direct sequencing of DNA from bacterial cells without cloning; this procedure is starting to become fashionable, but in the early 1990s that was not the case. I also had to figure out how to enrich the mutations because knocking out the HA synthase with a transposon was pretty rare, but we also had a background of nonspecific synthase mutations. The bacteria do not like working harder than they have to; they want to be easy slackers not wasting energy making HA polymer. If you are not careful, then you will have spontaneous synthase mutations and then how can you tell if it is a spontaneous mutation happening at the same time as your genetic intervention with these transposons? Therefore, I had to figure out a way to fish out the rare ones and then quickly test if they were the right one or not. When you do a genetic disease pedigree, sometimes you have familial heredity and you can actually track down that it came from the mother and it is recessive or dominant. On the other hand, with this HA synthase project sporadic mutations also came up. You can never really track down the gene from a sporadic mutation because you don't know where to look, you don't have any markers like the transposon to help out. It was definitely a pain because nobody else really knew what the HA synthase gene was; in retrospect, it resembled a few other enzymes, but back in 1992–93, nobody could really put two and two together, so it was something where you were learning as you went along, and Nature made things difficult quite often. It took about six months to do a step that nowadays takes a week or so—so it was really a hard work.

Was this your post doctoral work?

Yes.

And where did you do your Ph.D.?

At the University of California at Irvine. We were working on sperm-egg interaction; we were trying to figure out the structure—function relationship. My advisor was Charles Glabe at the Department of Molecular Biology and Biochemistry. But I was working with sugars already as an undergraduate trying to decipher how plants recognize sugars from pathogenic fungi as danger signals. Actually, that is how I stumbled into glycobiology. I decided to do work study while I was at Harvard and I was looking at the different things that were available and one professor said something about sugar chemistry and biology. From our undergraduate classes I knew that almost everybody was doing transcription and protein structure and similar things and I really did not see why I should compete with everybody else, I thought I would rather be a pioneer, so I signed up for that. I took three years of independent study in the lab of Arthur Ayers in the Cellular and Developmental Biology department.

Back in the 1960s there was this great controversy between the molecular biologists and the development biologists.

I was there during 1980—1984, but they still had their different buildings. I was in the old brick building with the elevator with the metal slats and no air-conditioning while all the biochemists were in the glass air-conditioned modern building.

Did you encounter any of the big names at Harvard?

Yes, I did meet some of them and they all were very kind and helpful. Some of the big-name chemists and physicists were my teachers. There were also many good stories about them. I remember one: Frank Westheimer was telling us how around World War II they were doing a process to make penicillin, the antibiotic, and one of the intermediates was red. One time they had an equipment failure and the reaction vessel broke and all that red liquid spilled on the floor and when his supervisor saw this he said "That better be blood on the floor!"

Blood rather than the compound.

Yes. I learned there that it is inevitable that you make mistakes during your work at one time or another. I also learned that I should not worry if I read something in the literature and I could not reproduce it; you have to try once, a second and a third time, but if it does not work, maybe the literature is wrong and you are right. For example, there was this hyaluronan synthase, the very first one we found, in principle, it was already cloned before I got to the lab by somebody else but as it turned out, it was totally wrong. The scientist cloned, purified, characterized the wrong protein, it did not have any activity but in the mean time we thought that it was right. So we tried to reproduce but we could not and I learned that if an experiment doesn't work one or two times it is probably not you, the problem must be something else. Experiments are supposed to be reproducible.

You need self-confidence – but it may also be simply arrogance...

You have to be a little arrogant, I think. You have to give certain experiments a shot; just because it didn't work for somebody else, does not mean that it could not work for you. But I still remember trying to do one of my first sugar derivatives back as an undergraduate. I was adapting a synthesis by a really famous biochemist, Pedro Cuatrecasas, who invented affinity chromatography for identifying the insulin receptor. I was using a chemistry that supposedly should have worked for my goal, but it did not. Then I went back and looked at his paper and I realized that he never did a direct proof, it was just an indirect proof; in that paper, he said that this synthesis must have worked because the other did not or competed. And I wasted about six or eight months on it before I realized the situation. So I tried it in a totally different way and my new way worked. Now I make it a point to tell my students, give it a shot a couple of times, check everything very carefully and if it still is not right then just go and try something different.

How did you get into Harvard?

Applied.

From where?

I grew up in Maryland and I had a good opportunity, because I always liked science and I read a lot so I got a scholarship to a boarding school, the McDonogh School in Maryland. They appreciated the sciences as much as I did and I took all kinds of labs that were sometimes even better than the ones in college, so I learned organic chemistry and was playing around in the anatomy laboratory, and physics, and other things as well. I was also on the wrestling team and my coach was from Harvard, so I thought, I might as well try, and I did. And I got in. I got in, in part, because I had an idea about a new kind of laser, while I was in high-school and I did a little back of the envelope estimate and then I wrote it all up in hand as my application essay. Later on, I think, it was a good thing to be at Harvard since I met Nicholaas Bloembergen, a laser expert and Nobel laureate (Physics 1981), who thought my idea was interesting, but maybe not practical due to a technical issue that I would not have guessed about as a high school student.

What is the most striking difference between Harvard and Oklahoma?

The whole state of Oklahoma is smaller than the city of Boston so there are probably fewer resources and fewer people to bump into, but we have top caliber people as well. I think that the human brain can do a lot of good no matter where it is.

Of course, but you understand what my question means. You spent years at Harvard University and now you are teaching and doing research in Oklahoma, so the question inevitably arises, do you think you can compete?

We are trying to think smart and work smart. Of course, there are more resources there, maybe more colleagues to talk to, it probably is easier to get funding at Harvard. If you look at some of the projects that get funded at Harvard and there are four or five projects that are pretty similar, then you wonder why they get that much money; maybe it is because of the clout. But I don't want to sound bitter. Sometimes you have initial ideas for pursuing in a grant project and you have people, the reviewer or others in the field, say that your ideas are wrong or certain work cannot be done. Then a couple of years later we would actually do the experiments, and it worked, just as it happened with the hyaluronan synthases making different size polymers depending on the species. The critics did not think that the work made any difference in the world or it would work at all and, by golly, here we are.

You are bringing up another problem: funding and recognition. We have on record about 15 interviews with people in this field. You are saying that you don't want to sound bitter and you are not sounding bitter at all, but we have heard much bitterness about difficulties in getting funding or in getting promoted, because they are told that the field is out of the mainstream.

You definitely have to prove yourself a little bit more, maybe it is because there are too many fads or weird ideas, like molecular imprinting of water which was bogus, to give one example. You certainly don't want to seem too crazy but you don't want to be boring either. I think, it just would be nicer if the funding would be spread a little bit more, but who knows, maybe the grants now will do better. We have different sources at the moment. I try to do basic science. Every time I do an experiment, I try to milk it for everything it's worth academically, try to get what is the hypothesis, what is the basic discovery? We also always try to think about ways to make new compounds that can help my lab, and also help other labs or ultimately patients; so we have actually been funded by the Oklahoma Center for Advancement of Science and Technology (OCAST). This means that the State of Oklahoma realizes that there is wealth that is untapped.

I helped starting three companies. Paul Weigel and I started *Hyalose* to commercialize the recombinant technologies that we worked out for hyaluronan, basically by bacterial-fermentation or by enzymatic syntheses. As I told you at the beginning, we can now control the size of the synthesized HA molecules. The second company I started is *Choncept* that focuses on the development of new technology for the production of chondroitin from fermentation of recombinant bacteria. And then, I also started a heparin company, called *Heparinex*, whose goal is to synthesize heparinoid compounds for different purposes, such as anticoagulants, medical device applications, and others.

We have gotten collaborative OCAST grants with laboratories at the University and the companies. When these sugar-based companies put in money into research, OCAST matches it. When the company put in $300,000, then OCAST matched it with $300,000, and this will make your money go a little farther and we have basic science in the university.

You mean that your company subsidizes your research at the University?

Yes. So basically there are usually multiple components besides OCAST grants. Typically my lab does some of the pilot work and some of the maybe more demanding instrument-wise experiments and the company does more of the developmental and scale up work and they are right across the street from each other, a quarter mile away.

How does separation work? I mean, this is a state University which subsidizes your research and then you apply it in your company.

Well, everybody wins. The state has more high-paying jobs—my former students and some other local students actually worked at the company. The company gets good recognition and more access to instruments because of the university; the university owns about 5 or 10% of the company, so they have equity. Thus, if the company does well, then the university gets licensing fees and royalties. The state of Oklahoma passed a law that allowed the faculty to have equity and ownership of companies. So there is a little bit more incentive, but it doesn't stop me from doing my regular teaching and service to the University.

How much teaching do you do?

It depends from year to year, but about 20 hours a year. It is not much direct class time, it is a medical school where research is relatively more important.

So you have three companies. Any of them paying taxes yet?

I think so. One company, Hyalose, has been around since 2000, the others started around 2002.

A company that pays taxes has become profitable, right?

I think, one of them is close to being profitable, the other two are still early ventures. We are trying; but basically we don't want to do everything by ourselves. For example, we could try to scale up and do huge vats of hyaluronan fermentation, but that would mean a lot of technology, it would need a lot of capital, so we rather found another company, Novozymes AS, to do that. We supply the information, the genes, and the intellectual property to allow them to get into the market. We are acting as a partner to people who are already experts in that area. I like to stay a scientist, trying to figure out how these catalysts work and figure out new leads. We try to do the same with the other sugar companies; our teams try to take the risk out of any endeavor, take it to the next two or three steps of progress as well as be support for whoever the industry partner is. We're looking for partners for the other companies right now (news: Heparinex and Choncept entered into a co-development agreement with Biological E, Ltd. in late 2007 and early 2008, respectively).

How long have you known Bandi [Endre A. Balazs]?

I just met him for the first time in 2000; he came up to me at a conference and introduced himself, a very nice guy. He asked: can you really do what you said you can do?

What was that?

Building these sugars step by step. I showed the audience a little animation, where we could add one sugar at a time and I assured him that yes, we can do it. And it has gotten better since 2000. It turned out to be pretty remarkable; nobody really expected that it worked that way.

Paul DeAngelis with Endre A. Balazs at the Charleston meeting, Charleston, South Carolina, 2007 (photograph by M. Hargittai)

Before you met, did you know of him?

Sure, everybody knows him, in name. I had to because we are making hyaluronan a different way than he was, and he is kind of the benchmark. This was about the time when his company, Biomatrix was merging with Genzyme. Probably the most striking thing that catches all the peoples' eyes is that he named his yacht after hyaluronic acid.

His what?

His yacht, his boat. After hyaluronic acid.

I didn't know he had a boat.

Maybe, he doesn't have it anymore, but I liked the story – maybe somebody was just teasing me, you'll have to ask him.

No, I have been to his villa in France and that is named after NIF-NaHA.

So, it's not the yacht it's the villa. Anyway, I thought it was a boat, and things like that get people's attention at first because when you're doing science you're saying, well, geez, am I going to starve doing this? Is it going to be satisfying, am I going to do something that nobody's going to notice? It is worrisome. So when you hear good stories like somebody chased a dream and got something and it worked out for him, it is always good to hear.

I can imagine that he is an inspiration. But he is also very much into basic science.

Oh, yes, you've got to be. If you don't have good science, the technology is not going to come out and you won't be the first person to do it. So trying to get intellectual property protection, the patents and all, isn't going to happen without good science, so it is always best to be the pioneer and then there is no question, you don't have to fight for it.

Some people think that they can go directly to the application and be successful in that.

Only if they are very lucky. The whole reason that we know how to harness and use these enzymes is because we did the basic science, we did things step by step and made models and thought about it a lot. Once we knew the enzymes' characteristics, it was a different thing. It is like when you are trying to put together a baseball team or a football team and you need somebody to block and somebody to run, you are not going to make the slowest guy your runner, so you have to know the characteristics of everything – then you can assemble the team and do what you need to win. I think, if you don't do the basic work, then you won't be able to imagine the next step.

You said that your hyaluronan is too expensive, say, for medical applications.

It depends on the application. For the chemoenzymatic "made in a test tube" synthetic HA version, this is true; that is expensive now. The other version, the bacterial fermentation HA, is already out on the market.

How do you make sure that this is pure hyaluronan?

We run the tests. We have to pass the pharmacopiea-style tests of HA-percent purity and all the other things.

I would like to understand this. Bandi's way of testing was with the monkeys' eyes, he didn't look for percentages, he just tested whether it caused inflammation in the monkeys' eyes or not.

Good practical test if you're not a monkey.

It was a very practical test. I understand that today this is different.

There are several extra tests, but I think that if you can show it does not cause inflammation in that test, that is good too, but I am not sure if it is required anymore. I think that today there is more analytical technology; they have different rules but it is still kind of old fashioned. Some of the tests that they are doing are not that exact, so you can imagine that contaminants could slip by. But it is better to do those tests rather than go to FDA clinical Phase I or Phase II trials and have them fail. Most HA is used as a medical *device*, so there are different rules. But I have not gotten into these aspects very deeply; I've been staying in basic science. Actually, the companies are really good because we have business people doing the negotiations and the contracts and I just keep an eye on that and they keep me informed and get my opinion.

Are you the owner?

No, I am officially chief scientist and director.

We know how the information transfers from DNA to proteins, and how proteins are made. How are these polysaccharides made? What directs their synthesis?

When the sugars are made, the fidelity of the information transfer is maintained by having an enzyme that does a specific sugar-transfer onto a group. So the enzyme knows what it should hold on to and what it should add on and then the next enzyme activity would say, alright, now that next sugar is there, I will grab on and add on to it, so it's very short range.

I understand but these enzymes are just executing something. But the information originally must come from somewhere else...

Polysaccharides have been around for a long time. In fact, hyaluronic acid probably has not been around as long as other things, just about half a billion years and for some reason cells thought it was good to have it around. HA was easy to move around in, to percolate through, and they have learned how to use it as maybe the third letter in the alphabet of the glycosaminoglycan sugar code. Chondroitin was probably the second one but the first one was probably heparin or heparin-like molecules, because every animal on the planet has some kind of heparin and only some of them have chondroitin, so why heparin was the number one choice, who knows? It was probably a kind of random accident, just like the difference between D and L amino acids; it is just the way things are cooked up in Nature, it is kind of like the Rube Goldberg approach...

Do I understand this correctly that the question I asked you cannot be answered now? You are saying the enzymes do this and that, but the enzymes are just another protein...

Yes. DNA gives them information for their structure to do a certain activity.

So there is information in the DNA about targeting these sugars?

I don't know if the DNA knows any better, I don't know how far it goes back. I think it is just a matter of if you put the right molecules in the right context they will make the right material. So, it is a combination of a lot of things to make it. But can the DNA tell you to make a different sugar? Yes, if you have the right mutation and probably that is what happens.

We know the genetic code. But we don't have such a set of information about how sugars are made, or how these enzymes are directed to make them, and yet another question, which is a sub-question of this, do these enzymes decide the length of these sugar molecules?

We don't know how they do that yet, in a live animal it could be that when they run out of sugar precursor, maybe that will stop or it could be that once the chain is so big, all the water moving around the Brownian motion may have enough force knocking on it that it rips it away.

People talk so much about aging today. As I understand, part of aging is that you produce shorter sugar molecules...

Well, it could be, because you are making shorter ones because you are running out of fuel, or you have less enzyme, or it could be that you are not turning it over as fast and you are seeing more degraded material. The brand new one, if you could watch it, was probably just as long but if your replacement HA is not as quick appearing, then all you see are the smaller degradation fragments, maybe that is what is happening.

Is this being investigated?

It is a tough thing to do. If you imagine that just to do a study on a rat, old rats cost $200-300 a piece, so that is not even probably a good model because they die pretty quickly. So these are tough questions. I usually steer clear of cell biology, I stay with single molecules or a group of molecules because then one little research group like mine can get an answer. I don't have an army of people, I would not even like to; I prefer to have a close-knit group. But these aging questions are very tough and it is going to be a lot more work and time before we will know the answer. I don't think we're going to be finished with glycobiology and hyaluronan this century.

My last question: Do I see it correctly that there is a shift in which molecular weight hylauronan is better? There used to be a preference of high molecular weight, but today I see that there are lots of advantages with low molecular weight as well.

That is probably depending on the cell and the condition, either one could be good. It's part of the code.

Not for the same purpose.

Not for the same purpose. It turns out that there are a couple of antagonistic ying and yang effects, big hyaluronan is good for cell proliferation in certain cell types but small molecular weight will kill other ones, so I think we're just learning the code and we don't know everything yet.

Summary

by Paul L. DeAngelis

Throughout my scientific career, I have focused on glycobiology, the science studying the roles that complex carbohydrates play in living systems. Currently, my laboratory is researching polysaccharide biosynthesis at the molecular level. In particular, we are exploring the production of an essential class of polymers called glycosaminoglycans; these carbohydrate molecules are essential for higher animals are utilized as well as virulence factors for certain pathogenic bacteria. The enzymes that catalyze glycosaminoglycan synthesis, called synthases, have proven novel and fascinating.

Training and Research

As an undergraduate researcher at Harvard in the laboratory of Dr. Arthur Ayers for three years, I explored the carbohydrate structures of fungal pathogens that the plant hosts detected as "foreign"; the plants then respond by secreting poisons to kill the invading fungus. I designed and created a series of synthetic structural mimics for the fungal molecules to identify the essential features.

As a graduate student at University of California, Irvine, with Dr. Charles Glabe, I elucidated some of the details surrounding the sperm/egg interaction during fertilization. My experiments proved that sulfate groups were critical elements of the egg surface sugars; in contrast, the leading theory at the time was that a lectin-like interaction was key for fertilization. I also found that certain residues of the sperm adhesive protein specifically bound the egg sugars.

As a postdoctoral researcher in the laboratory of Dr. Paul Weigel at the University of Texas Medical Branch at Galveston, I began the study of polysaccharide biosynthesis. I proposed and executed a plan to identify the enzyme that produces the hyaluronic acid [HA] capsule of the human bacterial pathogen, Group A Streptococcus. This enzyme was unique in the glycobiology field, as it was the first enzyme proven to transfer two distinct sugars; in contrast, the usual "dogma" of Glycobiology is that one enzyme transfers one sugar. The identification of the streptococcal enzyme also allowed me to predict a candidate, a sequenced frog gene with no proven function, for the elusive vertebrate HA synthase enzyme.

Current Research

As an independent investigator at the University of Oklahoma Health Sciences Center, I have discovered two new HA microbial synthases (besides the streptococcal enzyme) as well as confirmed the identity of the vertebrate HA synthases. The main contributions to the field was the further delineation of conserved residues that are most likely essential for function as well as the observation of a new class of enzyme. The first discovery was that a virus that infects algae was found to encode a HA synthase. This finding had two important impacts: (a) the initial discovery of HA in the plant kingdom (no other known plant polymer is similar) and (b) the initial, and as yet only, account of a virus encoding a glycosyltransferase (in all known cases, the virus normally pirates the host cell system and does not encode any such enzyme). The sequence for the virus enzyme is very similar to the vertebrate and streptococcal enzymes. Certain regions of the enzymes from the various sources are identical or very similar, implying that these residues are important for structure or function. In a second discovery, I discovered a new bacterial HA synthase from the Gram-negative bacterium *Pasteurella multocida*, the causative agent of fowl cholera and pasteurellosis. The *P. multocida* enzyme had a distinct sequence and does not resemble the vertebrate, streptococcal, or viral HA synthases. Therefore, at least two independent means have evolved to synthesize the HAS polysaccharide from the same precursors. The *P. multocida* enzyme had distinct reaction mechanism from the vertebrate and streptococcal enzyme.

In addition to HA synthases, I recently reported the identification and cloning of the first chondroitin synthase from any source. The enzyme resembles the *P. multocida* HA synthase, but it has different sugar transfer specificity. I also discovered two new heparosan (unsulfated, unepimerized heparin) synthases; they are very distinct from the HA and chondroitin synthases. The biosynthesis of the three major glycosaminoglycans is being studied in my laboratory.

After 30 years of study by several groups around the world, I definitively elucidated the molecular directionality of HA biosynthesis for one of the HA synthases. My laboratory also used molecular biology and enzymology approaches to conclusively show that the *P. multocida* HA synthase contains two distinct domains that are each responsible for transferring one of the sugars.

The basic science knowledge on synthases obtained above was then utilized by my laboratory to make various glycosaminoglycans with defined structures. Polymers with very narrow size distributions were made by either step-wise reactions for oligosaccharides or by synchronized reactions for polysaccharides. Such reagents should be useful to tease apart the biological effects attributed to this class of carbohydrates as well as facilitate production of better therapeutics. In addition, the synthesis of novel polysaccharides with new chemical functionalities was developed. These reagents are useful for understanding the nature of sugar/protein binding specificity as well as potentially creating therapeutic embodiments such as anticoagulants, tissue engineering scaffolds or drug-conjugates.

Current Research Goals

My laboratory has three main research thrusts on polysaccharide biosynthesis: (1) pursuit of basic science knowledge of catalysis, (2) exploration of disease processes with defined sugar tools, and (3) development of novel biomaterials. The catalytic mechanisms of polysaccharide production are, for the most part, unknown. The glycosaminoglycans hyaluronic acid, chondroitin and heparosan were chosen for study, as these polymers are important for medicine and biotechnology. The tools of enzymology, molecular biology, biochemistry and carbohydrate chemistry are utilized to unravel this puzzle. Due to the difficulties with understanding polymerization at the molecular level, data derived from all these approaches are required to develop and to test our theories.

Bibliography*

Hyaluronan-Related Publications

1. DeAngelis, P.L., Papaconstantinou, J., and Weigel, P.H. (1993). Molecular cloning, identification, and sequence of the hyaluronan synthase gene from Group A *Streptococcus pyogenes*. J Biol Chem 268 (26), 19181-19184.

2. DeAngelis, P.L., Papaconstantinou, J., and Weigel, P.H. (1993). Isolation of a *Streptococcus pyogenes* gene locus that directs hyaluronan biosynthesis in acapsular mutants and in heterologous bacteria. J Biol Chem 268 (20), 14568-14571.

3. DeAngelis, P.L., and Weigel, P.H. (1994). Immunochemical confirmation of the primary structure of streptococcal hyaluronan synthase and synthesis of high molecular weight product by the recombinant enzyme. Biochemistry 33 (31), 9033-9039.

4. DeAngelis, P.L., and Weigel, P.H. (1994). Rapid detection of hyaluronic acid capsules on group A streptococci by buoyant density centrifugation. Diagn Microbiol Infect Dis 20 (2), 77-80.

5. DeAngelis, P.L., Yang, N., and Weigel, P. H. (1994). The *Streptococcus pyogenes* hyaluronan synthase: sequence comparison and conversation amoung various group A strains. Biochim Biophys Res Commun 199 (1), 1-10.

6. DeAngelis, P.L., and Weigel, P.H. (1995). Characterization of the recombinant hyaluronic acid synthase from *Streptococcus pyogenes*. Dev Biol Stand 85, 225-229.

7. DeAngelis, P.L. (1996). Enzymological characterization of the *Pasteurella multocida* hyaluronic acid synthase. Biochem 35, 9768-9771.

8. DeAngelis, P.L., and Achyuthan, A. M. (1996). Yeast-derived recombinant DG42 protein of *Xenopus* can synthesize hyaluronan *in vitro*. J Biol Chem 271, 23657-23660.

9. DeAngelis, P.L., Jing, W., Graves, M. V., Burbank, D. E., and Van Etten, J. L. (1997). Hyaluronan synthase of *Chlorella* virus PBCV-1. Science 278, 1800-1803.

10. DeAngelis, P.L., Jing, W., Drake, R. R., and Achyuthan, A. M. (1998). Identification and molecular cloning of a unique hyaluronan synthase from *Pasteurella multocida*. J Biochem 273, 8454-8458.

---

* Provided by the interviewee.

11. Pummill, P. E., Achyuthan, A. M., and DeAngelis, P.L. (1998). Enzymological characterization of recombinant *Xenopus* DG42, a vertebrate hyaluronan synthase. J Biol Chem 273, 4976-4981.

12. Weigel, P., DeAngelis, P.L., and Papaconstantinou, J. (1998). Hyaluronate synthase gene and uses thereof. US 6,455,304 B1 (The Board of Regents of the University of Oklahoma, Norman, OK, assignee). September 24, 2002.

13. DeAngelis, P.L. (1999). Hyaluronan synthases: fascinating glycosyltransferases from vertebrates, bacterial pathogens, and algal viruses. Cell Mol Life Sci 56, 670-682.

14. DeAngelis, P.L. (1999). Molecular directionality of polysaccharide polymerization by the *Pasteurella multocida* hyaluronan synthase. J Biol Chem 274, 26557-26562.

15. Graves, M. V., Burbank, D. E., Roth, R., Heuser, J., DeAngelis, P.L., and Van Etten, J. L. (1999). Hyaluronan synthesis in virus PBCV-1-infected *Chlorella*-like green algae. Virology 257, 15-23.

16. DeAngelis, P.L., and Padgett-McCue, A. J. (2000). Identification and molecular cloning of a chondroitin synthase from *Pasteurella multocida* type F. J Biol Chem 275 (31), 24124-24129.

17. Jing, W., and DeAngelis, P.L. (2000). Dissection of the two transferase activities of the *Pasteurella multocida* hyaluronan synthase: two active sites exist in one polypeptide. Glycobiology 10, 883.

18. DeAngelis, P.L. (2001). Novel hyaluronan synthases from *Chlorella* viruses and *Pasteurella* bacteria. In *Glycoforum. Hyaluronan Today* (Eds. Hascall, V.C. and Yanagishita, M.) (Seikagaku Corporation Glycoforum) (Accessed at http://www.glycoforum.gr.jp/science/hyaluronan/HA19/HA19E.html) Tokyo (JP).

19. Heldermon, C., DeAngelis, P.L., and Weigel, P. H. (2001). Topological organization of the hyaluronan synthase from *Streptococcus pyogenes*. J Biol Chem 276 (3), 2037-2046.

20. Pummill, P. E., Kempner, E. S., Ellis, S., and DeAngelis, P.L. (2001). Functional molecular mass of a vertebrate hyaluronan synthase as determined by radiation inactivation analysis. J Biol Chem 276, 39832.

21. DeAngelis, P.L. (2002). Hyaluronan synthases: mechanistic studies and biotechnological applications. In *Hyaluronan Volume 1 Chemical, Biochemical and Biological Aspects* (Eds. Kennedy, J. F., Phillips, G. O., Williams, P.A., and Hascall, V.C.), Woodhead, Cambridge (UK), 227-236.

22. DeAngelis, P.L. (2002). Microbial glycosaminoglycan glycosyltransferases. Glycobiology 12 (1), 9R-16R.

23. DeAngelis, P.L., Gunay, N. S., Toida, T., Mao, W. J., and Linhardt, R. J. (2002). Identification of the capsular polysaccharides of Type D and F *Pasteurella*

multocida as unmodified heparin and chondroitin, respectively. Carbohydr Res 337 (17), 1547-1552.

24. Blundell, C. D., Mahoney, D. J., Almond, A., DeAngelis, P.L., Kahmann, J. D., Teriete, P., Pickford, A. R., Campbell, I. D., and Day, A. J. (2003). The link module from ovulation- and inflammation-associated protein TSG-6 changes conformation on hyaluronan binding. J Biol Chem 278 (49), 49261-49270.

25. DeAngelis, P.L., Oatman, L. C., and Gay, D. F. (2003). Rapid chemoenzymatic synthesis of monodisperse hyaluronan oligosaccharides with immobilized enzyme reactors. J Biol Chem 278 (37), 35199-35203.

26. Jing, W., and DeAngelis, P.L. (2003). Analysis of the two active sites of the hyaluronan synthase and the chondroitin synthase of *Pasteurella multocida*. Glycobiology 13, 661-671.

27. Pummill, P. E., and DeAngelis, P.L. (2003). Alteration of polysaccharide size distribution of a vertebrate hyaluronan synthase by mutation. J Biol Chem 278, 19808-19814.

28. Blundell, C. D., DeAngelis, P.L., Day, A. J., and Almond, A. (2004). Use of 15N-NMR to resolve molecular details in isotopically-enriched carbohydrates: sequence-specific observations in hyaluronan oligomers up to decasaccharides. Glycobiology 14 (11), 999-1009.

29. DeAngelis, P.L., and White, C. L. (2004). Identification of a distinct, cryptic heparosan synthase from *Pasteurella multocida* types A, D, and F. J Bacteriol 186 (24), 8529-8532.

30. Jing, W., and DeAngelis, P.L. (2004). Synchronized chemoenzymatic synthesis of monodisperse hyaluronan polymers. J Biol Chem 279 (40), 42345-42349.

31. Almond, A., Colebrooke, S. A., DeAngelis, P.L., Mahoney, D. J., Day, A. J., and Blundell, C. D. (2005). Dynamic conformational predictions for hyaluronan: using NMR to confirm aqueous simulations. In *Hyaluronan Structure, Metabolism, Biological Activities, Therapeutic Applications Volume I* (Eds. Balazs, E.A., and Hascall, V.C.), Matrix Biology Institute, Edgewater, NJ 07020 (USA), 3-6.

32. Almond, A., DeAngelis, P.L., and Blundell, C. D. (2005). Dynamics of hyaluronan oligosaccharides revealed by 15N relaxation. J Am Chem Soc 127 (4), 1086-1087.

33. Blundell, C. D., Almond, A., Mahoney, D. J., DeAngelis, P.L., Campbell, I. D., and Day, A. J. (2005). Towards a structure for a TSG-6.hyaluronan complex by modeling and NMR spectroscopy: insights into other members of the link module superfamily. J Biol Chem 280 (18), 18189-18201.

34. Bodevin-Authelet, S., Kusche-Gullberg, M., Pummill, P. E., DeAngelis, P.L., and Lindahl, U. (2005). Biosynthesis of hyaluronan: direction of chain elongation. J Biol Chem 280 (10), 8813-8818.

35. Colebrooke, S. A., Blundell, C. D., DeAngelis, P.L., Campbell, I. D., and Almond, A. (2005). Exploiting the carboxylate chemical shift to resolve degenerate resonances in spectra of 13C-labelled glycosaminoglycans. Magn Reson Chem 43 (10), 805-815.

36. Jing, W., O'Bar, A., Oatman, L. C., and DeAngelis, P.L. (2005). Production of defined monodisperse hyaluronan polmers with the *Pasteurella* hyaluronan synthase; new tools for invesigating HA Biology--"SelectHA". In *Hyaluronan: Structure, Metabolism, Biological Activities, Therapeutic Applications Volume I* (Eds. Balazs, E.A. and Hascall, V.C.), Matrix Biology Institute, Edgewater, NJ (USA), 155-158.

37. Pummill, P. E., and DeAngelis, P.L. (2005). Vertebrate hyaluronan synthase: functional unit mass, UDP-sugar precursor structural requirements, and product size control. In *Hyaluronan: Structure, Metabolism, Biological Activities, Therapeutic Applications Volume I* (Eds. Balazs, E.A. , and Hascall, V.C.), Matrix Biology Institute, Edgewater, NJ (USA), 165-171.

38. Widner, B., Behr, R., Von Dollen, S., Tang, M., Heu, T., Sloma, A., Sternberg, D., DeAngelis, P.L., Weigel, P. H., and Brown, S. (2005). Hyaluronic acid production in *Bacillus subtilis*. Appl Environ Microbiol 71 (7), 3747-3752.

39. Williams, K. J., Halkes, K. M., Kamerling, J. P., and DeAngelis, P.L. (2005). Critical elements of oligosaccharide acceptor substrates for the *Pasteurella multocida* hyaluronan synthase. J Biol Chem 281 (9), 5391-5397.

40. Almond, A., DeAngelis, P.L., and Blundell, C. D. (2006). Hyaluronan: the local solution conformation determined by NMR and computer modeling is close to a contracted left-handed 4-fold helix. J Mol Biol 358 (5), 1256-1269.

41. Blundell, C. D., DeAngelis, P.L., and Almond, A. (2006). Hyaluronan: the absence of amide-carboxylate hydrogen bonds and the chain conformation in aqueous solution are incompatible with stable secondary and tertiary structure models. Biochem J 396 (3), 487-498.

42. Jing, W., Michael Haller, F., Almond, A., and DeAngelis, P.L. (2006). Defined megadalton hyaluronan polymer standards. Anal Biochem 355 (2), 183-188.

43. Pummill, P. E., Kane, T. A., Kempner, E. S., and DeAngelis, P.L. (2007). The functional molecular mass of the *Pasteurella* hyaluronan synthase is a monomer. Biochim Biophys Acta 1770 (2), 286-290.

44. Tracy, B. S., Avci, F. Y., Linhardt, R. J., and DeAngelis, P.L. (2007). Acceptor specificity of the *Pasteurella* hyaluronan and chondroitin synthases and production of chimeric glycosaminoglycans. J Biol Chem 282 (1), 337-344.

45. Weigel, P. H., and DeAngelis, P.L. (2007). Hyaluronan synthases: A decade-plus of novel glycosyltransferases. J Biol Chem 282 (51), 36777-36781.

Timothy Hardingham, 2003
(photograph courtesy of T. Hardingham)

Timothy
Hardingham

Timothy E. Hardingham (b. 1942, Norfolk, UK) received his B.Sc. degree (1965) in Biochemistry as well as his Ph.D. (1968) and D.Sc. (1984) degrees at the University of Bristol. He held a fellowship (1968-71), was Deputy Head (1971-86), and subsequently Head of the Biochemistry Division (1986-94) at the Kennedy Institute of Rheumatology. He then relocated to become Professor of Biochemistry in the Wellcome Trust Centre for Cell-Matrix-Research, Faculty of Life Sciences, University of Manchester and is the founding Director of the UK Centre for Tissue Engineering, University of Manchester.

Dr. Hardingham received the Colworth Medal of the Biochemical Society of the UK (1978) and won the Roussel International Award for Scientific Research into Osteoarthritis (1989) and the Carol Nachman Inter-national Prize for Rheumatology (1991). He is a founding member of the International Society for Hyaluronan Sciences (ISHAS). He is also a member of several other scientific societies and has served on the editorial boards of different scientific journals.

Interview*

How did you get involved with the hyaluronan field?

I came into contact with glycosaminoglycans (GAG; then known as mucopolysaccharides) from the very start of my research career, which was as a Ph.D. student with a young lecturer in Bristol called Charles Phelps. Charles had been himself a student of Sandy Ogston. He did his D.Phil. in Oxford with Sandy, but then moved to Bristol and it was at Bristol, where I graduated and enrolled with Charles to do a Ph.D. Charles was trained as a biophysicist, but he chose a project for me that was very much synthetic chemistry and biochemistry. I always felt that I was to be the route by which he would gain insight into biochemical approaches. The first year of my work was a disaster. Charles wanted me to chemically synthesise nucleotide sugar intermediates for biosynthetic experiments. Their synthesis was a multistep process and we were not equipped for organic chemistry, with the need for ultra-high vacuum, inert gases and palladium catalysts, which all left me cold! Basically, I made very little headway in the first year and we decided to cut the losses and chose a different approach. Schiller and Dorfman had just published on mucopolysaccharide biosynthesis in young rat skin and so I set about investigating the nucleotide sugar intermediates involved in their biosynthesis. This approach to the problem better suited my interest, and perhaps more importantly, my skills. Work went well and I established techniques for in vivo radiolabelling with ^{14}C-glucose, by peritoneal injection in 3-day-old rats and then extracting and chromatographically separating the nucleotide sugar intermediates at various times from 30 min to 24h after the injection. The young rat skin at this age accounts for 25% of the total body weight and its rate of growth is very fast and glycosaminoglycan production is very active.

---

* This interview was recorded during the first meeting "Conversations on Hyaluronan" in St. Tropez, September 2002.

It therefore provided a good system for this analysis. Hyaluronan accounts for about 60 % of the glycosaminoglycan in the skin and so this was my first encounter with HA. The work was published in 2 papers in *The Biochemical Journal*, one on the sugar intermediates and one on the glycosaminoglycan composition of young rat skin.

Did you ever meet Ogston?

Yes, I met him, but much later, when I was no longer with Charles, and after Sandy had returned from Australia to take the position of Master of Trinity College, Oxford. The background to my visit to see Sandy was during a very important stage of my career and I'll outline that first, before describing my visit to Sandy Ogston in Oxford.

When I left Bristol as a new Ph.D. graduate, I went to London and worked with Helen Muir at the Kennedy Institute of Rheumatology. Helen was then a leading international figure in the protein-polysaccharide field. Her background, in contrast to Charles Phelps, was more chemistry than physics. She had made her name by identifying serine as the amino acid involved in the chemical linkage between chondroitin sulphate and protein. This she published in 1958 in *The Biochemical Journal* and this marked the "birth of proteoglycans", as until this point there was great controversy on the link, or lack of link, between protein and chondroitin sulphate. The views of Karl Meyer had led the field and had showed no protein linkage for HA and this appeared to provide the template for the other glycosaminoglycans, but as Helen's result began to establish, the other GAGs did not follow the pattern of HA, but were a new class of protein-polysaccharide conjugates, later known as proteoglycans. So Helen's group at the Kennedy was involved in gaining a better understanding of cartilage proteoglycans, which at the time were regarded as polydisperse and heterogeneous complexes formed of one or many protein-polysaccharide components.

Left to right: Con Tsiganos, Dick Heinegård, Tim Hardingham, Roger Ewins, Michael Dean, and Elsemaree Baxter at the Kennedy Institute in London, 1969 (all photographs courtesy of T. Hardingham)

Tim Hardingham and Roger Ewins at the Kennedy Inst about 1973, looking at the hexosamine analyser

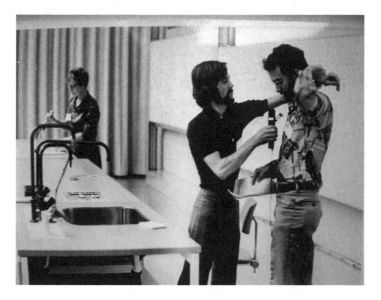

Tim Hardingham and Vince Hascall in Uppsala circa 1974
(the late Helen Muir in the background) and Tim fixing Vince's microphone.

Steve Carney, Tony Ratcliffe, Bruce Caterson, the late Helen Muir, Tim
Hardingham, and the late Mike Bayliss in the Kennedy Institute garden, 1987

I started to work with Helen in 1968 initially on the biosynthesis of cartilage proteoglycans. When I arrived at the lab Dick Heinegård was there on study leave from Lund and also Ken Brandt, who later became a leading rheumatologist back in the USA and a senior post-doc Con Tsiganos, who trained in Australia with Dennis Lowther, but came from Greece and who I worked closely with initially. It was a lively research environment and rather quickly we made interesting and important discoveries. The major discovery was the first identification of hyaluronan in cartilage as an organizer of cartilage proteoglycans. The discovery was surprising as it appeared to contradict newly published work in which Vince Hascall, working with Stan Sajdera, had established the principle of how the proteoglycans in cartilage formed supramolecular aggregates. But in their first papers they had no awareness of hyaluronan in the system, so their model involved aggregation of these large proteoglycans through a protein, which they had separated and called link-protein. In London we had tried to recapitulate these results, but our results were somewhat different, as in our hands link protein alone had no ability to aggregate proteoglycans and it was a great challenge for us to try and understand why the results differed.

How did you find out that hyaluronan had an important role?

Hyaluronan was identified by tracking down what was responsible for forming aggregates with proteoglycans in our test system. I assessed interaction by mixing active fractions with proteoglycan purified as decribed by Hascall and Sajdera, and chromatographing the mixture on a long (1,800mm) thin (9mm) cross-linked agarose gel filtration column. Active fractions moved the proteoglycan into the void volume of the column. This provided a simple, although not very rapid assay, as it took about a day (overnight) to run the column and analyse the column fractions. I tracked down a component that caused the formation of these aggregates and to do this I started with a density gradient fractionation of cartilage proteoglycan in 4M guanidine HCl. The active fraction from the gradient was low in protein and low in proteoglycan and I attempted to purify it from this fraction. From a range of techniques tried, ion exchange chromatography on Ecteola cellulose (anion exchanger) was the most successful, which suggested that the active fraction was negatively charged. On this column the active fraction eluted at lower ionic strength than proteoglycan and the protein content was now even lower and the UV absorbance showed there was negligible RNA/DNA, but it did still contain a significant amount of uronic acid. So a low charged uronic acid containing polymer, such as hyaluronan, was now surprisingly a candidate.

I then showed that, although the activity was unaffected by mild acid or mild alkali and it was insensitive to proteinase treatment, it was however degraded by hyaluronidase. I also prepared sufficient of the Ecteola cellulose fraction to do an infrared spectrum, which showed that the IR spectrum was very similar to hyaluronan and showed no trace of sulfate. I compared what we had extracted, with commercially available hyaluronan, and the commercial sample mimicked the properties I had with the component extracted from the tissue—so we had the proof of the identity that the active fraction was hyaluronan.. Experiments on the stoichiometry of interaction, assessed similarly by gel chromatography, showed its potency. Because each hyaluronan chain can bind up to over 100 proteoglycans, when they are mixed in equal amounts there is only a very modest effect, because each aggregate formed is one aggrecan per hyaluronan, but as the amount of hyaluronan in the mixture is reduced, each aggregate now contains several proteoglycans and when the hyaluronan is only 1% of the mixture, each aggregate contains ~100 proteoglycans and they are very large. So there is an optimum concentration of hyaluronan, which at ~1% of the proteogycan causes maximum aggregation.

This evidence that hyaluronan could cause proteoglycan aggregation was at this stage only a part of the story as there remained a major dilemma. At the Kennedy Institute we had a limited amount of biophysical equipment with no analytical ultracentrifugation as used by Hascall and Sajdera, so most of my results relied on viscometry and gel chromatography. Using these techniques I was able to isolate components from cartilage that would increase viscosity and form high molecular weight species when mixed with the cartilage proteoglycan. This effect as we now know is independent of any protein, but what I couldn't demonstrate, which was the essence of Vince and Stan's work, was the generation of a fast sedimenting species in the analytical centrifuge. With Helen, we didn't have our own centrifuge, so we had to do that work with a collaborator at St. Mary's Hospital Medical Centre, who had an analytical centrifuge. In hindsight, it was our unfamiliarity with the issues and our collaborator's experience with proteins that led him to do our experiments with concentrations that were too high! For at high concentration, as I found out later, you would never see the aggregated species, because the sedimentation behavior of these high molecular weight proteoglycans is so concentration-dependent that the sedimentation rate of monomeric species and aggregated species become the same at 4mg/ml, which was the concentration at which our collaborator typically studied small proteins!

You didn't vary the concentration?

Well, we were doing it through the collaborator and it was his advice that guided what concentration we needed. A high concentration was necessary to get a good image of the sedimentation profile, so you couldn't work at lower concentrations at that time with the optics on the ultracentrifuge being used. Our detective work had enabled us to identify hyaluronan as the agent, which caused the aggregation we detected by gel chromatography and viscometry. This was a fascinating discovery at the time as no-one thought hyaluronan was in cartilage, and an interation between a long chain polyanion and a high molecular weight branched polyanion, seemed to be a very challenging concept. It was also the first demonstration of a hyaluronan binding protein in extracellular matrix. Although at the time I demonstrated that purified hyaluronan isolated from any source could cause the effect detected by gel filtration and viscometry, we still couldn't understand why our results didn't mimic those of Vince and Stan Sajdera in the ultracentrifuge. So Helen suggested that we go and see Sandy Ogston, who was the biophysical "guru" who understood all these effects. So we took our data and our model of how proteoglycan from cartilage was binding to hyaluronan (see Figure 1).

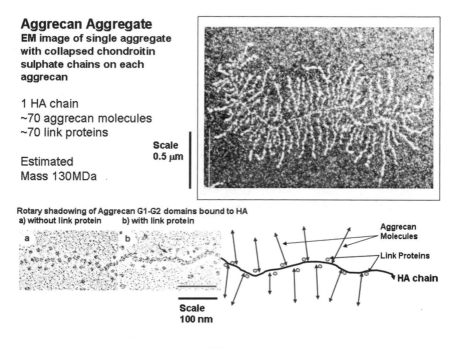

Aggrecan Aggregate
EM image of single aggregate with collapsed chondroitin sulphate chains on each aggrecan

1 HA chain
~70 aggrecan molecules
~70 link proteins

Estimated
Mass 130MDa

Scale
0.5 μm

Rotary shadowing of Aggrecan G1-G2 domains bound to HA
a) without link protein   b) with link protein

Aggrecan Molecules
Link Proteins
HA chain

Scale
100 nm

Figure 1.

At that time Sandy was back in Oxford, where he was now Master of Trinity College. It was a lovely summer day and we met in the Master's Garden at Trinity. It was a beautiful, peaceful environment and Sandy suggested we sat in the garden and we talked about our problems. There was blue sky, butterflies all around and he wanted me to explain what our observations were. I told him what evidence we had and what we felt we were missing. He said, well, gel chromatography was a very non-quantitative technique, it wasn't really what a numerate scientist would rely on. He said, "you have this model, with one large polyanion polymer, which was the cartilage proteoglycan (aggrecan), which has all these negatively charged chondriotin sulfate chains, and you're suggesting it binds to this other negatively charged polyanion, hyaluronan." While he was saying this, I was thinking that to Sandy, who is so used to these polymer properties, it must be sounding very unlikely that two polyanions can bind specifically together. He asked "what about the ultracentrifuge?" We had to tell him that we actually didn't see anything there. Sandy was stroking his chin and I felt that all was dissolving before my eyes. He was really feeling quite skeptical and I couldn't think of an argument that would be more persuasive. His view was that gel chromatography was the sort of thing in which you can get all sorts of artifacts—and he was the expert in that field. He worked and established theories on what the fundamentals of the technique were, so we left with the feeling that we convinced Sandy Ogston of nothing. He was skeptical of our evidence. On the other hand, I had been working on this for 3 years, which was a long time, so I had confidence that the effect was real, but it still took me maybe another year until we finally realized what the problem was. Eventually, we got our own ultracentrifuge, which was a more modern version with transmission optics and we could work at much lower concentrations—and then, suddenly, the door opened to understanding what we had seen and how it did create fast sedimenting species. But the lasting impression of that day, when we visited Sandy Ogston at Trinity College, always stuck with me. I had gone there with such excitement to persuade someone I respected so much in the whole field, of a new discovery concerning the biological function of these major ECM components, but I convinced him of nothing and that was a big, big anti-climax.

Was Helen also skeptical?

No. She had much less of a biophysical insight and she didn't pretend to understand that area, so she still had a belief in it, but realized we didn't have the evidence to persuade those that would challenge the concept in a rigorous way. I don't think that was unfair—it needed more substantial proof to carry it. Interestingly, it made us become more organized to gain that extra bit of proof, that extra bit of data that would be more persuasive for a skeptical audience.

In addition to Ogston, whom would you mention as influential on your career?

Vince has been one of the biggest influences on me in this field, because he has always been very open about scientific results. He was instrumental in setting standards about being open, because there was a bunch of scientists like Karl Meyer and Albert Dorfman, who were the forerunners and who were very combative and very secretive. I suppose that was more normal in those days. Vince was very influential in making it a field full of people that talked a lot with each other. It was a fast expanding field and I believe it is better to encourage others to think and get ideas; there was lots of opportunity for new things to be done the whole time. In many fields, science can be competitive and secretive as many people are working on the same things. They become paranoid about knowing what other people find out about what they do. If a field is young and developing there is ample scope for everyone to work non-competitively on aspects they make their own and Vince was a big influence in making this a friendly research community and this was greatly helped by other leading individuals like, Dick Heinegård, Larry Rosenberg, Bruce Caterson, Brian Toole and Koji Kimata and many others that followed.

I first met Vince quite soon after we figured out the meaning of our proteoglycan and hyaluronan experiments. It was at the International Congress of Biochemistry in Stockholm, in 1972. We then kept up some dialog and I later went to the States to work with him in 1975 at NIH funded by an MRC traveling Fellowship. That was good fun. There were many visitors to Vince's lab at NIH and I met and interacted with a whole range of new contacts. Vince was an excellent host and this was a most important learning experience for me. It was also where I first learnt cell culture. This was with a nice young American from Hawaii, Jim Kimura. We worked with Swarm rat chondrosarcoma cells and investigated the biosynthesis and secretion of cartilage proteoglycan and the site of proteoglycan aggregation with hyaluronan and link protein. This work involved major pulse-label studies with radioactive sulfate and we demonstrated quite elegantly the kinetics of synthesis and secretion of proteoglycan and we showed that aggregation was an extracellular event and that the link-protein added extra stability to the proteoglycan-hyaluronan bond, which is work we published in two *J. Biol. Chem.* papers. Looking back it always amazed me how much radioactive sulfate we would go through in an experiment, which was typically tens of millicuries and most of it ended up in disposable bins in the lab still within G25 columns we used for separating incorporated isotope from free sulfate. We established quite a production line and my record was running and counting the radioactivity in 80 of these G25 columns in a day!

I followed this work up when I returned to London and showed the function of link protein in stabilizing the proteoglycan aggregate with hyaluronan. This showed that in the absence of link protein proteoglycan binding to HA was reversible, but when aggregation was carried out with link protein the binding was much tighter and there was no detectible dissociation over 3 days under physiological conditions of pH and ionic strength. This established the principle that link protein "locked" the proteoglycan onto the hyaluronan chain and would therefore be important in determining its stability in the cartilage matrix. Later in collaboration with Van Mow at Columbia, New York, we showed how link protein had a major impact on the viscoelastic properties of proteoglycan aggregates and was therefore a key component in determining aggregate function in cartilage tissues.

In following up the biosynthesis of proteoglycans, link protein and hyaluronan I went on to show that hyaluronan was biosynthesized in a different cellular compartment from proteoglycan and link protein. This was based on the use of agents to disrupt the secretary pathway common to all proteins destined for secretion, which guided proteins from the rough endoplasmic reticulum through the Golgi, to secretory vesicles and out of the cell. The production of proteoglycan and link protein were both blocked by the ionophore monensin, as it prevented translocation in and out of the Golgi, but this had no affect of the production and secretion of hyaluronan. This fitted in with a model of hyaluronan biosynthesis at the cell surface quite separate from the secretory pathway and it also explained why aggregation was extracellular, as proteoglycan and hyaluronan were separate until the proteoglycan was secreted from the cell. Proteoglycan aggregation was thus an extracellular assembly mechanism to sequester and immobilize proteoglycan within the cartilage matrix and it is by this means that the extremely high concentration of proteoglycan (>50mg/ml) is maintained in cartilage, which creates the high osmotic swelling pressure and gives the tissue its compressive resilience and ability to withstand load.

You have also been involved with the molecular structure of hyaluronan, but could you specify your studies as molecular structure has a very broad meaning.

In early 1970s viscosimetry and gel chromatography of hyaluronan became common research tools. I followed the literature and although I didn't do much myself at this time on the properties of hyaluronan on its own, I became familiar with techniques that you could use to determine its molecular weight and molecular weight distribution. We extracted hyaluronan from cartilage. Until that time it was not thought to be a component of cartilage because it's only about 1 percent of the glycosaminoglycans there, so it was not picked up. But then we showed that it was present in all cartilaginous tissues at this level. So it was a "minor" component, but it had a major organizing function. We also developed in my lab at different times two assays for hyaluronan, based on its specific binding to aggrecan, the major cartilage proteoglycan.

More details of the molecular organization of hyaluronan with proteoglycan aggregates came from other techniques we became involved with. This included collaborative work I initiated with Jurgen Engel in Basel. By using rotary shadowing EM we were able to get detailed images of proteoglycan aggregates and the assembled complexes from the isolated sub-domains of the proteoglycan aggrecan with hyaluronan. By this time (1984-7) the first sequence structure of aggrecan was determined, which revealed its multi-domain structure. The rotary shadowing enabled the two N-terminal domains of aggrecan to be visualized and showed clearly that only one of the domains was involved in aggregation, even though both domains contained related putative hyaluronan binding sequences. This was also supported by the isolation of the separate domains and demonstration of the interaction between aggrecan G1 domain with hyaluronan and link protein and the inactivity of the isolated G2 domain. In these images (see Figure 1) the compact protein domains provide the most clearly identified structures and the hyaluronan is only evident from the way it links the domains together, but it also revealed the spacing of adjacent domains on the hyaluronan and provided evidence of non-cooperativity between adjacent G1 domains, but close association between G1 and link protein. The principles established in proteoglycan aggregation were later extended to other members of the aggrecan family, versican, neurocan and brevican, which all show properties of aggregation with hyaluronan.

The other area of structure where I have made a major contribution is in assessing hyaluronan solution structure and properties. A new approach to this issue was made possible when together with Phil Gribbon I developed in 1996-8, fluorescence recovery after photo-bleaching (confocal-FRAP) to assess intermolecular interactions of polymers in solution. The technique enables measurements of molecular diffusion to assess interaction in dilute, or concentrated solutions and most importantly, the measurements are made at equilibrium. The technique therefore has none of the problems associated with many biophysical techniques involving non-ideal effects of concentration boundaries, or gradients, or fluid flow and it can look at solution properties at high concentrations where intermolecular interactions are maximized. Our work showed unequivocally that hyaluronan behaved as a stiffened random coil, which at higher concentrations showed intermolecular interactions entirely predicted by entanglement. There was no evidence, under a broad range of supporting electrolyte, physiological pH and temperature, for "self-association" between hyaluronan chains, which had been proposed based on other indirect experiments. Hyaluronan thus behaves as a classic polymer and its viscoelastic properties can be entirely understood as a consequence of the stiffening provided by a range of dynamic hydrogen bonds between adjacent sugars. This is also compatible with its failure to form a "gel, as at any concentration, it remains a viscoelastic liquid. Incidentally, it is also compatible with the fact that hyaluronan can easily be separated by gel chromatography into different molecular weight fractions, which would not be possible with a strongly self-associating polymer.

As the confocal-FRAP technique can be used to measure tracer diffusion as well as self-diffusion it enabled the porosity of hyaluronan solutions to be determined and this permitted an evaluation of the anomalous behaviour of hyaluronan at pH 2.4 originally reported by Balazs. At this pH, hyaluronan was originally described by Balazs to form a viscoelastic putty. Indeed, self-diffusion measurements by confocal-FRAP showed a sharp fall of diffusion in a narrow range pH

2.2-2.7. This was compatible with an increase in size, or an increase in intermolecular interaction. The tracer diffusion measurements made using FITC-polystyrene beads showed that at pH 2.5 there was an increase in the apparent pore size of the solution. At the time this was a surprising result as it showed that the decreased self-diffusion was accompanied by an increase in porosity. However, with a little thought, it was clear that there was a simple explanation to these two changes. The decrease in self-diffusion at pH 2.5 was most likely caused by intermolecular chain association decreasing molecular mobility, but the clustering of chains caused by chain-chain interaction would also create an increase in the pore size of the hyaluronan network. This intermolecular interaction was clearly absent above pH 2.8 and below pH 2.2, so it appeared to be a special pH-dependent property that might involve the partial ionization of carboxyl groups, which occurred at pH 2.5, but not above, or below this pH. So this new technology gave us further insight into another old unresolved question.

My Perspective

Timothy Hardingham

Looking back, hyaluronan has been a thread running through my whole career and it has always had that combined interest of biophysics and biology, which has ideally matched my own interests. My interest in hyaluronan has spanned over 5 decades from the nineteen sixties until now (2008). What has changed remarkably in that time is our whole perception and understanding of biology and biological systems. There have also been revolutionary developments in the tools we have to investigate biological processes. The basic concepts of hyaluronan structure and physical properties were established when I started in this field, but the understanding of its biological function was poorly developed. It has been fascinating that as biology has advanced it has raised many new questions about hyaluronan and revealed many new aspects of hyaluronan function. My claim to fame in the hyaluronan world is that I discovered the first example of a hyaluronan-protein ligand interaction that was highly specific. This revealed an animal lectin function that was previously unexpected in extracellular matrix components in animal tissues and especially in proteoglycans, like aggrecan. So at the time it was very surprising, but we can now look back and see it as the first of many such interactions, which are now seen as common-place, to the extent that we are quite surprised if every matrix molecule doesn't interact with a myriad of others.

Where there is still room to gain greater understanding in biology, is in aspects of molecular events within tissues, where environments are crowded, water is more limited and nothing is at equilibrium. We have also yet to get a good handle on the temporal basis of biological events and indeed the priorities amongst all the molecular interactions that occur and how these change with time under the conditions that prevail in tissues. Hyaluronan, above all extracellular matrix components, plays an important role in maintaining the hydration of the ECM and commanding the water environment, which is essential for molecular traffic and generates the environment in which assembly of the structural elements in the matrix can occur. However, in addition to this fundamental function, hyaluronan also has an exquisite range of highly evolved functions that characterize the complexity of highly evolved organisms. So hyaluronan has presented us all with wonderfully varied challenges to research and its been a fun field to be in, not least because of the camaraderie of the generous and good humoured crowd that have been there.

Bibliography*

Hyaluronan-Related Publications

1. Hardingham, T., and Muir, H. (1972). The specific interaction of hyaluronic acid with cartilage proteoglycans. Biochim Biophys Acta 279, 401-405.

2. Hardingham, T., and Muir, H. (1973). Binding of oligosaccharides of hyaluronic acid to proteoglycans. Biochem J 135, 905-908.

3. Atkins, E. D. T., Hardingham, T., Isaac, D. H., and Muir, H. (1974). X-ray fibre diffraction of cartilage proteoglycan aggregates containing hyaluronic acid. Biochem J 141, 919-921.

4. Hardingham, T., and Muir, H. (1974). Hyaluronic acid in cartilage and proteoglycan aggregation. Biochem J 139, 565-581.

5. Hardingham, T., and Adams, P. (1976). A method for the determination of hyaluronate in the presence of other glycosaminoglycans and its application to human intervertebral disc. Biochem J 159, 143-147.

6. Hardingham, T., Ewins, R., and Muir, H. (1976). Cartilage proteoglycans. Structure and heterogeneity of the protein core and the effects of specific protein modifications on the binding to hyaluronate. Biochem J 157, 127-143.

7. Isles, M., Foweraker, A. R., Jennings, B. R., Hardingham, T., and Muir, H. (1978). Characterization of Proteoglycan and the Proteoglycan-Hyaluronic Acid Complex by Electric Birefringence. Biochem J 173, 237-243.

8. Nieduszynski, I.A., Sheehan, J., Phelps, C.F., Hardingham, T.E., and Muir, H. (1980). Equilibrium-binding studies of pig laryngeal cartilage proteoglycans with hyaluronate oligosaccharide fractions. Biochem J 185, 107-114.

9. Solursh, M., Hardingham, T.E., Hascall, V.C., and Kimura, J.H. (1980). Separate effects of exogenous hyaluronic acid on proteoglycan synthesis and deposition in pericellular matrix by cultured chick embryo limb chondrocytes. Dev Biol 75, 121-129.

10. Perkins, S. J., Miller, A., Hardingham, T. E., and Muir, H. (1981). Physical properties of the hyaluronate binding region of proteoglycan from pig laryngeal cartilage. Densitometric and small-angle neutron scattering studies of carbohydrates and carbohydrate-protein macromolecules. J Mol Biol 150 (1), 69-95.

---

* Provided by the interviewee.

11. Mitchell, D., and Hardingham, T.E. (1982). Monensin inhibits synthesis of proteoglycan, but not of hyaluronate, inchondrocytes. Biochem J 202, 249-254.

12. Ratcliffe, A., Tyler, J. A., and Hardingham, T.E. (1986). Articular cartilage cultured with interleukin 1. Increased release of link protein, hyaluronate-binding region and other proteoglycan fragments. Biochem J 238 (2), 571-580.

13. Mörgelin, M., Paulsson, M., Hardingham, T.E., Heinegård, D., and Engel, J. (1988). Cartilage proteoglycans. Assembly with hyaluronate and link protein as studied by electron microscopy. Biochem J 253, 175-185.

14. Fosang, A. J., and Hardingham, T.E. (1989). Isolation of the N-terminal globular protein domains from cartilage proteoglycans. Biochem J 261, 801-809.

15. Fosang, A. J., Hey, N. J., Carney, S.L., and Hardingham, T.E. (1990). An ELISA plate based assay for hyaluronan using biotinylated proteoglycan G1 domain (HA-binding region). Matrix 10, 306-131.

16. Fosang, A. J., Tyler, J. A., and Hardingham, T.E. (1991). Effect of interleukin-1 and insulin like growth factor-1 on the release of proteoglycan components and hyaluronan from pig articular cartilage in explant culture. Matrix 11 (1), 17-24.

17. Perkins, S. J., Nealis, A. S., Dunham, D. G., Hardingham, T.E., and Muir, I. H. (1992). Neutron and x-ray solution-scattering studies of the ternary complex between proteoglycan-binding region, link protein and hyaluronan. Biochem J 285 (Part 1), 263-268.

18. Gribbon, P., Heng, B.C., and Hardingham, T.E. (1999). The molecular basis of the solution properties of hyaluronan investigated by confocal fluorescence recovery after photobleaching. Biophysical J 77, 2210-2216.

19. Hardingham, T., Heng, B.C., and Gribbon, P. (1999). New approaches to the investigation of hyaluronan networks. Biochem Soc Trans 27 (2), 124-127.

20. Gribbon, P., Heng, B.C., and Hardingham, T. E. (2000). The analysis of intermolecular interactions in concentrated hyaluronan solutions suggest no evidence for chain-chain association. Biochem J 350 Part 1, 329-335.

21. Hardingham, T. (2004). Solution properties of hyaluronan. In *Chemistry and Biology of Hyaluronan* (Eds. Garg, H. G. and Hales, C.A.), Elsevier Ltd., Amsterdam (The Netherlands), 1-19.

22. Hardingham, T. (2005). Properties of hyaluronan in aqueous solution. In *Hyaluronan Structure, Metabolism, Biological Activities, Therapeutic Applications Volume I* (Eds. Balazs, E.A. and Hascall, V.C.), Matrix Biology Institute, Edgewater, NJ 07020 (USA), 67-78.

23. Papagiannopoulos, A., Waigh, T.A., Hardingham, T., and Heinrich, M. (2006). Solution structure and dynamics of cartilage aggrecan. Biomacromolecules 7 (7), 2162-2172.

24. Pothacharoen, P., Teekachunhatean, S., Louthrenoo, W., Yingsung, W., Ong-Chai, S., Hardingham, T., and Kongtawelert, P. (2006). Raised chondroitin sulfate epitopes and hyaluronan in serum from rheumatoid arthritis and osteoarthritis patients. Osteoarthritis and Cartilage 14 (3), 299-301.

Vincent C. Hascall (photograph courtesy of V. Hascall)

Vincent C. Hascall

Vincent C. Hascall, Jr. (b. 1940, Burwell, Nebraska) received his B.Sc. degree at the California Institute of Technology (1962) and his Ph.D. at Rockefeller University in New York City (1969). He was Assistant Professor (1964-74), Associate Professor (1974-1975) at the University of Michigan, and Fellow of the Swedish Medical Research Council in Lund, Sweden (1972-73). He spent 18 years at the National Institutes of Health (NIH) as a Senior Staff Fellow (1975-76), Research Chemist (1976-78), Instructor (1977-93), and as Chief of the Proteoglycan Chemistry Section of the Laboratory of Biochemistry, National Institute of Dental Research (1978-94). Since 1994 he has been at the Department of Biomedical Engineering in the Lerner Research Institute at the Cleveland Clinic in Cleveland, Ohio. He has been Associate Editor of the *Journal of Biological Chemistry (JBC)* since 1995, and has served on the Editorial Board of several other journals. He received numerous awards and distinctions, among them the Karl Meyer Award from the Society for Complex Carbohydrates, and honorary degrees from the University of Lund, Sweden (1986) and the University of Kuopio, Finland (2000). Three of his papers were recently featured as *JBC* classics in the issue celebrating the journal's centennial. He is a founding member of the International Society for Hyaluronan Sciences (ISHAS).

Interview*

How did you get into the hyaluronan field?

Even though I did not know it, my work with hyaluronan began in 1966-69, when I was a graduate student at the Rockefeller Institute, now Rockefeller University, where I worked with another graduate student by the name of Stanley Sajdera. The philosophy at Rockefeller was basically to let students develop their own projects with as little or as much input from the staff as was necessary.

Tell us a little about your background, education, teachers.

I grew up in a very small town, Longmont, north of Denver in Colorado, and I expected to go to the University of Colorado in Boulder. From Longmont we often went over to Boulder on weekends to play around so I knew that environment fairly well, and it was close to home. I also had a state scholarship that would have paid my tuition. However, I had to take the SATs, the scholar aptitude tests, and on that test they always ask you for up to 3 schools that you would like to send the results to. I didn't know what schools to send the results to, so I asked my track coach to help. Since his son was then a graduate student at Caltech, he said "well Caltech is a good school," so I put that down and never expected to be going there because I couldn't afford it. But it turned out that I got a National Merit Scholarship, which provided the funds necessary to go there. So I went there not really knowing what I was getting myself into. It was an extremely high powered school, and I came from a small town school that didn't have lots of background and lots of courses that one would need in order to feel comfortable going to Caltech. I still

---

* This interview was recorded during the first meeting "Conversations on Hyaluronan" in St. Tropez, September 2002.

remember the first lecture I ever had. It was a math teacher, Tom Apostle, and he started his lecture by saying that he was going to talk about area. Well, I thought that's great, I know what area is. But then he went into integral calculus, and that was the last thing I understood in the whole lecture. But I held on, I managed to pass, barely, my 1st quarter there. After the semester I went home to Colorado, and I didn't want to go back. However, my mother said, "you started it, you finish it", so I went back. After that I began to catch up with the other students. Eventually I managed to make my grades respectable if not outstanding and did get my degree.

I majored in biology. It looked attractive in many ways, and it seemed a more easy-going group. Much of Caltech was dominated by physics and math and high powered chemistry, and biology was just easier.

The person I related to most was named Ray Owens. He was sort of a geneticist-type and became the Chairman of the Department of Biology at the time I was there. Earlier the chairman was the Nobel laureate George Beadle, but he took the position of Chancellor at the University of Chicago. It was because of Owens that I ended up at Rockefeller. He suggested that I go to a science camp for boy scouts, being organized by a physician researcher, Rulon Rawson, in New York, as an instructor. I'd never been further east than Omaha, Nebraska, so I thought it would be fun to go to New York, so I applied for that. I taught two summers there, and while I was on the east coast, Dr. Rawson arranged that I should meet several people, including F.A.O. Schmidt at Yale and Alfred Mirsky at Rockefeller.

During my senior year at Caltech I applied to go to Rockefeller, Yale, and Harvard, not knowing exactly what I would do. The policy at Rockefeller was to bring a potential graduate student there for an interview, and the President of Rockefeller was personally involved in making the selections. At the end of interviewing with several people, including Dr. Mirsky, the President, Dr. Detlev Bronck, asked if I wanted to come. I said yes, and he said okay. Again, this wasn't something that I had planned, but I knew a little about Rockefeller and I thought it interesting to try. Then Stan Sadjera, who also came to Rockefeller from Caltech, and I sort of drifted down into a laboratory in the basement of one of the buildings way out of the way. We were working in a lab that was run by Dominic Dziewiatkowski. He was interested in cartilage and in particular in proteases that were involved in breaking down cartilage. Stan and I occupied this lab in the basement and began to putter around with cartilage. Stan was going to go after the protease, and I was going to go after analyzing the substrates, which at that time were called protein polysaccharides but now are referred to as proteoglycans. After about 4 or 5 years there, our mentor, Dr. Dziewiatkowski, went to the University of Michigan, and that left Stan and myself entirely on our own. Stan began to play with denaturing reagents to try to see if he could use them to extract the proteases from cartilage, and one of those was guanidineHCl that Gertrude Perlman, who was a protein chemist at Rockefeller, had been using to denature proteins like pepsin and renature them. Stan was treating slices of cartilage with 4 molar guanidine hydrochloride solutions.

One day, I still remember that day, we were going in the elevator up to go to lunch, and he said "I don't believe this. I extracted the cartilage slices with this guanidine solution, and the slices don't look all that different. But all the proteoglycans are in the solution and no longer in the tissue." All the procedures up to that point relied on high speed homogenization to release the proteoglycans from the tissue, and that was the work that Maxwell Schubert was doing. Schubert and Larry Rosenberg were down at NYU, so Stan and I once every couple of weeks would go down and talk with them to exchange ideas and information to keep current with the protein polysaccharide field. In any event, what happened was that we had stumbled onto a procedure that actually denatures the aggregates of proteoglycan that are in the cartilage, and allows them to come out of the tissue. Then when you lower the denaturing agent the aggregates reform, so both of us had to change totally our thesis.

I'd been doing lots of physical chemical measurements on protein polysaccharide solutions, so I went back and redid them on these aggregate solutions. Then we figured out a way to purify the monomer from the aggregate. We did that in density gradients that were run in the presence of the denaturing agent, and what happened was that because the chondroitin sulfate is dense all the proteoglycan monomers would go to the bottom and some proteins would go to the top of the gradient. We knew that if we put them all back together we'd get back the aggregate by removing the denaturing agent, so we called the 4 molar guanidine solution a dissociative solvent. Then under associative conditions we purified aggregates, while under dissociative conditions they would come apart and we could remove this protein, which we named 'link protein'. We didn't know there was any hyaluronan in the aggregates, so I was working with hyaluronan but I didn't know it. When I refer to that stage of my career, I refer to hyaluronan as the stealth molecule.

Formally, Dr. Dziewiatkowski was our mentor until he left, and all this work that Stan and I eventually published together, was done while we had no formal mentor. John Gregory was assigned to be our mentor but only for the last year. He knew enough about carbohydrate chemistry so he was a reasonable person for that choice. He was one of those people who, unless you went and pounded on him, you'd never get any feedback, and both Stan and I were pretty reclusive and shy, so we tended to rely more on each other than on seeking outside help. I learned more from Stan during my graduate years than I did from anyone else. Stan and I graduated in 1969, and I took a job at the University of Michigan, where Dr. Dziewiatkowski was now the Director of the Dental Research Institute, and he invited both of us to work there. I chose to go, but Stan chose to stay. Sadly, he was killed very tragically about 3 or 4 years after that. We lost a really brilliant individual, certainly the one who had the most influence on shaping my graduate career.

Since we didn't know there was hyaluronan in proteoglycan aggregates, we had to come up with a model that explained all our data, and we came up with a beautiful model. In this model the link protein was bifunctional because we knew it had two interactions in the aggregate, so we figured that the proteoglycan was also bifunctional. In my thesis I drew a model in which the proteoglycan has two globular domains, one at either end, with chondroitin sulfate chains in the middle, which actually turns out coincidentally to be reasonably accurate for the family. Then the link protein had two binding sites, one of which would interact with the C terminal and the other with the N terminal end of the monomer. So the link protein was named for the wrong reason. A few years later when I was working with Dick Heinegård at the University of Lund, Sweden for a year on a sabbatical from Michigan, he and I sorted out the aggregate structure, in which hyaluronan enters the picture.

Tim Hardinghan and Helen Muir showed that if you take the monomer proteoglycan prepared the way Stan and I did, and then added a small amount of hyaluronan, you'd get a major increase in the viscosity of the solution. This indicated that the monomer was actually interacting with the hyaluronan. They couldn't show that it was stable in an ultracentrifuge for technical reasons, but it turns out that it is the link protein that is necessary.

When did you become aware of the importance of hyaluronan?

That was about 1972. I went to Michigan in 1969 and in 1972 there was a Gordon conference that was organized by Al Dorfman and Karl Meyer, and Stan and I were invited there. Some people had come from Sweden, Sven Gardell, Torvard Laurent, and Dick Heinegård, and Dick invited me to work with them. The next year they got a Swedish medical research fellowship for me, and I went to Lund, Sweden, and spent a year there. Shortly after I got there, we saw an abstract from Hardingham and Muir that was going to be presented at a meeting, and it said that if you put the monomer onto hyaluronan you would get this aggregation. So that solved the puzzle immediately, it was the missing piece of the puzzle.

I also knew the work that John Gregory had started doing after both Stan and I had left Rockefeller. While we were there, all the time we would ask John if he would like to start working with us because there were so many things to do, but he would never do it. When we left, he felt it was okay for him to start working on this topic. He was a very-very careful researcher. When Stan and I were working on this topic, we purified the aggregate and put it back in the 4 molar guanidine and ran these dissociative density gradients. We just cut the tube in half and compared the bottom half with the top half, and the bottom half would have the monomer, and the top half would have the link protein. It turns out that the top half also had the hyaluronan because it would float above the proteoglycan because it has a much lower density than the proteoglycan does.

As I said, Dr. Gregory did a more thorough job. He cut his tubes into six fractions, and he took the bottom sixth, which is where most of the proteoglycan was, and he would add it back to the top sixth, which was where the link protein was. But he wouldn't get aggregates However, if he used the top three fractions with the bottom sixth, he would get aggregates. He actually postulated that there were two links, he called them link-1 and link-2. I knew about link-1, and the Hardingham-Muir experiment said that link-2 was probably hyaluronan. This made sense because it was deeper in the gradient. So Dick and I rethought our model, and we came up with a new model, which is the correct one. In fact, this was my second hyaluronan story, the first one being the one in which I didn't know I was working with hyaluronan. In the second one we sorted out what its role was in this particular biology. I had three papers with Stan in 1969, and later three with Dick; those are probably the papers that are definitive in redefining the structure of the non-collagenous part of the cartilage matrix. The first discovery was that guanidineHCl will dissociate proteoglycan aggregates and the second one that the hyaluronan is in the middle of the process.

How would you assess the major steps in the development of the hyaluronan field?

Obviously the hyaluronan field was running great guns independent of what I've told you. The fact that hyaluronan ends up playing a part of the biology that I was involved with, would be considered almost a curiosity by the mainstream hyaluronan people. This is so because the amount of hyaluronan in cartilage is very small compared to the amount of proteoglycan, and therefore the properties of the cartilage are dominated by the proteoglycan. Until fairly recently, most of my research was related to the proteoglycan field rather than the hyaluronan field, and thus I wasn't involved with the major events that have been going on in the hyaluronan field. It is basically the last 15 years that I have been involved more intensively with hyaluronan for some very interesting reasons. I am sure this will keep me very happy and busy for the next decade at least, but these weren't directions that I necessarily planned to go into.

What were those reasons?

In 1975, I was recruited by Karl Piez to the National Institute of Dental Research at NIH to develop a proteoglycan research group. This was an opportunity that I could not pass up and resulted in 18 years of fun and productive research. However, it was not until the late 1980s that hyaluronan once again intruded into my research. At that time, Masaki Yanagishita was studying the metabolism of heparan sulfate proteoglycans in ovarian granulosa cells. A very talented reproductive biologist from Italy, Antonia Salustri, knew this work and asked if she could spend a sabbatical year in my laboratory learning about proteoglycans, which she did. Her research interest was in ovulation, and she wanted to study the synthesis of the hyaluronan-based matrix during cumulus oophorus expansion. Her work initiated a series of studies that have continued in my laboratory to the present.

This process involves the cumulus cells around the oocyte under hormonal instruction upregulating an enzyme, hyaluronan synthase II, which begins to make a hyaluronan matrix. That matrix then expands the cumulus oophorus so at the time of ovulation the oocyte is sitting inside this very large cumulus cell oocyte complex, which is all hyaluronan-based. This project is now dovetailing extremely interestingly with two other biologies that I am involved with. Interestingly, many people consider the expansion of the cumulus oophorus as an inflammatory process. It turns out that the players that are necessary to form the hyaluronan matrix in the ovulation model are the same ones that reappear in inflammation responses.

Inflammation is another topic that I am involved with and that I got into by accident or perhaps better to say, by being in an environment that is permissive to the exchange of ideas. I was sitting in my office at the Cleveland Clinic one day when I got a phone call from someone in colorectal surgery who wanted to see me. Her name is Carol de la Motte and she's a technician.[7] She wanted to run some data by me that was a puzzle to her. They were working with human colon smooth muscle cells isolated from normal human colon, and they were interested in Chron's disease and inflammatory bowel disease. What they had been doing for the past 4 or 5 years was to look at cytokine stimulation of smooth muscle cells. Without going into details, they were exploring the effect of viruses because there is a viral etiology to asthma or to Chron's disease. Someone who is susceptible often has a real bad flare after a viral infection. She thought that there was something very strange about how the monocytes bind to smooth muscle cells treated with virus; they sort of clump together on what look like long seaweed strands and if you swirl the medium around they look like algae. I thought that sounds familiar, so I suggested that they try to use some hyaluronidase and see what happens. Indeed, after that most of the monocytes came loose. So what's happening is that the smooth muscle cells in response to the pathogen are actually upregulating a pathway that includes synthesizing hyaluronan in a new context. In fact, they're already synthesizing hyaluronan in a normal context that the monocytes don't see, but in this new context they do. Apparently, a smooth muscle cell that has been infected with the virus is using its last metabolic energy to put out hyaluronan with a structure now that surveying monocytes recognize as a problem. So they destroy the hyaluronan and fight the invader; but in a Chron's patient or in an asthmatic patient, they get out of hand and you have an overreaction and a clinical problem. At the moment what we're focusing on is trying to figure out what that new structure is, what are the other molecules that are in that new structure that allows the monocyte to become activated and aggressive. I think that we are in the middle of a major host defense and clean up mechanism that's very important, and the fact that hyaluronan is in the middle of it is a big surprise to everybody. It's so surprising that it's hard for me to get NIH to give me money to continue the work on this topic because the prevailing opinion is that hyaluronan is an inert space filler.

---

[7] Since the time of the interview, she has received a Ph.D. for her work on this project from the University of Cardiff.

I am also working on a third hyaluronan based model that is connected with the epidermis, and it is interesting how I got into that. I was still at NIH in 1993, when a husband and wife team, Markku and Raija Tammi from Finland told me that they would like to come and work with me for a while at NIH. By that time I knew that I was going to leave NIH. I ended up at the Cleveland Clinic, and part of my package to go there was that the Clinic would provide salaries to support this couple for two years. They came and helped me set up the lab. Their area of interest was in epidermal biology, and they had shown that—quite surprisingly—the intercellular space around keratinocytes in the epidermis is a hyaluronan based matrix. This is surprising because when you look at the classic morphology of the epidermis you see pictures of keratinocytes without any intercellular space. All the desmosomes are linking all the cells together, and they look like they are on zippers. Actually, we believe that that is an artifact because when you fix tissues for electron microscopy, the structures collapse and you lose the hyaluronan. When we did freeze substitution fixation on the epidermis, we saw that instead of about 1-2% intercellular space there's more like 15%, so the hyaluronan is actually creating highways of matrix through the epidermis. This is very important because nutrients have to get into the epidermis by diffusion and waste materials have to go out by diffusion. The other surprising thing that the Tammis had also discovered was that the metabolism of hyaluronan in the epidermis is extremely fast, so the half life of hyaluronan in the epidermis is about a day. Since there is a basement membrane under the epidermis, all the metabolism is being handled by the cells in the tissue, and that means that the cells are making it and also breaking it down; it's a continuously differentiating tissue, and this makes it quite fascinating to work with it—but also it is extremely hard to work with.

One of my closest friends at Michigan was a person by the name of Don MacCallum. His interest was in epithelial tissues, and he had in his freezer a rat keratinocyte cell line that is still the most unique among all the models of epidermal biology in that if you grow this cell line on a collagen substrate at an air-liquid interface, it will form an epidermis. We have been playing with that model to explore different aspects of how hyaluronan synthesis is regulated, how it is modulated, how it alters the differentiation program, how it affects stratification, what are the hyaluronidases that catabolize it, and how cell surface CD44 is involved in that process. This has become a major biological model that is hyaluronan based.

The last topic that we're interested in is diabetes. We got into that basically through the inflammation project. One of my colleagues, Aimin Wang, was interested in mesangial cell biology and wanted to know if these cells would respond to the viral stimulus in the same way the smooth muscle cells do. He tested the viral response with a normal level and a high level of glucose, and found that the mesangial cells responded to the high glucose alone control by elaborating hyaluronan in this adhesive and monocyte activating structure. We have shown an increase of hyaluronan in diabetic rat glomeruli at the same time that you get monocyte/macrophage infiltration, and the histology showed abnormal puddles of hyaluronan with monocytes embedded in it. I think, we're seeing again another host response but to a different stimulus. The surprising thing to me in this particular study is that we've shown as clearly as possible that the intracellular signaling pathways that those cells respond to when they are attacked by the viral pathogen, are totally different from the intracellular signaling pathway that's activated by the high glucose, so there are two different intracellular routes. In the inflammatory model we want to understand the mechanism of activation and phagocytosis on the part of the monocytes, and in the diabetes situation we want to understand what the signaling pathway is that opens up that particular synthesis of that structure. In the oocyte project we want to figure out how TSG6 and IalphaI actually work together to make a structure. In the skin we just want to understand what is really involved in both synthesis and catabolism of the hyaluronan, and how is that regulated, and how does that interact, either passively or actively, with the program of differentiation that is required to make an epidermis. So within the past 8 years at the Cleveland Clinic I've stumbled into 4 major biologies, only one of which I was doing before I got there.

When Torvard drew the tree of the development of the hyaluronan field, in the crown there are the clinical applications done by Bandi. Now you are describing whole new areas of potential clinical applications so that the tree is expected to blossom further.

I would hope so. Bandi's genius is of course to see how he can take the basics into something that is going to be very beneficial in a clinical sense, and I've never gotten beyond the basics. So my whole modus operandi has been to understand how the biology works, and I've never really thought much about how to interfere with that biology.

I wonder how the properties of hyaluronan, for example, its molecular weight influence those actions that you are observing.

There's a lot of smoke out there, and one of the reasons I think we're here is to try to determine what's real and what's not real. Part of it is that you go back to hyaluronan preparations; some preparations had endotoxins in them, so when you use that preparation and you get a response from, say, some leukocytes, is it the endotoxin or is it the hyaluronan that caused it? There are results that argue that hyaluronan that has one million Dalton molecular weight has a different biology from the hyaluronan that has five million Dalton molecular weight. I find it very difficult to imagine how that cell could distinguish five from one, but that 1 million preparations may have had a contaminant or it may be so polydisperse that what's causing the differences are actually the small pieces of hyaluronan.

How did you get to know Bandi?

Well, we knew of each other's research, but our interests were not very close. He was interested in the pure molecule and its physical properties, how he could get it free of other things; also in how inflammatory and how viscous it is—and I wasn't. I was more into the cell biology questions. Then, one day I got a phone call from Glyn Phillips asking me to be the scientific chairman of the hyaluronan 2000 conference, during which they planned to honor Bandi's 80th birthday. I was surprised, but I accepted. It was then that I started to interact in a more formal and informal way with Bandi. I think we both found that we have a variety of background information that is complementary and doesn't overlap that much. I can wander through a lot of the cell biology and enzyme stuff; whereas when it comes to the application side he's dominating the agenda. He also said that he wants to organize another meeting that relates to cell surface receptors and to how they interact with hyaluronan, which is a blossoming area and has a fairly short history but obviously one that is very important. I think that we work remarkably well together; he's just a wonderful person to work with. After the HA 2000 meeting in Wrexham, he suggested that his Matrix Biology Institute would take the major initiative in terms of organizing the 2003 international conference and that he wanted me to be the scientific chairman again. I said fine if we could have it in Cleveland. The reason for that was mostly that there are probably eight or nine major projects on hyaluronan going on in the Cleveland area, at Case Western University and at the Clinic, which means that by having it at the Clinic, 60 or 80 people could come to the conference, whereas if it were somewhere else some of them could not go. In any event Bandi laughed and said that would be okay. And that's what our plans are.[8]

There are many people in the Cleveland area working on hyaluronan-related projects; is it due to your influence?

Much of it is now that there is a hyaluronan matrix involved in inflammations. There are other projects, for example, Arnold Caplan and his group at Case Western is involved with hyaluronan in stem cell research. I've interacted with them even before I went to Cleveland, so that's not surprising. Another program there is that of Joe Hollyfield. He's got a major interest in the role of hyaluronan in the interphotoreceptor matrix; he may have gotten involved because of the cross talk and joint seminars at the Clinic. Any information developed in one project is dispersed throughout the network very readily.

---

[8] The HA2003 Conference in Cleveland was a great success!

Is there a shift from the chemical and physical properties to the cell biological and clinical applications?

I don't think the whole emphasis is moving. But lots of the new emphasis has to go in that direction. One of the major applications of hyaluronan is in matrix formation and tissue engineering, and that is clearly something that Bandi has pushed through his divinyl sulfone crosslinking methodology. But now there must be 10 to 15 companies out there that in various ways are looking at how to modify hyaluronan so that it can become a slowly dissolvable substance, by esterifying the carboxyl groups or by cross-linking through a variety of ways. I think that area needs much more work, but it's probably an area where a lot of that work will be done behind closed doors because of the patent issues. For example, at the Clinic, one of my proteges, Tony Calabro, has now developed a cross-linking procedure for hyaluronan where cells will survive. Now you can have a crystal clear matrix with chondrocytes embedded in it, and the versatility of that is enormous. His cross-linking procedure opens up the possibility of forming matrices around viable cells, whereas with most of the other cross-linking procedures you can't do it.

Do you do anything patentable?

No, I've never even entertained the idea. But I can see the point. If I were Tony and doing the same thing, maybe I would patent that procedure. But I'd give it to the Clinic, which is a tax-exempt foundation. But it is the biggest clinical center in Cleveland.

References

1. Sajdera, S. W.; Hascall, (1969) V. C. "Proteinpolysaccharide Complex from Bovine Nasal Cartilage. A Comparison of Low and High Shear Extraction Procedures" J Biol Chem 244, 77–87.
2. Hascall, V. C.; Sajdera, S. W. (1969) "Proteinpolysaccharide Complex from Bovine Nasal Cartilage. The Function of Glycoprotein in the Formation of Aggregates" J Biol Chem 244, 2384–2396.

3. Heinegård, D.; Hascall, V. C. (1974) "Aggregation of Cartilage Proteoglycans. III. Characteristics of the Proteins Isolated from Trypsin Digests of Aggregates" J Biol Chem 249, 4250–4256.

4. Kresge, N.; Simoni, R. D.; Hill, R. L. (2007) "Proteoglycans and Orchids: the Work of Vincent Hascall" J Biol Chem 282, e35-e37.

Bibliography*

Hyaluronan-Related Publications

1. Hascall, V.C., and Sajdera, S. W. (1969). Proteinpolysaccharide complex from bovine nasal cartilage. The function of glycoprotein in the formation of aggregates. J Biol Chem 244 (9), 2384-2396.

2. Sajdera, S. W., and Hascall, V.C. (1969). Proteinpolysaccharide complex from bovine nasal cartilage: A comparison of low- and high-shear extraction procedures. J Biol Chem 244, 77-87.

3. Hascall, V.C., and Heinegård, D. (1974). Aggregation of cartilage proteoglycans. II. Oligosaccharide competitors of the proteoglycan-hyaluronic acid interaction. J Biol Chem 249 (13), 4242-4249.

4. Hascall, V.C., and Heinegård, D. (1974). Aggregation of cartilage proteoglycans. I. The role of hyaluronic acid. J Biol Chem 249 (13), 4232-4241.

5. Heinegård, D., and Hascall, V.C. (1974). Aggregation of cartilage proteoglycans. III. Characteristics of the proteins isolated from trypsin digests of aggregates. J Biol Chem 249 (13), 4250-4256.

6. Hascall, V. (1977). Interaction of cartilage proteoglycans with hyaluronic acid. J Supramol Structure 7, 101-120. Also published in *Cell Surface Carbohydrates and Biological Recognition* (Eds. Marchesi, V., Ginsburg, V., Robbins, P. and Fox, C.), Alan R. Liss, Inc, New York (1977), pp. 181-200.

7. Faltz, L., Caputo, C., Kimura, J., Schrode, J., and Hascall, V. (1979). Structure of the complex between hyaluronic acid, the hyaluronic acid-binding region, and the link protein of proteoglycan aggregates from the Swarm rat chondrosarcoma. J Biol Chem 254 (4), 1381-1387.

8. Faltz, L. L., Reddi, A. H., Hascall, G. K., Martin, D., Pita, J. C., and Hascall, V.C. (1979). Characteristics of proteoglycans extracted from the Swarm rat chondrosarcoma with associative solvents. J Biol Chem 254 (4), 1375-1380.

---

* Provided by the interviewee.

9. Heinegård, D., and Hascall, V.C. (1979). The effects of dansylation and acetylation on the interaction between hyaluronic acid and the hyaluronic acid-binding region of cartilage proteoglycans. J Biol Chem 254 (3), 921-926.

10. Kimura, J. H., Hardingham, T. E., Hascall, V.C., and Solursh, M. (1979). Biosynthesis of proteoglycans and their assembly into aggregates in cultures of chondrocytes from the swarm rat chondrosarcoma. J Biol Chem 254 (8), 2600-2609.

11. Kimura, J. H., Hardingham, T. E., and Hascall, V.C. (1980). Assembly of newly synthesized proteoglycan and link protein into aggregates in cultures of chondrosarcoma chondrocytes. J Biol Chem 255 (15), 7134-7143.

12. Solursh, M., Hardingham, T. E., Hascall, V.C., and Kimura, J. H. (1980). Separate effects of exogenous hyaluronic acid on proteoglycan synthesis and deposition in pericellular matrix by cultured chick embryo limb chondrocytes. Dev Biol 75, 121-129.

13. Stevens, R. L., and Hascall, V.C. (1981). Characterization of proteoglycans synthesized by rat chondrosarcoma chondrocytes treated with multiplication-stimulating activity and insulin. J Biol Chem 256 (4), 2053-2058.

14. Kimata, K., Kimura, J. H., Thonar, E. J., Barrach, H. J., Rennard, S. I., and Hascall, V.C. (1982). Swarm rat chondrosarcoma proteoglycans. Purification of aggregates by zonal centrifugation of preformed cesium sulfate gradients. J Biol Chem 257 (7), 3819-3826.

15. Mason, R. M., d'Arville, C., Kimura, J. H., and Hascall, V.C. (1982). Absence of covalently linked core protein from newly synthesized hyaluronate. Biochem J 207, 445-457.

16. Mason, R. M., Kimura, J. H., and Hascall, V.C. (1982). Biosynthesis of hyaluronic acid in cultures of chondrocytes from the swarm rat chondrosarcoma. J Biol Chem 257 (5), 2236-2245.

17. Thonar, E. J.-M., Kimura, J. H., Hascall, V.C., and Poole, A. R. (1982). Enzyme-linked immunosorbent assay analyses of the hyaluronate-binding region and the link protein of proteoglycan aggregate. J Biol Chem 257 (23), 14173-14180.

18. Chang, Y., Yanagishita, M., Hascall, V.C., and Wight, T. N. (1983). Proteoglycans synthesized by smooth muscle cells derived from monkey (Macaca nemestrina) aorta. J Biol Chem 258, 5679-5688.

19. Wight, T. N., and Hascall, V.C. (1983). Proteoglycans in primate arteries. III. Characterization of the proteoglycans synthesized by arterial smooth muscle cells in culture. J Cell Biol 96 (1), 167-176.

20. Campbell, M. A., Handley, C. J., Hascall, V.C., Campbell, R. A., and Lowther, D. A. (1984). Turnover of proteoglycans in cultures of bovine articular cartilage. Arch Biochem Biophys 234 (1), 275-289.

21. Caputo, C., Kimura, J., and Hascall, V. (1984). Effect of puromycin on cartilage proteoglycan structure and capacity to bind hyaluronic acid. Arch Biochem Biophys 230 (2), 594-604.

22. Poole, A. R., Reiner, A., Mort, J. S., Tang, L. H., Choi, H. U., Rosenberg, L. C., Caputo, C. B., Kimura, J. H., and Hascall, V.C. (1984). Cartilage link proteins. Biochemical and immunochemical studies of isolation and heterogeneity. J Biol Chem 259 (23), 14849-14856.

23. Lamberg, S. I., Yuspa, S.H., and Hascall, V.C. (1986). Synthesis of hyaluronic acid is decreased and synthesis of proteoglycans is increased when cultured mouse epidermal cells differentiate. J Invest Dermatol 86 (6), 659-667.

24. Stevens, J. W., and Hascall, V.C. (1986). N-terminal carbamylation of the hyaluronic acid-binding region and the link protein from the chondrosarcoma proteoglycan aggregate. J Biol Chem 261 (33), 15442-15449.

25. Luyten, F. P., Hascall, V.C., Nissley, S. P., Morales, T. I., and Reddi, A. H. (1988). Insulin-like growth factors maintain steady-state metabolism of proteoglycans in bovine articular cartilage explants. Arch Biochem Biophys 267 (2), 416-425.

26. Morales, T. I., and Hascall, V.C. (1988). Correlated metabolism of proteoglycans and hyaluronic acid in bovine cartilage organ cultures. J Biol Chem 263 (8), 3632-3638.

27. Morales, T. I., and Hascall, V.C. (1989). Effects of interleukin-1 and lipopolysaccharides on protein and carbohydrate metabolism in bovine articular cartilage organ cultures. Connect Tissue Res 19 (2-4), 255-275.

28. Salustri, A., Yanagishita, M., and Hascall, V. (1989). Synthesis and accumulation of hyaluronic acid and proteoglycans in the mouse cumulus cell-oocyte complex during follicle-stimulating hormone-induced mucification. J Biol Chem 264, 13840-13847.

29. Hascall, V., Yanagishita, M., Salustri, A., and Morales, T. I. (1990). The use of radiolabeled glucosamine as a precursor for measuring hyaluronan synthesis. In Methods in Cartilage Research (Eds. Maroudas, A. and Kuettner, K.), Academic Press 132-137.

30. Salustri, A., Ulisse, S., Yanagishita, M., and Hascall, V.C. (1990). Hyaluronic acid synthesis by mural granulosa cells and cumulus cells in vitro is

selectively stimulated by a factor produced by oocytes and transforming growth factor-B. J Biol Chem 265, 19517-19523.

31. Salustri, A., Yanagishita, M., and Hascall, V. (1990). Mouse oocytes regulate hyaluronic acid synthesis and mucification by FSH-stimulated cumulus cells. Dev Biol 138, 26-32.

32. Salustri, A., Yanagishita, M., Underhill, C. B., Laurent, T. C., and Hascall, V.C. (1992). Localization and synthesis of hyaluronic acid in the cumulus cells and mural granulosa cells of the preovulatory follicle. Dev Biol 151, 541-551.

33. Calvo, J. C., Gandjbakhche, A. H., Nossal, R., Hascall, V., and Yanagishita, M. (1993). Rheological effects of the presence of hyaluronic acid in the extracellular media of differentiated 3T3-L1 preadipocyte cultures. Arch Biochem Biophys 302 (2), 468-475.

34. Camaioni, A., Hascall, V.C., Yanagishita, M., and Salustri, A. (1993). Effects of exogenous hyaluronic acid and serum on matrix organization and stability in the mouse cumulus cell-oocyte complex. J Biol Chem 268 (27), 20473-20481.

35. Salustri, A., Yanagishita, M., Camaioni, A., Tirone, E., and Hascall, V.C. (1993). Proteoglycan and hyaluronic acid synthesis by granulosa cells: regulation by an oocyte factor and gonadotropins. In *Ovarian Cell Interactions: Genes to Physiology* (Eds. Hsueh, A. J. W. and Schomberg, D. W.), Springer-Verlag Press, New York, 38-48.

36. Tirone, E., Siracusa, G., Hascall, V.C., Frajese, G., and Salustri, A. (1993). Oocytes preserve the ability of mouse cumulus cells in culture to synthesize hyaluronic acid and dermatan sulfate. Dev Biol 160 (2), 405-412.

37. Calabro, A., and Hascall, V. (1994). Differential effects of brefeldin A on chondroitin sulfate and hyaluronan synthesis in rat chondrosarcoma cells. J Biol Chem 269, 22764-22770.

38. Goldin, E., Imai, Y., Kaneski, C. R., Pentchev, P. G., Brady, R. O., and Hascall, V.C. (1994). Mucolipidosis IV fibroblasts synthesize normal amounts of hyaluronic acid. J Inherit Metab Dis 17 (5), 545-553.

39. Midura, R. J., Evanko, S. P., and Hascall, V.C. (1994). Parathyroid hormone stimulates hyaluronan synthesis in an osteoblast-like cell line. J Biol Chem 269 (18), 13200-13206.

40. Midura, R. J., Salustri, A., Calabro, A., Yanagishita, M., and Hascall, V.C. (1994). High-resolution separation of disaccharide and oligosaccharide alditols from chondroitin sulphate, dermatan sulphate and hyaluronan using CarboPac PA1 chromatography. Glycobiology 4 (3), 333-342.

41. Hashimoto-Uoshima, M., Hascall, V.C., MacCallum, D. K., and Yanagishita, M. (1995). Biosynthesis of proteoglycans and hyaluronic acid by rat oral epithelial cells (keratinocytes) in vitro. Arch Biochem Biophys 316 (2), 724-732.

42. Camaioni, A., Salustri, A., Yanagishita, M., and Hascall, V.C. (1996). Proteoglycans and proteins in the extracellular matrix of mouse cumulus cell-oocyte complexes. Arch Biochem Biophys 325 (2), 190-198.

43. Fülöp, C., Kamath, R. V., Li, Y., Otto, J. M., Salustri, A., Olsen, B. R., Glant, T. T., and Hascall, V.C. (1997). Coding sequence, exon-intron structure and chromosomal localization of murine TNF-stimulated gene 6 that is specifically expressed by expanding cumulus cell-oocyte complexes. Gene 202 (1-2), 95-102.

44. Fülöp, C., Salustri, A., and Hascall, V.C. (1997). Coding sequence of a hyaluronan synthase homologue expressed during expansion of the mouse cumulus-oocyte complex. Arch Biochem Biophys 337, 261-266.

45. Tirone, E., D'Alessandris, C., Hascall, V.C., Siracusa, G., and Salustri, A. (1997). Hyaluronan synthesis by mouse cumulus cells is regulated by interactions between follicle-stimulating hormone (or epidermal growth factor) and a soluble oocyte factor (or transforming growth factor beta1). J Biol Chem 272 (8), 4787-4794.

46. Weigel, P., Hascall, V., and Tammi, M. (1997). Minireview. Hyaluronan synthases. J Biol Chem 272 (22), 13997-14000.

47. Goodstone, N. J., Hascall, V.C., and Calabro, A. (1998). Differential effects of Staphylococcus aureus alpha-hemolysin on the synthesis of hyaluronan and chondroitin sulfate by rat chondrosarcoma chondrocytes. Arch Biochem Biophys 350 (1), 26-35.

48. Hascall, V.C., Fulop, C., Salustri, A., Goodstone, N. J., Calabro, A., Hogg, M., Tammi, R., Tammi, M., and MacCallum, D. (1998). Metabolism of hylauronan. In *The Chemistry, Biology and Medical Applications of Hyaluronan and its Derivatives Proceedings of the Wenner-Gren Foundation International Symposium held in honor of Endre A Balazs, Stockholm, Sweden, September 18-21,1996* (Ed. Laurent, T.C.), Portland Press Ltd., London (UK), 67-76.

49. Tammi, R., MacCallum, D., Hascall, V.C., Pienimäki, J.-P., Hyttinen, M., and Tammi, M. (1998). Hyaluronan bound to CD44 on keratinocytes is displaced by hyaluronan decasaccharides and not hexasaccharides. J Biol Chem 273 (44), 28878-28888.

50. de la Motte, C. A., Hascall, V.C., Calabro, A., Yen-Lieberman, B., and Strong, S. A. (1999). Mononuclear leukocytes preferentially bind via CD44

to hyaluronan on human intestinal mucosal smooth muscle cells after virus infection or treatment with poly(I•C). J Biol Chem 274 (43), 30747-30755.

51. Salustri, A., Camaioni, A., Di Giacomo, M., Fulop, C., and Hascall, V.C. (1999). Hyaluronan and proteoglycans in ovarian follicles. Hum Reprod Update 5 (4), 293-301.

52. Calabro, A., Hascall, V.C., and Midura, R. J. (2000). Adaptation of FACE methodology for microanalysis of total hyaluronan and chondroitin sulfate composition from cartilage. Glycobiology 10 (3), 283-293.

53. Calabro, A., Midura, R. J., Hascall, V.C., Plaas, A., Goodstone, N. J., and Rodén, L. (2000). Structure and biosynthesis of chondroitin sulfate and hyaluronan. In *Proteoglycans: structure, biology and molecular interactions* (Ed. Iozzo, R.V.), Marcel Dekker, Inc., New York, 5-26.

54. Hascall, V.C. (2000). Hyaluronan, a common thread. Glycoconj J 17 (7-9), 607-616.

55. Hascall, V.C., Tammi, R., Tammi, M., Hunziker, E., and MacCallum, D. K. (2000). Does keratinocyte hyaluronan determine the volume of extracellular space in the epidermis? In *New Frontiers in Medical Sciences: Redefining Hyaluronan (Proceedings of the Symposium held in Padua, Italy, 17-19 June 1999)* (Eds. Abatangelo, G. and Weigel, P.), Elsevier, Amsterdam, 31-40.

56. Lesley, J., Hascall, V.C., Tammi, M., and Hyman, R. (2000). Hyaluronan binding by cell surface CD44. J Biol Chem 275 (35), 26967-26975.

57. Plaas, A. H. K., West, L., Midura, R. J., and Hascall, V.C. (2000). Disaccharide composition of hyaluronan and chondroitin/dermatan sulfate--analysis with fluorophore-assisted carbohydrate electrophoresis. In *Methods in Molecular Biology Volume 171: Proteoglycan Protocols* (Ed. Iozzo, R.V.), Humana Press, Inc., Totowa, NJ (USA), 117-128.

58. Tammi, R. H., Tammi, M. I., Hascall, V.C., Hogg, M., Pasonen, S., and MacCallum, D. K. (2000). A preformed basallamina laters the metabolism and distribution of hyaluronan in epidermal keratinocyte "organotypic" cultures grown on collagen matrices. Histochem Cell Biol 113, 265-277.

59. Mahoney, D. J., Aplin, R. T., Calabro, A., Hascall, V.C., and Day, A. J. (2001). Novel methods for the preparation and characterization of hyaluronan oligosaccharides of defined length. Glycobiology 11 (12), 1025-1033.

60. Mukhopadhyay, D., Hascall, V.C., Day, A.J., Salustri, A., and Fülöp, C. (2001). Two distinct populations of tumor necrosis factor-stimulated gene-6 protein in the extracellular matrix of expanded mouse cumulus cell-oocyte complexes. Arch Biochem Biophys 394 (2), 173-181.

61. Pienimäki, J.-P., Rilla, K., Fülöp, C., Sironen, R. K., Karvinen, S., Pasonen, S., Lammi, M. J., Tammi, R., Hascall, V.C., and Tammi, M. (2001). Epidermal growth factor activates hyaluronan synthase 2 (Has2) in epidermal keratinocytes and increases pericellular and intracellular hyaluronan. J Biol Chem 276, 20428-20435.

62. Tammi, R., Rilla, K., Pienimäki, J.-P., MacCallum, D. K., Hogg, M., Luukkonen, M., Hascall, V.C., and Tammi, M. (2001). Hyaluronan enters keratinocytes by a novel endocytic route for catabolism. J Biol Chem 276 (37), 35111-35122.

63. Calabro, A., Oken, M. M., Hascall, V.C., and Masellis, A. M. (2002). Characterization of hyaluronan synthase expression and hyaluronan synthesis in bone marrow mesenchymal progenitor cells: predominant expression of HAS1 mRNA and up-regulated hyaluronan synthesis in bone marrow cells derived from multiple myeloma patients. Blood 100, 2578-2585.

64. de la Motte, C. A., Hascall, V.C., Drazba, J. A., and Strong, S. A. (2002). Poly I:C induces mononuclear leukocyte-adhesive hyaluronan structures on colon smooth muscle cells: IαI and versican facilitate adhesion. In *Hyaluronan Volume 1* (Eds. Kennedy, J.F., Phillips, G.O., Williams, P.A. , and Hascall, V.C.), Woodhead, Cambridge, UK, 381-388.

65. Hascall, V.C. (2002). Karl Meyer--Discoverer of hyaluronan. In *Hyaluronan Volume 1 Chemical, Biochemical and Biological Aspects* (Eds. Kennedy, J. F., Phillips, G. O., Williams, P. A. , and Hascall, V.C.), Woodhead Publishing, Cambridge, UK, 17-23.

66. Lesley, J., English, N., Hascall, V.C., Tammi, M., and Hyman, R. (2002). Hyaluronan binding by cell surface CD44. In *Hyaluronan Volume 1* (Eds. Kennedy, J. F., Phillips, G. O., Williams, P. A. , and Hascall, V.C.), Woodhead, Cambridge, UK, 341-348.

67. McDonald, J. A., and Hascall, V.C. (2002). Hyaluronan minireview series. J Biol Chem 277 (7), 4575-4579.

68. Pasonen-Seppanen, S., Tammi, R., Tammi, M., Hogg, M., Hascall, V.C., and MacCallum, D. K. (2002). Hyaluronan metabolism and distribution in stratified differentiated cultures of epidermal keratinocytes. In *Hyaluronan Volume 1* (Eds. Kennedy, J. F., Phillips, G. O., Williams, P. A. , and Hascall, V.C.), Woodhead, Cambridge, UK, 511-516.

69. Rilla, K., Lammi, M. J., Sironen, R. K., Hascall, V.C., Midura, R. J., Tammi, M., and Tammi, R. (2002). Hyaluronan synthase 2 (HAS2) regulates migration of epidermal kerationocytes. In *Hyaluronan Volume 1* (Eds.

Kennedy, J. F., Phillips, G. O., Williams, P. A., and Hascall, V.C.), Woodhead, Cambridge, UK, 557-560.

70. Rilla, K., Lammi, M. J., Sironen, R. K., Törrönen, K., Luukkonen, M., Hascall, V.C., Midura, R. J., Hyttinen, M., Pelkonen, J., Tammi, M., and Tammi, R. (2002). Changed lamellipodial extension, adhesion plaques and migratin in epidermal keratinocytes containing constitutively expressed sense and antisense *hyaluronan synthase 2 (Has2)* genes. J Cell Sci 115, 3633-3643.

71. Tammi, M., Pienimäki, J. P., Rilla, K., Fülöp, C., Lammi, M. J., Sironen, R. K., Midura, R., Hascall, V.C., Luukkonen, M., Törrönen, K., Lehto, T., and Tammi, R. (2002). EGF regulates HAS2 expression controls epidermal thickness and stimulates kerationocyte migration. In *Hyaluronan Volume 1* (Eds. Kennedy, J.F., Phillips, G.O., Williams, P.A. , and Hascall, V.C.), Woodhead, Cambridge, UK, 561-570.

72. Tammi, R., Rilla, K., Pienimäki, J. P., Hogg, M., MacCallum, D. K., Hascall, V.C., and Tammi, M. (2002). Intracellular hyaluronan in epidermal keratinocytes. In *Hyaluronan Volume 1* (Eds. Kennedy, J. F., Phillips, G.O., Williams, P.A., and Hascall, V.C.), Woodhead, Cambridge, UK, 517-524.

73. Toole, B. P., and Hascall, V.C. (2002). Hyaluronan and tumor growth. Am J Pathol 161 (3), 745-747.

74. de la Motte, C. A., Hascall, V.C., Drazba, J. A., Banyopadhyay, S. K., and Strong, S. A. (2003). Mononuclear leukocytes bind to specific hyaluronan structures on colon mucosal smooth muscle cells treated with polyinosinic acid:polycytidylic acid. Inter-α-trypsin inhibitor is crucial to structure and function. Am J Pathol 163 (1), 1-13.

75. Fülöp, C., Szántó, S., Mukhopadhyay, D., Bárdos, T., Kamath, R. V., Rugg, M. S., Day, A. J., Salustri, A., Hascall, V.C., Glant, T. T., and Mikecz, K. (2003). Impaired cumulus mucification and female sterility in tumor necrosis factor-induced protein-6 deficient mice. Development 130, 2253-2261.

76. Gordon, L. B., Harten, I. A., Calabro, A., Sugumaran, G., Csoka, A. B., Brown, W. T., Hascall, V., and Toole, B. P. (2003). Hyaluronan is not elevated in urine or serum in Hutchinson-Gilford Progeria Syndrome. Hum Genet 113 (2), 178-187.

77. Knepper, M. A., Saidel, G. M., Hascall, V.C., and Dwyer, T. (2003). Concentration of solutes in the renal inner medulla: interstitial hyaluronan as a mechano-osmotic transducer. Am J Physiol Renal Physiol 284 (3), F433-446.

78. Mack, J. A., Abramson, S. R., Ben, Y., Coffin, J. C., Rothrock, J. K., Maytin, E. V., Hascall, V.C., Largman, C., and Stelnicki, E. J. (2003). *Hoxb13*

knockout adult skin exhibits high levels of hyaluronan and enhanced wound healing. Faseb J 17 (10), 1352-1354.

79. Majors, A.K., Austin, R.C., de la Motte, C.A., Pyeritz, R.E., Hascall, V.C., Kessler, S.P., Sen, G., and Strong, S.A. (2003). Endoplasmic reticulum stress induces hyaluronan deposition and leukocyte adhesion. J Biol Chem 278 (47), 47223-47231.

80. Hascall, V.C., Majors, A. K., De La Motte, C. A., Evanko, S. P., Wang, A., Drazba, J. A., Strong, S. A., and Wight, T. N. (2004). Intracellular hyaluronan: a new frontier for inflammation? Biochim Biophys Acta 1673 (1-2), 3-12.

81. Karousou, E. G., Militsopoulou, M., Porta, G., De Luca, G., Hascall, V.C., and Passi, A. (2004). Polyacrylamide gel electrophoresis of fluorophore-labeled hyaluronan and chondroitin sulfate disaccharides: application to the analysis in cells and tissues. Electrophoresis 25 (17), 2919-2925.

82. Selbi, W., de la Motte, C., Hascall, V., and Phillips, A. (2004). BMP-7 modulates hyaluronan-mediated proximal tubular cell-monocyte interaction. J Am Soc Nephrol 15 (5), 1199-1211.

83. Wang, A., and Hascall, V.C. (2004). Hyaluronan structures synthesized by rat mesangial cells in response to hyperglycemia induce monocyte adhesion. J Biol Chem 279 (11), 10279-10285.

84. Zhuo, L., Hascall, V.C., and Kimata, K. (2004). Inter-α-trypsin Inhibitor, a Covalent Protein-Glycosaminoglycan-Protein Complex. J Biol Chem 279 (37), 38079-38082.

85. de la Motte, C. A., Drazva, J., Bandyopahhyay, S., Majors, A. K., Hascall, V.C., and Strong, S. A. (2005). Viral stimuli induce novel hyaluornan cable structures on colon smooth muscle cells that bind leukocytes externally and nuclei internally. In *Hyaluronan: Structure, Metabolism, Biological Activities, Therapeutic Applications Volume I* (Eds. Balazs, E.A. , and Hascall, V.C.), Matrix Biology Institute, Edgewater, NJ 07020 (USA), 109-116.

86. Grande-Allen, K. J., Vesely, I., and Hascall, V.C. (2005). Identification, localization, and function of proteoglycans in normal and diseased valves and valvular cell cultures. In *Hyaluronan: Structure, Metabolism, Biological Activities, Therapeutic Applications Volume II* (Eds. Balazs, E.A. and Hascall, V.C.), Matrix Biology Institute, Edgewater, NJ (USA), 887-890.

87. Lopez, S., Hascall, V.C., and Mahendroo, M. (2005). Regulated expression of HAS2 during cervical ripening. In *Hyaluronan: Structure, Metabolism, Biological Activities, Therapeutic Applications Volume II* (Eds. Balazs, E.A. and Hascall, V.C.), Matrix Biology Institute, Edgewater, NJ (USA), 703-711.

88. Mack, J. A., Abramson, S. R., Ben, Y., Coffin, J. C., Rothrock, J. K., Maytin, E. V., Hascall, V.C., Largman, C., and Stelnicki, E. J. (2005). *Hoxb13* knockout adult skin exhibits high levels of hyaluronan and enhanced wound healing. In *Hyaluronan: Structure, Metabolism, Biological Activities, Therapeutic Applications Volume II* (Eds. Balazs, E.A. and Hascall, V.C.), Matrix Biology Institute, Edgewater, NJ (USA), 791-796.

89. Majors, A. K., Austin, R. C., De La Motte, C. A., Pyeritz, R. E., Zhou, J., Hascall, V.C., Clark, B. A., Kessler, S. P., Sen, G., and Strong, S. A. (2005). Endoplasmic reticulum stress alters the structure and function of hyaluronan. In *Hyaluronan: Structure, Metabolism, Biological Activities, Therapeutic Applications Volume II* (Eds. Balazs, E.A. and Hascall, V.C.), Matrix Biology Institute, Edgewater, NJ (USA), 591-595.

90. Pasonen-Seppänen, S., Tammi, M., Törrönën, K., MacCallum, D., Hascall, V.C., Maytin, E., and Tammi, R. (2005). Retinoic acid upregulates hyaluronan production but retards keratinocyte differentiation. In *Hyaluronan: Structure, Metabolism, Biological Activities, Therapeutic Applications Volume II* (Eds. Balazs, E.A. and Hascall, V.C.), Matrix Biology Institute, Edgewater, NJ (USA), 565-569.

91. Rugg, M. S., Willis, A. C., Mukhopadhyay, D., Hascall, V.C., Fries, E., Fülöp, C., Milner, C. M., and Day, A. J. (2005). Characterization of complexes formed between TSG-6 and inter-α-inhibitor that act as intermediates in the covalent transfer of heavy chains onto hyaluronan. J Biol Chem 280 (27), 25674-25686.

92. Straach, K. J., Shelton, J. M., Richardson, J. A., Hascall, V.C., and Mahendroo, M. S. (2005). Regulation of hyaluronan expression during cervical riping. Glycobiology 15, 55-65.

93. Tammi, R. H., Pasonen-Seppanen, S., Kultti, A., Hyttinen, J. M., MacCallum, D., Hascall, V.C., and Tammi, M. I. (2005). Hyaluronan degradation in epidermis. In *Hyaluronan: Structure, Metabolism, Biological Activities, Therapeutic Applications Volume I* (Eds. Balazs, E.A. and Hascall, V.C.), Matrix Biology Institute, Edgewater, NJ (USA), 241-245.

94. Wang, A., and Hascall, V.C. (2005). Hyperglycemia induces hyaluornan-mediated monocyte adhesion to rat mesangial cells. In *Hyaluronan: Structure, Metabolism, Biological Activities, Therapeutic Applications Volume II* (Eds. Balazs, E.A. and Hascall, V.C.), Matrix Biology Institute, Edgewater, NJ (USA), 781-786.

95. Zhang, X. L., Selbi, W., de la Motte, C., Hascall, V., and Phillips, A. O. (2005). Bone morphogenic protein-7 inhibits monocyte-stimulated TGF-

beta1 generation in renal proximal tubular epithelial cells. J Am Soc Nephrol 16 (1), 79-89.

96. Zhuo, L., Salustri, A., Atsumi, F., Kawano, M., Wu, J., Shen, L., Ogura, A., Yasue, H., Hascall, V.C., and Kimata, K. (2005). Role of serum-derived hyaluronan-associated protein in the construction of cumulus matrix and oocyte maturation. In *Hyaluronan: Structure, Metabolism, Biological Activities, Therapeutic Applications Volume II* (Eds. Balazs, E.A. and Hascall, V.C.), Matrix Biology Institute, Edgewater, NJ (USA), 731-735.

97. Selbi, W., de la Motte, C. A., Hascall, V.C., Day, A. J., Bowen, T., and Phillips, A. O. (2006). Characterization of hyaluronan cable structure and function in renal proximal tubular epithelial cells. Kidney Int 70 (7), 1287-1295.

98. Vigetti, D., Ori, M., Viola, M., Genasetti, A., Karousou, E., Rizzi, M., Pallotti, F., Nardi, I., Hascall, V.C., De Luca, G., and Passi, A. (2006). Molecular cloning and characterization of UDP-glucose dehydrogenase from the amphibian Xenopus laevis and its involvement in hyaluronan synthesis. J Biol Chem 281 (12), 8254-8263.

99. Pasonen-Seppanen, S. M., Maytin, E. V., Torronen, K. J., Hyttinen, J. M. T., Hascall, V.C., MacCallum, D. K., Kultti, A. H., Jokela, T. A., Tammi, M. I., and Tammi, R. H. (2008). All-trans Retinoic Acid-Induced Hyaluronan Production and Hyperplasia Are Partly Mediated by EGFR Signaling in Epidermal Keratinocytes. J Invest Dermatol 128 (4), 797-807.

Edited Books

1. Kuettner, K. E., Schleyerbach, R., and Hascall, V.C., eds. (1986). *Articular Cartilage Biochemistry*. Raven Press, New York, NY (USA).

2. Kuettner, K. E., Schleyerbach, R., Peyron, J. G., and Hascall, V.C., eds. (1992). *Articular Cartilage and Osteoarthritis*. Raven Press, New York, NY (USA).

3. Hascall, V.C., and Yanagishita, M., eds. (1997-). *Glycoforum. Hyaluronan Today (Accessed at http://www.glycoforum.gr.jp/)*. Seikagaku Corporation Glycoforum, Tokyo (JP).

4. Kennedy, J.F., Phillips, G.O., Williams, P.A., and Hascall, V.C., eds. (2002). *Hyaluronan. Volume 1. Chemical, Biochemical and Biological Aspects*. Woodhead, Cambridge (UK), 577 pgs.

5. Kennedy, J. F., Phillips, G.O., Williams, P.A., and Hascall, V.C., eds. (2002). *Hyaluronan. Volume 2. Biomedical, Medical and Clinical Aspects.* Woodhead, Cambridge (UK), 517 pgs.

6. Kuettner, K.E., and Hascall, V.C., eds. (2002). *The Many Faces of Osteoarthritis.* Birkhäuser Verlag AG, Basel, Switzerland (CH).

7. Balazs, E.A., and Hascall, V.C., eds. (2005). *Hyaluronan. Structure, Metabolism, Biological Activities, Therapeutic Applications (2 Volumes).* Matrix Biology Institute, Edgewater, NJ 07020 (USA), 912 pgs.

Koji Kimata, 2007 (photograph courtesy of K. Kimata)

Koji Kimata

Koji Kimata (b. 1941 in Tajimi City, Gifu prefecture, Japan) is Professor Emeritus at the Institute for Molecular Science and Medicine, Aichi Medical University in Nagakute, Japan. He received his B.S. (1964), M.S. (1966), and Ph.D. (1975) degrees in Biochemistry from Nagoya University. He started to work at the Department of Chemistry of Nagoya University in 1967, where he stayed till 1987. He was visiting associate at the National Institute of Dental Research, NIH, Bethesda, Maryland. He became Associate Professor at the Institute for Molecular Science of Medicine, Aichi Medical University in 1987 and Professor and Director of the Institute in 1991. He retired from the professorial position in 2007, and became director of a newly established facility, the Research Complex for the Medicine Frontiers at the same university. Dr. Kimata is on the editorial board of several scientific journals. He was president of the Japanese Matrix Club (2001-2003) and of the Japanese Society for Connective Tissue Research (2003-2005), and is still an active member of many Japanese and international scientific societies. He is a founding member of the International Society for Hyaluronan Sciences (ISHAS).

Interview*

Please, tell us something about yourself.

I was professor of Institute for Molecular Science of Medicine at the Aichi Medical University but I just retired. I am 65 years old and that is retirement age in most Japanese universities. But I got a new position at the University, and am going to advise the graduate students on how to do experiments and also on other topics.

Where did you grow up?

I grew up in Tajimi City, Gifu prefecture, in central Honshu. Tajimi City is famous for the production of china and, generally, ceramics. I went to school there and then I started my university studies at the University of Nagoya, where I studied at the Department of Chemistry. My original specialty is biochemistry. I received both my Master's degree and Ph.D. at Nagoya University. The topic that originally interested me was in limb buds, specifically chick limb buds and how it happens that cells differenciate into cartilage and bone for the limb bud. My professor was interested in glycosaminoglycans in the extracellular matrix. This was in the early 1960s and at that time not so many people were yet interested in those polysaccharides. In fact, they were not even called that way then, they called them mucopolysaccharides. I started to work on the analysis of the glycosaminoglycan compositions of cartilage and the bone and also on the relationship between cells and the matrix and on how they "talk to each other" to give a signal to make cartilage and bone.

What kind of actual experiments did you do?

---

* The interview was recorded during the Hyaluronan Meeting in Charleston, South Carolina, April 2007.

We got cells from small tissues of chicken limb buds and cultured them in specific media and put some polysaccharides in them and then looked at the effects, whether there followed growth or not. Then I was also interested in how to make a matrix. Of course, the mucopolysaccharides are major molecules of the cartilage matrix and are very important for its function, so I got interested in how to make these kinds of polymers. I think that was the beginning of how I got interested in hyaluronan because it is one of the major polysaccharides in the cartilage matrix. We got some good results and published them.

Later, I went to study abroad, to the United States, to George Martin, who was very famous that time in the extracellular matrix community. He was the one who discovered laminin, a protein unique to the basement membrane and important in the normal, ordered growth of epithelial cells. He was that time at the National Institute of Dental Research and was kind enough to invite me to study in his institute as a visiting scientist, not as a postdoctoral fellow. Unfortunately, I could only spend two years in his laboratory because at that time it was not allowed to go abroad for a longer period if you had a position at a university. I was at that time already an assistant professor at Nagoya University.

But the two years I spent in Dr. Martin's laboratory were very useful to me. He had a wide knowledge about the extracellular matrix. He was especially interested in tumor matrix—I think that was the time when he started to work on the biology of cancer and he also recommended me to do that. George Martin had his laboratory on the fourth floor and at that time Vincent Hascall was on the first floor; that is when I got to know him. Dr. Martin was not pushing about what I was doing, he basically said that I could do what I liked, so I went downstairs and started to collaborate with Vince and started with proteoglycan aggregates in tumor cartilage. But I also have to say that I was stimulated by Dr. Martin's interest in cancer. That is the reason why I am so much interested in hyaluronan because hyaluronan is produced by tumor cells.

Did you know that already at that time?

No, not yet. There were only a few reports that time about this. After my stay at Dr. Martin's lab I went back to Japan and started to work on the extracellular matrix in cancer tissues. I think that it was a very original work. First, I studied the matrix of mammary gland tumors. At that time many people tried to isolate malignant cells and benign cells separately from a tumor cell line. Some Japanese scientists established the cell line that was very easy to metastasize even though the original one was benign; so I compared the matrix in the benign mammary gland tumor cell line with the one in the malignant one. I found that the malignant mammary gland tumor cells produced a hundred times more hyaluronan than the benign cells did. The benign cells made almost none.

Does this hyaluronan stay in the malignant cell or does it go into the blood stream?

It stays around the cells. So I hypothesized that, considering the biological properties of hyaluronan, hyaluronan maybe makes cells more migratory, which is beneficial for their metastatic malignancy, and also that the hyaluronan coat around the cells causes some kind of resistency to the leukocyte cells. It is a kind of host cell self defense. We published this work around 1983.

This was over twenty years ago and even today we still do not know much about the relationship between hyaluronan and cancer.

That is true. But many things are clearer now. An example is the receptors, the CD44 or RHAMM. At that time we did not know anything about them and now we do. At that time we did not know how cells make hyaluronan. I mean biochemical mechanisms for the synthesis. We did not know anything about that.

The synthesis of hyaluronan is still not fully understood.

Right. Hyaluronan has a very specific mechanism compared to the mechanisms for other glycosaminoglycans because hyaluronan doesn't have core-proteins. For example, in case of chondroitin sulfate or heparin sulfate; core-proteins are initiators for the synthesis but it is still not known how hyaluronan synthesis starts.

But hyaluronan is found in the rooster comb and the umbilical cord where there are always proteins...

For example, for the biosynthesis of chondroitin sulfate a coprotein is there and to its serine residues the transferases add xylose and two galactose and then glucuronosyl and N-acetylgalactosaminyl transferase sequentially work to make long chains. But in the case of hyaluronan, this is not the case, so how do you think that polysaccharide can be made?

I have no idea.

We thought that there must be some proteins. As you know, the hyaluronan molecule is very long, it has a high molecular weight, about 1000 kD or more. If it has any core-proteins, it must be very difficult to find them. So we purified hyaluronan as much as possible and then we found that some were covalently bound to proteins. So, we thought that there must be core-proteins and we succeeded in isolating them. But, although we tried labeling the proteins with radio isotope, we couldn't label them. Then, eventually we found that the proteins originated from the serum and those proteins covalently attached to hyaluronan after hyaluronan was synthesized and secreted to the matrix. So again, we had to ask how hyaluronan is made. Finally, we took a different method. I think, it was a good idea at that time to isolate hyaluronan synthase enzymes, which may be a clue to understand the mechanisms of the synthesis. We tried to isolate hyaluronan synthase and we used molecular biological techniques. We used mouse mammary carcinoma FM3A cells with a high activity to synthesize hyaluronan in the presence of carcinogens to change the DNA. And we got mutants with almost no activity to synthesize hyaluronan. So we had hyaluronan-producing cells and others which could not make hyaluronan, and we compared the RNA message levels. We then isolated a cDNA for the messenger RNA, which is specifically expressed in the original FM3A cells and not expressed in the mutants and confirmed that the cloned cDNA is responsible for synthesis of hyaluronan. This technique is called expression cloning. That is the story of how we first found a hyaluronan synthase; so we succeeded in isolating a cDNA for hyaluronan synthase. The hyaluronan synthase that we found, people now call HAS1, because that was the first such hyaluronan synthase; then later other people found HAS2 and HAS3.

Are you related to companies?

No, not now. But I used to be involved in some projects in collaboration with the Seikagaku Corporation. That was the first company that succeeded in applying hyaluronan to a therapeutic medicine in Japan as far as I know. But I retired from that, too.

How long have you known Bandi?

Bandi is a very famous person. I have known him for a long time. When I started to study hyaluronan, I read his books, at that time his books were very special and important for that kind of study. In person, I met him three years ago for the first time.

How strong is hyaluronan-related research in Japan?

It is quite strong. There is the Seikagaku Corporation that first used hyaluronan for therapy, to cure osteoarthritis, in particular. And I think Dr. Balazs had been involved with that application even before them.

Coming back to your career, what would you say was your greatest success in science?

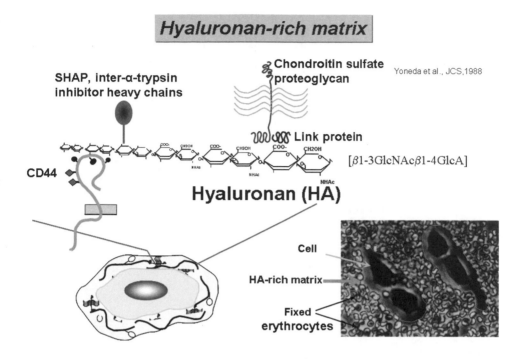

Illustration for SHAP (courtesy of K. Kimata)

I think, if I myself have to decide what my own success was, one is the discovery of the SHAP, and the other is the isolation of cDNA for hyaluronan synthase.

Now that you are retired, are you still involved with research in this field?

Yes, I am. I would say, I am deeply involved in research. I am now a chief of the Research Complex for the Medicine Frontiers as well as Professor Emeritus in Aichi Medical University. My obligation is not only to make arrangements to organize the collaboration between medical scientists in Aichi Medical University and industrial scientists but also to do my own research with graduate students so as to introduce and guide medical doctors how to do experiments, especially biochemical and molecular biochemical ones.

What is SHAP?

SHAP stands for Serum-derived Hyaluronan-Associated-Proteins. We isolated this SHAP-hyaluronan complex from the extracellular matrices of mouse cells that were cultured in the presence of serum, back in the early 1990s, as I already mentioned it briefly above.[1] To make a long story short, it is now getting clear how SHAP plays a role in hyaluronan functions. This molecule makes hyaluronan strings close together so that inflammatory cells easily adhere to the strand for the activation.

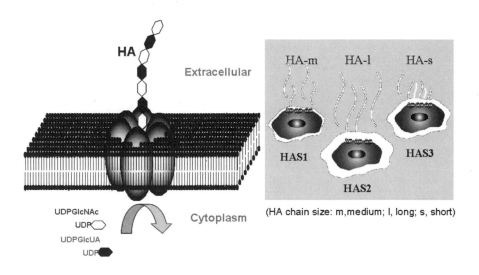

Mammalian hyaluronan synthases and different characteristics of hyaluronan and the hyaluronan-marix that they generated (courtesy of K. Kimata)

What do you expect the next important breakthrough will be in the HA field?

Recently, there have been many reports to describe that fragments of hyaluronan (that is, smaller molecules) have some unique functions that the long ones do not have. For example, long hyaluronan molecules never show such an activity, but smaller ones accelerate angiogenesis, and that is interesting to me. This means that somehow angiogenic cells recognize the size of hyaluronan molecules, even though the size of hyaluronan fragments varies from report to report. The mechanisms for the size recognition are important for the further understanding of hyaluronan functions. In addition, there are many hyaluronan binding proteins—including SHAP that we discovered— that may modify its three-dimensional structure and its functions. If general concepts were found for those modifications, they would be very helpful in understanding how hyaluronan functions. I should like to emphasize here that those understandings are certainly beneficial for the therapeutic application of hyaluronan.

What are the questions in this field that you would like to see the answer to most?

In my opinion, it would be very interesting to know what kinds of molecules could interact with hyaluronan. Binding molecules are important for the constructions of structures of those macromolecular complexes whose major component is hyaluronan. Binding molecules, such as CD44, a hyaluronan receptor, are important for the signal transduction of hyaluronan into cells.

Will hyaluronan in particular and the extracellular matrix in general ever be considered as important in the scientific community as proteins or DNA?

Frankly speaking, this has not happened until now. But, most scientists now start to consider the extracellular matrix and in particular, hyaluronan, as important as proteins or the DNA. If you look at the literature, you can see how it is described that many of the knockout genes of mice for extracellular matrix molecules and hyaluronan synthase can be lethal; thus, you can easily understand their importance. Proteins and the DNA are one side and extracellular matrix and hyaluronan as the environmental factors are the other side. Both are important. No life would have been created without interactions between the environment, the proteins, and the DNA.

Anything else that you would like to add?

Nothing in particular.

Reference

1 Yoneda, M., Suzuki, S., Kimata, K. (1990). Hyaluronic acid associated with the surfaces of cultured fibroblasts is linked to a serum-derived 85-kDa protein. J Biol Chem 265, 5247-5257.

Bibliography*
Hyaluronan-Related Publications

1. Kimata, K., Honma, Y., Okayama, M., Oguri, K., Hozumi, M., and Suzuki, S. (1983). Increased synthesis of hyaluronic acid by mouse mammary carcinoma cell variants with high metastatic potential. Cancer Res 43 (3), 1347-1354.

2. Yamagata, M., Yamada, K. M., Yoneda, M., Suzuki, S., and Kimata, K. (1986). Chondroitin Sulfate Proteoglycan (PG-M-like Proteoglycan) is Involved in the Binding of Hyaluronic Acid to Cellular Fibronectin. J Biol Chem 261 (29), 13526-13535.

3. Yoneda, M., Shimizu, S., Nishi, Y., Yamagata, M., Suzuki, S., and Kimata, K. (1988). Hyaluronic acid-dependant change in the extracellular matrix of mouse dermal fibroblasts that is conducive to cell proliferation. J Cell Sci 90 (Part 2), 275-286.

4. Yoneda, M., Yamagata, M., Suzuki, S., and Kimata, K. (1988). Hyaluronic acid modulates proliferation of mouse dermal fibroblasts in culture. J Cell Sci 90 (Part 2), 265-273.

5. Yoneda, M., Suzuki, S., and Kimata, K. (1990). Hyaluronic acid associated with the surfaces of cultured fibroblasts is linked to a serum-derived 85-kDa protein. J Biol Chem 265 (9), 5247-5257.

6. Huang, L., Yoneda, M., and Kimata, K. (1993). A serum-derived hyaluronan-associated protein (SHAP) is the heavy chain of the inter α–trypsin inhibitor. J Biol Chem 268 (35), 26725-26730.

7. Zhao, M., Yoneda, M., Ohashi, Y., Kurono, S., Iwata, H., Ohnuki, Y., and Kimata, K. (1995). Evidence for the covalent binding of SHAP, heavy chains of inter-α-trypsin inhibitor, to hyaluronan. J Biol Chem 270 (44), 26657-26663.

8. Itano, N., and Kimata, K. (1996). Molecular cloning of human hyaluronan synthase. Biochem Biophys Res Commun 222, 816-820.

---

* Provided by the interviewee.

9. Itano, N., and Kimata, K. (1996). Expression Cloning and Molecular Characterization of HAS Protein, a Eukaryotic Hyaluronan Synthase. J Biol Chem 271 (17), 9875-9878.

10. Spicer, A. P., Seldin, M. F., Olsen, A. S., Brown, N., Wells, D. E., Doggett, N. A., Itano, N., Kimata, K., Inazawa, J., and McDonald, J. A. (1997). Chromosomal localization of the human and mouse hyaluronan synthase genes. Genomics 41, 493-497.

11. Watanabe, H., Cheung, S. C., Itano, N., Kimata, K., and Yamada, Y. (1997). Identification of hyaluronan-binding domains of aggrecan. J Biol Chem 272 (44), 28057-28065.

12. Yamada, Y., Itano, N., Zako, M., Yoshida, M., Lenas, P., Niimi, A., Ueda, M., and Kimata, K. (1998). The gene structure and promoter sequence of mouse hyaluronan synthase 1(mHAS1). Biocheim Journ 330 (1223-1227).

13. Ichikawa, T., Itano, N., Sawai, T., Kimata, K., Koganehira, Y., Saida, T., and Taniguchi, S. (1999). Increased synthesis of hyaluronate enhances motility of human melanoma cells. J Invest Dermatol 113 (6), 935-939.

14. Itano, N., Sawai, T., Yoshida, M., Lenas, P., Yamada, Y., Imagawa, M., Shinomura, T., Hamaguchi, M., Yoshida, Y., Ohnuki, Y., Miyauchi, S., Spicer, A. P., Mcdonald, J. A., and Kimata, K. (1999). Three isoforms of mammalian hyaluronan synthases have distinct enzymatic properties. J Biochem 274, 25085-25092.

15. Takada, Y., Sakiyama, H., Kuriiwa, K., Musuda, R., Inoue, N., Nakagawa, K., Itano, N., Saito, T., Yamada, T., and Kimata, K. (1999). Metabolic activities of partially degenerated hypertrophic chondrocytes: gene expression of hyaluronan synthases. Cell Tissue Res 298, 317-325.

16. Yamada, Y., Itano, N., Narimatsu, H., Kudo, T., Hirohashi, S., Ochiai, A., Niimi, A., Ueda, M., and Kimata, K. (1999). Receptor for hyaluronan-mediated motility and CD44 expressions in colon cancer assessed by quantitative analysis using real-time reverse transcriptase-polymerase chain reaction. Jpn J Cancer Res 90 (9), 987-992.

17. Perissinotto, D., Iacopetti, P., Bellina, I., Doliana, R., Colombatti, A., Pettway, Z., Bronner-Fraser, M., Shinomura, T., Kimata, K., Morgelin, M., Lofberg, J., and Perris, R. (2000). Avian neural crest cell migration is diversely regulated by the two major hyaluronan-binding proteoglycans PG-M/versican and aggrecan. Development 127 (13), 2823-2842.

18. Yoneda, M., Zhao, M., Zhuo, L., Watanabe, H., Yamada, Y., Huang, L., Nagasawa, S., Nishimura, H., Shinomura, T., Isogai, Z., and Kimata, K. (2000). Roles of inter-α-trypsin inhibitor and hyaluronan-binding proteoglycans in hyaluronan-rich matrix formation. In *New Frontiers in*

Medical Sciences: Redefining Hyaluronan (Proceedings of the Symposium held in Padua, Italy, 17-19 June 1999) (Eds. Abatangelo, G., and Weigel, P.), Elsevier, Amsterdam, The Netherlands, 21-30.

19. Yoshida, M., Itano, N., Yamada, Y., and Kimata, K. (2000). In vitro synthesis of hyaluronan by a single protein derived from mouse HAS1 gene and characterization of amino acid residues essential for the activity. J Biol Chem 275, 497-506.

20. Kimata, K., and Zhuo, L. (2001). SHAP, a protein covalently bound to hyaluronan. In *Glycoforum Hyaluronan Today* (Eds. Hascall, V.C. and Yanagishita, M.) (Seikagaku Corporation Glycoforum)(Accessed at http://www.glycoforum.gr.jp/science /hyaluronan/HA22/HA22E.html), Tokyo (JP).

21. Kimata, K., and Zhuo, L. (2001). [Dissecting the structure and function of the extracellular hyaluronan-rich matrix by gene manipulation]. Seikagaku 73 (6), 429-438.

22. Sawai, T., Itano, N., Yoshida, M., and Kimata, K. (2001). Regulation of hyaluronan synthase: negative effects on the hyaluronan synthetic activity of the mutated HAS protein that has no enzymatic activity. Int Congress Series 1223, 183-187.

23. Tominaga, A., Tajima, S., Ishibashi, A., and Kimata, K. (2001). Reticular erythematouc mucinosis syndrome with an infiltratino of factor XIIIa+ and hyaluronan synthase 2+ dermal dendrocytesq. Br J Derm 145, 141-145.

24. Zhuo, L., Yoneda, M., Zhao, M., Yingsung, W., Yoshida, N., Kitagawa, Y., Kawamura, K., Suzuki, T., and Kimata, K. (2001). Defect in SHAP-hyaluronan complex causes severe female infertility. J Biol Chem 276 (11), 7693-7696.

25. Itano, N., Atsumi, F., Sawai, T., Yamada, Y., Miyaishi, O., Senga, T., Hamaguchi, M., and Kimata, K. (2002). Abnormal accumulation of hyaluronan matrix diminishes contact inhibition of cell growth and promotes cell migration. Proc Natl Acad Sci U S A 99 (6), 3609-3614.

26. Itano, N., and Kimata, K. (2002). Mammalian hyaluronan synthases. IUBMB Life 54, 195-199.

27. Yada, T., Maeda, H., Sakura, Y., and Kimata, K. (2002). Hyaluronan during liver regeneration after partial hepatectomy: transient accumulation in the tissue and elevation of the serum concentration. In *Hyaluronan Volume 2 Biomedical, Medical and Clinical Aspects* (Eds. Kennedy, J.F., Phillips, G.O., Williams, P.A., and Hascall, V.C.), Woodhead, Cambridge (UK), 209-216.

28. Zhao, M., Yoneda, M., Zhuo, L., Huang, L., Watanabe, H., Yamada, Y., Nagasawa, S., Nishimura, H., and Kimata, K. (2002). Proteoglycan enhances

the formation of the SHAP-Hyaluronan complex and its effect in hyaluronan-rich matrix. In *Hyaluronan Volume 1 Chemical, Biochemical and Biological Aspects* (Eds. Kennedy, J.F., Phillips, G.O., Williams, P.A. , and Hascall, V.C.), Woodhead, Cambridge (UK), 487-500.

29. Matsumoto, K., Shionyu, M., Go, M., Shimizu, K., Shinomura, T., Kimata, K., and Watanabe, H. (2003). Distinct interaction of versican/PG-M with hyaluronan and link protein. J Biol Chem 278 (42), 41205-41212.

30. Yingsung, W., Zhuo, L., Morgelin, M., Yoneda, M., Kida, D., Watanabe, H., ishiguro, N., iwata, H., and Kimata, K. (2003). Molecular heterogeneity of the SHAP-Hyaluronan complex. J Biol Chem 278 (35), 32710-32718.

31. Itano, N., Sawai, T., Atsumi, F., Miyaishi, O., Taniguchi, S., Kannagi, R., Hamaguchi, M., and Kimata, K. (2004). Selective expression and functional characteristics of three mammalian hyaluronan synthases in oncogenic malignant transformation. J Biol Chem 279 (18), 18679-18687.

32. Kakizaki, I., Kojima, K., Takagaki, K., Endo, M., Kannagi, R., Ito, M., Maruo, Y., Sato, H., Yasuda, T., Mita, S., Kimata, K., and Itano, N. (2004). A novel mechanism for the inhibition of hyaluronan biosynthesis by 4-methylumbelliferone. J Biol Chem 279 (32), 33281-33289.

33. Takeo, S., Fujise, M., Akiyama, T., Habuchi, H., Itano, N., Matsuo, T., Aigaki, T., Kimata, K., and Nakato, H. (2004). In vivo hyaluronan synthesis upon expression of the mammalian hyaluronan synthase gene in Drosophila. J Biol Chem 279 (18), 18920-18925.

34. Yamada, Y., Itano, N., Hata, K., Ueda, M., and Kimata, K. (2004). Differential regulation by IL-1beta and EGF of expression of three different hyaluronan synthases in oral mucosal epithelial cells and fibroblasts and dermal fibroblasts: quantitative analysis using real-time RT-PCR. J Invest Dermatol 122 (3), 631-639.

35. Yamada, Y., Itano, N., Narimatsu, H., Kudo, T., Morozumi, K., Hirohashi, S., Ochiai, A., Ueda, M., and Kimata, K. (2004). Elevated transcript level of hyaluronan synthase1 gene correlates with poor prognosis of human colon cancer. Clin Exp Metastasis 21 (1), 57-63.

36. Yoshida, M., Sai, S., Marumo, K., Tanaka, T., Itano, N., Kimata, K., and Fujii, K. (2004). Expression analysis of three isoforms of hyaluronan synthase and hyaluronidase in the synovium of knees in osteoarthritis and rheumatoid arthritis by quantitative real-time reverse transcriptase polymerase chain reaction. Arthritis Res Ther 6 (6), R514-520.

37. Itano, N., Kakizaki, I., Mita, S., Endo, M., Takagaki, K., and Kimata, K. (2005). A mechanism for 4-methylumbelliferone-mediated inhibition of hyaluronan biosynthesis. In *Hyaluronan Structure, Metabolism, Biological*

Activities, Therapeutic Applications Volume I (Eds. Balazs, E.A. and Hascall, V.C.), Matrix Biology Institute, Edgewater, NJ (USA), 147-153.

38. Zhuo, L., Salustri, A., Atsumi, F., Kawano, M., Wu, J., Shen, L., Ogura, A., Yasue, H., Hascall, V. C., and Kimata, K. (2005). Role of serum-derived hyaluronan-associated protein in the construction of cumulus matrix and oocyte maturation. In *Hyaluronan: Structure, Metabolism, Biological Activities, Therapeutic Applications Volume II* (Eds. Balazs, E.A. and Hascall, V.C.), Matrix Biology Institute, Edgewater, NJ (USA), 731-735.

39. Koyama, H., Hibi, T., Isogai, Z., Yoneda, M., Fujimori, M., Amano, J., Kawakubo, M., Kannagi, R., Kimata, K., Taniguchi, S., and Itano, N. (2007). Hyperproduction of hyaluronan in neu-induced mammary tumor accelerates angiogenesis through stromal cell recruitment: possible involvement of versican/PG-M. Am J Pathol 170 (3), 1086-1099.

40. Kakizaki, I., Itano, N., Kimata, K., Hanada, K., Kon, A., Yamaguchi, M., Takahashi, T., and Takagaki, K. (2008). Up-regulation of hyaluronan synthase genes in cultured human epidermal keratinocytes by UVB irradiation. Arch Biochem Biophys 471 (1), 85-93.

41. Kishida, T., Yabushita, H., Wakatsuki, A., Zhuo, L., and Kimata, K. (2008). Hyaluronan (HA) and serum-derived hyaluronan-associated protein (SHAP)-HA complex as predictive markers of cervical ripening in premature labor. Connect Tissue Res 49 (2), 105-108.

42. Koyama, H., Kobayashi, N., Harada, M., Takeoka, M., Kawai, Y., Sano, K., Fujimori, M., Amano, J., Ohhashi, T., Kannagi, R., Kimata, K., Taniguchi, S., and Itano, N. (2008). Significance of tumor-associated stroma in promotion of intratumoral lymphangiogenesis: pivotal role of a hyaluronan-rich tumor microenvironment. Am J Pathol 172 (1), 179-193.

43. Ohno-Jinno, A., Isogai, Z., Yoneda, M., Kasai, K., Miyaishi, O., Inoue, Y., Kataoka, T., Zhao, J. S., Li, H., Takeyama, M., Keene, D. R., Sakai, L. Y., Kimata, K., Iwaki, M., and Zako, M. (2008). Versican and Fibrillin-1 Form a Major Hyaluronan-Binding Complex in the Ciliary Body. Invest Ophthalmol Vis Sci.

44. Zhu, L., Zhuo, L., Watanabe, H., and Kimata, K. (2008). Equivalent involvement of inter-alpha-trypsin inhibitor heavy chain isoforms in forming covalent complexes with hyaluronan. Connect Tissue Res 49 (1), 48-55.

Cheryl Knudson, 2008 (photograph courtesy of C. Knudson)

Cheryl Knudson

Cheryl Knudson (b. 1954 in Pomona, California) received her B.A. degree at Pomona College (1976) and her Ph.D. at the University of Southern California, Los Angeles (1981). She was a postdoctoral fellow at Tufts University School of Medicine (1981-85) in Boston. In 1985 she moved to Chicago, where she was first Assistant Professor (1985-93), Associate Professor (1993-2000), and finally Professor (2000-2006) at Rush Medical College, Rush-Presbyterian-St. Luke's Medical Center in Chicago. Since March 2006, she has been Professor and Chair at the Department of Anatomy & Cell Biology of East Carolina University. She received several honors and awards, among them the Tilllson Prize in Physics (1976), The Exceptional Mentor Award from the Graduate College of Rush University (2003), and many scholarships. She is member of several scientific societies and is a founding member of the International Society of Hyaluronan Sciences (ISHAS).

Interview*

What was your road to science?

When I was a little girl in school, in San Diego, California, I had a wonderful teacher. He exposed us to lots of different ideas from earth sciences to biological sciences and some chemistry. He had a big impact on me. I was also involved with the science fair in the San Diego area; at first doing experimental projects for it and then later also organizing it. I think that teacher and becoming involved with this group of students to organize a science fair influenced my decision to study biology at Pomona College. Pomona was a wonderful environment; it is part of a consortium of colleges including also Harvey Mudd, the Honnold Library and Scripps College nearby and that made it possible to have contact with many different people.

My advisor at Pomona College suggested to me the University of Southern California for graduate studies. I wanted to teach and the program at USC offered me more opportunity to be mentored in teaching than the other schools I considered. For my thesis I worked on the neural crest in the head. I used the chick embryo as the model system, and we looked at the role of the pattern in the mesoderm, how it affected the neural crest cells, when they left the cranial neural tube and started to migrate into the head; how they used the pathway set up or pre-established in the mesoderm. Then we became interested in one of the major extracellular matrix molecules in the head of the embryo, known as hyaluronan—so that was when I first started working on hyaluronan, quite a while ago. I injected hyaluronidase in chick embryos. We made a little window in the eggshell, opened it up and with a pulled glass needle injected the hyaluronidase. Then the neural

---

* This interview was recorded during the second meeting "Conversations on Hyaluronan" in St. Tropez, June 2003.

crest cells stopped migrating because the hydrated hyaluronan-dependent space in which to invade and the spaces between other cells of the mesoderm also condensed.

Basically in my thesis project I was looking at mechanisms, by which these neural crest cells knew their migration pattern, had their information. The question was, was this because they had the information intrinsically or were they gathering information in the extracellular matrix as cues? And so we tried some of those combination experiments where you take the neural crest cells down from the tail, or trunk, and implant them up in the head, and see if they still know how to find their way. In fact, we found that yes, they do, and so there is a lot of information in the mesoderm in the extracellular matrix. Then my thesis advisor, Dr. Stephen Meier, and his postdoctoral mentor Dr. Betty Hay, suggested that I go and work with Dr. Bryan Toole at Tufts because they thought that Bryan would be a good match for me. And that's where I went for my postdoctoral work.

What is your overall impression of hyaluronan research?

I think that there are two different but interacting groups. There are the groups of the physical chemists who are studying the molecule itself and the properties of the molecule; that aspect is more physiology and more mathematical. That is a big part of the hyaluronan field and I always learn something new in this area when I attend a hyaluronan meeting. The other group is involved with how this molecule interacts with proteins, how does hyaluronan interact with aggregating proteoglycans, how does hyaluronan interact with the cell surface, that is the part that I have been most focused on. I have the feeling that the field of hyaluronan is much smaller compared to the field of other extracellular matrix molecules, but interest continues to grow. When you think of the field of integrins, that's a huge field, and all the different molecules as integrin ligands and all that seems much more popular—and maybe easier to do. It's all protein and if you you're trained as a protein chemist or molecular biologist, you look at protein structures and you can do the manipulations and mutations, whereas in the hyaluronan field, it may be more difficult. So I think that the hyaluronan field is more challenging. I wonder if sometimes people come into the field and become frustrated, and then they leave and go back to studying proteins because that seems to be more straightforward. At the same time, the people who stay in the hyaluronan field have a little more tenacity and are able to try and think of a different way to do things because it's not as simple. I think that people who work in this field seem more patient, more cooperative, and able to face difficult problems and not back away, rather keep going forward.

Do you mean that this is a little less glamorous field than the other field?

I think now there is the popular literature in hyaluronan and that seems to be growing faster in notoriety than the actual serious science of hyaluronan... I don't know, about being glamorous. But research that's related to disease processes is quite the preferred type of science nowadays. If you're studying osteoarthritis as more people have the diagnosis of osteoarthritis, it may become popular. My area of research has a little to do with that—or at least with the basic biology of the chondrocytes that can be related to changes with respect to osteoarthritis, so that makes it more attractive, perhaps also to the funding agencies. I think that all aspects where hyaluronan relates to disease processes make it as a molecule, more glamorous. Non-scientists seem to want scientists to work on something that impacts disease processes.

Do you have a sense of the history of the field, where it started?

Some; mainly from listening to Bandi (Dr. Balazs) and Torvard (Dr. Laurent) and reading their work. Although I am not exactly a newcomer, I have pursued topics outside of the initial areas of research in hyaluronan, in the sense that I am interested in how the cells are interacting with the molecule, rather than the biophysical properties of the molecule or the isolation/characterization of the enzymes, the synthases or the hyaluronidases.

What do you consider your most important result in the field of hyaluronan research?

It is how the cells respond to changes in the hyaluronan environment. How hyaluronan is broken down by free radicals or otherwise changed in the extracellular matrix remains unclear but hyaluronan must go through these changes during the course of its life as a molecule. The cells are able to sense those changes and respond to those changes. Because hyaluronan is in all the different tissues and all the cells have experience with that molecule; they have to encounter it, they seem to respond to it. Those are the mechanisms we need to unravel.

It is interesting to observe that embryonic cells are clearly responsive and undergo morphogenesis and healing. Hyaluronan being such an important molecule in the embryo, its ability to function in the embryo to organize other molecules and present other molecules to cells in the embryo is fundamental. When gradients of molecules are established, the edges of a tissue can be determined, and tissues within one organism can undergo different sets of differentiation processes.

What would you like to achieve?

I'd like to figure out how hyaluronan influences molecular gradients, maybe using embryonic cells as a model initially and then see if a mature, differentiated cell could also use that same kind of information, which I think it can. I don't think an adult cell loses all the capacity to respond to these growth factors. But again, it's hard to know because with so many of the experiments that we do; we take the cells out of the whole embryo, out of the whole organism and use a cell culture model, and ask how those cells respond to exogenous factors in the presence of endogenous factors.

You don't use human embryo material…

No. We use chicken and mouse embryo material. We also use some human donor tissue, mature tissues of a range of ages, but not embryonic tissues. So, again, we have model systems and we study if we can adapt those models to determine how human cells respond. We use a lot of bovine material as well, fetal bovine as well as adult bovine tissues.

Do you get enough support for your research?

My main support is from an NIH grant and then also an NIH program project grant. So I'd say baseline support. Sometimes the expense of certain experiments hinders that direction of investigation. It also is difficult to recruit talented people and to offer them a good salary or to keep them because after they have some experience working with me, they are able to move on to another position, where they can get a better salary. So I would say we worry about that too much and it can be a distraction from concentrating on the science itself. I worry about writing my grant applications, making sure my applications are well-organized and well-presented; about resubmissions and that is stressful to me. But those efforts to write grants to obtain funding are necessary.

You are married and you have children.

Yes; and I have two children. It is interesting that there are quite a few married couples involved with hyaluronan studies; Torvard and Ulla Laurent; Anna Engstrom-Laurent and Claude Laurent (see photographs) and, of course, Endre Balazs and Janet Denlinger, just to mention a few.

Did having children delay your becoming an independent scientist?

Yes. I think so, but I think that our choice of joining the Rush Medical College Faculty was a very good choice because that school at that time was very family oriented. There are several husbands and wives who work together there either in the same department or different departments of the school.

Cheryl Knudson, Anna Engstrom-Laurent and Claude Laurent at a meeting at the
Ciba house in London (photograph courtesy of W. Knudson)

From left to right: Cheryl Knudson, Torvard Laurent, Anna Engstrom-Laurent, and
Ulla Laurent at a meeting in Sätre Brunn, Sweden, 1991
(photograph by and courtesy of W. Knudson)

Is it a denominational school?

Yes, it originally had a Presbyterian affiliation. But it was not really due to any influence of the church, but rather the Office of the President and the Office of the Dean that reflected the concepts of being family oriented. The physicians who held those posts liked to talk about their children and about their families. The president is an infectious disease physician and his wife is a surgical nurse, just to give you examples. The sense of the family and the loyalty of the faculty to that university made it such that even though my progress wasn't as fast as other people's, I was still encouraged to stay.

Your husband is in the same field.

Yes, he's in the same field. Warren and I have adjoining laboratories and have successful professional collaboration on our NIH-sponsored research. If you look at our publications we have a lot of publications as co-authors together. When we first came to Rush, our department chairman Dr. Klaus Kuettner and also Dr. Vince Hascall suggested that we should not work together, rather, we should pursue very separate areas of research in order to develop more of our personal identity. But after a while both men changed their minds and advised us to work together.

Where did you meet?

Warren and I met in Bryan Toole's lab. I went to work in Bryan's lab because I looked at him as more of a cellular biochemist, and Warren went to Bryan's lab thinking of Bryan as more of a biologist. And so we had a very different training as graduate students and we saw him very differently. And we have worked on hyaluronan ever since.

How does it work?

It works great. And I think we're very lucky because we understand our daily experiences, we can appreciate each other's daily assignments, and daily worries, because we share them, during the course of the day and the week.

Do you talk science at home?

Yes, we do.

Warren and Cheryl during the Hyaluronan Meeting in St. Tropez, 2003
(photograph by M. Hargittai)

With the children present?

At the beginning, when they were very little, I used to read my grant applications out loud to them because they didn't care, they didn't know what it was about, they just liked to listen to their mother. So I'd just read it out loud to see how it sounded to me, and they would just listen to me and fall asleep. They used the back sides of the first drafts of my grants to color on at home. So, there were all the blank back sides of the paper to draw on and also they would turn them over and make patterns of the words on the draft side of the grant. So, they've been involved in this grant writing process.

How do you feel about the project that would systematize the hyaluronan literature in a critical way?

I think that it's an enormous project. It seems like a good idea to have it. When I read an article that has historical perspective, I enjoy that article very much. Now this project will be generating a collection of all of these papers.

Do you think that graduate students would read this?

Yes I think they would. Actually, I direct a special topics course in cell biology. As an assignment, I ask the students to think of a particular question. I ask them to make a reading list, so they have 8 or 10 papers that were published prior to 1985 and then 10 papers that are more current. Then I ask them to use that reading list, to compare and contrast the historical perspective and the current concepts of their question. I've been doing this with our graduate students for maybe 4 years now. So of course it's a small focused area that they are looking at and a small list of papers but that helps them to look at some of the older papers. They all enjoy reading those papers because otherwise they're reading the most current papers only and they wouldn't read the older papers, so I give it out as an assignment. Now these students continue to look at some of the older papers on their own because they have had that experience. I think, it's interesting that, somehow, separately, I came up with an idea similar to Bandi's, although only on a much smaller scale, with my students.

Would you like to add something?

I think, I have been adopted by all these scientists in the hyaluronan field, and part of that may be because my Ph.D. advisor died at a young age unexpectedly and so I became a scientific orphan at that moment. I always felt adopted by these talented and creative people and have been very fortunate to be part of this group. The first meeting of hyaluronan scientists was in France, and that was my first trip to Europe.   It is lovely to be here again; thank you.

I think that writing these assignments for the Hyaluronan Library will help me come up with some ideas to put together into a new grant just from reading some of these older papers, and seeing some of the suggestions or speculations that were made and that have never been followed up.   Just as my students have enjoyed reading some of these historical papers, I think I will enjoy it, too.

Bryan Toole and I are going to look at the section on hyaluronan and aging and that's very important to the NIH, as the Aging Institute (NIA) is growing and they are interested in new ideas. Reading these papers in the field of hyaluronan and aging will help me to be able to construct a grant with a different, better background, not just a focused approach, to have a little bit broader approach. Sometimes we have to be too focused and everything has to be so clear; some say to write your NIH grant you have to have attempted most of the proposed experiments and submit all those data in your proposal.   Maybe this new project will develop a new way to present a field with lots of unanswered questions that would be attractive to the funding by the NIH. But this project will also help me to do better science by having a stronger background, to be able to conceive interesting experiments that are not just driven by the current technology, but driven by the questions that need to be answered. Sometimes we are just saying "I can do this experiment because we now have this methodology." This project may help us to go back and review thoughtfully the questions that need to be answered.   Then we can determine if we have or need to develop methodology best-suited to answer those questions.   That's what I see that in this project as an overall goal, that will help not just me but everyone, to see the unanswered problems.

Addendum

Since this interview in June, 2003, Cheryl Knudson was elected by the faculty to serve as University Marshall for the 2005 Rush University Commencement. While a member of the faculty at Rush University Medical Center in Chicago she mentored five students who received their Ph.D.s from Rush University and led the development and implementation of the core curriculum for the Graduate College of Rush University as its inaugural Director. She was Co-Director of the Minority High School Summer Research Program in Biochemistry that mentored and trained inner city Chicago high school students and teachers. She is active in the peer-review process; she served a four-year term as a member of the OBM-2 NIH study section and a six year term, the final two as Chair, on the Cell Biology study section of the Arthritis Foundation.

In late 2005, Cheryl Knudson and Warren Knudson joined the faculty at East Carolina University. In March 2006 Cheryl Knudson was appointed as Professor and Chair, Department of Anatomy and Cell Biology at the Brody School of Medicine at East Carolina University in Greenville, North Carolina. Currently she is serving as a member of the National Institute for Arthritis and Musculoskeletal and Skin Diseases Board of Scientific Counselors, Associate Editor of the journal *Connective Tissue Research* and Vice President of the International Society for Hyaluronan Sciences.

Her research interests include hyaluronan-cell interactions in the assembly of the pericellular matrix and the regulation of cellular events in the cortical cytoplasm. Her current research focuses on the differential responses by cells to growth factors as dependent on the composition of the extracellular matrix and the interactions between hyaluronan and CD44 during differentiation, aging and disease.

Summary

by Cheryl Knudson

The interaction between hyaluronan and cell surfaces is an important means of communication between the extracellular matrix and cells. In cartilage, cell-matrix interactions are the primary means for chondrocytes to sense changes in the extracellular environment, and signal a reparative response. Hyaluronan binding to the CD44 receptor is a key player in such interactions. The mechanisms by which chondrocytes sense changes in the extracellular matrix—especially changes that induce a metabolic response, have been difficult to unravel. The role of integrins is only part of the story.

Our studies have demonstrated that chondrocytes tether proteoglycan aggregates through the binding of hyaluronan to the receptor CD44 and that matrix assembly and retention is regulated by the expression of functional CD44. Disruption of CD44-hyaluronan interactions (by antisense approaches, hyaluronan oligosaccharides, cytoskeletal disruption) results in cartilage damage coupled with enhanced biosynthesis. We found that human chondrocytes express both exon19-containing and exon20-containing CD44 mRNA. To study the function of CD44exon19, a point mutation was made to introduce a premature stop codon resulting in COOH-terminal truncation of 67 amino acids identical to CD44exon19. Cells expressing CD44HΔ67 cannot bind hyaluronan. Also, CD44HΔ67 functions as a dominant negative (DN-CD44) when expressed in articular chondrocytes in the background of the endogenous CD44 as these cells no longer exhibit the capacity to retain a pericellular matrix. Therefore, since hyaluronan-CD44 interactions are required for the retention of proteoglycan in the matrix, the relationship between these two components is crucial to cartilage homeostasis. The predicted inability CD44exon19 to interact with cytoskeletal and signaling components suggest mechanisms whereby DN-CD44 modulates CD44 signaling activity.

To explore pathways that utilize CD44 to transduce changes in the matrix to alter chondrocyte metabolism, a yeast two hybrid (Y2H) screen was performed. This led to the interesting discovery that Smad1, a signaling partner associated with bone morphogenetic protein (BMP) receptors, interacts with the cytoplasmic tail domain of CD44 and this was validated by a variety of approaches. This interaction has important effects on chondrocyte responsiveness to BMP and the interaction is sensitive to changes in the extracellular matrix. Thus our investigations continue on the dual role of CD44 as a matrix receptor and a binding partner of Smad1 and how this role may represent a mechanism for cells to "sense" and "respond" to changes in their extracellular environment.

The diminished response of osteoarthritic chondrocytes to local growth factors, such as endogenous BMPs, is one hypothesis that may explain, in part, the reduced capacity of these cells to maintain the critical balance of extracellular matrix synthesis and degradation. One prominent feature of osteoarthritic cartilage is an inherent failure to retain proteoglycan-rich extracellular matrix. As a working hypothesis we argue that a loss of hyaluronan-CD44 interactions gives rise to signaling events that alter chondrocyte metabolism. To address whether CD44 plays an important role in BMP signaling in situ, particularly in chondrocytes, a loss-of-function approach using the DN-CD44 was taken. Transfected chondrocytes over-expressing DN-CD44 exhibited no pericellular coats and no nuclear translocation of endogenous Smad1 after BMP-7 treatment but rather retained the cytoplasmic localization of Smad1, similar to non-stimulated chondrocytes.

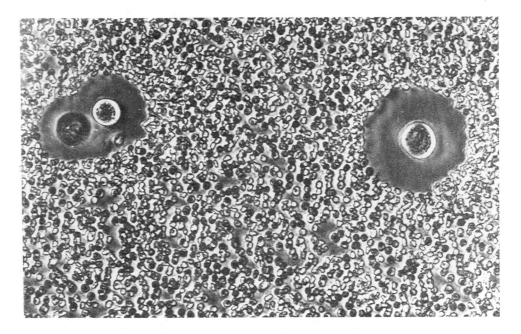

The chondrocyte "pericellular coat" visualized by the particle exclusion assay is dependent on the hyaluronan scaffold (photomicrograph by C. Knudson)

Another approach to model matrix loss is the use of *Streptomyces* hyaluronidase, an enzyme with high specificity for its substrate hyaluronan. *Streptomyces* hyaluronidase pretreatment diminished Smad1 phosphorylation and its signaling activities, including the nuclear translocation of either Smad1 or Smad4 in BMP-7-stimulated articular chondrocytes. Loss of hyaluronan-CD44 interactions also resulted in decreased Smad1 phosphorylation in other cells stimulated with BMP-7. This negative effect on Smad1 –mediated signaling events can be rescued by the re-addition of extracellular hyaluronan. Thus, our results suggest that restoration of hyaluronan-CD44 interactions at the cell surface enhances the chondrocyte response to BMP-7. Furthermore, we have determined that these CD44 effects are highly specific for Smad1 in that alterations in hyaluronan or CD44 have no effect on Smad2-mediated signaling (e.g, signaling induced by TGFβ). These results naturally led us to the question: how do the matrix/CD44 effects on the BMP pathway fit into the overall biology of cell-matrix interactions in cartilage? Interestingly, while observing the effects of matrix loss on Smad1-mediated signaling, we also noted that changes in hyaluronan-CD44 interactions initiated other signaling cascades. Some of these cascades resulted in the stimulation of matrix turnover genes (such as MMP-3, MMP-13, iNOS) while others affected a stimulation of matrix repair genes including collagen II, COMP, aggrecan, HAS-2 and endogenous BMP-7. In matrix-intact chondrocytes, clustered CD44 receptors occupied in a multivalent fashion with high-molecular-mass hyaluronan represent the quiescent state of the cells. We postulate that for these cells, CD44 signaling is initiated by disruption of hyaluronan-CD44 interactions and thus declustering of CD44. As such this becomes an exciting new chondrocyte-based model that closely mimics the early stage of osteoarthritis namely, "attempted repair" in which there is a robust anabolic repair response coincident with enhancement of matrix degradation. This has led us to hypothesize that alterations in the hyaluronan-rich matrix (or CD44 itself), initiate or impact several signaling cascades, including BMP-7/Smad1; cascades that may be independent or interdependent, the end result of which is a degradative response coincident with attempted repair.

Bibliography*
Hyaluronan-Related Publications

1. Anderson, C. B. (1981). The role of metameric pattern in the distribution of cranial neural crest cells in the chick embryo. Ph.D. Thesis.

2. Anderson, C. B., and Meier, S. (1981). The influence of the metameric pattern in the mesoderm on migration of cranial neural crest cells in the chick embryo. Dev Biol 85 (2), 385-402.

3. Anderson, C. B., and Meier, S. (1982). Effect of hyaluronidase treatment in the distribution of cranial neural crest cells in the chick embryo. J Exper Zool 221 (3), 329-335.

4. Knudson, C., and Toole, B. (1985). Fluorescent morphological probe for hyaluronate. J Cell Biol 100 (5), 1753-1758.

5. Knudson, C. B., and Toole, B. P. (1985). Changes in the pericellular matrix during differentiaton of limb bud mesoderm. Dev Biol 112 (2), 308-318.

6. Knudson, C. B., and Toole, B. P. (1987). Hyaluronate-cell interactions during differentiation of chick embryo limb mesoderm. Dev Biol 124 (1), 82-90.

7. Knudson, C. B., and Toole, B. P. (1988). Epithelial-mesenchymal interaction in the regulation of hyaluronate production during limb development. Biochem Int 17 (4), 735-45.

8. Toole, B. P., Munaim, S. I., Welles, S., Knudson, C. B. (1989). Hyaluronate-cell interactions and growth factor regulation of hyaluronate synthesis during limb development. Ciba Found Symp. 143, 138-145; Discussion 145-149.

9. Knudson, C. B., and Knudson, W. (1990). Similar epithelial-stromal interactions in the regulation of hyaluronate production during limb morphogenesis and tumor invasion. Cancer Letters 52 (2), 113-122.

10. Knudson, W., and Knudson, C. B. (1991). Assembly of a chondrocyte-like pericellular matrix on non-chondrogenic cells. J Cell Sci 99 (2), 227-235.

---

* Provided by the interviewee.

11. Hua, Q., Knudson, C. B., and Knudson, W. (1993). Internalization of hyaluronan by chondrocytes occurs via receptor-mediated endocytosis. J Cell Sci 106 (1), 365-375.

12. Knudson, C. (1993). Hyaluronan receptor-directed assembly of chondrocyte pericellular matrix. J Cell Biol 120 (3), 825-834.

13. Knudson, C. B., and Knudson, W. (1993). Hyaluronan-binding proteins in development, tissue homeostasis, and disease. FASEB J 7 (13), 1233-1241.

14. Knudson, W., Bartnik, E., and Knudson, C. B. (1993). Assembly of pericellular matrices by cos-7 cells transfected with cd44 lymphocyte-homing receptor genes. Proc Natl Acad Sci U S A 90 (9), 4003-4007.

15. Chow, G., Knudson, C. B., Homandberg, G., and Knudson, W. (1995). Increased expression of CD44 in bovine articular chondrocytes by catabolic cellular mediators. J Biol Chem 270 (46), 27734-27741.

16. Knudson, C. B., Munaim, S. I., and Toole, B. P. (1995). Ectodermal stimulation of the production of hyaluronan-dependent pericellular matrix by embryonic limb mesodermal cells. Dev Dyn 204 (2), 186-91.

17. Maleski, M. P., and Knudson, C. B. (1996). Hyaluronan-mediated aggregation of limb blud mesenchyme and mesenchymal condensation during chondrogenesis. Exp Cell Res 225 (1), 55-66.

18. Maleski, M. P., and Knudson, C. B. (1996). Matrix accumulation and retention in embryonic cartilage and in vitro chondrogenesis. Connect Tissue Res 34 (1), 75-86.

19. Knudson, W., Aguiar, D., Hua, Q., and Knudson, C. (1996). CD44-anchored hyaluronan-rich pericellular matrices: An Ultrastructural and biochemical analysis. Exp Cell Res 228 (2), 216-228.

20. Chow, G., Nietfeld, J., Knudson, C., and Knudson, W. (1998). Antisense inhibition of chondrocyte CD44 expression leading to cartilage chondrolysis. Arthritis Rheum 41 (8), 1411-1419.

21. Knudson, C. (1998). Hyaluronan-cell interactions during chondrogenesis and matrix assembly. Cells & Materials 8, 33-56.

22. Knudson, C. B. (1998). Hyaluronan in embryonic cell adhesion and matrix assembly. In *The Chemistry, Biology and Medical Applications of Hyaluronan and its Derivatives* (Ed. Laurent, T. C.), Portland Press Ltd., London, 161-168.

23. Knudson, C. B., Nofal, G. A., Pamintuan, L., and Aguiar, D. J. (1999). The chondrocyte pericellular matrix: a model for hyaluronan-mediated cell-matrix interactions. Biochem Soc Trans 27 (2), 142-147.

24. Nishida, Y., Knudson, C. B., Nietfeld, J. J., Margulis, A., and Knudson, W. (1999). Antisense inhibition of hyaluronan synthase-2 in human articular

chondrocytes inhibits proteoglycan retention and matrix assembly. J Biol Chem 274 (31), 21893-21899.

25. Aguiar, D. J., Knudson, W., and Knudson, C. B. (1999). Internalization of the hyaluronan receptor CD44 by chondrocytes. Exp Cell Res 252 (2), 292-302.

26. Knudson, W., and Knudson, C. B.(1999).The hyaluronan receptor, CD44. In *Glycoforum. Hyaluronan Today* (Eds. Hascall, V.C. and Yanagishita, M.) (Seikagaku Corporation Glycoforum)(Accessed at http://www.glycoforum.gr.jp /science/hyaluronan/HA10/HA10E.html).

27. Nishida, Y., Knudson, C. B., Eger, W., Kuettner, K. E., and Knudson, W. (2000). Osteogenic protein 1 stimulates cell-associated matrix assembly by normal human articular chondrocytes. Arthritis Rheum 43 (1), 206-214.

28. Knudson, W., Casey, B., Nishida, Y., Eger, W., Kuettner, K. E., and Knudson, C. B. (2000). Hyaluronan oligosaccharides perturb cartilage matrix homeostatis and induce chondrocytic chondrolysis. Arthritis Rheum 43 (5), 1165-1174.

29. Nishida, Y., Knudson, C. B., Kuettner, K. E., and Knudson, W. (2000). Osteogenic protein-1 promotes the synthesis and retention of extracellular matrix within bovine articular cartilage and chondrocyte cultures. Osteoarthritis Cartilage 8 (2), 127-36.

30. Jiang, H., Knudson, C. B., and Knudson, W. (2001). Antisense inhibition of CD44 tailless splice variant in human articular chondrocytes promotes hyaluronan internalization. Arthr Rheum 44 (11), 2599-2610.

31. Knudson, C. B., and Knudson, W. (2001). Cartilage proteoglycans. Seminars Cell Devel Biol 12 (2), 69-78.

32. Kurtis, M. S., Tu, B. P., Gaya, O. A., Mollenhauer, J., Knudson, W., Loeser, R. F., Knudson, C. B., and Sah, R. L. (2001). Mechanisms of chondrocyte adhesion to cartilage: role of ß1-integrins, CD44, and annexin V. J Orthop Res 19 (6), 1122-1130.

33. Jiang, H., Peterson, R. S., Wang, W., Bartnik, E., Knudson, C. B., and Knudson, W. (2002). A requirement for the CD44 cytoplasmic domain for hyaluronan binding, pericellular matrix assembly, and receptor-mediated endocytosis in COS-7 cells. J Biol Chem 277 (12), 10531-10538.

34. Knudson, C. B., Nofal, G. A., Chow, G., and Peterson, R. S. (2002). CD44: The link between hyaluronan and the cytoskeleton. In *Hyaluronan Volume 1* (Eds. Kennedy, J. F., Phillips, G. O., Williams, P. A. , and Hascall, V. C.), Woodhead, Cambridge, UK, 331-340.

35. Knudson, C. B., Rousche, K. T., Peterson, R. S., Chow, G., and Knudson, W. (2002). CD44 and cartilage matrix stabilization. In *The Many Faces of*

Osteoarthritis (Eds. Kuettner, K. E., and Hascall, V.), Birkhauser Verlage AG, Basel, Switzerland, 219-230.

36. Knudson, W., Chow, G., and Knudson, C. B. (2002). CD44-mediated uptake and degradation of hyaluronan. Matrix Biol 21 (1), 15-23.

37. Nofal, G. A., and Knudson, C. B. (2002). Latrunculin and Cytochalasin decrease chondrocyte matrix retention. J Histochem Cytochem 50 (10), 1313-1324.

38. Rousche, K. T., and Knudson, C. B. (2002). Temporal expression of CD44 during embryonic chick limb development and modulation of its expression with retinoic acid. Matrix Biol 21 (1), 53-62.

39. Knudson, C. B. (2003). Hyaluronan and CD44: strategic players for cell-matrix interactions during chondrogenesis and matrix assembly. Birth Defects Research C Embryo Today 69 (2), 174-196.

40. Nishida, Y., Knudson, C. B., and Knudson, W. (2003). Extracellular matrix recovery by human articular chondrocytes after treatment with hyaluronan hexasaccharides or *Streptomyces* hyaluronidase. Mod Rhematol 13, 62-68.

41. Knudson, C. B., and Knudson, W. (2004). Hyaluronan and CD44: modulators of chondrocyte metabolism. Clin Orthop (427 Suppl), S152-62.

42. Knudson, W., and Knudson, C. B. (2004). An update on hyaluronan and CD44 in cartilage. Current Opinion Orthop 15, 369-375.

43. Nishida, Y., Knudson, C. B., and Knudson, W. (2004). Osteogenic protein-1 inhibits matrix depletion in a hyaluronan hexacaccharide-induced model of osteoarthritis. Osteoarth Cartilage 12 (5), 374-382.

44. Ohno-Nakahara, M., Honda, K., Tanimoto, K., Tanaka, N., Doi, T., Suzuki, A., Yoneno, K., Nakatani, Y., Ueki, M., Ohno, S., Knudson, W., Knudson, C. B., and Tanne, K. (2004). Induction of CD44 and MMP expression by hyaluronidase treatment of articular chondrocytes. J Biochem (Tokyo) 135 (5), 567-75.

45. Peterson, R. S., Andhare, R. A., Rousche, K. T., Knudson, W., Wang, W., Grossfield, J. B., Thomas, R. O., Hollingsworth, R. E., and Knudson, C. B. (2004). CD44 modulates Smad1 activation in the BMP-7 signaling pathway. J Cell Biol 166 (7), 1081-1091.

46. Knudson, W., and Knudson, C. B. (2005). The hyaluronan receptor, CD44-- An update. In *Glycoforum. Hyaluronan Today* (Eds. Hascall, V.C. and Yanagishita, M.) (Seikagaku Corporation Glycoforum) (Accessed at http://www.glycoforum.gr.jp /science/hyaluronan/HA10a/HA10aE.html).

47. Nishida, Y., Knudson, W., Knudson, C. B., and Ishiguro, N. (2005). Antisense inhibition of hyaluronan synthase-2 in human osteosarcoma cells

inhibits hyaluronan retention and tumorigenicity. Exp Cell Res 307 (1), 194-203.

48. Ohno, S., Im, H. J., Knudson, C. B., and Knudson, W. (2005). Hyaluronan oligosaccharide-induced activation of transcription factors in bovine articular chondrocytes. Arthritis Rheum 52 (3), 800-809.

49. Ohno, S., Ohno-Nakahara, M., Knudson, C. B., and Knudson, W. (2005). Induction of MMP-3 by Hyaluronan Oligosaccharides in Temporomandibular Joint Chondrocytes. J Dent Res 84 (11), 1005-1009.

50. Chow, G., Knudson, C. B., and Knudson, W. (2006). Expression and cellular localization of human hyaluronidase-2 in articular chondrocytes and cultured cell lines. Osteoarthritis Cartilage 14 (9), 849-858.

51. Iacob, S., and Knudson, C. B. (2006). Hyaluronan fragments activate nitric oxide synthase and the production of nitric oxide by articular chondrocytes. Int J Biochem Cell Biol. 38 (1): 123-133.

52. Ohno, S., Im, H. J., Knudson, C. B., and Knudson, W. (2006). Hyaluronan oligosaccharides induce MMP-13 via transcriptional activation of NFkB and p38 MAP kinase in articular chondrocytes. J Biol Chem 281 (26), 17952-17960.

53. Ohno, S., Schmid, T., Tanne, Y., Kamiya, T., Honda, K., Ohno-Nakahara, M., Swentko, N., Desai, T. A., Tanne, K., Knudson, C. B., and Knudson, W. (2006). Expression of superficial zone protein in mandibular condyle cartilage. Osteoarthritis Cartilage 14 (8), 807-813.

54. Hosono, K., Nishida, Y., Knudson, W., Knudson, C. B., Naruse, T., Suzuki, Y., and Ishiguro, N. (2007). Hyaluronan Oligosaccharides Inhibit Tumorigenicity of Osteosarcoma Cell Lines MG-63 and LM-8 in Vitro and in Vivo via Perturbation of Hyaluronan-Rich Pericellular Matrix of the Cells. Am J Pathol 171 (1), 274-286.

Warren Knudson, 2008 (photograph courtesy of W. Knudson)

Warren Knudson

Warren Knudson (b. 1953, in Illinois) received his B.Sc. in Biology at Elmhurst College (1975) and his M.Sc. (1979) and Ph.D. (1982), both in Biochemistry, at the University of Illinois. He was a postdoctoral fellow at Tufts University School of Medicine (1981-85) in Boston. In 1985 he became Assistant Professor at Rush Medical College, Rush-Presbyterian-St. Luke's Medical Center in Chicago, then Associate Professor (1993-2000), and Professor (2000-2006). Currently he is Professor at the Department of Anatomy & Cell Biology at East Carolina University. He is a member of several scientific societies. . He is active in the peer-review process; having served a five-year term as a member of the SBSR NIH study section and a three-year term on the Cell Biology study section of the Arthritis Foundation. He is also a founding member of the International Society of Hyaluronan Sciences (ISHAS).

Interview*

When did you become interested in hyaluronan?

My graduate thesis dealt with the use of hyaluronidase in sequencing glycosaminoglycans. However, I began my interest in hyaluronan when I thought about working for Bryan Toole at Tufts University in Boston. During my graduate studies I became interested in glycosaminoglycans through my work on chondroitin sulfate. We were primarily interested in developing methods to sequence sulfated glycosaminoglycans. Using compositional analyses we knew that changes in glycosaminoglycan subtypes likely played an important role in cell behavior but had few ways available, at the time, to test this directly. Then, I read about the work of Bryan Toole and knew immediately that this was the kind of work I would like to do. Bryan had made the observation that the levels of hyaluronan seemed to increase when cell migration was in full swing, and especially the migration of undifferentiated cells. The inverse relationship was also present. As the cells began to differentiate the level of hyaluronan would become reduced and cell migration ended. So, I became very interested in hyaluronan, a glycosaminoglycan that appeared to have direct effects on cell behavior. My thought was that I could use my background in glycosaminoglycan chemistry but, at the same time, test the effects of glycosaminoglycans on cells in a biological setting. So I went to work with him, I believe this was in the fall of 1981. At that time Bryan was revitalizing his laboratory. Cheryl Anderson and another postdoctoral fellow, Ron Goldberg had just joined as well, so there were three of us—the fresh face of Bryan's new laboratory at Tufts.

---

* This interview was recorded during the second meeting "Conversations on Hyaluronan" in St. Tropez, June 2003.

Bryan Toole (front left) and Torvard Laurent (front right) during the 1985 meeting on hyaluronan (photograph courtesy of W. Knudson)

When I began in Toole's lab, I took up the tumor project that was in progress. We started looking at tumor-host cell interactions. We knew from his earlier observations that a lot of hyaluronan accumulated around invasive tumors. Carcinomas, in particular were enriched in hyaluronan, and Bryan already had some preliminary evidence that this build-up seemed to be facilitating the invasion. But what we wanted to know was "what was the cellular source of all this hyaluronan?" Was the hyaluronan synthesized by the tumor cells or, was the hyaluronan made by the normal host cells in response to the tumor?

How did you know that hyaluronan facilitated the invasion?

That was, of course, the question, whether the hyaluronan was there in what we would call a desmoplastic response to wall off the tumor, or was it there to facilitate invasion. We really had no idea, we knew that there was a correlation with development, that on the onset of migration hyaluronan would accumulate. This coincident pattern made sense as a mechanism to facilitate migration but we really didn't know. One of the things Bryan did was to grow a rabbit tumor, called a V2 carcinoma, in a nude mouse. This tumor grows well in the nude mouse but as a benign tumor. It has a very thick capsule, suggesting that the host does a very good job at walling off the tumor. Coincidentally, this capsule is very low in hyaluronan. However, when the same tumor is grown in rabbits, the natural host, it is highly invasive and metastatic, and there the levels of hyaluronan were three-fold higher in the surrounding connective tissue. The rabbit tumors would build up something like a capsule around the tumor, but this capsular tissue contained extensively-spread invading tumor cells. And, the rabbit capsule was very enriched in hyaluronan. If the hyaluronan was used by the host to retard tumor invasiveness its concentration would have been expected to be higher in the nude mouse tumors. However, other interpretations of the data are also possible. Nonetheless, regardless of the role of hyaluronan, the cellular source in these tumors was still unknown. To begin to look at which cells were involved we set up in vitro co-cultures of tumor cells together with normal fibroblasts. What we eventually determined was that the tumor cells had the ability to stimulate the normal fibroblasts to synthesize more hyaluronan.

There were some early clues when we started this project. Another close associate of Bryan, Dr. Chitra Biswas, had already made similar observations but in regard to the degradative enzymes associated with these same tumors, in particular, type 1 collagenase which is now known as MMP1. What she found was that most of the degradative enzymes in an invasive tumor were not generated by the tumor cells themselves. Interestingly, these enzymes were synthesized by the stromal cells surrounding the tumor, seemingly in response to the presence of the tumor cells. So the pattern was already there, tumor cells did have a capacity to alter the metabolism of surrounding normal stromal cells. What we wanted to know was whether a similar kind of mechanism was responsible for the build-up of tumor-associated hyaluronan. I should also note here that Chitra served as a co-mentor for my postdoctoral work in Bryan's laboratory. Sure enough, when we set up in vitro co-cultures of tumor cells and fibroblasts, there was a big jump in the amount of hyaluronan produced—being synthesized by the normal cells. In fact, many of the carcinoma cell types we investigated synthesized very little hyaluronan on their own. However, when placed together with normal cells, hyaluronan synthesis was enhanced 3-fold above what either of the cell types synthesized independently. Admittedly, we weren't the first ones to actually show this interaction. For example, about the same time, Dr. Merv Merrilees had shown that conditioned medium removed from the tumor cells, when added to normal fibroblasts, could stimulate the fibroblasts production of hyaluronan. This suggested that soluble factors, derived from the tumor cells, were stimulating the fibroblasts to synthesize additional hyaluronan. However, when we added the conditioned media of human LX-1 lung carcinoma cells to normal fibroblasts, nothing happened. We were a little perplexed. Eventually what we found was that direct cell-cell contact between tumor cells and fibroblasts was necessary for the enhancement of hyaluronan. At the time, names for these kinds of events were just being developed. Since names like paracrine effects, autocrine effects, or endocrine effects were just not appropriate, they came up with a new name called a juxtaocrine effect to best describe this mechanism where the two cells required direct contact for stimulation to occur. As for the purification of the factor or factors responsible, this just made the problem more difficult. We had to prepare membranes from the tumor cells and add the crude or semi-purified membranes back to the fibroblasts or vice versa. What we found was that there did exist proteins within the LX-1 plasma membrane that when added to cultures of fibroblasts, the cells would be stimulated to produce more hyaluronan. After many years of follow-up work, the identity of the elusive protein remains unknown. We have looked at several other carcinomas and they also have membrane-localized hyaluronan-stimulating potential. Bryan has published work subsequently that the collagenase-stimulator factor, EMMPRIN can also stimulate hyaluronan synthesis in fibroblasts. Whether another factor, distinct from EMMPRIN, still exists, remains to be determined.

An important offshoot of this project was work that dealt with the hyaluronan receptor, a matrix receptor that had been just recently characterized on SV-3T3 cells in Bryan's laboratory when our tumor work began. Cheryl had also just detected hyaluronan receptor activity on early chick chondrocytes. We developed a working hypothesis that these carcinoma cells stimulated the production of hyaluronan in adjacent stromal fibroblasts so as to establish a hyaluronan-rich environment through which to migrate. Bryan's original concept was that the hyaluronan-rich matrix provided opened-up spaces – perhaps making the tissue more hydrated and permissive for cell migration, be it tumor cells or embryonic cells. In this way, the newly-synthesized stromal hyaluronan would serve as a leading substratum for migrating cells. But the question remained as to whether the migrating cells also used the hyaluronan-rich matrix to adhere or interact in such as way as to promote invasion/migration. An ability of the tumor cells to interact or "crawl" through hyaluronan-rich matrices assumed the presence of a functioning hyaluronan receptor. This question was one of the questions that I carried with me when I left Bryan's laboratory to take up my first faculty position as an Assistant Professor of Biochemistry.

In January of 1985, I became an Assistant Professor at Rush Medical School in Chicago, where I continued working on hyaluronan projects—projects that I had started in Bryan Toole's lab. In one early study we found that a human tumor cells, derived from bladder transitional cell carcinoma, had the ability to bind hyaluronan. We characterized the binding site and found that the receptor on these cells had similar characteristics as the SV40 3T3 cell receptor. For example, the hyaluronan receptor was stable to fixation and the binding increased with increase in ionic strength. I worked on this project together with my first graduate student in Chicago, Ray Nemec. Like the SV-3T3 cells, the glutaraldehyde-fixed carcinoma cells could be used as cell-affinity column. Once fixed and washed, we poured the cells into a column and added tritium-labeled hyaluronan which bound to the hyaluronan receptors expressed by these cells. The labeled hyaluronan could then be eluted by more stringent conditions or released using buffers containing hexasaccharides of hyaluronan to displace off the bound hyaluronan.

Ray Nemec also worked with me to purify the tumor-derived hyaluronan stimulatory factor, which was my main goal. We knew it was a protein present in membranes and we could detect the activity but it was very hard to fractionate it and get it down to an individual band. In subsequent years, working with Dr. Tibor Glant at Rush, we isolated blocking monoclonal antibodies to this putative stimulatory factor and used these to screen a human cDNA expression library. This provided some intriguing candidates but verifying the results for function proved increasingly difficult. I had my first NIH grant, a "young investigator grant" on that, but without a purified factor, I wasn't able to continue my research in this direction. And that's when Cheryl and I really started working together. Why we went to Rush in the first place was that there was a new chairman of Biochemistry at Rush, Dr. Klaus Kuettner. He was building a department with a focus on connective tissue research. He offered the two of us equivalent tenure-track Assistant Professorships if we would move to Chicago. And, he promised that each of us would have our own laboratory, both of us would be on a tenure track, yet we could work in the same department. As I mentioned, she was working along the line of hyaluronan in chondrogenesis and I was along the line of hyaluronan in tumor invasion. So, in a sense, we were looking at hyaluronan function at the earliest period of life (namely, embryonic development) as well as hyaluronan events that occur at later stages in life (such as tumorigenesis). In the first few years we tried to keep our careers separate so that our work could be recognized by our peers as individuals. She eventually evolved from studying early mesenchymal cells that became chondrogenic, to characterization of cell-matrix interactions in mature chondrocytes. As before, she was primarily characterizing the hyaluronan binding activity on chick and bovine articular chondrocytes. She wrote a paper on what she found: that she could add hyaluronan back to matrix-depleted chondrocytes, together with some added proteoglycan, and the cells would re-establish pericellular coats, a hyaluronan-rich structure that Bryan Toole was well-known for. But the paper reviewers asked her, well you're adding hyaluronan and aggrecan proteoglycan back to these chondrocytes, maybe these molecules are binding due to an aggrecan receptor already present on chondrocytes; how do you know it is a hyaluronan receptor? Perhaps the added-back components are stimulating new synthesis of hyaluronan and aggrecan. It was at this point when we really started collaborating. I had my human bladder carcinoma cells – these are epithelial cells – they have very little extracellular matrix but they have a high expression of hyaluronan receptor, what would later to be identified as CD44. So we took those human tumor cells that had no capacity to make cartilage proteoglycan, and we added purified cartilage molecules to them. I must add that these carcinoma cells do not exhibit pericellular matrices, so you would see no glycocalyx or halo surrounding the cells. But if we added the purified hyaluronan and cartilage proteoglycan to these cells, they could grab these matrix macromolecules out of solution and organize them into this pericellular matrix or coat around them. The coat looked just like those on chondrocytes. The matrix could exclude particles from the cell up to about 1 cell-diameter in width. It looks like a jel-like coating that surrounds the cells. With this project we looked at a completely different cell line that had the same binding sites on the surface. In addition, the cells did not have to be alive. Glutaraldehyde-fixed carcinoma cells (or chondrocytes) could also capture soluble matrix macromolecules and re-establish a pericellular matrix.

Then we went back to look at some other cell types, particularly at the SV3T3 cells, that Dr. Charles Underhill had originally characterized in Bryan Toole's lab. These transformed cells also did not exhibit a pericellular matrix; while the nontransformed 3T3 cells do have a matrix. On the other hand the SV3T3 cells have an increased number of hyaluronan receptors. We did the same thing as before, we added purified hyaluronan and proteoglycan to the SV-3T3 cells and, sure enough, they assembled a large surrounding pericellular matrix. We tried other carcinoma cell lines--cells that had a high expression of hyaluronan receptor activity. Every one that we tried was able to form the matrix; on the other hand, we had some human tumor cells derived from non-invasive bladder papillomas that had very little expression of any binding activity and they did not have this capacity to form the matrix. So this work really suggested that in order to form a pericellular matrix you needed hyaluronan, hyaluronan receptors and a small amount of proteoglycan. A few years later, in the early 1990s, the hyaluronan receptor that Dr. Underhill had originally characterized on SV-3T3 cells, was identified as the lymphocyte homing receptor CD44. To determine if our hyaluronan receptor activity was also CD44, we obtained an expression plasmid containing full-length CD44 from our colleague at Hoescht in Germany, Dr. Eckart Bartnik. We transfected COS7 cells, a monkey kidney epithelial cell line, which, fortunately for our studies, was CD44-negative. When these cells were not transfected they did not exhibit pericellular matrices even if we added hyaluronan or hyaluronan plus proteoglycan, nothing would happen, the particles would just bury the cells. But if we transfected them first with CD44 and then added hyaluronan *and* proteoglycan, the cells established huge pericellular matrices just like those surrounding the chondrocytes. So we concluded from this that CD44 had the capacity to function as a hyaluronan receptor with all the characteristics we had observed on chondrocytes as well as a variety of tumor cells. I would say that it was from this point onward that Cheryl has been and remains a close collaborator. Her research evolved from chondrogenesis to the adult chondrocyte and I came from the tumor invasiveness to using tumor cells as mock chondrocytes, with the final result that we both ended up working on chondrocytes. Cheryl also had her own grant at that time as well, an R29 young investigator award. Nonetheless, we next put together our first grant working together as a team; a project in the renewal of a SCOR grant in the Department of Biochemistry at Rush.

Out of that project, my research moved into a new area, cartilage catabolism. Cartilage is a strange tissue. It is avascular, it is aneural, and receives its nutrients and oxygen by diffusion. The same goes for its catabolism, most of the turnover of the cartilage extracellular matrix occurs locally by the activity of resident chondrocytes. Little was known about how the hyaluronan of cartilage was metabolized as no hyaluronan fragments could be found and no extracellular-acting hyaluronidase had been identified. One suggestion was that hyaluronan was internalized by chondrocytes for degradation intracellularly in lysosomes. If correct, this would likely implicate or require that a hyaluronan receptor be present on the chondrocytes. At the time we had characterized what we thought was the principal receptor present in cartilage, and had just demonstrated that chondrocytes do, in fact, express CD44 and that CD44 was responsible for binding hyaluronan to the cell surface. So, since we were already actively working on the principal hyaluronan receptor, the question came to us: is CD44 involved in the internalization and degradation of the hyaluronan? So we began work with this question. Charles Underhill was addressing this same question in human tumor cells with one of his post docs. We began to look at our chondrocytes in culture and sure enough, these cells have the ability to specifically bind fluorescein or tritium-labeled hyaluronan (we have a lot of different tags) to the cell surface, internalize it and deliver the internalized hyaluronan to the lysosome. The internalized hyaluronan was both of high molecular mass and present as small oligosaccharides.

It was at this point that I wrote a grant along the lines of hyaluronan metabolism in cartilage, because again, at the time this was an area that was severely understudied. Cheryl was also involved with this, but she then spread out to a different area to look more at cell-matrix interactions and signal transduction. This is pretty much how I see our work separating out, even when we collaborate in a general theme, she's probably more involved in cell matrix interactions and cartilage repair whereas I have focused more on hyaluronan catabolism. So we then went to our model systems, our COS7 cells, and made transient transfections with full length CD44; the CD44-positive cells not only bound the hyaluronan but could also internalize and degrade hyaluronan. Further this occurred selectively, that is only in the successfully transfected COS7 cells that could now be distinguished using red or green fluorescent proteins. Since this worked we could begin to explore the effect of a whole series of mutations in CD44. CD44 is essential for anchoring and retaining hyaluronan in chondrocytes, but it's also the same receptor that's involved in turning over the hyaluronan. So the bigger question arises namely, how do cells control the use of CD44 for these two, somewhat diametric roles? How do the functions change in chondrocytes such as in osteoarthritis—a condition where there's a lot of turnover and not very much synthesis? Inflammatory cytokines like IL1 will cause the chondrocytes to become more catabolic like in osteoarthritis, and when we look at this model we see large increases in CD44. So it would appear that when the cell wants to turn-over more hyaluronan, it synthesizes more CD44. However, under different conditions we can induce a high level of synthesis repair in cartilage. For example, treating chondrocytes with the anabolic growth factor BMP7 stimulates the cells to synthesize more collagen, aggrecan, hyaluronan and interestingly, more CD44. Thus, when a cell wants to enhance the retention of extracellular matrix, it synthesizes more CD44. This suggests that the control of CD44 *function* is not due to transcriptional regulation. So we began to look within the cell to determine mechanisms used by cells to control these two different functions. We still don't know what that is, but we're going to. We know that CD44 is a single-pass transmembrane receptor containing a 70 amino acid cytoplasmic tail. Using the assumption that cellular control occurred via interactions with the cytoplasmic tail, we modified or mutated almost every site or putative domain within the tail known to participate in either for signaling or for interacting with cytoskeleton. Our hypothesis is that one of these sites acts as a *switch*, regulating components that might be involved in the internalization in some cases versus the signaling or anchoring or matrix assembly.

Do you have any rivalry between yourself and your wife?

I would say yes or no, maybe some. I mentioned, when we first went to Bryan Toole's lab there were three post docs and we all had a certain amount of rivalry, because we were all trying hard, we were all trying to get grants, and naturally, we were sort of competing with each other to be successful. Then the same thing, when we were on our tenure track as Assistant Professors, we had a certain degree of collegial rivalry between each other as well as the other Assistant Professors in the department as well. But really, between ourselves, it was probably less and we combine this with a good deal of mutual support. I should also note that in our field of hyaluronan and connective tissue research, we don't have very ambitious and cutthroat scientists; I think that we're a friendlier bunch.

Warren and Cheryl during a hyaluronan meeting in France, 1988
(photographs courtesy of W. Knudson)

Who of the two of you is more ambitious? As it is usually more difficult for women to advance, and you are at about the same level, my guess would be that she may be more ambitious.

Right. We think about that too. In my opinion, the generation of women scientists who came before Cheryl were more aggressive in style as that was how you had to be to make it in a man's world. I don't believe Cheryl had to be this way to succeed. I believe she was probably the first generation that made it just by working hard and being creative but otherwise, normal. That is not to say that there are probably a lot of things that she has to do that I don't have to do. I can just sort of "be", and I probably fit easier into the normal mold of what people are looking for. Cheryl has said this before. When I was an Assistant Professor, I'd be standing with a group of some colleagues who were also Assistant Professors and she'd look and say, "This is a Kodak moment here." I think what she would like is to be able to be just a normal, friendly person, without having to be a tyrant to be successful at science. I don't know that she's achieved that, but I think she has; anyway, that was one of her goals.

How much did having children set her back?

I don't think it set her back very much; we had our children after we were already post docs, so we were already older. She took a three-month maternity leave when both of our children were born and then went back to work. When our first daughter Kathleen was born this worked out especially well. Cheryl wrote a grant and went on maternity leave while the grant was being reviewed. At the end of the leave, the grant had been funded and she could return to work with renewed excitement. It also worked out because we both contribute a lot at home. I was able to cover for her in some situations, when she needed to work and vice versa, so I think that having our children hasn't been that much of a burden. But, that's not to say that there are still no sociological differences. She still has the worry almost everyday, should I be going to work or should I be staying home.

Hired help?

Yes, we had nannies and various kinds of daycare. At different times, when they were young we went to a daycare where they had other small children to play with. And, the daycare was close to where we lived so they stayed in the same community. Then we had a primary school teacher who just wanted to stay at home and have some children for daycare and I think it worked out pretty well. When they were older and they had more things going on, we would have someone come in during the day or just come in after school and be there for them until we would get home. So yes, we did.

Do you discuss science over dinner?

No, not generally. Well, there are always times when it would come up. Our children have actually been very good that way, because they took control over whatever was going on. So they have been very good at sort of shocking us out of work issues, because when we come home we have all sorts of things we need to do. But there also was a lot of work at home that needed to be done. We didn't have a maid or someone to come in and do the cooking. When our children were younger, we had someone to watch them after school, but not to clean the house or whatever, so we still have to do all the domestic chores ourselves. We were also very active with our children; cub scout leaders, boy scouts, brownies, girl scouts, soccer coaches, baseball coaches, Sunday school teachers, piano concerts, viola concerts, home work coaches and so forth. It makes for a busy but enriching life experience.

But it should also be said that we really enjoy working together. So, it's not really an issue to talk about science at home and it has been beneficial for both of us. Like when I have a grant application to write, a 25-page grant, I'll look at it and read it two or three times and I think it's good. Then I give it to her and she'll read it and just rip it to pieces. "Why do you say it this way?" "Your English here could be better, your grammar isn't good here" and so forth. So I'll go back and fix it, and then again back and forth to Cheryl for more reworking. This also goes on in reverse. I've gone over her grants a few times and come up with some new ideas and say let's try this and that has been very productive. It's like having an editorial assistant who was also a good scientist who could actually not only read it and know what you want to say and what you want to do, but also to think that's a stupid experiment that you're going to get killed for doing it that way. So you know what I mean… That has helped both our careers. I think we give each other a lot of support.

Nowadays, departments like to invite women if not for other reasons but for improving their statistics about the composition of their staff. What if she gets a very attractive job offer from somewhere else?

Well, then she and I would have to decide. But, both of us are flexible and supportive of each other. Interestingly, one of the advantages of moving to Chicago originally was that since there are six medical schools in the city as well as other universities, we thought that if it didn't work out at Rush, one or both of us could always go to a neighboring school. Fortunately, our careers progressed well at Rush, likely better than other places we could have settled.

Addendum

by Warren Knudson

In 2002 to 2003, I served as the acting Chairman of the Department of Biochemistry at Rush. Later in 2003, I was named the Ralph and Marion C. Falk Endowed Chair Professor of Biochemistry at Rush Medical College and also served as the Associate Chairman for the new incoming chair, Dr. Ted Oegema. In March of 2006, after 21 years in Chicago, we moved to the Department of Anatomy and Cell Biology at the Brody School of Medicine at East Carolina University in Greenville, North Carolina. Cheryl accepted the new position of Chairman and Professor of Anatomy and Cell Biology at East Carolina.

My area of interest continues to concern the overall metabolism of hyaluronan. My laboratory has explored the expression and function of hyaluronan synthases, hyaluronidases and the hyaluronan receptor CD44 in articular chondrocytes as well as a variety of cell lines. Working together with a graduate student, Sai Thankamony, we determined that palmitoylation of particular cysteine residues within the transmembrane and cytoplasmic tail of CD44 (C^{286} in particular) regulated the function of CD44 as an endocytosis receptor. I currently serve on the Editorial Board of the journal *Osteoarthritis and Cartilage* and am one of the founding members of the International Society for Hyaluronan Sciences. Our daughter, Kathleen graduated from Oberlin College in 2007 in Chemistry and our son, Jason graduates in 2008 from Occidental College in Diplomacy and World Affairs.

Cell surface Fl-HA   **Intracellular Fl-HA**

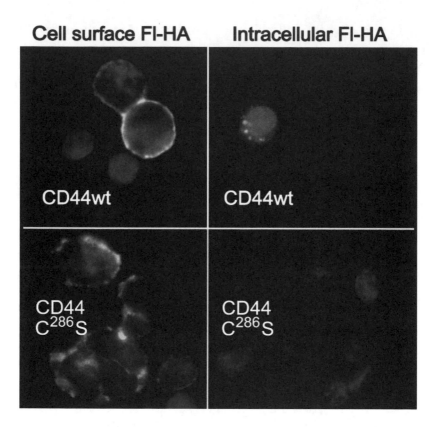

Hyaluronan is bound and internalized in COS-7 cells transfected with CD44. Fluorescein-conjugated hyaluronan (Fl-HA) is bound (left panels) and internalized (right panels) by CD44-transfected COS-7 Cells.   COS-7 cells typically display ~50% level of transfection efficiency for plasmid DNA.   The nuclei of all cells are shown in blue fluorescence (DAPI staining).   COS-7 cells transfected with either CD44Hwt (top left panel) or mutated CD44H-C[286]A (lower left panel), bind Fl-HA to the cell surface (green fluorescence).   However, whereas Fl-HA is internalized by CD44Hwt transfected cells (top right panel), endocytosis of HA does not occur in cells transfected with CD44H-C[286]A.   Thus, molecular events involving this amino acid (palmitoylation of C[286] and transit into lipid rafts) are required for the endocytosis of Fl-HA in these cells.

Bibliography*
Hyaluronan-Related Publications

1. Knudson, W., Biswas, C., and Toole, B. (1984). Interactions between human tumor cells and fibroblasts stimulate hyaluronate synthesis. Proc Natl Acad Sci USA 81, 6767-6771.

2. Knudson, W., Biswas, C., and Toole, B. P. (1984). Stimulation of glycosaminoglycan production in murine tumors. J Cell Biochem 25, 183-196.

3. Orkin, R. W., Knudson, W., and Toole, B. P. (1985). Loss of hyaluronate-dependent coat during myoblast fusion. Dev Biol 107, 527-530.

4. Nemec, R. E., Toole, B. P., and Knudson, W. (1987). The cell surface hyaluronate binding sites of invasive human bladder carcinoma cells. Biochem Biophys Res Comm 149 (1), 249-257.

5. Nemec, R. E., Toole, B. P., and Knudson, W. (1987). The cell surface hyaluronate binding sites of invasive human bladder carcinoma cells. Biochem Biophys Res Commun 149 (1), 249-257.

6. Toole, B. P., Knudson, C. B., Knudson, W., Goldberg, R. L., Chi-Rosso, P. G., and Biswas, C. (1987). Hyaluronate-cell interactions in morphogenesis and tumorigenesis. In *Mesenchymal-Epithelial Interactions in Neural Development NATO, ISI Series H, Volume 5* (Eds. Wolff, J. F., Sievers, J., and Berry, M.), Springer-Verlag, Berlin (Germany), 267-278.

7. Knudson, W., and Toole, B. P. (1988). Membrane association of the hyaluronate stimulatory factor from LX-1 human lung carcinoma cells. J Cell Biochem 38 (3), 165-177.

8. Pauli, B. U., and Knudson, W. (1988). Tumor invasion: a consequence of destructive and compositional matrix alterations. Hum Pathol 19 (6), 628-639.

---

* Provided by the interviewee.

9. Toole, B. P., Knudson, C. B., Munaim, S. I., Knudson, W., Welles, S., and Chi-Rosso, G. (1988). Hyaluronate-cell interactions and regulation of hyaluronate synthesis during embryonic limb development. In *Biological Mechanisms of Tooth Eruption and Root Resorption* (Ed. Davidovitch, Z.), EBSCO Media, Birmingham, AL (USA), 35-41.

10. Knudson, W., Biswas, C., Li, X.-Q., Nemec, R. E., and Toole, B. P. (1989). The role and regulation of tumour-associated hyaluronan. In *The Biology of Hyaluronan CIBA Foundation Symposium No 143* (Eds. Evered, D., and Whelan, J.), John Wiley & Sons, Chichester (UK), 150-169.

11. Li, X.-Q., Thonar, E., and Knudson, W. (1989). Accumulation of hyaluronate in human lung carcinoma as measured by a new hyaluronate ELISA. Conn Tiss Res 19 (2-4), 243-253.

12. Toole, B. P., Knudson, C. B., Munaim, S. I., Knudson, W., Welles, S., and Chi-Rosso, G. (1989). Hyaluronate-cell interactions and regulation of hyaluronate synthesis during embryonic limb development. In *Development, Aging and Repair* (Eds. Abatangelo, G., and Davidson, J. M.), Fidia Research Series, Volume 18, Padova (IT), 41-50.

13. Knudson, C. B., and Knudson, W. (1990). Similar epithelial-stromal interactions in the regulation of hyaluronate production during limb morphogenesis and tumor invasion. Cancer Letters 52, 113-122.

14. Knudson, W., and Knudson, C. B. (1991). Assembly of a chondrocyte-like pericellular matrix on non-chondrogenic cells. J Cell Sci 99, 227-235.

15. Lindqvist, U., Chichibu, K., Delpech, B., Goldberg, R. L., Knudson, W., Poole, A. R., and Laurent, T. C. (1992). Seven different assays of hyaluronan compared for clinical utility. Clin Chem 38 (1), 127-132.

16. Hua, Q., Knudson, C. B., and Knudson, W. (1993). Internalization of hyaluronan by chondrocytes occurs via receptor-mediated endocytosis. J Cell Sci 106, 365-375.

17. Knudson, C. B., and Knudson, W. (1993). Hyaluronan-binding proteins in development, tissue homeostasis, and disease. FASEB J 7 (13), 1233-1241.

18. Knudson, W., Bartnik, E., and Knudson, C. B. (1993). Assembly of pericellular matrices by cos-7 cells transfected with cd44 lymphocyte-homing receptor genes. Proc Natl Acad Sci U S A 90 (9), 4003-4007.

19. Chow, G., Knudson, C. B., Homandberg, G., and Knudson, W. (1995). Increased expression of CD44 in bovine articular chondrocytes by catabolic cellular mediators. J Biol Chem 270 (46), 27734-27741.

20. Knudson, W., and Knudson, C. B. (1995). Hyaluronan and hyaluronan binding proteins in tumor extracellular matrix. In *Tumor Matrix Biology* (Ed. Adany, R.), CRS Press, Cleveland, Ohio (USA), 55-79.

21. Sharif, M., George, E., Shepstone, L., Knudson, W., Thonar, E., Cushnaghan, J., and Dieppe, P. (1995). Serum hyaluronic acid level as a predictor of disease progression in osteoarthritis of the knee. Arthritis Rheum 38 (6), 760-767.

22. Knudson, W. (1996). Tumor-associated hyaluronan. Providing an extracellular matrix that facilitates invasion. Am J Pathol 148 (6), 1721-1726.

23. Knudson, W., Aguiar, D., Hua, Q., and Knudson, C. (1996). CD-44-anchored hyaluronan-rich pericellular matrices: An Ultrastructural and biochemical analysis. Exp Cell Res 228 (2), 216-228.

24. Knudson, W., and Kuettner, K. E. (1997). Proteoglycans. In *Primer on the Rheumatic Diseases, 11th Edition* (Ed. Klippel, J. H.), Arthritis Foundation, Atlanta, Georgia (US), 33-38.

25. Chow, G., Nietfeld, J., Knudson, C., and Knudson, W. (1998). Antisense inhibition of chondrocyte CD44 expression leading to cartilage chondrolysis. Arthritis Rheum 41 (8), 1411-1419.

26. Knudson, W. (1998). Hyaluronan in malignancies. In *The Chemistry, Biology and Medical Applications of Hyaluronan and its Derivatives Proceedings of the Wenner-Gren Foundation International Symposium held in honor of Endre A Balazs, Stockholm, Sweden, September 18-21, 1996* (Ed. Laurent, T. C.), Portland Press Ltd., London (UK), 169-179.

27. Knudson, W. (1998). The role of CD44 as a cell surface hyaluronan receptor during tumor invasion of connective tissue. Frontiers in Bioscience 3, 604-615.

28. Aguiar, D. J., Knudson, W., and Knudson, C. B. (1999). Internalization of the hyaluronan receptor CD44 by chondrocytes. Exp Cell Res 252, 292-302.

29. Knudson, W., and Knudson, C. B. (1999). The hyaluronan receptor, CD44. In *Glycoforum Hyaluronan Today* (Eds. Hascall, V. C. , and Yanagishita, M.), (Seikagaku Corporation Glycoforum, Tokyo, Japan). (Accessed at http://www.glycoforum.gr.jp/science /hyaluronan/HA10/HA10E.html), (March 30, 1999), Tokyo (JP).

30. Nishida, Y., Knudson, C. B., Nietfeld, J. J., Margulis, A., and Knudson, W. (1999). Antisense inhibition of hyaluronan synthase-2 in human articular chondrocytes inhibits proteoglycan retention and matrix assembly. J Biol Chem 274 (31), 21893-21899.

31. D'Souza, A. L., Masuda, K., Otten, L. M., Nishida, Y., Knudson, W., and Thonar, E. J. (2000). Differential effects of interleukin-1 on hyaluronan and proteoglycan metabolism in two compartments of the matrix formed by articular chondrocytes maintained in alginate. Arch Biochem Biophys 374 (1), 59-65.

32. Knudson, W., Casey, B., Nishida, Y., Eger, W., Kuettner, K. E., and Knudson, C. B. (2000). Hyaluronan oligosaccharides perturb cartilage matrix homeostatis and induce chondrocytic chondrolysis. Arthritis Rheum 43 (5), 1165-1174.

33. Nishida, Y., D'Souza, A. L., Thonar, E. J.-M. A., and Knudson, W. (2000). Stimulation of hyaluronan metabolism by interleukin-1α in human articular cartilage. Arthritis Rheum 43 (6), 1315-1326.

34. Nishida, Y., Knudson, C. B., Eger, W., Kuettner, K. E., and Knudson, W. (2000). Osteogenic protein 1 stimulates cells-associated matrix assembly by normal human articular chondrocytes: up-regulation of hyaluronan synthase, CD44, and aggrecan. Arthritis Rheum 43 (1), 206-214.

35. Nishida, Y., Knudson, C. B., Kuettner, K. E., and Knudson, W. (2000). Osteogenic protein-1 promotes the synthesis and retention of extracellular matrix within bovine articular cartilage and chondrocyte cultures. Osteoarthritis Cartilage 8 (2), 127-136.

36. Jiang, H., Knudson, C. B., and Knudson, W. (2001). Antisense inhibition of CD44 tailless splice variant in human articular chondrocytes promotes hyaluronan internalization. Arthr Rheum 44 (11), 2599-2610.

37. Knudson, C. B., and Knudson, W. (2001). Cartilage proteoglycans. Seminars Cell Devel Biol 12, 69-78.

38. Knudson, W., and Kuettner, K. E. (2001). Proteoglycans. In *Primer on the Rheumatic Diseases, 12th Edition* (Ed. Klippel, J. H.), Arthritis Foundation, Atlanta, Georgia (US), 42-49.

39. Kurtis, M. S., Tu, B. P., Gaya, O. A., Mollenhauer, J., Knudson, W., Loeser, R. F., Knudson, C. B., and Sah, R. L. (2001). Mechanisms of chondrocyte adhesion to cartilage: role of ß1-integrins, CD44, and annexin V. J Orthop Res 19, 1122-1130.

40. Jiang, H., Peterson, R. S., Wang, W., Bartnik, E., Knudson, C. B., and Knudson, W. (2002). A requirement for the CD44 cytoplasmic domain for hyaluronan binding, pericellular matrix assembly, and receptor-mediated endocytosis in COS-7 cells. J Biol Chem 277 (12), 10531-10538.

41. Knudson, C. B., Rousche, K. T., Peterson, R. S., Chow, G., and Knudson, W. (2002). CD44 and cartilage matrix stabilization. In *The Many Faces of Osteoarthritis* (Eds. Kuettner, K. E. , and Hascall, V.), Birkhauser Verlage AG, Basel, Switzerland, 219-230.

42. Knudson, W., Chow, G., and Knudson, C. B. (2002). CD44-mediated uptake and degradation of hyaluronan. Matrix Biol 21, 15-23.

43. Knudson, W., and Loeser, R. F. (2002). CD44 and integrin matrix receptors participate in cartilage homeostatsis. Cell Mol Life Sci 59, 36-44.

44. Knudson, W., Nishida, Y., and Peterson, R. S. (2002). Maintenance of cartilage extracellular matrix: the participation of HAS-2 and CD44. In *Hyaluronan Volume 2* (Eds. Kennedy, J. F., Phillips, G. O., Williams, P. A., and Hascall, V. C.), Woodhead, Cambridge, UK, 319-328.

45. Embry, J. J., and Knudson, W. (2003). G1 domain of aggrecan cointernalizes with hyaluronan via a CD44-mediated mechanism in bovine articular chondrocytes. Arthritis Rheum 48 (12), 3431-3441.

46. Nishida, Y., Knudson, C. B., and Knudson, W. (2003). Extracellular matrix recovery by human articular chondrocytes after treatment with hyaluronan hexasaccharides or *Streptomyces* hyaluronidase. Modern Rheumatol 13, 62-68.

47. Knudson, C. B., and Knudson, W. (2004). Hyaluronan and CD44: modulators of chondrocyte metabolism. Clin Orthop Related Res (427 Suppl), S152-S162.

48. Knudson, W., and Knudson, C. B. (2004). An update on hyaluronan and CD44 in cartilage. Current Opinion Orthop 15, 369-375.

49. Knudson, W., and Peterson, R. S. (2004). The hyaluronan receptor: CD44. In *Chemistry and Biology of Hyaluronan* (Eds. Garg, H. G. , and Hales, C. A.), Elsevier, Ltd., Amsterdam, 83-123.

50. Nishida, Y., Knudson, C. B., and Knudson, W. (2004). Osteogenic protein-1 inhibits matrix depletion in a hyaluronan hexasaccharide-induced model of osteoarthritis. Osteoarthritis Cartilage 12, 374-382.

51. Ohno-Nakahara, M., Honda, K., Tanimoto, K., Tanaka, N., Doi, T., Suzuki, A., Yoneno, K., Nakatani, Y., Ueki, M., Ohno, S., Knudson, W., Knudson, C. B., and Tanne, K. (2004). Induction of CD44 and MMP expression by hyaluronidase treatment of articular chondrocytes. J Biochem (Tokyo) 135 (5), 567-575.

52. Peterson, R. S., Andhare, R. A., Rousche, K. T., Knudson, W., Wang, W., Grossfield, J. B., Thomas, R. O., Hollingsworth, R. E., and Knudson, C. B.

(2004). CD44 modulates Smad1 activation in the BMP-7 signaling pathway. J Cell Biol 166 (7), 1081-1091.

53. Chow, G., and Knudson, W. (2005). Characterization of promoter elements of the human HYAL-2 gene. J Biol Chem 280 (29), 26904-26912.

54. Knudson, W., and Knudson, C. B. (2005). The hyaluronan receptor, CD44-- An update. In *Glycoforum. Hyaluronan Today* (Eds. Hascall, V.C. and Yanagishita, M.) (Seikagaku Corporation Glycoforum (Accessed at glycoforum.gr.jp/science/hyaluronan /HA10a/HA10aE.html) (January 13, 2005), Tokyo (JP).

55. Knudson, W., and Peterson, R. S. (2005). Cellular regulation of CD44- mediated catabolism of hyaluronan. In *Hyaluronan: Structure, Metabolism, Biological Activities, Therapeutic Applications Volume I* (Eds. Balazs, E.A., and Hascall, V. C.), Matrix Biology Institute, Edgewater, NJ (USA), 213-220.

56. Nishida, Y., Knudson, W., Knudson, C. B., and Ishiguro, N. (2005). Antisense inhibition of hyaluronan synthase-2 in human osteosarcoma cells inhibits hyaluronan retention and tumorigenicity. Exp Cell Res 307 (1), 194- 203.

57. Ohno, S., Im, H. J., Knudson, C. B., and Knudson, W. (2005). Hyaluronan oligosaccharide-induced activation of transcription factors in bovine articular chondrocytes. Arthritis Rheum 52 (3), 800-809.

58. Ohno, S., Knudson, C. B., and Knudson, W. (2005). Transcriptional activation by hyaluronan oligosaccharide in chondrocytes. In *Hyaluronan: Structure, Metabolism, Biological Activities, Therapeutic Applications Volume II* (Eds. Balazs, E. A. , and Hascall, V. C.), Matrix Biology Institute, Edgewater, NJ (USA), 513-518.

59. Ohno, S., Ohno-Nakahara, M., Knudson, C. B., and Knudson, W. (2005). Induction of MMP-3 by Hyaluronan Oligosaccharides in Temporomandibular Joint Chondrocytes. J Dent Res 84 (11), 1005-1009.

60. Chow, G., Knudson, C. B., and Knudson, W. (2006). Expression and cellular localization of human hyaluronidase-2 in articular chondrocytes and cultured cell lines. Osteoarthritis and Cartilage 14, 849-858.

61. Chow, G., Knudson, C. B., and Knudson, W. (2006). Letter to the Editor. Human hyaluronidase-2 is localized intracellularly in articular chondrocytes and other cultured cell lines. Osteoarthritis Cartilage 14 (12), 1312-1314.

62. Embry, J. J., Fosang, A. J., and Knudson, W. (2006). Extracellular hyaluronan binding is necessary for the intracellular accumulation of ITEGE epitope in bovine articular chondrocytes. Arthritis Rheum 54, 443-454.

63. Ohno, S., Im, H. J., Knudson, C. B., and Knudson, W. (2006). Hyaluronan oligosaccharides induce MMP-13 via transcriptional activation of NFkB and p38 MAP kinase in articular chondrocytes. J Biol Chem 281 (26), 17952-17960.

64. Ohno, S., Schmid, T., Tanne, Y., Kamiya, T., Honda, K., Ohno-Nakahara, M., Swentko, N., Desai, T. A., Tanne, K., Knudson, C. B., and Knudson, W. (2006). Expression of superficial zone protein in mandibular condyle cartilage. Osteoarthritis Cartilage 14 (8), 807-813.

65. Thankamony, S. P., and Knudson, W. (2006). Acylation of CD44 and Its Association with Lipid Rafts Are Required for Receptor and Hyaluronan Endocytosis. J Biol Chem 281 (45), 34601-34609.

66. Hosono, K., Nishida, Y., Knudson, W., Knudson, C. B., Naruse, T., Suzuki, Y., and Ishiguro, N. (2007). Hyaluronan Oligosaccharides Inhibit Tumorigenicity of Osteosarcoma Cell Lines MG-63 and LM-8 in Vitro and in Vivo via Perturbation of Hyaluronan-Rich Pericellular Matrix of the Cells. Am J Pathol 171 (1), 274-286.

Torvard C. Laurent, 2002 (photograph courtesy of T. Laurent)

Torvard C. Laurent

Torvard C. Laurent (b. 1930, Stockholm, Sweden) received his Bachelor of Medicine degree (1950), his License in Medicine (1958), and his Doctor of Medicine (equivalent of a Ph.D., 1958) at the Karolinska Institute in Stockholm. He was instructor at the Karolinska Institute (1949-52, 1955-58), research fellow at the Retina Foundation in Boston, MA, (1953-54, 1959-61), Associate Professor at the University of Uppsala, Sweden (1961-66), and Professor of Medical and Physiological Chemistry at the University of Uppsala (1966-96). He has been member of numerous prestigious scientific boards both in Sweden and internationally.

He is member of the Royal Swedish Academy of Sciences (1982) and served as its President between 1991 and 1994. He was Member of the Nobel Committee for Chemistry (1992-2000) and Chairman of the Board of Trustees of the Nobel Foundation (1994-2001). He is Member of the Academia Europaea and other academies. He received a very large number of awards, among them The Prize of King Oscar II (1965), the Pharmacia Award (1986), the King Carl XVI Gustav Gold Medal (1994), and the "l'Ordre National du Merite au Grade de Commandeur" of France (2000). A laboratory at Pharmacia was named after him (1993). He, edited three books, served on the editorial boards of six journals and is a founding member of the International Society of Hyaluronan Sciences (ISHAS). The Sixth International Conference of ISHAS (Cleveland, Ohio 2003) celebrated his contributions to hyaluronan research.

Interview[*]

Although you stopped doing hyaluronan research some time ago, you have remained in the field and must have a perspective on its development.

The field is moving very fast. I wish I could follow everything that has been written in the last years but most of my information is from discussions with colleagues. I regret that I cannot be more involved any more, but with my other activities it would not be possible. When I am meeting with colleagues, such as here and now, I am happy that I can follow the discussion and that I still remember a lot.

I do believe that I have a perspective on the development of the field and I have been asked at various occasions to talk and write about the history of hyaluronan research. I have met most of the ground-breaking scientists in the field starting with Karl Meyer who discovered hyaluronan in 1934.

Do you have an idea how many people are involved in this field of research?

It is difficult to say but we could make an estimate. At the last meeting on hyaluronan in Wales in 2000, I think there were about 300-400 people present. Of course, there is quite a strong interest at the moment from industry, and a number of the people were industrial representatives, but maybe half of them were from academia. Of course, not everyone who is involved in academia went to the meeting, so this is just a very rough estimate.

The studies of proteins and nucleic acids are much larger fields than the polysaccharides....

---

[*] This interview was recorded during the second meeting "Conversations on Hyaluronan" in St. Tropez, June 2003. An earlier, longer interview with Torvard Laurent appeared in Hargittai, I., *Candid Science II: Conversations with Famous Biomedical Scientists*, (ed. Hargittai, M.), Imperial College Press, London, 2002.

That is true, but even so, there are plenty of people interested in polysaccharides. Not only that, but people are also divided according to which particular polysaccharide they are studying, each polysaccharide by now has its investigators. Just take two other related polysaccharides that are very much studied at present: heparin and heparan sulfate. Heparin is of importance in medicine as an anticoagulant and has a lot of medical applications. Heparan sulfate turns out to be a very unusual polysaccharide, because it can vary its structure depending on where it is found in the organism; it can contain different amounts of iduronic acid instead of glucuronic acid, it can contain different amounts of sulfate at various sites on the chain. In this way there can be a number of binding sites on heparan sulfate for specific proteins. Thus hyaluronan is not the only polysaccharide in this field, which is interesting; there are many others.

Is there an interaction between these different polysaccharide fields?

Of course. All of them grew out from the same field, the glycosaminoglycan field, but they have become more and more specialized. Naturally, we still talk to each other and I can tell you that one of my younger colleagues, who is now a professor in our department, is probably the leading expert on heparin and heparan sulfate. But as in science in general, when a field grows, it is separated into smaller compartments, and this is what has happened here as well.

You have risen to the top in science, but I wonder about the others. My impression is that it is rather difficult to get high recognition in this field, like membership in national academies of sciences, and there are even having difficulties in getting promotion and funding. What may be the reason?

I may not have reached the top in sciences.

But position-wise you did.

Position-wise, yes. You wonder why the scientists you have met here have not been elected to academies and positions at top universities.

First of all I think that all of them are highly respected scientists. In an historical perspective the leading persons in the earlier generation such as Karl Meyer, Albert Dorfman, Sandy Ogston and Helen Muir have received honorary degrees and belonged to the National Academy of Sciences or the Royal Society even if they have not actively participated as officers of the academies. The persons who are here today belong to a younger generation and furthermore represent only the fraction of the field which studies structures. On the other hand, these are the active people now in research and when people are recognized and become members of academies, then they are usually already beyond that stage. It's much better to interact with the young active people when you discuss the current issues.

You said the central topic here is structure. However, there seems to be relatively little known about the metrical aspects of structure in this field.

The primary structure actually was determined in the 1950s and that was settled then. We know exactly that and what we are discussing now is the conformation of the polysaccharide in solution.

The primary structure is the sequence.

It's the sequence of the sugars and the linkages between them. And then it is the conformation of this chain that we are discussing now. We do have various kinds of X-ray structures of fibers of these polymers in 2-fold and 4-fold conformation. But the question is, what does it look like in solution, and there I would say we are still arguing. John Scott has been one of the foremost persons in this field.

Wouldn't the NMR technique help in giving a similar level of structure like the X-ray diffraction crystal in solution?

The problem is that hyaluronan is not like a protein, where you have a defined tertiary structure with a greatly limited intramolecular flexibility, on which you can unambigously use NMR. Hyaluronan is a much, much larger molecule, with many more conformations, so you really cannot talk about a fixed three-dimensional structure. What we are discussing are hydrogen bonds and configurations around the single chain, and I think we all agree that it is probably a stiff chain, which is stiffened by intramolecular intrachain hydrogen bonds. However, we are not aware of how many of these there are as an average.

But if it's a stiff chain it should be easier to investigate...

Yes. But when you discuss stiffness it is something relative to something else and now we discuss it relative to other polysaccharide chains.

Then there are the complexes when hyaluronan is attached to a protein, studying their structure would also be of importance...

Of course. I believe that a lot of the future of the biological function can be revealed by studies of protein-hyaluronan complexes. What has turned up from a biological point of view in recent years is that short oligosaccharides have different biological effects than high molecular weight polysaccharides. We now know that proteins often occur in complexes with other macromolecules that create a certain biological effect. If we think in these terms it is most probable that the biological effects of hyaluronan are exerted via multi-macromolecular complexes and that the hyaluronan chain might let two or three or more proteins bind next to each other. However, if you have a short oligosaccharide, where only one or two proteins can bind instead of more, then that would have a different effect on the signaling system of the cell. Such complex formation most probably occurs on the surface of the cell membrane, where we have hyaluronan binding proteins. I believe that in the future we will have to isolate the hyaluronan binding proteins, even from cell membranes, but it's not easy.

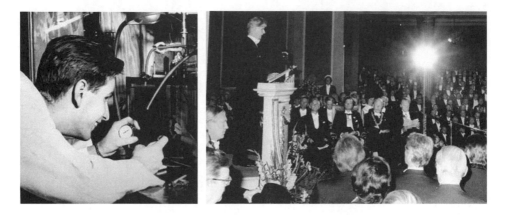

Left: Torvard Laurent in Boston, 1953; *right:* graduation lecture, "Modern medicine is founded on basic research," given at the 500th anniversary of Uppsala University on September 30, 1977 (photograph courtesy of T. Laurent)

Torvard and Ulla Laurent in 1998 (photograph courtesy of T. Laurent)

Left: Ernst Barany, Professor of Pharmacology and Endre A. Balazs outside Uppsala University on the occasion of Balazs's receiving an honorary MD in 1967, *right:* Sandy Ogston receiving an honorary doctorate in Medicine from T. Laurent at the 500th anniversary of Uppsala University in 1977 (photograph courtesy of T. Laurent)

Torvard Laurent as President of the Royal Swedish Academy of Sciences with Carl XVI Gustaf, King of Sweden, and Carl-Olof Jacobsson, permanent secretary of the academy in 1992 (photograph courtesy of T. Laurent)

Does this also mean that hyaluronan may be very important within the cell, not only in the intercellular region?

It could be but its main function is probably on the cell surface. We now know that hyaluronan, or its oligosaccharides, can induce cells to do various things. Short oligosaccharides can induce cells to make more blood vessels, angiogenesis. We know that short hyaluronan oligosaccharides can induce macrophages to phagocytose other things. And we know that certain cells migrate along hyaluronan and that there are receptors on the cell surface that recognize hyaluronan when they move, and all these cellular functions go via a signal transduction system from the cell membrane into the cell and here we have a large very interesting field to study.

I have asked everyone among this group of interviewees about what they consider to be the seminal steps in the development of this field. Most of them entered the field quite a few years ago, but they were not keen to elaborate on this question. Is it only my impression that there is generally scarce information concerning the whole development from the early days?

Your impression may be correct. We have all been young and have not been able to see far backward. It's very often when we get old that we get interested in history and the historical background of our field. Which were the seminal discoveries? The first one was, of course, the isolation of hyaluronan by Karl Meyer, which he described in 1934. Other people had isolated it earlier but described it incorrectly. Karl Meyer was definitely a very important person in this field. He and his collaborators determined the primary structure of the polysaccharide in the 1950s and they were able to do it by using new techniques that polysaccharide chemists hadn't been using before. Karl Meyer introduced enzymatic procedures to determine the structure and that was definitely a seminal step.

I would also say that the physico-chemical work by Sandy Ogston in Oxford was very important and he was very influential, although you can argue that he was doing his studies on a product that wasn't a pure hyaluronan because it contained proteins as well.

Undoubtedly, he has had a great influence on the thinking of this scientific community; not the least I myself have been very much influenced by Sandy Ogston.

The third person to really point out is Endre Balazs, because he has had a drive that I haven't seen in any other person in the field to really propose practical applications of hyaluronan. Without him, in my opinion, the field would never have developed the way it has.

Bandi, who is a medical doctor by training, has had a tremendous interest in the physical chemistry of hyaluronan.

He has been interested in everything that has come his way, and he also understood the advantage of choosing collaborators with the background knowledge of the various techniques he has used. When I met him in the early 1950s, he had no interest in physical chemistry, he was a biologist, he was interested in tissue culture and how these polysaccharides would affect living cells. And I would say his interest in physical chemistry pretty much arose when we found that the viscosity of hyaluronan varied with ionic strength and described the polyelectrolyte viscosity of hyaluronan, which people hadn't realized before. Then we tried to sterilize hyaluronan with ultraviolet irradiation and the polysaccharide was degraded so the viscosity dropped dramatically. These two things induced him to use physical chemical techniques to study hyaluronan and its degradation. Bandi attracted people with expertise and asked them to work on his problems and that has been his great strength.

As you know, Baruch S. Blumberg shared the 1976 Nobel Prize in Physiology or Medicine with D. Carleton Gajdusek; the citation said, "for their discoveries concerning new mechanisms for the origin and dissemination of infectious diseases." Blumberg's work concerned specifically Hepatitis B, but in his younger years he worked on hyaluronan.

I met him at that time when he worked on hyaluronan. He had been working with Karl Meyer and then Karl Meyer sent him over to Sandy Ogston. There he worked on the same kind of problems that I worked on at that time. Then he disappeared from the horizon in our field and it was not until suddenly he got the Nobel Prize for something completely different that I recognized that he was the same person I had met previously.

If you were now 25 or 30 years old would you choose this field again today?

When you are young you really don't know what you are going into, therefore it is always circumstances that decide where you will end up. I was a medical student, I was asked to become an unpaid instructor in histology, and I got into it without knowing what it was all about. In the histology department I met Bandi and he was the one who engaged me in hyaluronan research. Without that I would never have ended up in this field.

Then you stayed in it throughout your entire research career…

Yes, I stayed because I found it interesting. But on the other hand, if I hadn't gotten a position in Uppsala I might have become a clinician, so you never know.

But you didn't answer my question.

I suppose that I probably would do the same thing that I did as a young boy, I would take the opportunity which was the closest one. If I had the possibility to go to a charismatic person no matter what he did, I would probably do that.

That's a heavy statement.

Yes. But I think very few people in advance can determine what would be interesting and continue that their whole life.

Just recently you were president of the Royal Swedish Academy of Sciences, chairman of the Nobel Foundation's Board of Trustees, so you have a tremendous overview of science. Are you saying that you would still not try to pick a certain field, rather, you would pick a certain person?

Yes, I think so, because the person that helps you to develop is the one you are working with and educated by. Hans Krebs once wrote an article in *Nature* about how to become a Nobel laureate, and he showed that the easiest way to become a Nobel laureate was to be the pupil of a Nobel laureate. He could show this with different examples of long chains. A charismatic person, who can induce interest in young people, is extremely important. It is rather interesting that we have had a number of high-level schools that have depended upon charismatic persons. I can just mention Niels Bohr and his school in Copenhagen in theoretical physics, or you could mention Rutherford in England and the school he actually started in physics. Or you could think of the Medical Research Council's laboratory in Cambridge and the start of molecular biology and the charismatic people that were there.

Do you think that this holds today as much as it did 50 years ago?

Yes, I believe so. It's still the personality that is very important. One example is Bandi Balazs and his personality.

Two years ago we spent three months at the Laboratory of Molecular Biology in Cambridge and I didn't feel that sizzling intellectual atmosphere that other people had described earlier, just as you did now. But many of the great people who started that laboratory are gone.

But every school will have to die in the end.

What do you think will be Bandi's main legacy?

In my opinion it is that he really made this field into a medically very interesting field. Without him we wouldn't have the enormous industrial interest in this field. But I also think that his importance would be the enthusiasm that he has induced in so many of his collaborators. He will be remembered for that.

What do you feel will be your legacy?

I'm not so sure that there will be so much of a legacy….

What would you like it to be?

I would like to be remembered by my pupils.

I asked Jim Watson what would be his legacy, and you would expect him to say the double helix, but he said it would rather be his books. Then, after a while, he added the institution of Cold Spring Harbor, but not the discovery.

I would like to be remembered, if I will be remembered, for the way I have run my laboratory and I hope that my pupils will remember me positively for that.

What do you think of Bandi's idea of trying to put together the Encyclopedia of Hyaluronan?

I think, it is a very interesting project, in fact, a unique project within a field, and I think it's very characteristic for Bandi to come up with an idea like this. If he succeeds, it will become a good encyclopedia. It will show the strength of the mode of media we have for information and how to collect information; not only collect, but also trying to find out what is right and what is wrong in the information. In a big computer you can have all the information but it is not digested.

Someone suggested that they should present the literature but not make judgments, what you are saying is different.

Of course, we should make judgments, it is absolutely essential that we do.

This is a rather well-defined field. Do you think that other fields that may be much larger can follow this example?

Every large field can be subdivided into smaller fields in the same way that this is a small part of the extracellular matrix research or the polysaccharide research. I'm sure it could be done with other fields as well. It's only a question of how you limit it. For example, we can discuss the physical chemical behavior of this polysaccharide, but we have to limit ourselves to that and not go into discussing the techniques and the background of the techniques that we use, we have to take those for granted. Of course, we have to know if the techniques are correct or not.

The whole idea of making this Encyclopedia came about because of Bandi's generosity. If there is not such private potential, how can this happen?

If this works out well, I'm pretty sure that NIH or other funding agencies could finance a second or third example.

You would advise them to do that.

Not until I have seen the results of this, but if it works out…

So does it mean that you have still doubts about this…

One would not be a scientist if one didn't have doubts.

Summary

by Torvard C. Laurent

My scientific career is described in reference [195] – i.e. my background, my teachers, in which laboratories I have worked, my co-workers and my other scientific interests outside the hyaluronan field.[9]

1. Characterization of the hyaluronan molecule

I defended my doctoral thesis "Physico-chemical studies on hyaluronic acid" [10] in 1957. It summarized the work described in publications [2-9]. The polymer was prepared from different tissues (umbilical cord, vitreous body, synovial fluid, cock's comb and skin) using different preparative techniques. By means of light-scattering and viscosity it was shown that the molecule had varying molecular weight – usually in the order of millions – and had the configuration of an extended random coil. At low ionic strength hyaluronan showed a typical polyelectrolyte behaviour and a similar conclusion was drawn from streaming dielectric measurements and titration. The intrinsic pK of hyaluronan was found to be 3.21 in good agreement with the pK of glucuronic acid.

It had been proposed that the high water content within the coil could be due to an extensive ordered water structure around the chain. This hypothesis was tested by x-ray diffraction but no hydration shell could be detected. Instead the expansion of the coil must be due to an inherent stiffness in the chain partly supported by the negative charges. When hyaluronan had been precipitated by cetylpyridinum ions (CPC) the precipitate could be dissolved in methanol. In this hydrophobic environment the coil contracted to a fifth of its volume indicating that

---

[9] Publication numbers cited in this text refer to the separate list of hyaluronan publications, following this summary.

the interaction with water and the charges on the chain are important for the native expanded coil structure.

Further physical chemical characterization of the hyaluronan chain was later carried out in my laboratory by Robert L. Cleland and Ove Wik.

2. Molecular weight fractionation of hyaluronan and other polyanions

Light-scattering studies on hyaluronan from the bovine vitreous body indicated a high degree of polydispersity [5]. Fractionation of the polysaccharide by precipitation with CPC at gradually decreasing ionic strengths yielded fractions of decreasing molecular weights [14]. Ionic exchange chromatography of corneal polysaccharides [17, 18] gave a similar fractionation of keratan sulphate and CPC-fractionation of heparin too [16]. A theoretical explanation to the molecular weight fractionation of polyanions with CPC was subsequently published [32]. Later when gel chromatography became available [29] it has become the most common method to fractionate the polysaccharides.

The importance of molecular weight fractionations of hyaluronan and other polysaccharides have been apparent since different lengths of the chains show different biological activities (for hyaluronan see e.g.Stern et al. J. Cell Biol. 85, 699 (2006) and for heparin reference [68]).

3. The formation of entangled hyaluronan networks

When hyaluronan fractions of different molecular weights were studied in the analytical ultracentrifuge the sedimentation rate varied strongly with concentration [14]. At infinite dilution the sedimentation rate mirrored the difference in molecular mass but at higher concentrations the S-value decreased rapidly and at concentrations above 0.2% all fractions sedimented with the same rate. It was concluded that hyaluronan formed an entangled network above 0.2% and the slow sedimentation was due to the high resistance to solvent flow through the network. The concept that hyaluronan forms entangled networks at physiological concentrations induced studies of the physical chemistry of such networks and their interactions with other macromolecules.

4. Restricted movements of macromolecules in polymer networks

That hyaluronan networks act as filters or sieves for other macromolecules was first shown by sedimentation in the ultracentrifuge [15]. Hyaluronan retards large molecules more than small ones. The diffusion is similarly retarded [21] and an empirical equation for the retardation as a function of the hyaluronan concentration and diameter of the globular molecules could be presented [21]. This equation was later given a theoretical explanation by Ogston et al. (Proc. R. Soc. (Lond.) A333, 297 (1973)). The sieve effect could be used to increase the resolution in the separation of macromolecules in the ultracentrifuge [22]. Other polymers than hyaluronan also act as sieves [28]. The transport of linear macromolecules through hyaluronan networks was faster than that of globular molecules of equal hydrodynamic volumes which was interpreted as a reptation mechanism [55].

Low molecular weight compounds like oxygen, nitrogen and water diffuse without restriction through hyaluronan networks [57].

The impediment of the rotational diffusion of globular molecules in hyaluronate and other polymer networks is very moderate [48, 50, 52] in agreement with the view that the restricted translational diffusion of macromolecules is due to sterical hindrance and not to friction exerted by the networks.

5. The exclusion of macromolecules from polymer networks

A three-dimensional chain network will for sterical reasons restrict the volume available to other macromolecules. Ogston calculated the available volume for a sphere in the presence of randomly distributed rods as a function of the concentration of rods and the diameters of the rods and the sphere (Trans. Faraday Soc. 54, 1754 (1958)). My work on molecular exclusion is based on Ogston's equation.

A new technique to separate macromolecules according to size by chromatography on dextran gels was described by Porath and Flodin in 1959 and termed gelfiltration. No physical explanation to the effect was available at the time. Using chromatographic data from a large number of proteins and several dextran gels of different concentrations we could show that the results were compatible with an exclusion of the proteins from the dextran gels and that the data followed Ogston's equations [29]. This paper has subsequently become a citation classic [153].

To further prove that gel chromatography works by exclusion (an entropy effect) it was studied at various temperatures [38]. Similarly the interaction between dextran and albumin was studied by lightscattering over a temperature interval [66]. The data confirmed that the interaction was essentially entropic in nature.

The exclusion by hyaluronan networks was either determined by equilibrium dialysis of proteins between hyaluronan solutions and buffers or by chromatography on hyaluronan gels. For the latter purpose hyaluronan was cross-linked [30]. The results were completely compatible with the steric exclusion from a network of extended rigid hyaluronan chains and thus confirmed the macromolecular structure of hyaluronan obtained by other techniques [31]. Gelchromatography was subsequently used to determine the structure of agarose gels [36].

6. Some consequences of steric exclusion

When a protein is mixed with a polymer its available volume decreases, resulting in an increased concentration or chemical activity. This has several interesting consequences of physiological importance.

a. The colloid osmotic pressure of a mixture of hyaluronan and albumin is considerably higher than the sum of osmotic pressures for the two components measured separately [23]. This has consequences for the regulation of hydration of extracellular compartments in the body.

b. The solubility of a protein decreases in the presence of a polymer and the effect is larger the larger the protein is [24, 25]. Interestingly, proteins like antigen-antibody complexes [33] and lipoproteins [37] are easily precipitated by various polymers. A graduate student, Krister Hellsing, specifically showed a clear effect of hyaluronan on immune precipitation (Biochem. J. 112, 475 (1969)). Also the solubility of sodium urate decreases in high concentrations of chondroiti-4 sulphate [27] which could explain the precipitation of uric acid in gout.

c. The increase in chemical activity due to exclusion also effects chemical equilibria. This was verified in studies of enzyme reactions in the presence of polymers [46].

d. Exclusion effects the conformation of other macromolecules. Equilibria between two conformations are moved towards the most compact one. This was verified in experiments with polynucleotides which prefer a helix conformation rather than a random coil conformation in the presence of a neutral polymer [53]

7. The formation of dissipative structures in mixed polymer systems

In our studies on the diffusion of polyvinylpyrrolidone (PVP) in dextran solutions [75] we recorded a very rapid transport of PVP at high dextran concentrations – many times higher than its free diffusion in water [67]. The explanation was found when we labelled PVP with a blue dye. If PVP and dextran where mixed and placed in the lower compartment of a diffusion cell and only dextran in the top compartment macroscopic symmetric structures (blue fingers) moved from the lower compartment upwards. Similarly colorless fingers moved downwards. After a while the structures dissipated and the cell was filled with a homogenous solution [69]. The phenomenon could be explained by an osmotically driven water transport from the dextran solution to the mixed PVP-dextran solution and an inversion of density [72, 78, 79, 80, 84, 93, 191]. The discovery is an example of what Prigogine has termed dissipative structures i.e. when a system is far from equilibrium it may take a shortcut towards equilibrium by forming well-defined structures which then disappear.

Comper has subsequently studied dissipative structures in connective tissue polysaccharide systems and discussed the importance for the formation of biological structures and transport in vivo (see e.g. J. theor. Biol. 145, 497 (1990)).

8. Determination of hyaluronan concentrations

Analyses of hyaluronan concentration have gradually increased in specificity and sensitivity. During the 1950s and 1960s simple color reactions for uronic acid and hexosamine were used. In 1969 we published an isotope dilution technique to determine hyaluronan in individual samples of aqueous humour [42]. It had a sensitivity of 0.4 microgram. When it was found that proteoglycans specifically bind to hyaluronan the binding portion could be used for specific assays. Such an assay was first described by Anders Tengblad in my laboratory (Biochem. J. 185, 101 (1980)). He labelled the protein with radioactive iodine and partitioned it between a hyaluronan-substituted gel and free hyaluronan in a fluid. The radioactivity bound to the gel is related to the concentration of free hyaluronan in the sample. By this technique he could determine 5 nanogram specifically. This became a turning point in hyaluronan research. Subsequently a number of assays were designed and seven of them used in clinical research were compared and gave essentially the same results [136]

Hyaluronan was measured for the first time in untreated samples of lymph, blood and urine in 1981 [70]. Lymph had at least 10-fold higher concentrations than blood plasma and it was concluded that plasma hyaluronan at least partly originated from extravascular compartments and carried to blood via lymph. Urinary excretion could not be the main route for removal of serum hyaluronan.

The hyaluronan concentration in blood serum from healthy persons is within the range of 10-100 ng/ml and increases with age over 50 years [86]. There are no differences between sexes. Many animals often show higher serum levels than man. Newborn children display very high levels but these drop to normal at an age of one year [152].

Hyaluronan levels have subsequently been determined in a number of body fluids such as lymph [94], urine [101], aqueous humour (Ulla Laurent, Arch. Ophthalmol 101, 129 (1983)), amniotic fluid (Dahl et al, Biochem. Med 30, 280 (1983)), and cerebrospinal fluid [179].

In order to study the distribution of hyaluronan in the organism, rat tissues were separated, proteolytically digested and hyaluronan extracted. A rat weighing 250 g contained 40-60 mg hyaluronan. More than half was found in the skin and a quarter in the skeleton and supporting structures. Less than 10% were found in striated muscles [108]. If the data of the rat could be extrapolated to humans a man should contain 15 g of hyaluronan.

The availability of hyaluronan-binding protein which could be labelled with a dye made it possible to visualize hyaluronan in histological sections. This has been used extensively by my younger co-workers, especially Claude Laurent.

9. Turnover of hyaluronan in the vascular system

In 1981 Robert Fraser came to my laboratory. He had synthesized a tritium-labelled hyaluronan in tissue culture. We injected it intravenously in rabbits and followed its disappearance [71]. It had a half-life of 2.5-4.5 minutes and was taken up mainly by the non-parenchymal cells of the liver and some in the spleen. After a while the radioactivity was found in tritiated water. Prior injection of excess unlabelled hyaluronan prevented the uptake of labelled polysaccharide. Intravenous injection of tritium-labelled hyaluronan in humans showed a similar rapid clearance as in rabbits [83]. A detailed study of the kinetics of disappearance of hyaluronan injected in sheep blood gave values of maximal uptake capacity [121]. This study was then repeated in man [162].

Injection of carbon-14-labelled hyaluronan in a rat and whole body autoradiography [81] confirmed that the hyaluronan was essentially concentrated in liver but also in spleen, lymph nodes and bone marrow. It was subsequently shown both by studies in cell culture [77,85] and by in situ studies using light- and electronmicroscopic autoradiography [87] that the liver endothelial cells were responsible for the uptake. More recently it has been shown that also Kupffer cells can take up and degrade hyaluronan [147] but their contribution is small compared to that of the endothelial cells. A key enzyme in the degradation, N-acetylglucosamine-6-phosphate deacetylase, was only found in the liver endothelial and Kupffer cells but not in hepatocytes [102,117,124].

Studies on hyaluronan in urine [101] showed an excretion of hyaluronan of low molecular weight (4000 -12000) indicating that it came from plasma after glomerular filtration. The weight-average molecular weight of hyaluronan in plasma is in the order of 100.000 and in lymph ten times higher [94]. Apparently, large moleules are preferentially taken up in the liver and small excreted in urine. Studies on the hyaluronan concentration in different vascular beds of man [92] confirm that hyaluronan is removed when passing the liver and kidneys.

Subsequently it was shown by perfusion of labelled hyaluronan that lymph nodes are important sites for its catabolism [109]. Only a minor part of the hyaluronan in lymph reaches the general circulation.

10. The scavenger properties of liver endothelial cells

At the time when we discovered that hyaluronan is taken up in the liver a Norwegian graduate student, Bård Smedsröd, had joined our group. He was able to isolate liver endothelial cells and grow them in cell culture and show that they metabolize hyaluronan [76, 77]. The cells carry receptors for hyaluronan and the polysaccharide is endocytosed and degraded [85]. A detailed study of the binding of hyaluronan fractions of varying molecular weights gave the number of receptors per cell and the binding constants. The receptor also bound chondroitin-4 sulphate [91]. The uptake of chondroitin sulphate proteoglycans was followed morphologically [106]. The in vivo uptake of hyaluronan in liver endothelial cells was also confirmed with hyaluronan labelled with radioactive iodine [111,114]. The hyaluronan receptor was subsequently characterized (McCourt et al. Hepatology 30, 1276 (1999)) and shown to be identical to stabilin (Politz et al, Biochem. J. 362, 155 (2002)). Receptors for collagen chains were also present on liver endothelial cells [96].

The discoverey that liver endothelial cells are important scavenger cells changed the common notion that only the Kupffer cells (i.e. macrophages) had this task in the liver [123]. Bård Smedsröd has continued to study the various scavenger functions of the liver endothelial cells.

11. Studies on hyaluronan concentration and turnover under normal and pathological conditions in individual tissue compartments

After the successful studies of hyaluronan turnover in blood the techniques developed for this purpose were used for turnover studies in individual tissues or compartments. Often an external collaborating group or a graduate student concentrated their research efforts on a specific organ under normal and pathological conditions.

a. *Vascular compartment.* It soon became apparent that certain diseases displayed pathological serum levels of hyaluronan. Anna Engström-Laurent described in her thesis in 1985 the effect in inflammatory diseases and liver affections. In rheumatoid arthritis increased levels were noted especially in the morning. Apparently, hyaluronan is accumulated in the inflammed joints during night time and released into the general circulation when the patients start moving in the morning. This explains the well-known symptom of "morning stiffness" (Arthr. Rheum. 30, 1333 (1987)). In liver cirrhosis very high serum levels are noticed (e.g. Hepatology 4, 638 (1985)) due to an impaired uptake in the liver [90, 104].

Increased levels are also found in patients with mesotheliomas [107] and it was later shown that mesothelioma cells produce factors which stimulate fibroblasts to produce hyaluronan [154]. Sören Berg has described high plasma levels under septic conditions [110, 151] which can be explained by decreased liver uptake [151,165]) or increased hyaluronan flow in lymph [120]. In postsurgical conditions increased levels [161] can be due to infusion of physiological salt solutions leading to increased lymph flow [163]. Henning Onarheim in Bergen studied increase of serum hyaluronan in burn injury which apparently also is due to increased lymph flow [128, 129, 135, 146]. Patients with eclampsia have high plasma levels [191]. A review of hyaluronan as a disease marker describes further conditions [176].

b. *Skin.* The major part of hyaluronan is found in skin [108]. In collaboration with Rolf Reed in Bergen and his american associates. the half-life of hyaluronan injected in skin was found to be in the order of a day [126] indicating a removal by lymph flow. When hyaluronan was measured in prenodal lymph, and the lymph flow increased by increased venous pressure an increased washout was noted [127, 160]. However, when tritium labelled hyaluronan was injected in similar experiments it was shown that the lymphatic removal was small compared to the local turnover [175].

c. *Joints.* The observation cited above that hyaluronan is accumulated during night in inflamed joints and causes morning stiffness led to studies of the cause of the hyaluronan production. It was found that hyaluronan was localized around proliferating cells. Cytokines from macrophages seemed to induce the proliferation [141]. Hyaluronan labelled with iodine-125-tyramine-cellbiose was injected into rabbit knee joints and the degradation products, which remain intracellularly, were traced. They were found either in the joint tissues indicating a local degradation or in the liver [140]. Further studies on hyaluronan in joints by members of the research group are cited in reviews e.g. [171].

d. *Eye and Ear.* Ulla Laurent measured concentration, molecular weight and turnover of hyaluronan in eye compartments. She defended her thesis in 1982. When tritium hyaluronan was used to study the turnover in the anterior chamber the degradation could be followed by measuring tritiated water in blood [103]. In a later paper (Exp Eye Res 57, 435 (1993)) when hyaluronan was labeled with iodine-125-tyramine-cellobiose it was shown that all degradation took place in the liver.

Claude Laurent defended his thesis on hyaluronan in the middle ear in 1988. He has published extensively on the presence and turnover of hyaluronan in ear tissues and its clinical use in otolaryngology.

e. *Lung and pleura.* Roger Hällgren and his collaborators in Uppsala were interested in the diagnostic use of lung lavage fluid. They found a six-fold increase in patients with adult respiratory distress syndrome (ARDS) and on the same time a 30-fold increase in the serum concentrations [113]. Subsequently high levels of hyaluronan in lung lavage have been found in a number of pulmonary conditions e.g. sarcoidosis, farmer's lung, and quartz-induced fibrosis.

The hyaluronan in lymph from sheep lung was followed at increased pressure in the lung circulation. The lymph flow and the amount of hyaluronan washed out of the lung increased in parallel. About 2% of lung hyaluronan was removed per day via lymph under normal conditions [105]. The experiments were repeated in dogs with similar results [164]. The turnover of hyaluronan in the pleural space was determined with tritium labelled polysaccharide in rabbits and half-lives of 8-15 hrs were recorded [150].

f. *Abdominal organs. Liver.* In order to explain the high serum hyaluronan levels under septic conditions James Alston-Smith studied the effects of endotoxin on hyaluronan uptake by liver cells. No effect [134] or a moderate decrease in capacity [148] was found. A reason for high serum levels is rather a decreased perfusion of the liver [151,165] and increased production of hyaluronan in other tissues. Interestingly, the stellate cells (lipocytes) in the liver increase production of hyaluronan after endotoxin treatment [156] and hyaluronan accumulates around portal vessels [169].

Alvin Wells described the increase of hyaluronan in rejected grafted *kidneys* and the accumulation could be correlated with the edema in the tissue [125, 145, 155, 158].

Rolf Reed and collaborators described that *intestinal* hyaluronan is washed out by lymph flow [137], The lymphatic flux of hyaluronan increases during fat absorption [144].

g. *Female reproductive tract and the fetus.* Salustri et al. followed the hormone-driven synthesis of hyaluronan in the preovulatory follicle during the maturation of the oocyte [142].

Greta Edelstam studied the hyaluronan distribution in the female reproductive tract with special reference to changes in the tubae in infertility [133]. The hyaluronan turnover was also studied in peritoneal fluid in experimental aseptic peritonitis [149] and in patients with genital inflammation [159].

Lauritz Dahl described in his thesis [1989) the concentration and molecular weight of hyaluronan in human amniotic fluid and he also injected labelled hyaluronan in sheep fetuses to study the turnover. The hyaluronan in amniotic fluid comes from the urine of the fetus and to a certain amount from the lungs. It is removed when the fetus swallows it. The fetus has a very high catabolic activity in its liver.

The hyaluronan content during fetal development of the lung was followed in rabbits [132]. It was initially high and decreased towards term but increased again after birth.

Hans Johnsson studied in his thesis (defended in 2001) the lung hyaluronan content in prematurely born rabbits. Oxygen exposure neonatally results in increased hyaluronan and water content of the lungs [188]. Surfactants and N-acetylcystein are often sprayed in the lungs of prematurely born babies. It was shown that N-acetylcystein can promote hyaluronan production in fetal human lung fibroblasts in vitro [182].

12. Hyaluronan biosynthesis

Paraskevi Heldin joined my group as a postdoc and in her first paper she described that platelet-derived-growth-factor BB (PDGF-BB) stimulated hyaluronan synthesis in human fibroblasts [112]. She has independently pursued this line together with her graduate students and continued the studies of hyaluronan biosynthesis. I have taken part in a few investgations. PDGF-BB can induce hyaluronan synthesis in liver fat storing cells but not in liver endothelial cells [130]. PDGF-AA has no effect. Receptors for PDGF-BB are found on the fat storing cells and for PDGF AA on the endothelial cells [130]. The mechanism by which PDGF-BB activates hyaluronan synthase was studied in mesothelial cells and found to involve protein synthesis, tyrosine phosphorylation and activation of protein kinase C [138]. Mesothelioma cells were found to produce factors that promote hyaluronan synthesis in mesothelial cells [154]. A review on hyaluronan biosynthesis was published in 2000 [189].

13. Reviews

I have organized two symposia on hyaluronan, which have been published as books i.e. "The Biology of Hyaluronan" in 1988 (Ciba Foundation Symposium 143) and "The Chemistry, Biology and Medical Applications of Hyaluronan and its Derivatives" in 1996 (Wenner-Gren International Series vol. 72).

A number of reviews have been written on the physical chemistry of concentrated polymer systems and physiological functions of hyaluronan [39, 40, 41, 44, 45, 49, 54, 64, 74, 82, 170 and 190]. Similarly, reviews have been published on the metabolic turnover of hyaluronan [88, 89, 95, 96, 98, 100, 116, 118, 119, 122, 131, 139, 143, 167, 168, 172, 174, 176, 177, 178, 180, 181, 183, 185, 186, 187, 196]. Some articles have dealt with the history of hyaluronan research [184, 192, 193 and 194]

Bibliography*

Hyaluronan-Related Publications

1. Balazs, E.A., Högberg, B., and Laurent, T.C. (1951). The biological activity of hyaluron sulfuric acid. Acta Physiol Scand 23, 168-178.

2. Balazs, E.A., and Laurent, T.C. (1951). Viscosity function of hyaluronic acid as a polyelectrolyte. J Polymer Sci 6 (5), 665-667.

3. Jacobson, B., and Laurent, T.C. (1954). Streaming dielectric data of hyaluronic acid. J Colloid Sci 9 (1), 36-40.

4. Laurent, T.C., and Gergely, J. (1955). Light scattering studies on hyaluronic acid. J Biol Chem 212, 325-333.

5. Laurent, T.C. (1955). Studies on hyaluronic acid in the vitreous body. J Biol Chem 216, 263-271.

6. Laurent, T.C. (1957). A comparative study of physico-chemical properties of hyaluronic acid prepared according to different methods and from different tissues. Arkiv för Kemi 11 (54), 487-496.

7. Laurent, T.C. (1957). A study of cetylpyridinium hyaluronate in methanol solution. Arkiv för Kemi 11 (55), 497-501.

8. Laurent, T.C. (1957). On the hydration of macromolecules: X-ray diffraction studies on aqueous solutions of hyaluronic acid. Arkiv för Kemi 11 (56), 503-512.

9. Laurent, T.C. (1957). The amorphous x-ray diffractogram of hyaluronic acid. Arkiv för Kemi 11 (57), 513-518.

10. Laurent, T.C. (1957). Physico-Chemical Studies on Hyaluronic Acid (Thesis). Almqvist & Wiksells boktryckeri AB, Uppsala, Sweden, 28 pp.

11. Balazs, E.A., Laurent, T.C., and Laurent, U. B. G. (1959). Studies on the structure of the vitreous body. VI. Biochemical changes during development. J Biol Chem 234, 422-430.

---

* Provided by the interviewee.

12. Balazs, E.A., Laurent, T.C., Laurent, U. B. G., DeRoche, M. H., and Bunney, D. M. (1959). Studies on the structure of the vitreous body. VIII. Comparative biochemistry. Arch Biochem Biophys 81, 464-479.

13. Balazs, E.A., Laurent, T.C., Howe, A. F., and Varga, L. (1959). Irradiation of mucopolysaccharides with ultraviolet light and electrons. Radiation Res 11 (2), 149-164.

14. Laurent, T.C., Ryan, M., and Pietruszkiewicz, A. (1960). Fractionation of hyaluronic acid. The polydispersity of hyaluronic acid from the bovine vitreous body. Biochim Biophys Acta 42, 476-485.

15. Laurent, T.C., and Pietruszkiewicz, A. (1961). The effect of hyaluronic acid on the sedimentation rate of other substances. Biochim Biophys Acta 49, 258-264.

16. Laurent, T.C. (1961). Studies on fractionated heparin. Arch Biochem Biophys 92 (2), 224-231.

17. Anseth, A., and Laurent, T.C. (1961). Studies on corneal polysaccharides. I. Separation. Exp Eye Res 1, 25-38.

18. Laurent, T.C., and Anseth, A. (1961). Studies on corneal polysaccharides. II. Characterization. Exp Eye Res 1, 99-105.

19. Laurent, U. B. G., Laurent, T.C., and Howe, A. F. (1962). Chromatography of soluble proteins from the bovine vitreous body on DEAE-cellulose. Exp Eye Res 1, 276-285.

20. Anseth, A., and Laurent, T.C. (1962). Polysaccharides in normal and pathologic corneas. Invest Ophthalmol 1, 195-201.

21. Laurent, T.C., Björk, I., Pietruszkiewicsz, A., and Persson, H. (1963). On the interaction between polysaccharides and other macromolecules II. The transport of globular particles through hyaluronic acid solutions. Biochim Biophys Acta 78, 351-359.

22. Laurent, T.C., and Persson, H. (1963). On the interaction between polysaccharides and other macromolecules III. The use of hyaluronic acid for the separation of macromolecules in the ultracentrifuge. Biochim Biophys Acta 78, 360-366.

23. Laurent, T.C, and Ogston, A.G. (1963). The interaction between polysaccharides and other macromolecules. 4. The osmotic pressure of mixtures of serum albumin and hyaluronic acid. Biochem J 89, 249-253.

24. Laurent, T.C. (1963). The interaction between polysaccharides and other macromolecules. 5. The solubility of proteins in the presence of dextran. Biochem J 89, 253-257.

25. Laurent, T.C. (1963). The interaction between polysaccharides and other macromolecules. VI. Further studies on the solubility of proteins in dextran solutions. Acta Chem Scand 17, 2664-2668.

26. Gregory, J. D., Laurent, T.C., and Rodén, L. (1964). Enzymatic degradation of chondromucoprotein. J Biol Chem 239, 3312-3320.

27. Laurent, T.C. (1964). Solubility of sodium urate in the presence of chondroitin-4-sulphate. Nature 202 (4939), 1334-1335.

28. Laurent, T.C., and Persson, H. (1964). The interaction between polysaccharides and other macromolecules VII. The effect of various polymers on the sedimentation rates of serum albumin and α-crystallin. Biochim Biophys Acta 83, 141-147.

29. Laurent, T.C., and Killander, J. (1964). A theory of gel filtration ands its experimental verification. J Chromatog 14, 317-330.

30. Laurent, T.C., Hellsing, K., and Gelotte, B. (1964). Cross-linked gels of hyaluronic acid. Acta Chem Scand 18 (1), 274-275.

31. Laurent, T.C. (1964). The interaction between polysaccharides and other macromolecules. 9. The exclusion of molecules from hyaluronic acid gels and solutions. Biochem J 93, 106-112.

32. Laurent, T.C., and Scott, J. E. (1964). Molecular weight fractionation of polyanions by cetylpyridinium chloride in salt solutions. Nature 202 (4933), 661-664.

33. Hellsing, K., and Laurent, T.C. (1964). The influence of dextran on the precipitin reaction. Acta Chem Scand 18, 1303-1306.

34. Laurent, T.C. (1966). In vitro studies on the transport of macromolecules through the connective tissue. Fed Proc 25, 1128-1134.

35. Bettelheim, F. A., Laurent, T.C., and Pertoft, H. (1966). Interaction between serum albumin and acidic polysaccharides. Carbohydrate Res 2, 391-402.

36. Laurent, T.C. (1967). Determination of the structure of agarose gels by gel chromatography. Biochim Biophys Acta 136, 199-205.

37. Iverius, P. H., and Laurent, T.C. (1967). Precipitation of some plasma proteins by the addition of dextran or polyethylene glycol. Biochim Biophys Acta 133, 371-373.

38. Öbrink, B., Laurent, T.C., and Rigler, R. (1967). Studies on the temperature dependence of chromatography on a dextran gel Sephade G-200. J Chromatog 31, 48-55.

39. Laurent, T.C. (1968). The exclusion of macromolecules from polysaccharide media. In *The Chemical Physiology of Mucopolysaccharides* (Ed. Quintarelli, G.), Little, Brown & Co., Boston, 153-170.

40. Laurent, T.C., Öbrink, B., Hellsing, K., and Wasteson, Å. (1969). On the theoretical aspeccts of gel chromatography. In *Modern Separation Methods of Macromolecules and Particles (Progr Separation Purification)* (Ed. Gerritsen, T.), Wiley-Interscience, 199-218.

41. Laurent, T.C., Wasteson, Å., and Öbrink, B. (1969). Macromolecular properties of glycosaminoglycans (mucopolysaccharides) and proteoglycans. In *Aging of Connective and Skeletal Tissue Thule International Symposia* Nordiska Bokhandelns förlag, Stockholm, Sweden, 65-80.

42. Laurent, T.C., Bárány, E., Carlsson, B., and Tidare, E. (1969). Determination of hyaluronic acid in the microgram range. Anal Biochem 31 (1-3), 133-145.

43. Cleland, R. L., Stoolmiller, A. C., Roden, L., and Laurent, T.C. (1969). Partial characterization of reaction products formed by the degradation of hyaluronic acid with ascorbic acid. Biochim Biophys Acta 192, 385-394.

44. Laurent, T.C. (1970). The structure and function of the intercellular polysaccharides in connective tissue. In *Capillary Permeability* (Eds. Crone, C., and Lassen, N. A.), Munksgaard, Copenhagen, Denmark, 261-277.

45. Laurent, T.C. (1970). Structure of hyaluronic acid. In *The Chemistry and Molecular Biology of the Intercellular Matrix Vol II Glycosaminoglycans and Proteoglycans* (Ed. Balazs, E.A.), Academic Press, London, 703-732.

46. Laurent, T.C. (1971). Enzyme reactions in polymer media. Eur J Biochem 21 (4), 498-506.

47. Helting, T., Ögren, S., Lindahl, U., Pertoft, H., and Laurent, T. (1972). Glycosaminoglycan synthesis in mouse mastocytoma. Biochem J 126 (3), 587-592.

48. Laurent, T.C., and Öbrink, B. (1972). On the restriction of the rotational diffusion of proteins in polymer networks. Eur J Biochem 28, 94-101.

49. Laurent, T.C. (1972). The ultrastructure and physical-chemical properties of interstitial connective tissue. Pflugers Arch 336 (Suppl.), S21-S42.

50. Preston, B. N., Öbrink, B., and Laurent, T.C. (1973). The rotational diffusion of albumin in solutions of connective-tissue polysaccharides. Eur J Biochem 33, 401-406.

51. Atkins, E. D., and Laurent, T.C. (1973). X-ray-diffraction patterns from chondroitin 4-sulphate, dermatan sulphate and heparan sulphate. Biochem J 133 (3), 605-606.

52. Öbrink, B., and Laurent, T.C. (1974). Futher studies on the rotation of globular proteins in polymer solutions. Eur J Biochem 41, 83-90.

53. Laurent, T.C., Preston, B. N., and Carlsson, B. (1974). Conformational transitions of polynucleotides in polymer media. Eur J Biochem 43, 231-235.

54. Laurent, T.C. (1975). The properties and functions of connective tissue polysaccharides. In *Structure of Fibrous Proteins Colston Papers No 26* (Eds. Atkins, E. D. T. , and Keller, A.), Butterworths, London (UK), 27-33.

55. Laurent, T.C., Preston, B. N., Pertoft, H., Gustafsson, B., and McCabe, M. (1975). Diffusion of linear polymers in hyaluronate solutions. Eur J Biochem 53, 129-136.

56. Öbrink, B., Pertoft, H., Iverius, P. H., and Laurent, T.C. (1975). The effect of calcium on the macromolecular properties of heparan sulfate. Connect Tissue Res 3 (2), 187-193.

57. McCabe, M., and Laurent, T.C. (1975). Diffusion of oxygen, nitrogen and water in hyaluronate solutions. Biochim Biophys Acta 399, 131-138.

58. Öbrink, B., Laurent, T.C., and Carlsson, B. (1975). The binding of chondroitin sulphate to collagen. FEBS Lett 56 (1), 166-169.

59. Laurent, T.C., Sundelöf, L.-O., Wik, K. O., and Wärmegård, B. (1976). Diffusion of dextran in concentrated solutions. Eur J Biochem 68, 95-102.

60. Laurent, T.C. (1977). Interaction between proteins and glycosaminoglycans. Fed Proc 36 (1), 24-27.

61. Laurent, T.C., Hallén, A., and Pearce, R. H. (1977). The interaction of plasma proteins with extracellular material in connective tissue. In *9th European Conference Microcirculation, Antwerp 1976 Bibl Anat* (Ed. Lewis, D.H.), Karger, Basel, Antwerp, 224-227.

62. Laurent, T.C., Pertoft, H., Preston, B. N., Sundelöf, L. O., Wik, K. O., and Öbrink, B. (1977). Diffusion of macromolecules through compartments containing polysaccharides. In *9th European Conference Microcirculation, Antwerp 1976 Bibl Anat*, (Ed. Lewis, D.H.), Karger, Basel, 489-492.

63. Pearce, R. H., and Laurent, T.C. (1977). Exclusion of dextrans by meshworks of collagenous fibres. Biochem J 163 (3), 617-625.

64. Comper, W. D., and Laurent, T.C. (1978). Physiological function of connective tissue polysaccharides. Physiol Rev 58 (1), 255-315.

65. Laurent, T.C., Tengblad, A., Thunberg, L., Höök, M., and Lindahl, U. (1978). The molecular-weight dependence of the anti-coagulant activity of heparin. Biochem J 175, 691-701.

66. Comper, W. D., and Laurent, T.C. (1978). An estimate of the enthalpic contribution to the interaction between dextran and albumin. Biochem J 175 (2), 703-708.

67. Laurent, T.C., Preston, B. N., and Sundelöf, L. O. (1979). Transport of molecules in concentrated systems. Nature 279 (5708), 60-62.

68. Thunberg, L., Lindahl, U., Tengblad, A., Laurent, T.C., and Jackson, C. M. (1979). On the molecular-weight-dependence of the anticoagulant activity of heparin. Biochem J 181 (1), 241-243.

69. Preston, B. N., Laurent, T.C., Comper, W. D., and Checkley, G. J. (1980). Rapid polymer transport in concentrated solutions through the formation of ordered structures. Nature 287 (5782), 499-503.

70. Laurent, U. B. G., and Laurent, T.C. (1981). On the origin of hyaluronan in blood. Biochem International 2 (2), 195-199.

71. Fraser, J. R. E., Laurent, T.C., Pertoft, H., and Baxter, E. (1981). Plasma clearance, tissue distribution and metabolism of hyaluronic acid injected intravenously in the rabbit. Biochem J 200, 415-424.

72. Preston, B. N., Laurent, T.C., Comper, W. D., and Checkley, G. J. (1981). Further studies on the kinetcs of structured flows of polyvinylpyrrolidone-dextran systems. Proc 2nd Australian Thermodynamics Conference Royal Australian Chemical Institute Physical Chemistry Division, February 15j-19, 1981 (Melbourne University, Parkville, Australia), 516-525.

73. Dahl, I. M. S., and Laurent, T.C. (1982). Synthesis of glycosaminoglycans in corneal organ cultures. Exp Eye Res 34, 83-98.

74. Laurent, T.C., Preston, B. N., Comper, W. D., and Sundelöf, L.-O. (1982). The interactions in concentrated polysaccharide solutions. Progr Food Nutr Sci 6, 69-76.

75. Laurent, T.C., Preston, B. N., Sundelöf, L.-O., and Van Damme, M.-P. (1982). A versatile shear cell for diffusion measurements on small sample volumes allowing analytical recording of multicomponent transport, II. Applications. Anal Biochem 127, 287-292.

76. Smedsrød, B., Eriksson, S., Fraser, J. R. E., Laurent, T.C., and Pertoft, H. (1982). Properties of liver endothelial cells in primary monolayer cultures. In *Sinusoidal Liver Cells* (Eds. Knook, D. L., and Wisse, E.), Elsevier/North Holland Biomedical Press, Amsterdam, 263-270.

77. Eriksson, S., Fraser, J. R. E., Laurent, T.C., Pertoft, H., and Smedsrød, B. (1983). Endothelial cells are a site of uptake and degradation of hyaluronic acid in the liver. Exp Cell Res 144, 223-228.

78. Laurent, T.C., Preston, B. N., Comper, W. D., Checkley, G. J., Edsman, K., and Sundelöf, L.-O. (1983). Kinetics of Multicomponent Transport by Structured Flow in Polymer Solutions. 1. Studies on a Poly(vinylpyrrolidone)-Dextran System. J Phys Chem 87, 648-652.

79. Preston, B. N., Comper, W. D., Laurent, T.C., Checkley, G. J., and Kitchen, R. G. (1983). Kinetics of muticomponent transport by structured flow in polymer solutions. 2. Comparison of various transport techniques. J Phys Chem 87, 655-661.

80. Comper, W. D., Preston, B. N., Laurent, T.C., Checkley, G. J., and Murphy, W. H. (1983). Kinetics of multicomponent transport by structured flow in polymer solutions. 4. Relationships between the formation of structured flows and kinetics of polymer transport. J Phys Chem 87, 667-673.

81. Fraser, J. R. E., Appelgren, L. E., and Laurent, T.C. (1983). Tissue uptake of circulating hyaluronic acid. A whole body autoradiographic study. Cell Tissue Res 233, 285-293.

82. Preston, B. N., Laurent, T.C., and Comper, W. D. (1984). Transport of Molecules in connective tissue polysaccharide solutions. In *Molecular Biophysics of the Extracellular Matrix* (Eds. Arnott, S., Rees, D. A. , and Morris, E. R.), Humana Press, Clifton, NJ (USA), 119-162.

83. Fraser, J. R. E., Laurent, T.C., Engström-Laurent, A., and Laurent, U. B. G. (1984). Elimination of hyaluronic acid from the blood stream in the human. Clin Exp Pharmacol Physiol 11, 17-25.

84. Checkley, G. J., Comper, W. D., Edsman, K., Laurent, T.C., Preston, B. N., Sundelöf, L.-O., and Wells, J. D. (1984). Rapid transport of macromolecules in polysaccharide systems by means of dissipative structures. Biorheology 21 (1-2), 33-37.

85. Smedsrød, B., Pertoft, H., Eriksson, S., Fraser, J. R. E., and Laurent, T.C. (1984). Studies *in vitro* on the uptake and degradation of sodium hyaluronate in rat liver endothelial cells. Biochem J 223, 617-626.

86. Engström-Laurent, A., Laurent, U. B. G., Lilja, K., and Laurent, T.C. (1985). Concentration of sodium hyaluronate in serum. Scand J Clin Lab Invest 45, 497-504.

87. Fraser, J. R. E., Alcorn, D., Laurent, T. C., Robinson, A. D., and Ryan, G. B. (1985). Uptake of circulating hyaluronic acid by the rat liver. Cellular localization in situ. Cell Tissue Res 242, 505-510.

88. Laurent, T.C., Dahl, I. M. S., Dahl, L. B., Engström-Laurent, A., Eriksson, S., Fraser, J. R. E., Granath, K. A., Laurent, C., Laurent, U. B. G, Lilja, K.,

Pertoft, H., Smedsrød, B., Tengblad, A., and Wik, O. (1986). The catabolic fate of hyaluronic acid. Connect Tissue Res 15, 33-41.

89. Laurent, U. B. G., Engström-Laurent, A., and Laurent, T.C. (1986). Hyaluronsyra - en femtioåring som blivit kliniskt intressant. Nordisk Medicin 101, 8-10.

90. Fraser, J. R. E., Engström-Laurent, A., Nyberg, A., and Laurent, T.C. (1986). Removal of hyaluronic acid from the circulation in rheumatoid disease and primary biliary cirrhosis. J Lab Clin Med 107, 79-85.

91. Laurent, T.C., Fraser, J. R. E., Pertoft, H., and Smedsrød, B. (1986). Binding of hyaluronate and chondroitin sulphate to liver endothelial cells. Biochem J 234, 653-658.

92. Bentsen, K. D., Henriksen, J. H., and Laurent, T.C. (1986). Circulating hyaluronate: concentration in different vascular beds in man. Clin Sci 71, 161-165.

93. Wells, J. D., Edsman, K., Laurent, T.C., and Sundelöf, L.-O. (1986). Kinetics of multicomponent transport by structured flow in polymer solutions. 9. The dextran-poly (vinylpyrrolidone) system evaluated in terms of the osmotic flux model. J Phys Chem 90, 2425-2432 + appendix.

94. Tengblad, A., Laurent, U. B. G., Lilja, K., Cahill, R. N. P., Engström-Laurent, A., Fraser, J. R. E., Hansson, H. E., and Laurent, T.C. (1986). Concentration and relative molecular mass of hyaluronate in lymph and blood. Biochem J 236, 521-525.

95. Laurent, T.C., and Fraser, J. R. E. (1986). The properties and turnover of hyaluronan. In *Functions of the Proteoglycans Ciba Foundation Symposium 124* (Eds. Evered, D. , and Whelan, J.), Wiley, Chichester (UK), 9-29.

96. Smedsrød, B., Pertoft, H., Kjellen, L., Johansson, S., Eskild, W., and Laurent, T.C. (1986). Endocytyosis of connective tissue macromolecules by liver endothelial cells. In *Cells of the Hepatic Sinusoid, Volume I* (Eds. Kirn, A., Knook, D. L. , and Wisse, E.), The Kupffer Cell Foundation, Rijswijk, The Netherlands, 245-250.

97. Balazs, E.A., Laurent, T.C., and Jeanloz, R.W. (1986). Nomenclature of hyaluronic acid. Biochem J 235, 903.

98. Laurent, T.C. (1987). Structure, function and turnover of the extracellular matrix. Adv Microcirc 13, 15-34.

99. Roupe, G., Laurent, T.C., Malmström, A., Suurküla, M., and Särnstrand, B. (1987). Biochemical characterization and tissue distribution of the scleredema in a case of Buschke's disease. Acta Derm Venerol (Stockholm) 67, 193-198.

100. Laurent, T.C. (1987). Biochemistry of hyaluronan. Acta Otolaryngol (Stockh) 442 Suppl., 7-24.

101. Laurent, T.C., Lilja, K., Brunnberg, L., Engström-Laurent, A., Laurent, U. B. G., Lindqvist, U., Murata, K., and Ytterberg, D. (1987). Urinary excretion of hyaluronan in man. Scand J Clin Lab Invest 47, 793-799.

102. Campbell, P., Laurent, T.C., and Rodén, L. (1987). Assay and properties of N-acetylglucosamine-6-phosphate deacetylase from rat liver. Anal Biochem 166, 134-141.

103. Laurent, U. B. G., Fraser, J. R.E., and Laurent, T.C. (1988). An experimental technique to study the turnover of concentrated hyaluronan in the anterior chamber of the rabbit. Exp Eye Res 46, 49-58.

104. Henriksen, J. H., Bentsen, K. D., and Laurent, T.C. (1988). Splanchnic and renal extraction of circulating hyaluronan in patients with alcoholic liver disease. J Hepatol 6, 158-166.

105. Lebel, L., Smith, L., Risberg, B., Gerdin, B., and Laurent, T.C. (1988). Effect of increased hydrostatic pressure on lymphatic elimination of hyaluronan from sheep lung. J Applied Physiol 64, 1327-1332.

106. Smedsrød, B., Malmgren, M., Ericsson, J., and Laurent, T.C. (1988). Morphological studies on endocytosis of chondroitin sulphate proteoglycan by rat liver endothelial cells. Cell Tissue Res 253, 39-45.

107. Dahl, I. M. S., and Laurent, T.C. (1988). Concentration of hyaluronan in the serum of untreated cancer patients with special reference to patients with mesothelioma. Cancer 62, 326-330.

108. Reed, R. K., Lilja, K., and Laurent, T.C. (1988). Hyaluronan in the rat with special reference to the skin. Acta Physiol Scand 134 (3), 405-411.

109. Fraser, J. R. E., Kimpton, W. G., Laurent, T.C., Cahill, R. N. P., and Vakakis, N. (1988). Uptake and degradation of hyaluronan in lymphatic tissue. Biochem Journal 256, 153-158.

110. Berg, S., Brodin, B., Hesselvik, F., Laurent, T.C., and Maller, R. (1988). Elevated levels of plasma hyaluronan in septicaemia. Scand J Clin Lab Invest 48, 727-732.

111. Dahl, L. B., Laurent, T.C., and Smedsrød, B. (1988). Preparation of biologically intact radioiodinated hyaluronan of high specific radioactivity: coupling of ^{125}I-tyramine-cellobiose to amino groups after partial N-deacetylation. Anal Biochem 175 (2), 397-407.

112. Heldin, P., Laurent, T.C., and Heldin, C.-H. (1989). Effect of growth factors on hyaluronan synthesis in cultured human fibroblasts. Biochem J 258, 919-922.

113. Hällgren, R., Samuelsson, T., Laurent, T.C., and Modig, J. (1989). Accumulation of hyaluronan (hyaluronic acid) in the lung in adult respiratory distress syndrome. Am Rev Resp Dis 139, 682-687.

114. Dahl, L. B., Laurent, T.C., and Smedsrod, B. (1989). Radioiodinated hyaluronan. A tool for the study of liver endothelial cells. In *Cells of the Hepatic Sinusoid Volume 2* (Eds. Wisse, E., Knook, D. L., and Decker, K.), Kupffer Cell Foundation, Rijswijk, The Netherlands, 134-135.

115. Laurent, T.C. (1989). Chairman's introduction *and* Concluding remarks. In *The Biology of Hyaluronan Ciba Foundation Symposium Number 143* (Eds. Evered, D., and Whelan, J.), John Wiley & Sons, Chichester and New York, 1-5 and 286-288.

116. Fraser, J. R. E., and Laurent, T.C. (1989). Turnover and metabolism of hyaluronan. In *The Biology of Hyaluronan Ciba Foundation Symposium 143* (Eds. Evered, D., and Whelan, J.), John Wiley & Sons, Chichester and New York, 41-59.

117. Rodén, L., Campbell, P., Fraser, J. R. E., Laurent, T.C., Pertoft, H., and Thompson, J. N. (1989). Enzymic pathways of hyaluronan catabolism. In *The Biology of Hyaluronan CIBA Foundation Symposium 143* (Eds. Evered, D., and Whelan, J.), John Wiley & Sons, Chichester and New York, 60-85.

118. Engström-Laurent, A., and Laurent, T.C. (1989). Hyaluronan as a clinical marker. In *Clinical Impact of Bone and Connective Tissue Markers* (Eds. Lindh, E. , and Thorell, J. I.), Academic Press, London, UK, 235-252.

119. Laurent, T.C. (1989). Protein recognition of hyaluronan. Applications in clinical medicine. In *Protein Recognition of Immobilized Ligands* (Ed. Hutchens, T. W.), Alan R. Liss, Inc., New York, 169-178.

120. Lebel, L., Smith, L., Risberg, B., Laurent, T.C., and Gerdin, B. (1989). Increased lymphatic elimination of interstitial hyaluronan during E.coli sepsis in sheep. Am J. Physiol. 256, H1524-H1531.

121. Lebel, L., Fraser, J. R. E., Kimpton, W. S., Gabrielsson, J., Gerdin, B., and Laurent, T.C. (1989). A pharmacokinetic model of intravenously administered hyaluronan in sheep. Pharm Res 6 (8), 677-682.

122. Laurent, U. B. G., and Laurent, T.C. (1989). Catabolic fate of hyaluronan in the organism. In *Viscoelastic Materials: Basic Science and Clinical Applications* (Ed. Rosen, E. S.), Pergamon Press, Oxford, UK, 111-127.

123. Smedsrød, B., Pertoft, H., Gustafson, S., and Laurent, T.C. (1990). Scavenger functions of the liver endothelial cell. Biochem J 266, 313-327.

124. Campbell, P., Thompson, J. N., Fraser, J. R. E., Laurent, T.C., Pertoft, H., and Rodén, L. (1990). □acetylglucosamine-6-phosphate deacetylase in

hepatocytes, Kupffer cells and sinusoidal endothelial cells from rat liver. Hepatology 11, 199-204.

125. Wells, A. F., Larsson, E., Tengblad, A., Fellström, B., Tufveson, G., Klareskog, L., and Laurent, T.C. (1990). The localization of hyaluronan in normal and rejected human kidneys. Transplantation 50 (2), 240-243.

126. Reed, R. K., Laurent, U. B. G., Fraser, J. R. E., and Laurent, T.C. (1990). Removal rate of [³H]hyaluronan injected subcutaneously in rabbits. Am J Physiol 259, H532-H535.

127. Reed, R. K., Laurent, T.C., and Taylor, A. E. (1990). Hyaluronan in prenodal lymph from skin: changes with lymph flow. Am J Physiol 259, H1097-H1100.

128. Ferrara, J. J., Reed, R. K., Dyess, D. L., Townsley, M. I., Onarheim, H., Laurent, T.C., and Taylor, A. E. (1991). Increased hyaluronan flux from skin following burn injury. J Surg Res 50, 240-244.

129. Onarheim, H., Missavage, A. E., Gunther, R. A., Kramer, G. C., Reed, R. K., and Laurent, T.C. (1991). Marked increase of plasma hyaluronan after major thermal injury and infusion therapy. J Surg Res 50, 259-265.

130. Heldin, P., Pertoft, H., Nordlinder, H., Henrik-Heldin, C., and Laurent, T.C. (1991). Differential expression of platelet-derived growth factor α- and ß- receptors on fat-storing cells and endothelial cells of rat liver. Exp Cell Res 193, 364-369.

131. Laurent, T.C., and Fraser, J. R. E. (1991). Catabolism of hyaluronan. In *Degradation of Bioactive Substances: Physiology and Pathophysiology* (Ed. Henriksen, J. H.), CRC Press, Boca Raton, 249-265.

132. Allen, S. J., Sedin, G., Jonzon, A., Wells, A. F., and Laurent, T.C. (1991). Lung hyaluronan during development: a quantitative and morphologic study. Am J Physiol 260, H1449-H1454.

133. Edelstam, G. A. B., Lundkist, Ö. E., Wells, A. F., and Laurent, T.C. (1991). Localization of hyaluronan in regions of the human reproductive tract. J Cytochem Histochem 39, 1131-1135.

134. Fraser, J. R. E., Pertoft, H., Alston-Smith, J., and Laurent, T.C. (1991). Uptake of hyaluronan in hepatic endothelial cells is not directly affected by endotoxin and associated cytokines. Exp Cell Res 197, 8-11.

135. Onarheim, H., Reed, R. K., and Laurent, T.C. (1991). Elevated hyaluronan concentration in blood after major burns. Scand J Clin Lab Invest 51, 693-697.

136. Lindqvist, U., Chichibu, K., Delpech, B., Goldberg, R. L., Knudson, W., Poole, A. R., and Laurent, T.C. (1992). Seven different assays of hyaluronan compared for clinical utility. Clin Chem 38 (1), 127-132.

137. Reed, R. K., Townsley, M. I., Laurent, T.C., and Taylor, A. E. (1992). Hyaluronan flux from cat intestine: changes with lymph flow. Am J Physiol 262, H457-H462.

138. Heldin, P., Asplund, T., Ytterberg, D., Thelin, S., and Laurent, T.C. (1992). Characterization of the molecular mechanism involved in the activation of hyaluronan synthetase by platelet-derived growth factor in human mesothelial cells. Biochem J 283, 165-170.

139. Laurent, T.C., and Fraser, J. R. E. (1992). Hyaluronan. FASEB J 6 , 2397-2404.

140. Laurent, U. B. G., Fraser, J. R. E., Engström-Laurent, A., Reed, R. K., Dahl, L. B., and Laurent, T.C. (1992). Catabolism of hyaluronan in the knee joint of the rabbit. Matrix 12, 130-136.

141. Wells, A. F., Klareskog, L., Lindblad, S., and Laurent, T.C. (1992). Correlation between increased hyaluronan localized in arthritic synovium and the presence of proliferating cells. A role for macrophage-derived factors. Arthritis Rheum 35 (4), 391-396.

142. Salustri, A., Yanagishita, M., Underhill, C. B., Laurent, T.C., and Hascall, V. C. (1992). Localization and synthesis of hyaluronic acid in the cumulus cells and mural granulosa cells of the preovulatory follicle. Dev Biol 151, 541-551.

143. Laurent, T.C., Alston-Smith, J., Allen, S. J., Asplund, T., Berg, S., Dahl, I. M. S., Dahl, L. B., Edelstam, G. A. B., Forsberg, N., Engström-Laurent, A., Fraser, J. R. E., Gustafson, S., Heldin, P., Henriksen, J. H., Johnsson, H., Laurent, C., Laurent, U. B. G., Lebel, L., Lilja, K., Lindqvist, U., McCourt, P. A. G., Pertoft, H., Reed, R. K., Rodén, L., Smedsröd, B., Tengblad, A., Townsley, M. I., Wells, A., Wikström, T., and Ytterberg, D. (1992). Turnover of hyaluronan. In *Proc 2nd Joint Meeting On Carbohydrates, Grado, Italy, May 28-30, 1992 (organized by Società Chimica Italiana and Società Italiana di Biochimica)*, Grado, Italy, 11-14.

144. Reed, R. K., Townsley, M. I., Pitts, V. H., Laurent, T.C., and Taylor, A. E. (1992). Increased lymphatic flux of hyaluronan from cat intestine during fat absorption. Am J Physiol 263, G6-G11.

145. Tufveson, G., Gerdin, B., Larsson, E., Laurent, T., Wallander, J., Wells, A., and Hällgren, R. (1992). Hyaluronic acid accumulation: the mechanism behind graft rejection edema. Transplant Int 5 (Suppl. 1), 688-689.

146. Onarheim, H., Reed, R. K., and Laurent, T.C. (1992). Increased plasma concentration of hyaluronan after major thermal injury in the rat. Circulatory Shock 37, 159-163.

147. Alston-Smith, J., Pertoft, H., and Laurent, T.C. (1992). Endocytosis of hyaluronan in rat Kupffer cells. Biochem J 286, 519-526.

148. Alston-Smith, J., Pertoft, H., Fraser, J. R. E., and Laurent, T.C. (1992). Effects of endotoxin in hepatic endocytosis of hyaluronan. In *Hepatic Endocytosis of Lipids and Proteins* (Eds. Windler, E., and Greten, H.), W. Zuckschwerdt Verlag 119-126.

149. Edelstam, G. A. B., Laurent, U. B. G., Lundkvist, O. E., Fraser, J. R. E., and Laurent, T.C. (1992). Concentration and turnover of intraperitoneal hyaluronan during inflammation. Inflamm 16 (5), 459-469.

150. Allen, S. J., Fraser, J. R. E., Laurent, U. B. G., Reed, R. K., and Laurent, T.C. (1992). Turnover of hyaluronan in the rabbit pleural space. J Appl Physiol 73 (4), 1457-1460.

151. Berg, S., Jansson, I., Hesselvik, F. J., Laurent, T.C., Lennquist, S., and Walther, S. (1992). Hyaluronan: relationship to hemodynamics and survival in procine injury and sepsis. Crit Care Med 20, 1315-1321.

152. Lindqvist, U., and Laurent, T.C. (1992). Serum hyaluronan and amionterminal propeptide of type III procollagen. Variation with age. Scand J Clin Lab Invest 52, 613-621.

153. Laurent, T.C. (1993). History of a theory. J Chromatog 633, 1-8.

154. Asplund, T., Versnel, M. A., Laurent, T. C., and Heldin, P. (1993). Human mesothelioma cells produce factors that stimulate the production of hyaluronan by mesothelial cells and fibroblasts. Cancer Res 53, 388-392.

155. Wells, A., Larsson, E., Tufveson, G., Klareskog, L., and Laurent, T. (1993). Role of hyaluronan in chronic and acutely rejecting kidneys. Transplant Proceed 25, 2048-2049.

156. Alston-Smith, J., Pertoft, H., and Laurent, T.C. (1993). Hyaluronan synthesis by rat liver stellate cells is enhanced under endotoxic conditions. Matrix 13 (4), 313-322.

157. Harrison, N. K., McAnulty, R. J., Kimpton, W. G., Fraser, J. R. E., Laurent, T.C., and Laurent, G. J. (1993). Heterogeneity of type III procollagen N-terminal peptides in bronchoalveolar lavage fluid from normal and fibrotic lungs. Evidence for clearance of higher molecular weight peptides by lymphoid tissues. Europ Resp J 6, 1443-1448.

158. Wells, A., Larsson, E., Hanås, E., Laurent, T., Hällgren, R., and Tufveson, G. (1993). Increased hyaluronan in acutely rejecting human kidney grafts. Transplantation 55 (6), 1346-1349.

159. Edelstam, G. A. B., Lundkvist, Ö. E., Venge, P., and Laurent, T.C. (1994). Hyaluronan and myeloperoxidase in the human peritoneal fluid during genital inflammation. Inflammation 18, 13-21.

160. Reed, R. K., Townsley, M. I., Zhao, X., Ishibashi, M., Laurent, T.C., and Taylor, A. E. (1994). Lymphatic hyaluronan flux from skin increases during increased lymph flow induced by intravenous saline loading. Int J Microcir 14, 56-61.

161. Berg, S., Hesselvik, J. F., and Laurent, T.C. (1994). Influence of surgery on serum concentrations of hyaluronan. Crit Care Med 22 (5), 810-814.

162. Lebel, L., Gabrielsson, J., Laurent, T.C., and Gerdin, B. (1994). Kinetics of circulating hyaluronan in humans. Eur J Clin Invest 24, 621-626.

163. Berg, S., Engman, A., Hesselvik, J. F., and Laurent, T.C. (1994). Crystalloid infusion increases plasma hyaluronan. Crit Care Med 22, 1563-1567.

164. Townsley, M. I., Reed, R. K., Ishibashi, M., Parker, J. C., Laurent, T.C., and Taylor, A. (1994). Hyaluronan efflux from canine lung with increased hydrostatic pressure and saline loading. Am J Respir Crit Care Med 150, 1605-1611.

165. Rasmussen, I., Lebel, L., Arvidsson, D., Haglund, U., Laurent, T.C., and Gerdin, B. (1995). Hepatic extraction of hyaluronic acid in porcine peritonitis. Eur Surg Res 27, 1-10.

166. Laurent, T.C. (1995). Hyaluronan--an introduction. In *2nd International Workship on Hyaluronan in Drug Delivery Royal Society of Medicine Round Table Series 36* (Ed. Willoughby, D.A.). Royal Society of Medicine Press, London (UK), 2-4.

167. Laurent, T.C. (1995). Structure of the extracellular matrix and the biology of hyaluronan. In *Interstitium, Connective Tissue and Lymphatics Proceedings of the XXXII Congress of the International Union of Physiological Sciences, Glasgow, UK* (Eds. Reed, R. K., McHale, N. G., Bert, J. L., Winlove, C. P. , and Laine, G. A.), Portland Press, London, UK, 1-12.

168. Laurent, T.C., Laurent, U. B. G., and Fraser, J. R. E. (1995). Functions of hyaluronan. Ann Rheum Dis 54, 429-432.

169. Pertoft, H., Alston-Smith, J., Fraser, J. R. E., and Laurent, T.C. (1995). Hyaluronan accumulates around portal vessels in liver after endotoxin treatment of rats. J Endotoxin Res 2, 281-287.

170. Laurent, T.C. (1995). An early look at macromolecular crowding. Biophys Chem 57, 7-14.

171. Laurent, T.C., Fraser, J. R., Laurent, U. B., and Engström-Laurent, A. (1995). Hyaluronan in inflammatory joint disease. Acta Orthop Scand (Suppl. 266) 66, 116-120.

172. Laurent, T.C. (1995). Overview. In *Third International Workshop on Hyaluronan in Drug Delivery, Round Table Series 40* (Ed. Willoughby, D. A.), Royal Society of Medicine Press, London, 143-144.

173. Gustafson, S., Björkman, T., Forsberg, N., McCourt, P. A. G., Wikström, T., Lilja, K., Tinner, B., Fuxe, K., Westlin, J.-E., Liedholt, K., Lind, T., Westerberg, G., Bergström, M., Långström, B., de la Torre, M., Bergh, J., Hagberg, H., Glimelius, B., Lindhal, U., and Laurent, T.C. (1995). Studies on receptors for hyaluronan and the turnover of radioactively-labelled hyaluronan in mice and rats. In *2nd International Workshop on Hyaluronan in Drug Delivery. Round Table Series 36* (Ed. Willoughby, D.A.) Royal Society of Medicine Press, London (UK), 5-7.

174. Laurent, T.C., Laurent, U. B. G., and Fraser, J. R. E. (1996). The structure and function of hyaluronan: An overview. Immunol Cell Biol 74, A1-A7.

175. Reed, R.K., Laurent, U.B.G., King, S., Fraser, J.R.E., and Laurent, T.C. (1996). Effect of increased interstitial fluid flux on fractional catabolic rate of high molecular weight [3H] hyaluronan injected in rabbit skin. Acta Physiol Scand 156, 93-98.

176. Laurent, T.C., Laurent, U. B. G., and Fraser, J. R. E. (1996). Serum hyaluronan as a disease marker. Ann Med 28, 241-253.

177. Fraser, J. R. E., Cahill, R. N. P., Kimpton, W. G., and Laurent, T.C. (1996). Lymphatic system. In *Extracellular Matrix Volume 1: Tissue Function* (Ed. Comper, W. D.), Harwood Academic Publisher 110-131.

178. Fraser, J. R. E., and Laurent, T.C. (1996). Hyaluronan. In *Extracellular Matrix Volume 2, Molecular Components and Interactions* (Ed. Comper, W. D.), Harwood Academic Publishers 141-199.

179. Laurent, U.B.G., Laurent, T.C., Hellsing, Lilja, K., Persson, L., Hartman, M., and K., L. (1996). Hyaluronan in human cerebrospinal fluid. Acta Neurol Scand 94, 194-206.

180. Fraser, J. R. E., Laurent, T.C., and Laurent, U. B. G. (1997). Hyaluronan: its nature, distribution, functions and turnover. J Int Med 242 (1), 27-33.

181. Hascall, V. C., and Laurent, T.C. (1997). Hyaluronan: structure and physical properties. In *Glycoforum. Hyaluronan Today* (Eds. Hascall, V.C. and Yanagishita, M. (Seikagaku Corp.Glycoforum) (Accessed at

http://:www.glycoforum.gr.jp/science/hyaluronan
/HA01/HA01E.html)(Dec 15, 1997).

182. Johnsson, H., Heldin, P., Sedin, G., and Laurent, T.C. (1997). Hyaluronan
production *in vitro* by fetal lung fibroblasts and epithelial cells exposed to
surfactants of N-acetylcysteine. Uppsala J Med Sci 102, 199-210.

183. Laurent, T.C. (1998). The common origin of matrix biology and capillary
physiology. In *Connective Tissue Biology: Integration and Reductionism Wenner-
Gren Symposium Series No 71* (Eds. Reed, R. K. , and Rubin, K.), Portland
Press, London (UK), 1-7.

184. Laurent, T.C. (1998). Endre A. Balazs - a pioneer in hyaluronan research.
In *The Chemistry, Biology and Medical Applications of Hyaluronan and its
Derivatives. Wennwe-Gren Symposium Series No. 72* (Ed. Laurent, T.C.),
Portland Press Ltd., London, 3-5.

185. Fraser, J. R. E., Brown, T. J., and Laurent, T.C. (1998). Catabolism of
hyaluronan. In *The Chemistry, Biology and Medical Applications of Hyaluronan
and its Derivatives. Wennwe-Gren Symposium Series No. 72* (Ed. Laurent, T.C.),
Portland Press Ltd., London, 85-92.

186. Laurent, T.C. (1998). Hyaluronan as a clinical marker of pathological
processes. In *The Chemistry, Biology and Medical Applications of Hyaluronan and
its Derivatives. Wennwe-Gren Symposium Series No. 72* (Ed. Laurent, T.C.),
Portland Press Ltd., London, 305-313.

187. Balazs, E.A., and Laurent, T.C. (1998). Round table discussion: New
applications for hyaluronan. In *The Chemistry, Biology and Medical Applications
of Hyaluronan and its Derivatives. Wennwe-Gren Symposium Series No. 72* (Ed.
Laurent, T.C.), Portland Press Ltd., London, 325-336.

188. Johnsson, H., Eriksson, L., Jonzon, A., Laurent, T.C., and Sedin, G.
(1998). Lung hyaluronan and water content in preterm and term rabbit
pups exposed to oxygen or air. Pediatric Res 44, 716-722.

189. Heldin, P., and Laurent, T.C. (2000). Biosynthesis of hyaluronan. In
Carbohydrates in Chemistry and Biology. Volume 3 (Eds. Ernst, B., Sinay, P., and
Hart, G.), Wiley, Weinham 363-374.

190. Laurent, T.C., and Sundelöf, L. O. (2000). Spontaneous formation of
symmetrical structures in polymer solutions. In *Symmetry 2000 Wenner-Gren
International Series Volume 80* (Eds. Hargittai, I., and Laurent, T.C.), Portland
Press, London (UK), 329-335.

191. Berg, S., Engman, A., Holmgren, S., Lundahl, T., and Laurent, T.C.
(2001). Increased plasma hyaluronan in severe pre-eclampsia and
eclampsia. Scand J Clin Lab Invest 61, 131-138.

192. Laurent, T.C. (2002). "The Tree" – Hyaluronan Research in the 20th Century. In *Glycoforum. Hyaluronan Today* (Eds. Hascall, V.C. and Yanaghishita, M.) (Seikagaku Corporation Glycoforum) (Accessed at http://www.glycoforum.gr.jp/science/hyaluronan/HA23/HA23Ehtml) (March 15, 2002).

193. Laurent, T.C. (2002). Hyaluronan before 2000. In *Hyaluronan Volume 1 Chemical, Biochemical and Biological Aspects* (Eds. Kennedy, J.F., Phillips, G.O., Williams, P.A. , and Hascall, V.C.), Woodhead, Cambridge, UK, 3-16.

194. Laurent, T.C. (2002). Alexander G. ("Sandy") Ogston (1911-1996). In *Hyaluronan Volume 1 Chemical, Biochemical and Biological Aspects* (Eds. Kennedy, J.F., Phillips, G.O., Williams, P.A. , and Hascall, V.C.), Woodhead, Cambridge, UK, 25-28.

195. Laurent, T.C. (2003). A privileged life. In *Selected Topics in the History of Biochemistry: Personal recollections VII* (Eds. Semenza, G., and Turner, A.J.), Elsevier Science BV, Amsterdam.pp. 137-220.

196. Laurent, T.C. (2007). Hyaluronan research in Uppsala. Uppsala J Med Sci 112, 123-142.

Aled Phillips, 2007 (photograph by M. Hargittai)

Aled Phillips

Aled Phillips (b. in 1961 in Cardiff, Wales) is Professor in Nephrology and Director of the Institute of Nephrology at the School of Medicine, Cardiff University. He graduated from the Welsh National School of Medicine in 1986, and also completed a B.Sc. in Biochemistry. He started his career at the renal units of Cardiff University, and after a short stay at Kings College Hospital in London, he returned there. Dr. Phillips is Member of the American Society of Nephrology and the European Dialysis and Transplantation Society. He is member of the Editorial Board of the journal *Clinical Science*.

Interview*

Please tell me something about your background, your schooling, and your parents.

I guess the most important is my parents; my father is Professor Glyn Phillips, who was probably the biggest influence on where I am now in terms of my academic life. I'm a Welshman—and a proud Welsh-speaking Welshman—following my mother's influence. I was born in Cardiff, in South Wales, and spent the first 6 years of my life there. Most of my secondary school education was in Northeast Wales in a comprehensive education program, from there I went to Medical School back in Cardiff, where I qualified in 1986 and then trained as a nephrologist under the influence of Professor John Williams. I started my research career looking at mechanisms of fibrosis in renal disease.

Did you go to medical school because you planned to become a doctor?

Again, I think, it was my father's influence. He was a nonclinical scientist and we have had many discussions about what I would do with my career when we went to and from soccer matches when I was growing up. He planted in my mind that medicine was a very broad area where I did not necessarily have to make early decisions; where there were so many different specialties to go to. Also, I think my father had considered at one point going back into medicine because he felt that the combination of science and medicine opens some doors that were shut to scientists; so I think this is why I started in medicine. Having qualified in medicine, my first aim was to be a full-time clinician, and it was only under the influence of Professor John Williams, in the Institute of Nephrology that I became aware of the fact that, in addition to the clinical components of medicine I was

---

* This interview was recorded during the Hyaluronan Meeting in Charleston, South Carolina, April 2007.

enjoying, the intellectual challenge of academic work was also very attractive. It was only at that late stage that I committed myself to academic medicine, although it was not my intention from the beginning, to be honest.

Did you then go for a Ph.D.?

Well, I actually did an MD according to the system in the UK but it is equivalent with a Ph.D. I have been involved in research continuously every since.

And never have become a real clinician…

Oh no, no, I'm still a clinician, and I would say that about 30% of my time is still clinical work. I do both inpatient and outpatient clinical work, looking after patients with renal disease, both acute and chronic renal failure. Then, my other role now is Director of the Institute of Nephrology, which means that I am in charge of the research going on in our Institute.

Where do polysaccharides and, particularly, hyaluronan come into the picture?

There were two influences. When I came to the Institute of Nephrology, there was Dr. Malcolm Davies who had an interest in proteoglycans and tried to make me also interested in the topic. Of course, there was already my father's interest in proteoglycans and hyaluronan somewhere in the background, so I was cognizant of hyaluronan (HA) from a different aspect. Eventually, this background knowledge married to professor Malcolm Davies's work made me realize that there could be an interaction between the work that I had been doing—cytokine cell biology—and the matrix around the cells; so this is how I got into hyaluronan.

I find it interesting that you went into a field that may not have been in the very forefront of research—polysaccharides have not been considered as interesting as proteins or the DNA.

I don't feel that way. I guess that during the time when these influences were upon me people started to think differently about HA from being the filler and the "goo" to being functionally important. Looking at the cancer cell literature we saw lots of similarities in terms of regulation of cell fate and we were wondering whether this would also apply to our system and it did but in a very different way. Thus, we started to feel that hyaluronan at times could be responsible for maintaining normality or helping to revert to normality after injury. One of the major problems we face is that in case of renal injury if we repair by scarring there is going to be a progressive kidney failure. Therefore, if we could work out a way of manipulating this system and get back to normality without forming a scar that would be fantastic— that is the holly grail we are after. At that time I do not think that in medicine anybody was working in this area—so we thought that this would be an interesting and worthy field of research.

Please, describe your current research in a way that is understandable for a wider audience.

The specific aim is trying to understand why people have kidney failure. What we know at present is that if you have fibrous tissue in the kidney at the appearance of the disease you are likely to progress to end-stage organ damage which, of course, is quite devastating to the patients. What we have been trying to understand is why some people get a scar in their kidney that progresses and why some people do not get any scarring—and so they do not get end-stage kidney disease. The model we started was diabetes because about a quarter of the patients we worked with have got diabetic renal disease. We know that hyaluronan increases in the kidneys of diabetic patients. We had no real idea what this hyaluronan was doing in the kidney in terms of alteration of cell function. In theory the hyaluronan in the kidney could have either good or bad effects and the outcome would depend on how the hyaluronan was packaged and presented to the cells in terms of what the function it has on the cells. We are trying to understand what regulates the good side of hyaluronan or the bad side of hyaluronan and how that is put together.

So you do not yet know the answer to this question?

No, we can't answer it yet. But we are getting clues. I think it is the way the HA is packaged around the cells that seems to affect the response. We know, for instance, that hyaluronan can suppress the effects of TGFβ, which is a bad guy, but that's not always the response. We have to understand how you can have HA that always suppresses TGFβ and does not have other bad effects on the cells; that will give us the answers that we are looking for. We think that different isoforms of HA synthase may have an impact on how it suppresses TGFβ function; also some of the HA binding proteins may also have an influence.

I think you should explain what TGFβ means…

TGFβ stands for *T*ransforming *G*rowth *F*actor beta and it is the final common pathway for fibrosis in all organs including the kidney. We have been studying the regulation of its synthesis and also its signaling. TGFβ is a true fibrotic cytokine and it leads to scar formation and changes the cell phenotype into making cells aggressive scarring-type cells.

You mentioned scars several times already, what's the problem with them? Do they form in the kidney only if there is a problem?

It is a very important question. Obviously scars in the skin are a good thing, they are quick healing and they get rid of breaches, the defense mechanism of the body, if the scars are formed when you have an injury. However, the problem with the kidney is that once you have a scar that scar perpetuates further scarring which then leads to a fibrosed failed organ. So what we have here is that a body tries to repair itself but through that process eventually destroys itself. So what we need to do is to have a repair from injury that gets you back to normal without having the scar. As soon as you get the scar inside the kidney the scars get worse and worse and worse so I guess it is a scar in the wrong context that happens in the kidney.

By injury you do not necessarily mean a physical injury, like a car injury...

No, no! The injuries we are talking about are diseases and the predominant one is diabetes. Other causes include congenital abnormalities, infection and inflammatory diseases, all those things cause kidney problems. We call it injury – but it is not a trauma as such.

Do you have a large research group?

At the moment there are about 30 people in the Institute, a mixture of clinicians and scientists from all levels; Ph.D. students, graduate medical students undertaking further degrees, post docs and also some senior scientists. The Institute was set up, before I arrived to have an interaction between clinical and nonclinical academics. It was a nice plan to balance the understanding of basic science and also knowing its clinical application. I think the strength that we have is that we are always bearing in mind the patient at the end of the journey rather than just being a sterile academic exercise; the patient is at the end of what we do.

How does this work in practice? How do the Ph.D.s learn about the patient side?

This is possible because there are so many of us in the department that are clinicians. We always explain and teach the clinical problem to them; they're obviously not exposed to the patient. Although the majority of our work is basic science, we also have our own clinical investigation unit and thus they see the flow of patients that come through. The whole idea of the ethos of the institute is a bench-to-bedside; what we try to do is look at the mechanisms that we see and see how we can manipulate or test those hypotheses in patients. We do have an active clinical research program so I think that the Ph.D.s see that the clinic—if you like—is the reason for us being where we are.

We are involved with a big teaching hospital so again it's the medical school atmosphere we're in rather than a university atmosphere.

Are all the clinicians required to participate in research?

There was a time in the UK when you probably wouldn't progress in your career unless you had research. Things are changing a little at the moment because of political pressures; there is some downsizing of academia, and the pressure is to train more and more clinicians who can deliver patient care. There is less emphasis on giving academic training, which, I think, is a pity because then what we are lacking is clinical academics. These changes have happened over the last two-three years. I am afraid that this will be to the detriment of research and probably to us all because there is no doubt that the Ph.D.s benefit from working side by side with the clinicians.

Are the equipments and materials that you use for your research very expensive?

Yes, they are. We are fortunate that for many years we have been funded partly by a patient-based charity that was initially called the Kidney Research Foundation for Wales, now it is called the Kidney Wales Foundation. They still provide some of the infrastructure costs for us. While this is not nearly enough to run the Institute, it is a significant proportion of our core funding and the rest comes from grant monies. We are also lucky in that we've got quite a few collaborations with colleagues in Japan and other countries. We have a very active link with a renal unit in China that is sponsored by the International Society of Nephrology and that has been a great source of collaboration. Within these collaborations, we have junior doctors coming to us who have a thirst for academia, particularly the Chinese connection. This also supplements our own income.

I also wanted to ask you about international collaboration.

There are two types of collaboration; one of them is a purely academic link and that is driving forward the academic work; this is what we have with people like Bandi and others in the HA field. This type of collaboration certainly pushes the work forward. In the other type of collaboration, mostly with foreign countries, they send people over for research training and that, of course, is a collaboration of a different nature. In this case we are committed to train them but in the meantime they generate lots of data and information for us; an example is our connection with Nanjing, in China. In this collaboration we basically have a regular supply of young very enthusiastic junior doctors, who put in a lot of work in our hospital.

Before, I asked you about collaboration. Is there a competition between different groups in the same field?

I guess, in a way we are lucky because we're working in renal medicine, which is not an area where we would have to face too many competitors. My experience is that in the HA field people are helpful to each other rather than being competitive. The big players and also the others in that area are much more enthused about finding out the answers to questions than having a race to just publish first. Moreover, as I said, in renal medicine the subject matter is a little bit removed from some of the perceived competitors. I don't feel that it is an aggressive field; rather, I find it an inquiring field, which has a healthy collaborative nature in terms of the way that it is driven.

You are saying that the HA field is not that competitive. Considering, however, all the possibilities of practical applications, or the possibilities for starting a company that uses HA—I would think that it should be competitive.

I guess you are right if we are talking at the product level. But the area we are in is not the product to heal but rather manipulating the body's own HA that stops you becoming ill. We are a little bit away from the commercial end-point, from the therapeutic point, so we do not need to be quite as careful. At this point we are just trying to understand the processes that go on in the kidney. Perhaps when we get to the point where we will be able to manipulate the system, maybe it will get a bit touchier, I don't know. But at the moment what we have is just the thirst for understanding. At the beginning we thought that the question was if we can simply up or down regulate hyaluronan will that be a good thing. Now it is very clear that it will be much more complicated than that. It will have to be cell-specific; it will have to be environment specific, and also the packaging specific. Unfortunately, there are still lots of unknowns that we have to get around before we can really start thinking about the manipulation of HA in humans.

For an outsider, looking at the program of this conference, the role of HA seems to be incredibly widespread.

That is exactly right and one of the attractive things about working in this area. I think that the strength of this conference is also in its extensive coverage. You are rubbing shoulders with scientists from completely different areas and clinicians from different areas, people, with whom you probably would not have the opportunity to meet. As a clinical nephrologist where would I have the opportunity to talk to people who are interested in lung fibrosis, and skin injury, and all other different injuries? Probably, nowhere. But at this meeting I do and this is great. It broadens my outlook and I think it is fantastic. Looking at the different backgrounds of the participants, there are parallels, there are similarities, but there are also novel facts and you can learn a lot from seeing all the other systems and specialities. Maybe this is the reason why we are not so competitive; that all these people working on so widely different systems may draw support from each other rather than being a threat to each other.

Do you also teach?

Yes, I do. I teach medical undergraduates mainly, I don't teach science courses. I also teach some post graduate courses.

How do you divide your time?

Teaching, I would say less than 5%, clinical work about 25 - 30%, and then the rest of it would be what I would call academic work, which is between admininstration and school-politics nonsense and, finally, the things I enjoy, which is running the lab and chasing the guys in the lab and getting them productive. And that, I suppose, is still a good 30% of my time, probably.

You have mentioned your father's influence. When did it actually start?

Goodness, that is a difficult one. It started at a very early age. Our summer holidays were usually processions around Europe going from one scientific conference to the next. These were unbelievable holidays when we were driving around several different countries going from meeting to meeting and I guess it became the norm. Going away to meetings was something I thought was normal. So I guess from an early age that influenced the way we were.

This means that his influence was just by seeing how interesting his life was and not by his trying to convince you that this was very interesting.

No, to be fair to him, he has never ever—well, not that I have noticed anyway—pushed me in any particular direction. All he and my mother have ever really done was encouraging me to do things that I have enjoyed. What my father, I guess, did was show me opportunities, he sort of pointed me towards things, he didn't push me towards them, he just showed what was available. Also both my parents produced an environment that made it relatively easy to succeed. I talk about my father's influence but my mother was there every time; I remember, every time we had examination there was no question about not finding time to work; I'd come home from school and tea would be prepared for me and I would have coffee delivered to my room and my mother used to bring a particular type of sweet, which I used to love, the jelly babies and a big bag of those just so I could have an environment where work never became difficult. That sort of encouragement was more influential than anything; I guess, my mother probably is as influential if not more influential in terms of producing that environment than my father, but I guess the role model of understanding what academia was came from my father.

Are you an only child?

No, I have a sister and she works in industry. She works for Shell and for a while she lived in the States but now she and her husband are back working in London. Her career is completely different from mine. She had a degree in chemistry and also one in business studies; so I guess my father's influence was sort of there at that point in terms of the chemistry, but in terms of where she has gone she is much more into the commercial sector. So we have gone in very different directions in terms of our careers.

Do you have a family?

Oh, absolutely. I have a wife and three kids. The oldest one is a daughter, who is off to university in the next autumn and she is sadly thinking to do medicine as well. I have tried to dissuade her but I think she is going to do medicine. And then I have another daughter who is 15 and a son who is 11. I don't think that their careers are established yet; my son wants to be a rugby player so I'm not sure that my academic influence is going over him.

How about your wife?

My wife is a nurse. We have talked a lot about the early influences on my life and obviously that was my father and my mother. But since we have been married, the support that my wife has given me has been very important. I am here now in the States, just came from a meeting in Brazil, but my wife is holding the house together and it has been hard for her at times for different reasons. For example, in the early days I had to do many exams in my early medical career and subsequently. She has always kept the home going and has been there for the children, who are pretty well adjusted, it is all credit to her not to me so my debt is probably greatest to her to be honest.

The Phillips family. From left to right: Aled, son Dafydd, daughter Lowri, wife
Linda, and daughter Bethan on the top of Snowden summit in 2006
(photograph courtesy of A. Phillips)

Where do you live?

We live in Cardiff. I was born there and it is nice to be back. I feel that
is where I belong and where I am from. My wife is Welsh as well, so
that's quite nice.

What does it mean to be Welsh?

Everything. As I said I am a proud Welshman, a Welsh-speaking
Welshman. I think that it gives me an identity that I am very sure of. I
am very certain of where I am from and what my heritage is and I
think that sort of certainty in terms of your past and your identity
allows you to move on and have not arrogance but a sort of
confidence. I'm happy of who I am and where I come from and yes, I
think it is important to feel my "Welshness."

What language did you use in school?

My education was through the medium schools in Welsh. The language of my home with my wife and my children is also Welsh; my kids go to a Welsh medium education school and the way I think is Welsh not English, I guess. But it has had its problems. Although my social first language is Welsh, obviously in science and medicine it is English and sometimes if I am asked to give lectures about my work in Welsh that does become a little difficult to do because there is a definite separation of my social home life in Welsh and my professional life in English.

When did you start learning English?

I think that most kids just pick it up by diffusion, so I don't think I was formally taught English, I think it was just bilingual.

Much of your career is still ahead of you. But if I ask you about your scientific results so far, what would you pick as the most important?

A couple of years ago another group had published that the TGFβ receptors on the cell surface were in two pools, a signaling pool and a degradative pool. We had followed that up by showing that hyaluronan is a physiological stimulus that can push the receptors from one pool to the other and that starts to give us the key to try to manipulate the whole thing that we were talking about before, the fibrosis versus antifibrosis. We have been working on this topic since then and are trying to work out how to manipulate it, I think that to date that is probably the most important of our work and the one that may lead to something in the future.

Is it also the one you're most proud of?

No, the one I'm most proud of probably is one of my first publications when I started off. We were looking at the regulation of TGFβ, again, and at that time by glucose the context being diabetic renal disease.

The thrill of having a publication coming out in a high-quality international journal when I first started, I think that maybe was one of the things that fueled my enjoyment of what we were trying to do; so in a way that was a turning point for me.

What was the greatest challenge in your life that you can remember?

Socially or work wise?

Both.

The greatest challenge that I feel in terms of my life is to try and bring up well adjusted children. To make sure that you know that you are both a friend and a mentor and a role model to your children, I think, is very challenging and I think that is the one thing that I'd like to get right. This is the most important thing that I hope to get right, and that is probably my biggest challenge.

Do you have enough time for them?

Oh, that is difficult to answer while I am stuck in America, isn't it? But I hope so. I do like to try to spend time with them when I'm home, a lot of time. And certainly both my wife and myself try to put the children first in everything and maybe sometimes too much, both of us will sacrifice as much as we can to put the kids first.

What is your next goal to reach in science?

The goals that we have and what I want to do is to develop this bench-to-bedside approach that we have within the Institute. I think that we do quite good science and we are developing those in a way that I'm comfortable with and we have a strategy for the next few years—beyond that it is always difficult to guess. The goals and the challenges that we face is to take those observations from the laboratory end of our institution and move it into the clinical investigation unit and I think that is the challenge.

Going beyond your own field, what do you anticipate in hyaluronan research in the future?

That is a huge question, isn't it. I think that there are questions about regulation of synthesis of HA and regulation of assembly of HA matrices. The real challenge will be to understand why HA does what it does when it does and where it does it.

Is there anything else you think would be important to learn about you?

You have got all the skeletons out of the closet.

Summary

Investigations on Hyaluronan at the Institute of Nephrology, Cardiff University School of Medicine

by Aled Phillips

Our interest is in the role of hyaluronan (HA) in the regulation of fibrosis and its relationship to renal disease. The work can be divided into four main areas:
- Cell biology of HA in the epithelial cell
- Cell biology of HA in the fibroblast
- Understanding the transcriptional regulation of HAS isoforms
- Functional significance of HA in human renal disease.

The epithelial cell and HA

It is clear that in all renal diseases that the disease outcome is correlated to the degree of fibrosis in the renal cortex. The predominant cell type in the renal cortical interstitium is the proximal tubular epithelial cell. Although generally thought of as a cell type involved in the regulation of fluid and electrolyte balance this cell type is also a key player in initiation and perpetuation of renal injury. Our earlier studies demonstrated that disease associated stimuli such as glucose, an *in vitro* model of diabetic renal injury, and also pro-inflammatory cytokines were potent inducers of HA synthesis. In order to determine the functional significance of this alteration in HA synthesis we subsequently addressed the effects of exogenous HA on pro-fibrotic cell functions and also characterised the nature of endogenous cell associated HA in this cell type. By regulation of pro-fibrotic cytokine receptor movement in the cell membrane, through interaction with CD44 and activation of downstream intracellular signalling events, HA of high molecular weight attenuates pro-fibrotic cytokine action. In contrast low molecular weight HA, which has been shown by others to have pro-inflammatory effects on renal epithelial cell function does not influence pro-fibrotic cytokine action.

Endogenous HA in the renal proximal tubular cell is organised into both classical peri-cellular coats and also peri-cellular cables similar to those identified in the smooth muscle cells of the intestine. These two peri-cellular pools of HA serve different function with the peri-cellular coat promoting cell migration, an effect which is compatible with disease promoting activity. In contrast HA peri-cellular cables have a disease blunting function as they inhibit the direct interaction of inflammatory cells with the epithelial cell, an interaction which stimulates a pro-fibrotic response. Subsequent work examined the relative contribution of HA synthase isoforms and also hyaladherins to the formation of these two forms of peri-cellular HA.

HA and the fibroblast

In addition to the epithelial cell it is well established that fibrosis in the kidney as with other solid organs is driven by the fibroblast, and more specifically by the myofibroblast which represents and activated form of the fibroblast. During the differentiation/activation of the fibroblast into a myofibroblast we have demonstrated that there is a marked increase in HA generation. This is associated with an alteration in HA degradation and also the formation of a prominent HA pericellular coat. Within the kidney the aim is to allow repair following injury but to prevent scarring. As it is know that scar free healing is a feature of injury to the oral mucosa we are utilitising patient matched oral and dermal fibroblast in order to understand and ultimately take advantage of the mechanistic of scar free healing. These studies have also demonstrated that the formation of a scarring fibroblast phenotype (myofibroblast) is associated with the formation of a pericellular HA coat and inhibition of coat formation leads to resistance to myofibrobalstic differentiation. Similar conclusions are also being drawn from our work in a model of impaired wound healing associated with aging. In all of these models of fibroblast activation a recurrent theme is that there is a balance between synthesis, degradation and pericellular HA assembly related to hyaladherin expression, which dictate cell fate and fibroblast/myfibroblast phenotype.

Transcriptional regulation of HAS isoforms

Work in both epithelial and fibroblast cell types have suggested a HA synthase isoform specific phenotypes. This is the basis for ongoing work looking at the detailed molecular mechanisms which regulate transcriptional activation of HA synthases. To date the primary focus of the published work has been HAS2.

HA in the clinical setting

As a clinical department our ultimate goal is to influence disease outcome. Although the majority of the work that we have carried out involves in vitro studies of cell biology, we also have an active program of clinical research. The single most common cause of end stage renal failure in the world today is renal disease associated with diabetes mellitus, and this is the clinical focus of our disease associated studies. Utlising patient material we have explored potential associations of single nucleotide polymorphisms in HA synthase genes and disease progression, and also the association of HA distribution in renal tissue with potential markers of disease outcome.

Bibliography*

Hyaluronan-Related Publications

1. Jones, S., Jones, S., and Phillips, A. O. (2001). Regulation of renal proximal tubular epithelial cell hyaluronan generation: implications for diabetic nephropathy. Kidney Int 59, 1739-1749.

2. Stuart, G., Jones, S., Jones, M., and Phillips, A. O. (2002). Control of hyaluronan (HA) generation in renal proximal tubular epithelial cells. In *Hyaluronan Volume 1* (Eds. Kennedy, J.F., Phillips, G.O., Williams, P.A. and Hascall, V.C.), Woodhead, Cambridge, UK, 473-480.

3. Jones, S. G., Ito, T., and Phillips, A. O. (2003). Regulation of proximal tubular epithelial cell CD44-mediated binding and internalisation of hyaluronan. Int J Biochem Cell Biol 35 (9), 1361-1377.

4. Ito, T., Williams, J. D., Al-Assaf, S., Phillips, G. O., and Phillips, A. O. (2004). Hyaluronan and proximal tubular cell migration. Kidney Int 65 (3), 823-833.

5. Ito, T., Williams, J. D., Fraser, D., and Phillips, A. O. (2004). Hyaluronan attenuates transforming growth factor-beta1-mediated signaling in renal proximal tubular epithelial cells. Am J Pathol 164 (6), 1979-1988.

6. Ito, T., Williams, J. D., Fraser, D. J., and Phillips, A. O. (2004). Hyaluronan regulates transforming growth factor-beta1 receptor compartmentalization. J Biol Chem 279 (24), 25326-25332.

7. Selbi, W., de la Motte, C., Hascall, V., and Phillips, A. (2004). BMP-7 modulates hyaluronan-mediated proximal tubular cell-monocyte interaction. J Am Soc Nephrol 15 (5), 1199-1211.

8. Zhang, X. L., Selbi, W., de la Motte, C., Hascall, V., and Phillips, A. (2004). Renal proximal tubular epithelial cell transforming growth factor-beta1 generation and monocyte binding. Am J Pathol 165 (3), 763-773.

---

* Provided by the interviewee.

9. Zhang, X. L., Selbi, W., de la Motte, C., Hascall, V., and Phillips, A. O. (2005). Bone morphogenic protein-7 inhibits monocyte-stimulated TGF-beta1 generation in renal proximal tubular epithelial cells. J Am Soc Nephrol 16 (1), 79-89.

10. Selbi, W., Day, A. J., Rugg, M. S., Fulop, C., de la Motte, C. A., Bowen, T., Hascall, V. C., and Phillips, A. O. (2006). Overexpression of hyaluronan synthase 2 alters hyaluronan distribution and function in proximal tubular epithelial cells. J Am Soc Nephrol 17 (6), 1553-1567.

11. Selbi, W., de la Motte, C. A., Hascall, V. C., Day, A. J., Bowen, T., and Phillips, A. O. (2006). Characterization of hyaluronan cable structure and function in renal proximal tubular epithelial cells. Kidney Int 70 (7), 1287-1295.

12. Meran, S., Thomas, D., Stephens, P., Martin, J., Bowen, T., Phillips, A., and Steadman, R. (2007). Involvement of hyaluronan in regulation of fibroblast phenotype. J Biol Chem 282 (35), 25687-25697.

13. Phillips, A. (2007). The role of proximal tubular cells in interstitial fibrosis: understanding TGF-beta1. Chang Gung Med J 30 (1), 2-6.

14. Lewis, A., Steadman, R., Manley, P., Craig, K., de la Motte, C., Hascall, V., and Phillips, A. O. (2008). Diabetic nephropathy, inflammation, hyaluronan and interstitial fibrosis. Histol Histopathol 23 (6), 731-739.

15. Meran, S., Thomas, D. W., Stephens, P., Enoch, S., Martin, J., Steadman, R., and Phillips, A. O. (2008). Hyaluronan facilitates transforming growth factor-beta1-mediated fibroblast proliferation. J Biol Chem 283 (10), 6530-6545.

Glyn O. Phillips, 2008
(photograph by and courtesy of J. Denlinger)

Glyn O. Phillips

Glyn O. Phillips (b. 1927 in Rhosllannerchrugog, Wales) is currently Chairman of Research Transfer Ltd., Phillips Hydrocolloids Research Ltd., the Cellucon Trust, and the Wrexham Gums and Stabilizers Conferences. He is Visiting Professor and Fellow at the North East Wales Institute (University of Wales) where the "Glyn O. Phillips Hydrocolloids Research Centre" is located.

He graduated from the University of Wales in Chemistry and holds the degrees of B.Sc., Doctor of Philosophy (Ph.D.), and D.Sc. from this University, and is a Fellow of the Royal Society of Chemistry. He held leading positions at the North East Wales Institute and the Department of Chemistry and Applied Chemistry, University of Salford, England. He helped to set up the University of Benin, Nigeria in the 1970s.

Professor Phillips has been awarded many honors, including the Hopkins Medal of New York (1973), the Science and Technology Medal from the National Eisteddfod of Wales (2004) and the Gold Medal of the Food Hydrocolloids Trust (2007). He has been elected to several honorary memberships, and was awarded honorary doctorates by the University of Benin and University of Wales.

Glyn Phillips is Founder Executive Editor of the journal *Food Hydrocolloids*, and is Editor-in Chief of *Advances in Tissue Banking* and of the *International Journal of Cell and Tissue Banking*. He is a founding member of the International Society of Hyaluronan Sciences (ISHAS).

Interview*

Perhaps we start with your scientific background and how your interest in this field started.

I started my scientific career at the University of Wales in Bangor in the laboratory of Professor Stanley Peat FRS. He was one of the early carbohydrate chemists with an interest in enzymic syntheses. I elected to combine his carbohydrate interest with the kinetic and mechanistic studies of the previous Professor E. D. Hughes FRS. For my post-doctoral research I went to the Atomic Energy Research Establishment in Harwell whose director was the Nobel laureate Sir John Cockroft, who managed it more as an academic establishment. He really established a feeling of research and excitement in the radiation chemistry and physics field that is now more or less gone. It is sad that the word nuclear is presently regarded as a dirty word in many people's eyes and its many benefits largely ignored. Yes, I spent my postdoctoral years at Harwell and enjoyed it. I was able to look at the new study of the chemical effects of ionizing radiations on carbohydrates.

Did Cockroft carry over the atmosphere of the Cavendish Laboratory to Harwell?

It was the period immediately after the war. I went to Harwell in 1952 and stayed there until 1954. The resident scientists had come back from Chalk River in Canada and some from Los Alamos and there was a feeling that something different from the atomic bomb had to be built and for Cockroft this research establishment was the means. He had a vision of turning swords into plowshares and that nuclear energy could be an enormous benefit for mankind. His whole emphasis was

---

*This interview was recorded during the second meeting "Conversations on Hyaluronan" in St. Tropez, June 2003.

around the peaceful uses of nuclear energy, so there was great hope in the air and we all felt that we could do something worthwhile. The cynicism associated with all things nuclear that's developed by now, was not there at that time. Cockroft didn't emphasize the commercial aspects that are now dominating that field because he was more concerned about the academic developments; he'd come around regularly to the laboratories and wanted to know what you were doing. He wasn't a chemist but still he wanted to know why I was doing a particular experiment. It was very valuable and memorable for me to have these conversations with Sir John.

How did you feel about the atomic bomb?

I still regret it as disgraceful. Even less justified was the cold war race when the U.S.A., UK, and Russia built thousands of nuclear warheads, both of the atomic and hydrogen bombs types. The test explosions of the 1960s in particular poisoned the world. In Wales and other western regions of the UK we suffered disastrously from the nuclear fallout, which poisoned the grazing and so our food. Strontium-90 entered into our food chain and into the bones of children who have been growing up. My children's generation was unique since for the first time they had strontium-90 in their bones. Children died as a result of the test explosions who would otherwise have lived.

Why Wales in particular?

Generally in the western part of Britain the rainfall was higher and thus more of the pollutants fell on the ground; the soil was deficient in calcium and strontium took the place of calcium and stayed there a long time. The cows ate the grass, the children drank the milk and their strontium levels became extraordinary high. Indeed, these levels were higher than the Medical Research Council's guidelines at that time for urgent action to be taken. And it became clear that in the early 1960s when all the bombs were exploded, hundreds of them literally, that the world had to stop nuclear explosions in the atmosphere because of the poisoning. So I gradually realized that there was an enormously sinister aspect to nuclear energy and that sinister aspect has really poisoned the whole field by now. At that time I could go home to my mining village in North Wales to lecture and tell them that one ton of uranium produced the same amount of heat as burning your three million tons of coal and the miners commented – what a wonderful source of energy. If I gave that lecture in the same village now they'd tell me I was talking rubbish. At any rate, the 1950s was an extraordinarily interesting period in the nuclear field, there was hope on the one side and then there was the growth of the sinister side down the road from Harwell at the Atomic Weapons Research Establishment in Aldermaston.

After my period in Harwell I was appointed as a lecturer to the University of Wales in Cardiff and the nuclear establishment supported me and provided me with a Co-60 radiation source. Thus I could work on the effect of radiation on carbohydrates, which became very central to my research activities thereafter. More recently, in the last 10 years, I've been looking at the effects of radiation on connective tissue. I have been involved with setting up tissue banks in many parts of the world and I would not have been able to do that had I not laid a foundation of understanding the effects of radiation on connective tissue, including hyaluronan, earlier. Tissue banks throughout the world now use ionizing radiation to sterilize tissue grafts for use in surgery – more than one million per year in the U.S.A. alone.

What are the effects of radiation?

It depends on whether you have a living tissue or not. The effects on living tissue are very dramatic. For example, if you take the upper palate of a rat in vivo, which we studied extensively, very low doses—about 10 rads—of radiation would cause degradation of the two components, collagen and the glycosaminoglycans, and the matrix would in fact disintegrate. But if you took that same collagen outside the body—the rat tail collagen is used now as a suture in medicine—and sterilized it with 35 KGy, it would still be stable. Thus, there is a very big contrast between the effects on a living system and the effects on a system taken out of the body.

Why is this so?

Well, I believe it's because of the regularity of the system that exists in the connective tissue within the body. It is a highly organized regular basic situation whereas outside the body there are many dislocations and as the energy traverses and interacts with these dislocations a great deal of it is dissipated as heat. Besides, in these regular systems in the body many chain reactions can occur and these effects can travel for longer distances causing these changes. There are biological implications of this, of course, for example, the effects on the DNA within the system.

Has this regularity been studied by X-ray diffraction or some other method?

Most of the matrix structures are well established by now and there are beautiful regular patterns within the systems we are discussing in connection with hyaluronan, for example. But it's quite clear that when you study these things in vitro they are distinctly different from the same system in vivo. Considering hyaluronan, for example, when we talk about 2 million dalton as a high molecular weight, it could well be many times greater within the tissue itself as the extraction process inevitably changes the material. I wonder whether we really do study the material as it exists in Nature; I suppose it is an extrapolation that we are trying to do when we work on these systems in the laboratory and are trying to extrapolate to how they exist structurally in the animal and the human body. This is a subject we are actively investigating in association with Dr. Endre A. Balazs and comparing structures and animal molecular assemblies with the corresponding aggregate structures in the plant tissues.

From the studies of the structures of biological macromolecules we have learned that their water content has an important role...

Yes, I think water clearly has a very major influence on the overall structure of the matrix but very often it's not water as we know it. The water within the structural system of the connective tissue has various forms; some of it is bound directly to the macromolecule by OH groups usually about 13 molecules per disaccharide unit. Then there is what we've termed non-freezing bound water that doesn't freeze to give you ice-type structure and is thermodynamically different from free water. This has a lower dielectric constant and a lower energy of transition than regular water, and, finally, there is the free water. I think that in some ways an eyeball and an ice-cream are very similar to each other in terms of texture. You've got collagen, ascorbic acid, hyaluronan in an eyeball. In ice-cream you've got protein, water, fat; you add locust bean gum and a little additives such as carrageenan to give this wonderful product. No single ice crystal is formed when you freeze a good ice-cream since the water is bound within the whole system. As I moved from the connective tissue area to the food hydrocolloids area, I found it fascinating to look at these similar aspects of these two subjects. In one instance you are dealing with the connective tissue of animals and in the other the connective tissue of plants and trees.

I left Cardiff in 1967 to become Professor of Chemistry at the University of Salford, Manchester, England. That was shortly after the former Royal College of Advanced Technology became the University of Salford. They had great expectation for developing work, they had a very large chemistry department; it might not have been the best chemistry department but it was the largest. There were 90 faculty members in the department at that time because they did a lot of work with industry; they also had applied chemistry courses. The state-of-the-art Nuclear Centre was the target attraction for me to move there.

The name of the department was "chemistry and applied chemistry", so there was an emphasis on application.

Very much so. Many of the students had spent time in industry before coming to the University. It was an interesting time because this was the time before work with industry became fashionable. Nowadays everyone is rushing around looking for support from industry but at that time it was very suspicious if you were working with industry—

people said: "oh dear, this man is prostituting himself". Yet, it's very necessary that we should do this. If we want to establish research for a whole range of younger academics who are very keen to develop but without the resources to do so, it was necessary to look at a wider range of problems. I've found that whenever you took a problem from an industrial scene it was very much more difficult to solve than the one you chose yourself to play with. It was a very interesting period and with a greater range of resources and a greater range of people we moved from the pure polysaccharide area again into studying a wider range of radiation aspects using more and expensive equipment such as pulse radiolysis. We had bigger resources; for example, pulse radiolysis to study very fast reactions; we could look at reactions of the transient species existing only in nanoseconds.

Isn't it generally more characteristic of British science to consider practical problems at the starting point than in some other European countries?

I think this is true now but if you project back to 1967 it was not so. It is in later times that we are urged to go out and look for industrial money. It is unbelievable now that earlier all the money for students and resources and equipment came directly from university grants and you didn't need to look around anywhere for extra money for the capital facilities. But we were in a different situation in Salford because these resources weren't sufficient for the number of people who wanted to develop research. There were three types of staff there actually, one was the teachers who were already there when Salford had been a technical college and these were very good teachers; then it's been a College of Advanced Technology and the people there were all industrial people and then, finally, there came the whiz kids with the new professors. Now a department with only whiz kids would be, in my mind, a dreadful place, but the mix in Salford was just right – great teachers coming from the technical college, the people that were available from industry with great experience, and then the whiz kids who came with the professors who really wanted to burn the world up. It was a nice mix and it was a very profitable time; I found it extremely interesting and this is why I went there.

I left Cardiff because although it had a good chemistry department in the traditional sense but at the same time it was a very limiting place in that you couldn't extend beyond the bounds of the normal traditional academic area. At Salford I was able to move into more practical problems. For example, we started a company in association with Robert Harrison called Dairy Tech, in Atlanta, Georgia in the U.S.A. He was a leading salesman, who bought the company from the owner Charlie Morgan. Bob said, "I want to know what I'm selling." He wasn't a scientist, just a salesman. We looked at the stabilizers he was producing, locust bean gum, carboxy methyl cellulose, guar gum, carrageen, alginate, etc., and it was interesting that Dairy Tech became a highly technical company. And the two students that were working on that project became vice presidents of that company. It's just very exciting to see how the company changed in its technical knowledge at that time. I was asking Bob "why are you telling these competitors and user companies how to formulate this good ice cream? Aren't you afraid that they'll go and buy the material from somebody else 2 cents a pound cheaper?" and Bob said, "No, I don't worry; they'll know about the expertise and they'll come back" and they did. They got to realize that this company had more technical background and had more support and it grew to be the best technical stabilizer company. It has now been taken over by very much of the bigger companies and it was very profitable for all concerned. And we had several examples of that sort.

Another big program we had was with Aspro Nicolas. Ken Murton, the Vice President of Research and Development came to the conclusion that Aspro Nicolas was not big enough to go into the pharmaceutical business in a big way but he thought that if you looked back over the old pharmaceuticals and relook at them for new uses, you could get profitable products. We formed a consortium with the University of Manchester, the Square as they called the School of Pharmacy of the University of London, and Walter Elisa in Melbourne, Australia. That conglomerate, some in cell biology, some in chemistry, some in pharmacy, looked at several materials. One of them was heparin that had a lot of side effects and we developed a low molecular weight heparin with fewer side effects. These group projects were certainly interesting and exciting and they gave me a very useful insight into a broader range of areas. I felt that the benefits were going to be gained in areas that were crossing boundaries; crossing technical boundaries and industrial boundaries with academic interests. And I found this extremely exciting.

But I'm a Welshman and although I really enjoyed working in Salford my heart was in Wales. Then in 1975 I became head of a new institute in Wales, the Institute of Higher Education (NEWI), where four colleges were coming together; the college of education, two colleges of technology, and a college of arts to form one unit. This was an exciting task. I felt strongly that we needed a very strong research element and I brought with me many of my colleagues from Salford and many of the students into this Institute to continue the areas we had developed. We set up research as a full-time activity which freed these young scientists from a too demanding load of academic teaching.

By then you had already met Endre Balazs (Bandi) and you entered the hyaluronan field as well.

Yes, that's right. We met in 1963, with our association born out of controversy. I read their paper in *Experimental Eye Research* and they contradicted our work on radiation effects on carbohydrates. In those days it was a serious matter if somebody criticized your work. They claimed that a particular compound was not being formed, and yet I was looking at that paper and I could see it was there because those days you used to publish the chromatograms and you could see it wasn't there as the acid, it was there as the lactone; I could see it there. I was invited to give a talk at the Retina Foundation and I prepared to go there with all guns firing – but, of course, Bandi being the person he is, we ended up great friends and we've collaborated ever since. And he opened the door to me into hyaluronic acid. I'd never heard of hyaluronic acid previously. But Bandi had a considerable interest in the effects of free radicals on carbohydrates and particularly on hyaluronan. He had himself seen, already in the 1950s, that very-very low doses of radiation would cause changes in the molecular structure of hyaluronan. And it seemed unduly sensitive. This was the initial area of joint interest and collaboration.

Change in what sense?

Degradation changes, breakdown. Initial changes would not probably be complete breakdown but thereafter very small doses would break the molecular weight and change the size. And this observation on the very sensitivity of the connective tissue matrix itself was new, all the effects of radiation at that time had been on cells. The matrix was only regarded as a sort of a filler, a shock-absorber and the exciting work was considered to be the cells, changes in DNA, radiation chemistry of DNA, etc. We had what was called a Miller Conference in those days, Miller being a radiation scientist who worked also in Harwell, and everyone was concentrating on DNA and radiobiology and not a great deal of interest was taken on the effects of the matrix materials.

Bandi and I became very close friends and we had a very fruitful collaboration for many years. This was the time when he developed the Retina Foundation in Boston and he had many people coming to join him from Europe, from Sweden in particular, and he recruited American scientists also and several of them came to do Ph.D. degrees with us in Salford. Don Scheufle and Gerard Armand also came. We even exchanged secretaries, so there would be very good interaction between the systems! Bandi patiently taught me about hyaluronan. He had such a wide area of interest. Although he had a growing relationship to my field, he also had a close relationship to many other aspects, such as physiology, biochemistry, cell biology, and electron microscopy. There was not a subject or expertise he would not enter if it would help him understand the function of hyaluronan in the human body.

He had the molecule and he attacked it from so many different angles. The collaboration with us was centered very extensively on two major areas, one was the radiation effects and the other the free radical breakdown. At that time the feeling was growing that some of the breakdown in the body by disease was free-radical-oriented. For example, osteoarthritis that is due to the synovial fluid losing its viscoelasticity, could be due to free radical breakdown; it was speculated. Therefore, the fact that hyaluronan was very susceptible to free radical attack was an important aspect. We could develop the techniques to look at the interaction of hyaluronan with other small molecules, in particular with dyes. The observation of the material in the body itself by histological staining with dyes made it possible to see where it existed and what form it was in, etc. The molecular interactions, which were taking place between hyaluronan outside the body with various enzymes, with proteins, with other molecules, we could study using fast reaction techniques. Although it was not in any way directly related to the biological aspects, Bandi was interested in it and he had already himself looked at dye interactions, since after all he was a histologist as well! So, our collaboration grew and was maintained with Bandi. The other side of my interest was going much more into the food hydrocolloids area. This area has by now grown to be my major interest and activity. My current company is called Phillips Hydrocolloids Research Ltd.

Hydrocolloids are regarded as systems that are half way between solids and solutions. They are hydrophilic polymers, polysaccharides or proteins, and they very quickly hydrate in water to produce larger structures. I'm founding editor of the journal *Food Hydrocolloids*, published by Elsevier that has grown very rapidly in the last 20 years. We have developed new forms of hydrocolloid food products that are now used by many of the world's largest food companies. In association with a large Japanese company (San-Ei Gem FFI) the "Glyn O. Phillips Hydrcolloids Research Centre" was set up in old University NEWI and now flourishes I am glad to say.

An illustration of how Bandi's work has moved me into another field is the use of radiation thereafter for the protection of connective tissue. I started by using radiation for the breakdown of connective tissue and estimated the damage. But when we understood this, we could also add protectant systems that enable radiation to be used for the stabilization of connective tissue. Because of this, we were able to join with the International Atomic Energy Agency to set up tissue banks and now we have tissue banks in 30 countries, in Europe, Latin America, Asia, and the Pacific. I've assisted to set these up and managed them and now at the last count we had, 350,000 grafts have been used in transplant surgery. The alternative to using these for developing countries would have been to buy grafts from the United States or Europe. The equivalent cost in the States or in Europe would have been 55 million dollars. So the program has given economic benefits to the developing countries but even more so it made it possible to treat cancer, trauma, burns, paraplegics, and various leprosy sores. This would not have been possible otherwise and arose only because we can use radiation to sterilize and have the tissues safe after procurement from the human body. So I think that starting the work with Bandi with hyaluronan, the components of tissue, enabled us to move into the tissue area and thereafter to use it worldwide as a method of sterilization.

Just three weeks ago we had a joint meeting in the States of the Asia Pacific Association, Latin American Association, European Association and the American Association of Tissue Banking and it became clear that the Americans also have to move into this area to use radiation. Earlier they thought that this would not be necessary, but if you read the reports, you can learn that several people have died from Clostridium and other transmitted diseases from tissue banks because there was no end sterilization method used. I like to think of this as a sort of reverse technology transfer, when the people who came into the developing world as Experts and thus learned a technique so that they can apply radiation sterilization in the U.S.A. The seed that was started by Bandi has led to very active development and I think this is Bandi's genius, I use the word absolutely without equivocation. He himself had the vision when others didn't.

I have written about him in my foreword to the proceedings of a major hyaluronan meeting we held in his honor, in the year 2000 in our institution. Hyaluronan was a scientific novelty until Bandi took it in his hand, and he converted a scientific novelty into a major scientific and medical application. He led and others followed. Bandi organized several meetings to integrate all people working in the hyaluronan field together, to draw them into one unit. I'd like to feel that the meeting we held in his honor truly represented his achievements. We produced two large volumes based on the meeting; starting with the chemistry, the structure of the areas and all the knowledge that exists now about the molecule from different aspects; then the cell biology aspects, which is a new and rapidly developing aspect. All cell biologists are recognizing now that hyaluronan isn't a dead material in the tissue; it has a cell signaling function, it can transmit a signal to instruct the cell to do one thing or another. This, of course, led to an explosion to decide whether it is for disease study or for the normal functioning of cells. Then the third aspect has been medical application. The material is now being used for osteoarthritis, in the surgery of the eye, for adhesions, many new areas have been developing. Everybody is rushing into looking for new medical applications for this material. Here, again, Bandi led the way.

Endre A. Balazs and Glyn O. Phillips at the conference Glyn organized in Wales to celebrate Bandi's 80th birthday (photograph courtesy of G. O. Phillips)

Bandi himself first developed the field of applications to the eye, and now he has developed the use for osteoarthritis by supplementing diseased synovial fluid. And each of these areas required an ingredient from his past. All of these were due to integration of areas that he himself could see at that time but no one else. His faith in this area, his diligence and his continuing tenacity led him to carry on when other people gave up. He used his own money to protect his vision, so that eventually he was able to develop a major industry based on this. It is an act of genius, no question about this. The genius who knew the potential of the material scientifically but also had the way with all to be able to organize a business. That's a very rare if not unique combination. The fact that he could do this has made him special. He brought the breadth of the European-Hungarian world into a rather narrow American culture. European he was, in the broadest sense of the word, and he could then interact and bring all the people into the field in a global sense.

Do you think that he could have done this in Europe?

I don't think at that time because Europe was then in turmoil. He certainly couldn't have done this in Hungary. The after effects of the Second World War, the cold war rivalry, lack of resources, etc., would have been an insurmountable obstacle.

The opportunities certainly were there in America but he still had to overcome many difficulties. He set up the Retina Foundation, and then he had to change direction when things didn't work out entirely in that area. Then he became Research Professor at Columbia and at the same time he was preparing the industrialization of the system.

It was remarkable that he was offered the Columbia professorship.

Not really. He had an enormous publishing record in this field and I think that he was head and shoulders above anybody else. The Retina Foundation had gained support, he had major program grants from NIH in this area, he was well known in the academic sector, so I think they were very proud to get him there. And I think he enjoyed his time there, although I don't know that he was comfortable with all the people he had to deal with there. I think he found them rather narrow sometimes and not quick enough to move but still, in so doing, I think he himself was able to regroup after leaving the Retina Foundation and re-establish his priorities. And the priority was very clearly to develop this field now because at that time his publication record in all areas was enormous. He had kept the Retina Foundation as a major research center. European scientists came to a very thriving institution. There was accommodation for you to stay, and it was a home from home. You were always on the job enjoying yourself going back to your room, going back in seminars all day and night. There would always be something new we'd all discuss, there were biologists, chemists, electron microscopists, etc. I spent time with Bandi at the Retina Foundation several months one summer and there was this excitement being generated into the area. Columbia inherited all this and benefited greatly.

Where do you think the field goes from where it is now?

I can only extrapolate from that position we have in the two-volume publication I mentioned.[1] I think each of these areas will develop. I think all the structural aspects still haven't been solved in the necessary detail and I'm sure that hyaluronan chemical and physical modification will become important. Bandi himself has already developed hylan, a cross-linked material, so he set the trend. We know of techniques in which Japan has developed other types of gels from hyaluronan and patented these. There are structural modifications. So based on this structure, I think we will have new family of compounds of materials, each with a different aspect but keeping the base of hyaluronan. I'm sure that from a chemical point of view, we will have new materials to start off, which will have new functional properties. We'll be able to build function out of structure. The structure-function relationship will become much more precise, so that if we want to fabricate a material from this highly biocompatible source, then it will be possible because it is a raw material now that is available in large quantities throughout the world and becoming cheaper all the time. I think it will be a raw material source in the chemical sense for structure-functional work.

Will there be enough of this raw material?

Yes, there are two sources now. One is from rooster comb, and the other is a biosynthetic source by fermentation. Both of these are producing large quantities of materials, and both have their advocates. The amount of the materials is large because of its industrial applications. Cosmetics, for example, is a demanding area and here the quality need not be as high as for medical application and this again offers an outlet. I'm not a cell biologist, so I can't make predictions about this area but listening and reading to what's been happening, it is quite obvious that it is an area of incredible growth. Cell biologists are looking at hyaluronan in so many different ways. Whether cell biology and cell tissue culture work is truly relevant to the medical field, I'm not competent to judge. You must ask Bandi. My son is a physician researching in this area and he's finding again pathways, which depend on hyaluronan for their control. It gives me great pleasure that he too has discovered and made a friend of Bandi. They are now actively cooperating. How wonderful it is that his influence will now extend to another generation.

And the last one is the medical application areas which already are very significant. It can now be used alongside with what is now termed tissue engineering; to produce new systems. There are very few biomaterials that can be used despite all the efforts that have been made. Very few materials are already capable of being used in the body that had been synthesized outside the body. But now this material hyaluronan is available, so fabrication is possible in new systems such as tissue engineering and tissue culture, or in wound dressing systems. Production of laser skin is one example, many more of these developments technologically are possible, so the branches will grow. The seed was planted by Bandi, he cultured it, it grew into a small tree with quite strong branches, it grew faster as time went on during this period, and now it is a healthy large tree. But it is now also starting new trees. I don't think the model of a single tree is enough for now. It is planting its own trees elsewhere and I think we'll have a nice forest in due course—thanks to Endre Balazs.

Reference

1 Kennedy, J.F. Phillips, G.O. Williams, P.A. Eds.; Hascall, V.C. Guest Ed. *Hyaluronan.* Vols 1 and 2. (2002). Woodhead Publishing Ltd, Cambridge, England.

Bibliography[*]

Hyaluronan-Related Publications

1. Balazs, E.A., Davies, J., Phillips, G.O., and Young, M.D. (1967). Transient intermediates in the radiolysis of hyaluronic acid. Radiation Res 31 (2), 243-255.

2. Balazs, E.A., Phillips, G.O., and Young, M.D. (1967). Polyanions and their complexes. II. Light-induced paramagnetism in solid glycosaminoglycan-dye complexes. Biochim Biophys Acta 141 (2), 382-390.

3. Young, M.D., Phillips, G.O., and Balazs, E.A. (1967). Polyanions and their complexes. I. Thermodynamic studies of heparin-azure A complexes in solution. Biochim Biophys Acta 141 (2), 374-381.

4. Balazs, E.A., Davies, J.V., Phillips, G.O., and Scheufele, D.S. (1968). A study of polyanion-cation interactions using hydrated electrons. Biochem Biophys Res Commun 30 (4), 386-392.

5. Balazs, E.A., Davies, J.V., Phillips, G.O., and Scheufele, D.S. (1968). Polyanions and their complexes. Part III. Reactions of heparin, hyaluronic acid, sodium poly(ethylenesulphonate), sodium poly(styrenesulphonate), and sodium carboxy-methylcellulose with hydroxyl radicals and hydrated electrons. J Chem Soc 12 (Section C), 1420-1423.

6. Balazs, E.A., Davies, J.V., Phillips, G.O., and Scheufele, D.S. (1968). Polyanions and their complexes. Part IV. A pulse radiolysis study of the interation between methylene blue and heparin in aqueous solution. J Chem Soc 12 (Section C), 1424-1429.

7. Balazs, E.A., Davies, J.V., Phillips, G.O., and Scheufele, D.S. (1968). Polyanions and their complexes. Part V. Examination of polyanion-cation interaction using pulse radiolysis. J Chem Soc 12 (Section C), 1429-1433.

8. Davies, J.V., Dodgson, K.S., Moore, J.S., and Phillips, G.O. (1969). Pulse-radiolysis and spectral studies of the interaction of cetylpyridinium chloride

---

[*] Provided by the interviewee.

and methylene blue with connective-tissue glycosaminoglycans and related compounds. Biochem J 113, 465-471.

9. Phillips, G. O. (1970). Interaction between glycosaminoglycans and organic cations. In *The Chemistry and Molecular Biology of the Intercellular Matrix Volume II Glycosaminoglycans and Proteoglycans* (Ed. Balazs, E. A.), Academic Press, London (UK), 1033-1065.

10. Moore, J., Phillips, G.O., Davies, J., and Dodgson, K. (1970). Reactions of connective tissue and related polyanions with hydrated electrons and hydroxyl radicals. Carbohydrate Research 12, 253-260.

11. Moore, J. S., Phillips, G.O., Power, D.M., and Davies, J.V. (1970). Polyanions and their complexes. Part VII. Mechanism of methylene blue-polyanion interactions. J Am Chem Soc Section A, 1155-1159.

12. Armand, G., Baugh, P. J., Balazs, E.A., and Phillips, G.O. (1975). Radiation protection of hyaluronic acid in the solid state. Radiation Res 64 (3), 573-580.

13. Cundall, R. B., Murray, C. W., and Phillips, G.O. (1978). Spectrofluorimetric methods for estimating and studying the interactions of polysaccharides in biological systems. In *ACS Symposium Series No 77 Carbohydrate Sulfates* (Ed. Schweiger, R. G.), 67-81.

14. Diakun, G.P., Edwards, H.E., Allen, J.C., and Phillips, G.O. (1978). Analysis of glycosaminoglycans in urine by using acridine orange fluorescence. Biochem J 175, 573-577.

15. Edwards, H.E., Moore, J.S., and Phillips, G.O. (1978). Effects of ionizing radiations on human costal cartilage and exploration of the procedures to protect the tissue from radiation damage. Histochem J 10, 389-398.

16. Hall, A., Phillips, G.O., and Rasool, S. (1978). Action of ionizing radiations on a hyaluronate tetrasaccharide. Carbohydrate Research 62, 373-376.

17. Diakun, G. P., Edwards, H. E., Wedlock, D. J., Allen, J. C., and Phillips, G. O. (1978). The relationship between counterion activity coefficients and the anti-coagulant activity of heparin. Macromolecules 11 (6), 1110-1114.

18. Cundall, R. B., Lawton, J. B., and Murray, D. (1979). Interaction of acridine orange and polyanions: fluorimetric determination of binding strengths and the influence of simple electrolytes. J Chem Soc Perkin Trans II, 879-884.

19. Cundall, R. B., Lawton, J. B., Murray, D., and Phillips, G.O. (1979). Polyelectrolyte complexes. 2. Interaction between collagen and polyanions. Int J Biolog Macromolecules 1, 215-222.

20. Cundall, R. B., Lawton, J. B., Murray, D., and Phillips, G.O. (1979). Polyelectrolyte complexes. I. The effect of pH and ionic strength on the stoichiometry of model polycation-polanion complexes. Makromol Chem 180, 2913-2922.

21. Cundall, R. B., Lawton, J.B., Murray, D., Rowlands, D. P., and Phillips, G.O. (1979). Acridine orange as a fluorescent probe for the study of polyelectrolyte complexes. Polymer 20, 389-392.

22. Diakun, G. P., Edwards, H.E., Allen, J. C., Phillips, G.O., and Cundall, R. B. (1979). A simple purpose-built fluorimeter for the titrimetric assay of glycosaminoglycans. Anal Biochem 94, 378-382.

23. Gormally, J., Panak, J., Wyn-Jones, E., Dawson, A., Wedlock, D. J., and Phillips, G.O. (1981). A new method of determining the extent of binding of an ionic dye to a polyelectrolyte in solution. Analytica Chim Acta 130, 369-375.

24. Wedlock, D. J., Phillips, G.O., and Balazs, E.A. (1981). Sedimentation velocity of sodium hyaluronate - lysozyme mixtures. Int J Biol Macromol 3, 384-388.

25. Davies, A., Gormally, J., Wyn-Jones, E., Wedlock, D. J., and Phillips, G.O. (1982). A study of hydration of sodium hyaluronate from compressibility and high precision denitomertic measurements. Int J Biol Macromol Struct Func Interactions 4 (7), 436-438.

26. Lawton, J. B., and Phillips, G.O. (1982). The role of water in the metachromatic reaction. Makromol Chem 183, 1497-1509.

27. Phillips, G.O. (1982). Sterilisation of tissues by ionising radiations. In *Biological Principles of Tissue Banking* (Ed. Klen, R.), Pergamon Press, Oxford (UK), 117-123.

28. Balazs, E.A., Wedlock, D. J., and Phillips, G.O. (1983). Polymeric articles modified with hyaluronate. US 4,487,865 (Dec. 11, 1984). Dec. 11, 1984.

29. Davies, A., Gormally, J., Wyn-Jones, E., Wedlock, D. J., and Phillips, G.O. (1983). A study of factors influencing hydration of sodium hyaluronate from compressibility and high-precision densimetric measurements. Biochem J 213, 363-369.

30. Edwards, H. E., and Phillips, G.O. (1983). Radiation effects on human tissues and their use in tissue banking. Radiat Phys Chem 22 (3-5), 889-900.

31. Wedlock, D. J., and Phillips, G.O. (1983). Depolymerization of sodium hyaluronate during freeze drying. Int J Biol Macromol 5, 186-188.

32. Wedlock, D. J., and Phillips, G.O. (1984). Conductivity properties of hyaluronate salts in simple salt-free and sample salt-containing solutions. Int J Biol Macromol 6, 215-218.

33. Myint, P., Deeble, D.J., Beaumont, P.C., Blake, S. M., and Phillips, G.O. (1987). The reactivity of various free radicals with hyaluronic acid: steady-state and pulse radiolysis studies. Biochim Biophys Acta 925, 194-202.

34. Shimada, M., Uchida, T., Takigami, S., Nakamura, Y., and Phillips, G.O., (1988). Immobilization of hyaluronic acid on egg shell membrane. Sen-I Gakkaishi 44 (2), 106-110.

35. Blake, S., Deeble, D. J., Parsons, B. J., and Phillips, G.O. (1989). The effect of copper ions on the free radical chemistry of hyaluronic acid. Int J Radiat Biol 55 (5), 873.

36. Deeble, D. J., Parsons, B. J., Phillips, G.O., Myint, P., Beaumont, P. C., and Blake, S. M. (1989). Influence of copper ions on hyaluronic acid free radical chemistry. In *Free Radicals, Metal Ions and Biopolymers* Richelieu Press, London (UK), 159-182.

37. Myint, P., Deeble, D.J., and Phillips, G.O. (1989). The radiation chemistry of connective tissue: hyaluronic acid. In *Proceedings of an Advisory Group Meeting organized by the International Atomic Energy Agency, 14-17 November 1988*, Bologna, Italy: IAEA, 105-116.

38. Deeble, D.J., Bothe, E., Schuchmann, H., Parsons, B.J., Phillips, G.O., and von Sonntag, C. (1990). The kinetics of hydroxyl-radical-induced strand breakage of hyaluronic acid. A pulse radiolysis study using conductometry and laser-light-scattering. Z Naturforsch 45c (9/10), 1031-1043.

39. Deeble, D.J., Phillips, G.O., Bothe, E., Schuchmann, H., and von Sonntag, C. (1991). The radiation-induced degradation of hyaluronic acid. Radiat Phys Chem 37 (1), 115-118.

40. Shimada, M., Takigami, S., Kobayashi, N., Nakamura, Y., Williams, P.A., and Phillips, G.O. (1991). Immobilisation of hyaluronic acid on to cellulose. In *Cellulose: Chemical, Biochemical and Material Aspects* (Eds. Kennedy, J.F., Phillips, G.O., and Williams, P.A.), Woodhead, London (UK), 409-414.

41. Phillips, G.O. (1992). Molecular transformations in connective tissue hyaluronic acid. In *Viscoelasticity of Biomaterials* (Eds. Glasser, W. G., and Hatakeyama, H.), Amer Chem Soc Symp Series 489, New York, NY (USA), 168-183.

42. Takigami, S., Takigami, M., and Phillips, G.O. (1993). Hydration characteristics of the cross-linked hyaluronan derivative hylan. Carbohydr Polymers 22, 153-160.

43. Al-Assaf, S., Phillips, G.O., Deeble, D. J., Parsons, B., Starnes, H., and Von Sonntag, C. (1995). The enhanced stability of the cross-linked hylan structure to hydroxyl (OH) radicals compared with the uncross-linked hyaluronan. Radiat Phys Chem 46 (2), 207-217.

44. Takigami, S., Takigami, M., and Phillips, G.O. (1995). Effect of preparation method on the hydration characteristics of hylan and comparison with another highly cross-linked polysaccharide, gum arabic. Carbohydrate Polymers 26 (1), 11-18.

45. Al-Assaf, S., Meadows, J., Phillips, G.O., and Williams, P.A. (1996). The application of shear and extensional viscosity measurements to assess the potential of hylan in viscosupplementation. Biorheology 33, 319-332.

46. Gunning, A. P., Morris, V. J., Al-Assaf, S., and Phillips, G.O. (1996). Atomic force microscopic studies of hylan and hyaluronan. Carbohydr Polymers 30, 1-8.

47. Phillips, G.O. (1998). Degradation of hyaluronan systems by free radicals. In *The Chemistry, Biology and Medical Applications of Hyaluronan and its Derivatives* (Ed. Laurent, T. C.), Portland Press Ltd., London (UK), 93-112.

48. Shimada, M., Takigami, S., Uchida, T., Nakamura, Y., and Phillips, G.O.(1998). Immobilisation of hyaluronic acid on to silk fibroin. In *Cellulose: Structural and Functional Aspects* (Eds. Kennedy, J. F., Phillips, G.O. , and Williams, P. A.), John Wiley & Sons, Chichester (UK) and New York (USA), 323-328.

49. Al-Assaf, S., Hawkins, C. L., Parsons, B. J., Davies, M. J., and Phillips, G.O. (1999). Identification of radicals from hyaluronan (hyaluronic acid) and cross-linked derivatives using electron paramagnetic resonance spectroscopy. Carbohydrate Polymers 38, 17-22.

50. Balazs, E.A., Al Assaf, S., and Phillips, G.O. (1999). A new biomaterial tissue allograft: hylan, a hyaluronan derivative. In *Advances in Tissue Banking* (Eds. Phillips, G.O., Strong, D. M., von Versen, R., and Nather, A.), World Scientific Publishing, New York, NY USA, 355-397.

51. Al-Assaf, S., Meadows, J., Phillips, G.O., Williams, P. A., and Parsons, B. J. (2000). The effect of hydroxyl radicals on the rheological performance of hylan and hyaluronan. Int J Biol Macromol 27, 337-348.

52. Milas, M., Rinaudo, M., Roure, I., Al-Assaf, S., Phillips, G.O., and Williams, P. A. (2001). Comparative rheological behavior of hyaluronan from bacterial and animal sources with cross-linked hyaluronan (hylan) in aqueous solution. Biopolymers 59 (4), 191-204.

53. Al-Assaf, S., Phillips, G.O., Gunning, A.P., and Morris, V. J. (2002). Molecular interaction studies of the hyaluronan derivative, hylan A using atomic force microscopy. Carbohydrate Polymers 47, 341-345.

54. Al-Assaf, S., Williams, P.A., and Phillips, G.O. (2002). Molecular characterisation of hyaluronan and hylan using GPC MALLS and asymmetrical flow FFF-MALLS. In *Hyaluronan Volume 1 Chemical, Biochemical and Biological Aspects* (Eds. Kennedy, J. F., Phillips, G.O., Williams, P. A. , and Hascall, V. C.), Woodhead, Cambridge, UK, 55-66.

55. Milas, M., Rinaudo, M., Roure, I., Al-Assaf, S., Phillips, G.O., and Williams, P.A. (2002). Rheological behavior of hyaluronan, Healon and hylan in aqueous solutions. In *Hyaluronan Volume 1 Chemical, Biochemical and Biological Aspects* (Eds. Kennedy, J.F., Phillips, G.O., Williams, P.A., and Hascall, V.C.), Woodhead, Cambridge, UK, 181-194.

56. Parsons, B. J., Al-Assaf, S., Navaratnam, S., and Phillips, G.O. (2002). Comparison of the reactivity of different reactive oxidative species (ROS) towards hyaluronan. In *Hyaluronan Volume 1 Chemical, Biochemical and Biological Aspects* (Eds. Kennedy, J. F., Phillips, G.O., Williams, P. A. , and Hascall, V. C.), Woodhead, Cambridge (UK), 141-150.

57. Al-Assaf, S., Navaratnam, S., Parsons, B.J., and Phillips, G.O. (2003). Chain scission of hyaluronan by peroxynitrite. Arch Biochem Biophys 411 (1), 73-82.

58. Ito, T., Williams, J. D., Al-Assaf, S., Phillips, G.O., and Phillips, A. O. (2004). Hyaluronan and proximal tubular cell migration. Kidney Int 65 (3), 823-833.

Edited Books

1. Phillips, G.O., ed. (1966). *Energy Transfer in Radiation Processes, Chemical, Physical and Biological Aspects. Proceedings of the International Symposium held at Cardiff, United Kingdom, January 1965.* Elsevier, Amsterdam, 182 pgs.

2. Phillips, G.O., ed. (1968). *Energetics and Mechanisms in Radiation Biology. Proceedings of a NATO Advances Study Institute, Portmeirion, Wales, 1967.* Academic Press, New York, NY (US), xviii + 530 pgs.

3. Phillips, G.O., ed. (1970). *Radiation Chemistry of Carbohydrates, Fourth Periodical Seminar in Biophysics, 1969*. Consiglio Nazionale Delle Richerche, 91 pgs.

4. Phillips, G.O., Tallentire, A., and Triantafylou, N., eds. (1978). *Radiation Sterilisation: Irradiated Tissues and Their Potential Use*. North East Wales Institute, Clywd (UK), 242 pgs.

5. Edwards, H. E., Navaratnam, S., Parsons, B. J., and Phillips, G.O., eds. (1979). *Radiation Biology and Chemistry: Research Developments*. Elsevier, Amsterdam (The Netherlands), 505 pgs.

6. Phillips, G.O., von Versen, R., Strong, M. D., and Nather, A., eds. (1997). *Advances in Tissue Banking. Volume 1*. ed. Phillips, G.O. World Scientific, Singapore, London, Hong Kong and New Jersey (USA), 388 pgs.

7. Phillips, G.O., Strong, D. M., von Versen, R., and Nather, A., eds. (1998). *Advances in Tissue Banking. Volume 2*. ed. Phillips, G.O. World Scientific, Singapore, London, Hong Kong and New Jersey (USA), 451 pgs.

8. Phillips, G.O., Kearney, J. N., Strong, D. M., von Versen, R., and Nather, A., eds. (1999). *Advances in Tissue Banking. Volume 3*. ed. Phillips, G.O. World Scientific, Singapore, London, Hong Kong and New Jersey (USA), 466 pgs.

9. Phillips, G.O., ed. (2000). *Radiation and Tissue Banking. IAEA*. World Scientific, Singapore, 362 pgs.

10. Phillips, G.O., Strong, D. M., von Versen, R., and Nather, A., eds. (2000). *Advances in Tissue Banking. Volume 4*. ed. Phillips, G.O. World Scientific, Singapore, London, Hong Kong and New Jersey (USA), 377 pgs.

11. Phillips, G.O., and Nather, A., eds. (2001). *Advances in Tissue Banking. Volume 5*. ed. Phillips, G.O. World Scientific, Singapore, London, Hong Kong and New Jersey (USA), 575 pgs.

12. Kennedy, J. F., Phillips, G.O., Williams, P. A., and Hascall, V. C., eds. (2002). *Hyaluronan. Volume 1. Chemical, Biochemical and Biological Aspects*. Woodhead, Cambridge, UK, 577 pgs.

13. Kennedy, J. F., Phillips, G.O., Williams, P. A., and Hascall, V. C., eds. (2002). *Hyaluronan. Volume 2. Biomedical, Medical and Clinical Aspects*. Woodhead, Cambridge, UK, 517 pgs.

14. Phillips, G.O., ed. (2002). *Advances in Tissue Banking. Volume 6*. World Scientific, Singapore, London, Hong Kong and New Jersey (USA), 534 pgs.

15. Phillips, G.O., ed. (2003). *Allografts in Bone Healing: Biology and Clinical Applications. Volume 1. Bone Biology and Healing*. World Scientific, New Jersey (USA), 148 pgs.

16. Phillips, G.O., ed. (2003). *Allografts in Bone Healing: Biology and Clinical Applications. Volume 2. Morphogenic Protein and Collagen.* World Scientific, 148 pgs.

17. Phillips, G.O., ed. (2004). *Advances in Tissue Banking. Volume 7.* World Scientific, Singapore, London, Hong Kong and New Jersey (USA), 633 pgs.

18. Kennedy, J. F., Phillips, G.O., and Williams, P. A., eds. (2005). *Sterilisation of Tissues Using Ionising Radiations.* Woodhead Publishing and CRC Press, Cambridge (UK), 352 pgs.

Glenn Prestwich, 2007 (photograph by M. Hargittai)

Glenn D. Prestwich

Glenn Prestwich (b. in 1948 in the Panama Canal Zone) is Presidential Professor of Medicinal Chemistry at the University of Utah. He received his B.Sc. from the California Institute of Technology (1970) and his Ph.D. from Stanford University (1974). He spent three years as an NIH postdoctoral fellow at Cornell University and at the International Centre for Insect Physiology and Ecology in Nairobi, Kenya. Dr. Prestwich was Professor of Chemistry and of Biochemistry and Cell Biology at the University of New York at Stony Brook for about 20 years. He also served as Director of the New York State Center for Advanced Technology in Medical Biotechnology. He founded several small biotech companies, while being active at the University of Utah as Professor, and Director of two Utah Centers of Excellence. He is also a founding member of the International Society for Hyaluronan Studies (ISHAS).

Dr. Prestwich received many awards and distinctions and most recently was elected Fellow of the American Institute for Medical and Biological Engineering (2005). He was selected as a V100 Top Venture Entrepreneurs in Utah in 2005 and 2006, he received the TIAA-CREF "Greater Good" award (2006), was a Utah Business Magazine "Health Care Hero" for 2006, received the Governor's Medal for Science and Technology for 2006, and was awarded the 2008 Volwiler Research Award of the American Association of Colleges of Pharmacy.

Interview*

Please tell us something about your background and education.

I am a Navy brat; I was born in Panama, lived in California, New York, Maryland, and California again. Went to school at Caltech and then at Stanford for my Ph.D. in organic chemistry. After that I decided that it was time to keep traveling, so I went to Nairobi, Kenya, for three years as a post doctoral associate. I also switched from organic chemistry to the chemistry of understanding how insects communicate with each other. During those years I worked on termite communication, wrote an article for *Scientific American* on chemical warfare by termites and also did an article for *National Geographic* [1, 2] which I both photographed and wrote on African termites. A glue-squirting soldier termite, the kind from which I isolated many new molecules during the first decade of my career, is shown in Figure 1. So I have a history. I started off doing biology with a chemistry focus orientation back in the mid 1970s, when chemical biology did not even exist and the concept of interdisciplinary science was barely tolerated. Yet, I still got a good faculty position following that experience at the State University of New York at Stony Brook in the Chemistry Department. I was there for 19 years before moving to Salt Lake City in 1996. That is my short background.

Let us go back further and start with your interest in science—especially with that background of constantly moving to new places.

---

* This interview was recorded during the Hyaluronan Meeting in Charleston, South Carolina, April 2007, and was augmented in the spring of 2008.

Figure 1. Soldier *Trinervitermes bettonianus*
(1976, photograph by and courtesy of G. Prestwich)

In a somewhat funny way, my interest in science actually started as an interest in mathematics. I always loved astronomy, I always loved mathematics, and from the time I was a small child my father—who had graduated as a valedictorian in the Naval Academy—had helped me learn advanced mathematics; way in advance of what was actually taught in the class room. I remember, I would be doing fractions in second grade instead of in junior high and I doing calculus when I was in junior high school. It was great fun and I loved mathematics and I always wanted to be a mathematician. At the same time, I hated science fairs; I never participated in them because I thought that they were too staged. I did like chemistry as all little boys did, I suppose. I made horrible smells and blew things up in the basement with a chemistry set. Of course, you cannot get those kinds of chemistry sets anymore, the ones you can buy now are all too watered down and tame. So anyway, I had no idea what I really wanted to do; I only had the very specific idea about wanting to go to Caltech from the time I was in the eighth grade. So that is what I did. It was small, it had an absolute focus on science, a little bit of engineering but mostly on the basic sciences, and it was considered to be the best school in science in the world. I was set on going there. Every high school counselor I had said 'oh, you should apply to multiple schools, nobody that ever tried from this school to get there succeeded.' So I actually applied to other schools as well but when I got early acceptance from Caltech, I canceled all the other applications.

And what happened to your interest in mathematics?

I think, it is an interesting story. What happened was the following: Because I had so much mathematics before, I did not take the freshman mathematics course at Caltech and so I was one of maybe five freshmen who took sophomore mathematics. Then, all of a sudden, I realized that solving differential equations and integrating things under a curve, and doing full problems was not what mathematicians did; engineers did that, physicists did that, but mathematicians did things that were so abstract and boring and hard that I just I barely survived that course. So I did not do well there; physics had gotten to a level, where it was no longer fun-problems, it was very difficult, so I did not do well in physics either. So much for becoming an astrophysicist or a mathematician. On the other hand, biology at that time was a very descriptive science and I had no interest in that, but I had an absolutely fabulous inspiring chemistry professor. His name was Jürg Waser; he was Swedish, and he was a tall man with a personality that just extended many-many arm's lengths beyond his body size, which was already as I said quite large. He inspired many of us to become teachers and performers in the art of explaining chemistry, so I got sucked into chemistry. Because of my experience with mathematics it would have been logical to go into computational or theoretical chemistry—but I decided early on that I was not going to go to these fields, neither to physical chemistry. But I liked to cook and so I said, okay, if I like to cook and I like chemistry then I'll be an organic chemist.

What happened after Caltech?

After Caltech, I earned my Ph.D. degree with Professor W. S. Johnson at Stanford University. I became a natural products chemist trained in the total chemical synthesis. I loved the challenge of discovering new reactions and building complex molecules step-by-step. I developed a life-long set of friends in graduate school, and four of us are still in touch after 35 years. We'll talk soon about my return to Palo Alto after 30 plus years, this time as the scientific founder of a bay area based venture-capitalized company, Carbylan BioSurgery, developing modified HA as medical devices.

I nearly didn't complete graduate school, figuring that I had no future as an academic scientist, and worrying about the draft and Vietnam War. In 1971, I actually turned down two assignments in the Peace Corps—the first teaching mathematics in Kabul, and the second teaching chemistry to chemistry teachers at the Kenyatta Teachers College in Nairobi, Kenya. In any case, I settled down and finally completed my studies. Still, I felt insecure trying to compete with the likes of my graduate student and postdoc colleagues at Stanford, so I decided that I needed to expand my horizons into chemistry at the biological interface. My first assignment was to have been as a Visiting Assistant Professor of Chemistry at the University of Sao Paolo, under the auspices of an exchange sponsored by the National Academy of Sciences of the United States and of Brazil. In my last year of graduate school, I started learning Portuguese; but unexpectedly the program was cancelled after 6 or 7 years. Dr. Johnson came to me in his characteristic gruff voice and said: "Glenn, if you really want to do chemistry in an underdeveloped country, how about going to Kenya?"

Well, after turning down Nairobi once in 1971, I figured that lightning doesn't strike twice for no reason at all and so I interviewed with Dr. Jerry Meinwald (Cornell University) who happened to be giving a seminar at UC Santa Cruz that month, and poof! I was accepted to go to Africa rather than South America. I dropped out of Portuguese class and started learning Swahili instead (Yes, Stanford actually offered Swahili, taught by a native woman, for credit!). In June 1974 I finished my Ph.D. and headed for a 3-month training period in insect natural products and entomology at Cornell University. There, the renaissance men who became my role models—Dr. Thomas Eisner

—entomologist, chemical ecologist, photographer, musician, and Dr. Jerrold Meinwald—chemist, chemical ecologist, musician—taught me the basics of asking biologically interesting questions about insect chemical communication. In September 1974 I was off to the International Centre for Insect Physiology and Ecology (ICIPE) in Nairobi, where I worked until December 1976.

In Nairobi, I quickly discovered the excitement and frustration of working in a biologically rich but chemical-equipment-poor environment. Multistep synthesis under anhydrous conditions was not in the cards. Moreover, I had the only NMR and mass spectrometer for a several thousand mile radius, with the nearest serviceman 8 hr flight away in Frankfurt. Plus we had almost daily power and water outages. To get spectra of newly purified materials, I would set up camp in the instrument room, eat and sleep with my mass spec and rescue it by venting it when the oil diffusion pumps had to be shut down when power or water failed. Arrrgh! Still, I had brilliant biological collaborators, an international cadre of postdocs like myself augmented by the Who's Who of famous professors of insect physiology and ecology, and chemical ecology, and electron microscopy from all over the world. It was a fabulous place to make discoveries about chemical communication in insects. It was also a great place to do photography, and I took advantage of the wildlife – small and large – to hone my skills as a photographer. This ultimately led to the *National Geographic* experience, a commission by the German magazine Geo, and my wildlife photos appearing in *Ranger Rick*, *Natural History*, and elsewhere.

At ICIPE, I needed to work on one of five groups of arthropods: ticks, mosquitoes, termites, tsetse flies, or armyworms. I started on a tick project, but it became too political in the lab. The mosquitoes and tsetse were at different sites and the chemistry was less well appealing in terms of molecular complexity—plus these were disease vectors! The armyworm outbreaks had subsided—so no creatures to work on. Termites, however, were abundant, varied, and chemically understudied. Plus there was a very strong and interesting group of French, Dutch, German and Swiss termite behavior and physiologists there; I was naturally drawn into this exciting environment. In collaboration with my mentors Jerry Meinwald at

Cornell University, and Koji Nakanishi at Columbia Universtiy, we ended up identifying gazillions of totally bizarre structures from termite defense secretions, as well as some rather simple compounds with pheromonal activity in trail following queen cell construction.

Living away from television and most other forms of entertainment meant that I needed to entertain myself. I became an actor, working almost every night in the theatre—chorus, backstage, and eventually on stage in leading roles in plays and musicals. The love of music as a participant in a group continues to be an important part of my life to this day. The other activity that I learned in Nairobi which now greatly defines me as a person was learning to pilot an aircraft. I earned my pilot's license in 1975, and was privileged to fly my own postdoctoral advisors as well as visiting board of directors of ICIPE to game parks, to Lamu Island, and to field sites. Indeed, one of my passengers made the key introduction that led to my photographing and writing the *National Geographic* article on termites. Two images that capture the exciting work we did with termites are shown below. Figure 2a shows the small king and enormous egg-laying queen of a fungus-growing mound-building termite, while Figure 2b shows the slashing jaws of the soldier of the same termite species.

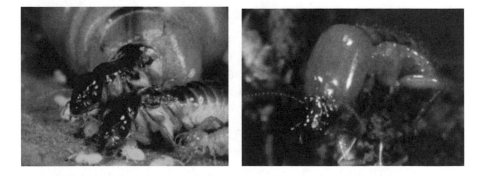

Figure 2a (left) and **b** (right) *Macrotermes subhyalinus*, Kenya
(1976, photograph by and courtesy of G. Prestwich)

At Stony Brook, I continued some of the postdoctoral work that I had started. I worked on chemical mechanisms of communication in termites and very soon realized that that was not going to be a long-term interest. So I started looking for ways to diversify my research portfolio, taking into account that I have always had a fairly short attention span. I decided that it was time to have a larger research group and I could only have one small research grant on termite chemistry so I had to look for something else. I started looking at metabolism in insects because that was what I had spent the last three or four years of my life doing. I did different methods of termite control that were based on chemically clever tricks, trying to fool the termites into eating things and then killing themselves after they'd eaten them. Then, I started looking at steroid metabolism in insects and that brought me into the area of hornworm chemistry. They are large agricultural pests that attack tobacco and tomato plants. Then I started expanding further to looking at pheromones, and looking into how insects, especially moths, communicate with each other. From moth pheromones, I started looking at juvenile hormones of insects which are the hormones that allow an insect to go from a larva to a pupa and then from a pupa to an adult in a controlled fashion, controlling the regulation of the genes during that transition that is metamorphosis.

During this changing process, starting in the early 1980s, I started making compounds that were radio-labeled. I was the only chemist who was interested in doing this and preparing compounds, so the entomologists would always come and ask if I could do this or that, and I'd say, "Sure!" All the other chemistry colleagues would say no, that is too boring. But I was interested in just about anything; so I tried, I would make stuff for them, and everybody wanted to have radioactively labeled compounds. So eventually I had a radioactivity laboratory for about 15 years at Stony Brook, which had the highest rating of any radioactivity laboratory in the synthetic chemistry sector of an academic environment. The only other place was at national laboratories or at pharmaceutical companies. So we would have, at any given time, about 50 Curies of tritiated pheromones, hormones, or steroids; about 10 Curies of ^{14}C labeled materials and another Curie here and there of ^{35}S and ^{32}P labeled materials. For example, we made a tritium-labeled version of disparlure, the gypsy moth pheromone (see Figure 3 for a photograph of a male gypsy moth) to study protein binding and enzymatic degradation. All of these were synthesized in what is called a "carrier-free way"; so they were not just tracers, each one had stoichiometric amounts of ^{14}C or tritium in it that allowed us to do a lot of really sensitive work studying pheromone perception, pheromone metabolism and so on. We also did a lot of photoaffinity labeling, which allowed us to use those materials to tag certain proteins and then study the tagged complexes. So that got me really tightly integrated with the insect biochemistry community.

Then, in the mid 1980s, there was this enormous crashing sound as the NIH budget went really low, the NSF budget went really low and all of the applied biology programs that were funding me took a nose dive. So I was involved in a crunch in funding that was not unlike what the young people are experiencing now. Mine was the Reagan-era crunch—as opposed to the Bush-era crunch. And the Reagan era crunch basically reduced my group size from 30ish down to eight and I had to completely abandon a lot of my projects. So I had to reinvent myself as a biological chemist doing mammalian biochemistry and not insect biochemistry—there just was no money in it anymore.

How did you learn about insects? You were, after all, a chemist....

That was done very much as a collaborative process and in fact one of the successes that I have had—if there is any secret to these at all—was the understanding that I can't do everything. I realized that the only way to get projects that are really interesting is to find the best biologist and to ask that person what he or she needs, and not the other way around, saying: "I have got this cool molecule, can you use it for me?" No, I have to ask: "What do you need?" "What can I make for you?" The underlying philosophy that I have had for the last 30 years in research is what I call "the marketing approach." I want to find out what the end-user wants and then I will make it for them. I have tried to stick with the end-user approach—and that has been very-very successful. In fact, that led me into the commercial sector because once I start making things for collaborators based on what they need, and what they want, then it is a fairly short mental leap to get into a customer orientation with a small company.

Figure 3. *Lymantri dispar* (1985, photograph by and courtesy of G. Prestwich)

So coming back to my story; we changed into mammalian biochemistry and I did that with the help of some on-campus, small-money grants that allowed me to do the work. Then I applied for some other grants, and some industrial money also came in and eventually we shifted into steroid metabolism in humans; inositol phosphate metabolism in the brain and later phosphoinositide signaling and, eventually, lysophosphotidic acid signaling. Then, along at the end of 1989-1990 came a completely serendipitous opportunity from one of my students who had worked on insect steroid metabolism. He finished his Master's degree, he was a Chinese gentleman, about 34 years old at the time and he needed to bring his family over from China. So he went to work for two years for MedChem in Woburn, Massachusetts, which is a hyaluronic acid company. They were selling AmVisc for ophthalmic surgery. Then the people at the company said that they wanted Jing Wen Kuo to come back to our laboratory, get his Ph.D. They would pay him during this time; they just wanted him to work on hyaluronic acid. I said: "What is hyaluronic acid?" I was an organic chemist, I worked on small molecules that were not larger than, say, 250-400 Dalton molecular weight; they were lipid soluble not water soluble. Then these people come and all of a sudden are asking me to work on something that was a million molecular weight, water soluble, and poorly characterized! I was thinking, why do I want to do this? And why would they want me to do this? But they said: "Well, you are a very good chemist and we want a new insight into this HA business because nobody is doing these kinds of chemical modification reactions." So I said, okay, you're paying for it, we will give it a try. So Jing Wen came to work in my laboratory. And, you know, what? Here, at this conference, I noticed that the company called Anika—that is the reincarnation of MedChem after they lost a patent infringement suit to Pharmacia—so Anika lists on their board about seven licensed patents on biscarbodiimide modification of HA—and most them have Prestwich as one inventor and Kuo as one of the other inventors. So this is how my life in HA started; through this carbodiimide crosslinking chemistry.

We eventually realized that that was not going to get us where we wanted to go with drug delivery or cell delivery, so we started looking for other ways to use that chemistry to make more flexible hyaluronic-acid-based hydrogels and then to modify other glycosaminoglycans and other proteins. But the story is that basically I was dragged into hyaluronic acid kicking and screaming; I didn't have any real interest in the project. For two years Jing Wen worked almost on his own with very little supervision from me because I thought, I don't really care about this project until I see something that I need to care about. That finally happened when we had these materials that he made towards the end of his dissertation. Then, the company continued funding another student and that led to the discovery that is the genesis of all the companies that are now involved with the thiol modifications. Interestingly, that was discovered by an Iranian graduate student, Tara Pouyani. She discovered it when I was off on sabbatical and sent me an email in which she wrote that she finally figured out how to make this modification work in high yield.

How much of your work is now connected with hyaluronan?

I would say, about 75 or 80%.

What else do you do?

I still have one small part of my group doing biomaterials and small molecules. But I am now letting the small molecules part finish up. That small molecule part was very important when I founded the company Echelon Biosciences, basically to commercialize and develop small phosphoinositide and other lipid reagents. This was when I was still very actively involved with research as the chief scientific officer and I also had active research grants. The logo and business strategy for this company is shown in Figure 4. Now I am letting that part of our research recede because we sold Echelon. From a year or so from now we will be doing only biomaterials, except that now I'm back involved with Echelon as their Chief Scientific Advisor and helping them regrow and expand their product portfolio.

Figure 4. Echelon's logo and business strategy (courtesy of G. Prestwich)

Originally you were only involved with research. How did you start to get involved with companies?

It was gradual; it was gradual in a sense and sudden in another sense. The sudden part of it was that while I was on sabbatical in 1991, I learned more about chemical biology. I learned with my own hands doing protein expression and enzyme measuring, enzyme reactions, and some of the initial work with structural NMR and NMR solution structures. At the end of that sabbatical, I got a phone call from the provost of my university at Stony Brook and he said that the director for the Center of Biotechnology has just resigned to go to Utah as the Vice President of Research, and he wanted me to take the job. I said, I don't want the job, I just spent 18 months learning to do all these experiments; I want to do great research, I want to do it with my own hands, and help students learn things by being in the lab with them. But the provost insisted on me taking that job. So I eventually said yes —but I asked for a lot. I asked for pay increase, I asked for a full time secretary, a full time post doc, etc., etc., and also for a commitment that I would only have to work that job 50% of my time and I would still be able to have 50% of it protected for research. So basically I was replacing my teaching responsibility with running this Center but not my research lab. So there I was, all of a sudden with this new job directing a biotechnology center. Just for the story; on my first day on the job I had to explain the Center to the Lt. Governor of the State of New York. I spent four years doing that job and I loved it. I loved the job, I loved working with faculty members who wanted to start companies, I loved working with companies who were trying to get established in the State of New York, I loved the idea of being part of building up the New York Biotechnology Complex from just a few startups to the robust entity that it is now. It was a lot of fun.

But in the process of helping out everybody else I realized that I could help out myself as well by learning about starting up companies with one of my friends, Dr. James Hayward, who had just started Collaborative Laboratories, Inc. And that is how my first company, Clear Solutions Biotech got started, based on some of my first work in the hyaluronan modification at Stony Brook. That company we sold later and the technology is now in Palo Alto with one of my other companies, now called Carbylan BioSurgery. It was an interesting route that started with this crazy opportunity with the hyaluronic acid in the late 1980s and then this almost magical offer of a job to run a Biotech Center and learn about commercialization. It was between 1992 and 1996 that I ran that Center and then I realized that I didn't really like New York that much and I didn't really like flatness and high population density and I hated, hated, HATED driving on the Long Island Expressway to do all the business that I was doing. I wanted an environment, where I could have no traffic, I could have mountains, interactive and friendly people, and less commuting with respect to business environment—so moving to Utah had all those things. It had a business community that was respectful of entrepreneurial scientists, and vice versa, it had clinicians that worked with engineers and worked with chemists and medicinal people hand in hand in an interactive way. So I realized that if I wanted to continue as an entrepreneur then moving to Utah would enhance everything; the science, the interdisciplinary end-user orientation, the business potential, and the business opportunities. And it's been a fantastic series of opportunities that have come from the way this small community of entrepreneurial researchers and science-savvy business people work together.

Are you involved with the University in Utah?

Yes, I am still at the University. The conflict of interest rules allow me to have a position there and have businesses as well. We have very liberal conflict of interest rules and I'm allowed to reduce my University percentage and use other percentage to do commercial activities. So usually I am between 80 – 95% at the university and the other percentages I am paid by one of my companies or by some other company. Right now I am 90% time with the University.

How many companies are you involved with?

It's hard to count—at least five or six, I think. Clear Solutions sold and the patents are licensed to Carbylan. Echelon was sold, but recently re-acquired by another company in Utah, and I am back on board as Chief Scientific Advisor. My third company was Sentrx Surgical, based on the whole portfolio of technologies from my lab with these synthetic extracellular matrices. When Sentrx was seeking to raise Series A financing, the opportunity arose to accept venture capital investment, and Carbylan BioSurgery was born in Palo Alto. In the process, Carbylan licensed only the human medical device applications, and so we formed Sentrx Animal Care in Salt Lake City for the veterinary applications in wound healing and adhesion prevention, and also Glycosan Biosystems in Salt Lake, which sells products for 3D cell culture, drug toxicity testing models, tumor xenograft models, and stem cell expansion and differentiaion. So, right now I am involved with those four, shown in Figure 5, plus a fifth that I'll mention later.

Figure 5. Startup companies in Salt Lake City, initiated by G. Preswich (courtesy of G. Prestwich)

In April 2007 I signed on with an energy-sector company, to be part of their team. In fact, I was recruited to lead their team to create a scientific advisory board and research directions in the area of the chemistry and the potential microbial resources that could be used in the environment from which oil and gas were extracted. By that I mean not where the oil is but what's around where the oil is. If you think about what you can get out of that environment you can find extremophiles that might be tolerant to pressure and high hydrocarbon levels that may be useful in bioremediation; there are definitely medicinal compounds that are in those kinds of high pressure oil-rich environments. This is just as there are biomarkers for shale oils from specific eras, there are small organic molecules that have potential medicinal value, and so I am going to put together a scientific team to help this company—it is called PaleoTechnology. Actually, our organizational meeting for that to kick off the selection of the SAB members and the research directions will be next Monday. I am looking forward to that; it's going to be a different thing. I figured, if I could jump into biomaterials knowing nothing about biomaterials, I can certainly jump into the energy sector knowing nothing about the energy sector.

Finally, University of Utah pulmonologist Tom Kennedy and I have just launched a company, GlycoMira ("astonishing sugars") to develop novel anti-inflammatory polysaccharides for rosacea, psoriasis, eczema, and other large-market inflammatory skin disorders. This was only conceived in February 2008, and incorporated in June 2008, but the company already has good traction. I hope to be able to tell more about these exciting HA-related products in a few years.

I wonder, why is having several small companies doing related things better than having one larger company that could do all the work?

We started out with a large one doing everything. But the trouble is when you have a company that is trying to do everything, it does nothing. If I have learned nothing else I learned this: a company is all about focus and focus means that the interesting science has to be reduced to boring practical accomplishments. That is, why I have not gone into wholeheartedly into any of my own companies because I'm better as the inventor and the explorer, not the captain of the ship who has to make sure that all of the oars have been properly sanded down and everything. I'm not good at running the company; I'm good at inventing stuff and being the visionary for the next generation of products. In fact, I'm quite good with marketing as well because I have a creative side and I can come up with compound product names pretty well and product packaging concepts that help guide the professionals bring that into an effective product.

I noticed something in your lecture that I am curious about: You talked about "3D cell culture." Would you elaborate on that?

Ever since people have been doing cell cultures, they used "tissue culture polystyrene," which is plastic, coated with polylysine or something else. Then cells are grown in a monolayer; they're seeded at subconfluent density and then they become confluent and then they stop growing. The problem with that is that, first of all, no cell in your body ever sees plastic. Then, of course, no cell ever grows in a monolayer with the exception of very few cell types and, finally, cells respond to the elasticity of the material and plastic has a 100kPa modulus. There is nothing in your body short of the hardest bones that has anything close to 100kPa elastic modulus, so it's unnatural for all sorts of reasons. Of course, it is convenient, it is cheap, and everybody does it, and tradition sometimes trumps science. But the only reason it trumps science is because there has not been a good alternative that is simple to use, affordable, and as versatile as tissue culture plastic.

In terms of end users we have the following strategy: if they want to compare it to what they've been doing so far, we say fine, take your tissue culture plastic and instead of growing the cells on the plastic here is our stuff; pour it into the wells and let it crosslink. It will make a gel, and the gel will be compliant, it will be less rigid and you can change that rigidity. Now if they grow your cells on it, they will see fantastic things; different genes being regulated, there is more physiological behavior—so I call this 2½ D because now they're growing their cells on a surface, which the cells can penetrate into and degrade, but they are still growing in 2D on an unnatural surface. So the only true 3D culturing occurs when a cell is encapsulated by the hydrogel, just as though it were encapsulated by a natural extracellular matrix. We have one of the few materials that actually provide the opportunity for a cell to be surrounded by extracellular matrix cues on all sides rather than just on a flat surface, one way or the other.

Are you selling this?

Yes, that's the Extracel product line, exactly. Figure 6 shows in schematic form the thinking we used to deconstruct the biological extracellular matrix (ECM) to make simple, approvable, versatile materials for the applications we just discussed.

Deconstructing the ECM

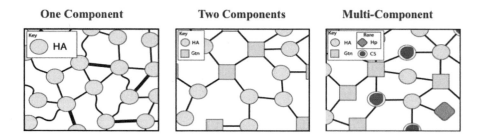

Figure 6. The synthetic ECM technology

You probably remember that Bandi made a remark after your talk.

I was so flattered; it was just a marvelous moment in my life to have the founder of so much of the science as well as the business of hyaluronic acid be so openly complimentary.

Yes, it was a very nice comment. But I would like to mention another aspect of his comment: he said that long ago, in the early 1980s he and Charles Weiss came up with the idea that this could be used for adhesion and they tried but they were not successful with the FDA. How did you manage that?

Well, adhesion is still tough, basically because the clinical trials are very expensive and it is very difficult to find a good end point. So we actually have the intention ultimately to do orthopedic adhesions as a way to get our material into the market and then have it used off label for other surgeries. Genzyme did this with a gynecological indication, it was approved for a gynecological indication, which was an easier end point and then it became used off label for many other things. We would go in first with an orthopedic use; we have really good data on tendon surgery.

How do you determine the best composition of the material for, say, adhesion or wound healing?

There are really two questions here. One is the scientific question, as a scientist I want to optimize a material for a given use because then you have the best material. And we have done that, we have done that with adding drugs, with changing compositions a number of different ways, and we have published papers on that. So that is one question. As a scientist we like to optimize things, to make them as cool, as interesting, as publishable, and as perfect as possible. The other thing is the business point of view. There you want one material that does everything because then you have one approval and one manufacturing, and then the same material is used for everything and that is all. At worst you have to reformulate it in different syringes, or put different labels on it with different instructions for the physician to use. But you have one approval, one manufacturing process, and life is good because then you can maintain your margins and still have affordable prices and have the minimum amount of regulatory nightmare.

So it may not be the optimal composition for any particular purpose for which it I sold.

It doesn't have to be, if it works better than anything else and if it is easy to use. The next to the last speaker today at the conference made the point that the excellence of the material, the performance of the material may have absolutely nothing to do with it, but if it can be done in five minutes instead of 45 minutes in the operating room, it is sold. That is ease. Ease of use. Simplicity of use. That is the user orientation. If you understand that from the beginning, you understand that a company wants one product, a physician wants something easy to use, a patient wants something that works. Those are your three users, if you build for those three, you are going to succeed. And there are very few, I would say fewer than 1%, of all the academic researchers in the world who truly understand this. It is not something that we learn in class or at the bench. You don't learn it until you are exposed to the concept of what a company has to do to be successful. Then if you bring those simple business principles back to the research lab, link marketing to research, then it becomes pretty obvious, how you should develop your research program and how you should avoid the research going in gazillions of directions like a stream flowing out of the delta and just keep the stream flowing in a narrow channel. That is your focus that is your product orientation.

How do you separate your university research and your work at these companies if they are related?

The hardest part of the separation is separating in my brain which brain should be active. Whether it is, one of the three companies' brains that is on or whether it is the academic brain that is on. It is easier when I am at a company because whatever we are talking about is company business and it is clear that is what I am doing. I am a company guy at that point. But when I am in my academic lab, I could have ideas that would be beneficial to one or the other company but I really had the idea in the university so who owns that intellectual, who owns my brain at any given time? It is really a judgment call and I have to make that.

The biggest issues though when it comes to conflict of interest is how you treat students in the laboratory where there is potential commercialization potential as well as the need to publicly disclose information. So you need to keep it quiet but you need to disclose it and that is always a dangerous balancing act. Now, for the past ten years it has been quite simple in my laboratory since we have had a conflict of interest policy, I actually helped the university people to write it. So the line in the sand is that if it is research and we can publish it, then students can work on it and then it is a university research. However, if it is product development and it is not really going to be published; it is more of a trade secret but not interesting research, it is not probing some fundamental question, it is just fixing something, then that is product research and the company does it.

Now I do have a line in the sand and the width of this line in the sand is what post docs can do for me and at what stage students can cross back and forth over that line. They can cross over if they are getting ready, if they are graduating and they are thinking about a non-academic career in a company; then that is when they can start crossing that line. My view of post docs is that they are apprentices for a career; they need to publish for their career but they also need career guidance and if part of their career guidance is learning how to do product development they can do it. I don't require it but they can do it, and it truly is part of their education.

Have you become rich with your companies?

Hardly. These are all development-stage companies and more money is going in than coming out. Still, selling the first companies, Clear Solutions and Echelon, were certainly not financial disasters. For me it also is fantastic to look at all the results that people came up with using our material. It is not that they are going to make you rich or famous but you live through their successes; so Echelon's products in lipids are enabling many-many papers in *Nature* and *Science* and *PNAS* and *Cell* and *Molecular Cell* and other journals appear. I look at these papers and I look at the things they are doing with the materials they bought from Echelon and I am saying, okay, I did the right thing!

Can you single out one of your results—either scientific or practical—that you are the most proud of?

Oh, boy! Actually one of the things I'm proud of is the fact that I'm making my father proud of me. I am an only child and he was an only child, and that is a special relationship. It was he who taught me, when I was about 13 years old, the difference between sales and marketing, and of course, I was interested in science and he was doing electronics marketing. I remember, I told one of my friends that he was selling electronic systems and he corrected me and said: no, no, I'm marketing electronic systems. I asked, "What's the difference?", and he said "In marketing you build what the customer wants, in sales you sell what you have to offer." And I said, "Oh", and, of course, that made no sense to me at all at the time, but sometime later I realized that that is essentially what I was doing in my career was I was going to a customer and asked what kind of chemicals do you need made? And then I went back to the lab and made them. I just wrote a short, invited personal opinion article for the *Journal of Cellular Biochemistry* and in the acknowledgements I acknowledged my father for teaching me the difference between marketing and sales. I sent him a copy of this paper and he said he cried all day. He had no idea that it had meant so much to me.

What was the greatest challenge?

Greatest challenge, oh boy. Trying to maintain a balanced life. My mom was always after me that I should do more volunteer work and I told her that I can't do volunteer work because I am too busy trying to succeed as a scientist. The balanced life part of it comes usually later. Now my volunteer work is singing, it's a personal satisfaction but also giving the gift of wonderful choral and symphonic music and being able to share that with other choristers and with the symphony, with the audience—it is a wonderful experience. Then being able to fly an airplane is another; now I spend about 30% of my time flying. I fly for Angel Flight West, a charitable organization that provides non-emergency medical transportation for those unable to afford it. This is a charitable thing. I donate time and money to fly children who have skeletal malformations and they need to go from some remote town to a hospital, or others with retinoblastoma, leukemia, bone marrow transplants. These patients, after I fly them, a number of times become friends. I'm the pilot and I'm flying them from their home to the hospital for chemotherapy treatment. There is this woman, for example, she is the brightest person, cheeriest-disposition person I have every seen. She had Stage IV metastatic breast cancer, she was given a six-month life expectance two years ago and she was still alive at the time of the interview, but died a few months later. She was as thin as a minute but she still managed to get in and out of the airplane. She flew with our Angel Flight pilots so much that she learned to fly the airplanes. She is 58 years old, we put her in the right seat, and she says okay can I fly now, and I said okay auto pilot is off, your airplane and she flies the airplane for an hour. It is wonderful to meet people that have that kind of positive attitude in the face of adversity.

Do you have your own family?

I have a family. My wife, Barbara Bentley, is an emeritus professor of ecology and evolution from Stony Brook and she spends a lot of time traveling. She does tropical ecology and she works and teaches in Costa Rica. Our daughter, Jocelyn Bentley-Prestwich, is 26; she graduated from Smith a few years ago and she has a landscape design, construction, and maintenance company (.jocelynalyssa.) in Oakland as well as playing in a band; she is an oboist. My son, Steve Carroll, is now 34 and is a manager at a furniture warehouse and apparently extremely well respected as a manager. He has achieved success in his own life as well as helped provide us with three grandchildren. I have a full life.

Plans for the future?

Plans for the future? I'm going to be moving up to Orcas Island and the San Juan Islands, Washington State. We are in the process of moving, slowly transitioning to that life style now. I will be moving from the academic sector to the industrial sector more fully within over the next three-four-year period. Whether I would be personally involved in my own companies or helping other faculty start companies, or being a consultant with venture capitalists, is still a question. But that is the area that I want to work in, the interface between business and science where the science is the interface between chemistry, biology, and engineering. In fact, since the interview, President Michael Young of the University of Utah appointed me as his Special Assistant for Faculty Entrepreneurs. This is a great privilege, since now it's actually part of my job description to mentor other faculty members in becoming entrepreneurs to commercialize their new technologies into products and companies.

Have I left out anything that would be important to convey?

I don't think so.

References

1 Prestwich, G.D. "The Chemical Defenses of Termites," *Scientific American*, pp. 78-87 (August 1983).
2 Prestwich, G.D. "Termites: Dweller in the Dark," *National Geographic*, **153**, 532-547 (April 1978).

Bibliography[*]

Hyaluronan-Related Publications

1. Prestwich, G., Kuo, J.-W., and Swann, D. (1990). N-acylurea and 0-acylisourea derivatives of hyaluronic acid. Canadian patent.

2. Kuo, J. W., Swann, D. A., and Prestwich, G. D. (1991). Chemical modification of hyaluronic acid by carbodiimides. Bioconjugate Chem 2 (4), 232-241.

3. Kuo, J.-W., Swann, D. A., and Prestwich, G. D. (1992). Water-insoluble derivatives of hyaluronic acid and their methods of preparation and use. US 5,356,883. October 18, 1994. (Research Foundation of State University of N.Y., Albany, NY (US); Anika Research, Inc., Woburn, MA (US), assignees).

4. Pouyani, T., Kuo, J., Harbison, G. S., and Prestwich, G. D. (1992). Solid-state NMR of N-Acylureas derived from the reaction of hyaluronic acid with isotopically-labeled carbodiimides. J Am Chem Soc 114, 5972-5976.

5. Pouyani, T., and Prestwich, G. D. (1993). Functionalized derivatives of hyaluronic acid. US 5,616,568. April 1, 1997 (Research Foundation of State University of New York, Albany, NY (US), assignee).

6. Kuo, J.-W., Swann, D. A., and Prestwich, G. D. (1994). Water-insoluble derivatives of hyaluronic acid and their methods of preparation and use. US 5,502,081. March 26, 1996 (Research Foundation of State University of New York, Albany, NY (US); Anika Research, Inc., Woburn, MA (US), assignees).

7. Pouyani, T., Harbison, G., and Prestwich, G. (1994). Novel Hydrogels of Hyaluronic Acid: Synthesis, Surface Morphology, and Solid-State NMR. J Am Chem Soc 116, 7515-7522.

---

[*] Provided by the interviewee.

8.   Pouyani, T., and Prestwich, G. D. (1994). Functionalized derivatives of hyaluronic acid oligosaccharides: Drug carriers and novel biomaterials. Bioconjugate Chem 5, 339-347.

9.   Pouyani, T., and Prestwich, G. D. (1994). Biotinylated hyaluronic acid: a new tool for probing hyaluronate receptor interactions. Bioconjugate Chem 5 (4), 370-372.

10.   Kuo, J.-W., Swann, D. A., and Prestwich, G. D. (1995). Water-insoluble derivatives of hyaluronic acid and their methods of preparation and use. US 6,013,679. January 11, 2000 (Anika Research, Inc., Woburn, MA (US); Research Foundation of State University of New York, Stony Brook, NY (US), assignees).

11.   Pouyani, T., and Prestwich, G. D. (1995). Method for making functionalized derivatives of hyaluronic acid. US 5,652,347. July 29, 1997 (Anika Research, Inc., Woburn, MA (US); Research Foundation of State University of New York, Stony Brook, NY (US), assignees).

12.   Prestwich, G. D., and Marecak, D. M. (1996). Functionalized derivatives of hyaluronic acid. US 5,874,417. February 23, 1999 (Research Foundation of State University of New York, Albany, NY (US), assignee).

13.   Vercruysse, K. P., Marecak, D. M., Marecek, J. F., and Prestwich, G. D. (1997). Synthesis and *in Vitro* degradation of new polyvalent hydrazide cross-linked hydrogels of hyaluronic acid. Bioconjugate Chem 8, 686-694.

14.   Kuo, J.-W., Swann, D. A., and Prestwich, G. D. (1998). Method for treating wounds using modified hyaluronic acid crosslinked with biscarbodiimide. US 6,096,727. August 1, 2000 (Anika Therapeutics, Inc., Woburn, MA (US); Research Foundation of State University of New York, Stony Brook, NY (US), assignees).

15.   Prestwich, G., Marecak, D. M., Marecek, J. F., Vercruysse, K., and Ziebell, M. (1998). Controlled chemical modification of hyaluronic acid: synthesis, applications, and biodegradation of hydrazide derivatives. JControlled Release (53), 93-103.

16.   Prestwich, G. D., Marecak, D. M., Marecek, J. F., Vercruysse, K. P., and Ziebell, M. R. (1998). Chemical modification of hyaluronic acid for drug delivery, biomaterials and biochemical probes. In *The Chemistry, Biology and Medical Applications of Hyaluronan and its Derivatives Proceedings of the Wenner-Gren Foundation International Symposium held in honor of Endre A Balazs, Stockholm, Sweden, September 18-21, 1996* (Ed. Laurent, T. C.), Portland Press Ltd., London (UK), 43-65.

17.   Vercruysse, K. P., and Prestwich, G. D. (1998). Hyaluronate derivatives in drug delivery. Critical Reviews™ in Therapeutic Drug Carrier Systems 15 (5), 513-555.

18.   Luo, Y., and Prestwich, G. D. (1999). Synthesis and selective cytotoxicity of a hyaluronic acid-antitumor bioconjugate. Bioconjugate Chem 10, 755-763.

19.   Vercruysse, K. P., Ziebell, M. R., and Prestwich, G. D. (1999). Control of enzymatic degradation of hyaluronan by divalent cations. Carbohydr Res 318 (1-4), 26-37.

20.   Luo, Y., Kirker, K. R., and Prestwich, G. D. (2000). Cross-linked hyaluronic acid hydrogel films: new biomaterials for drug delivery. J Controlled Release 69 (1), 169-184.

21.   Luo, Y., Ziebell, M. R., and Prestwich, G. D. (2000). A hyaluronic acid-taxol antitumor bioconjugate targeted to cancer cells. Biomacromolecules 1 (2), 208-218.

22.   Mason, M., Vercruysse, K. P., Kirker, K. R., Frisch, R., Marecak, D. M., Prestwich, G. D., and Pitt, W. G. (2000). Attachment of hyaluronic acid to polypropylene, polystyrene, and polytetrafluoroethylene. Biomaterials 21 (1), 31-36.

23.   Prestwich, G., Luo, Y., Ziebell, M., Vercruysse, K., Kirker, K., and MacMaster, J. (2000). Chemically modified hyaluronan: new biomaterials and probes for cell biology. In *New Frontiers in Medical Sciences: Redefining Hyaluronan (Proceedings of the Symposium held in Padua, Italy, 17-19 June 1999)* (Eds. Abatangelo, G., and Weigel, P.), Elsevier, Amsterdam (NL), 181-194.

24.   Luo, Y., and Prestwich, G. D. (2001). Hyaluronic acid-N-hydroxysuccinimide: a useful intermediate for bioconjugation. Bioconj Chem 12 (6), 1085-1088.

25.   Prestwich, G. (2001). Biomaterials from chemically-modified hyaluronan. In *Glycoforum. Hyaluronan Today.* (Eds. Hascall, V.C. and Yanagishita, M.) (Seikagaku   Corporation   Glycoforum)   (Accessed   at httpj://www.glycoforum.gr.jp/science/hyaluronan /HA18/HA18E.html) (March 29, 2001), Tokyo (JP).

26.   Ziebell, M., Zhao, Z., Luo, Y., Luo, B., Turley, E., A., and Prestwich, G. (2001). Peptides that mimic glycosaminoglycans: high-affinity ligands for a hyaluronan binding domain. Chem Biol 8, 1081-1094.

27. Day, A. J., and Prestwich, G. D. (2002). Hyaluronan-binding proteins: tying up the giant. J Biol Chem 277 (7), 4585-4588.

28. Kirker, K. R., Luo, Y., Nielson, J. H., Shelby, J., and Prestwich, G. D. (2002). Glycosaminoglycan hydrogel films as bio-interactive dressings for wound healing. Biomaterials 23, 3661-3671.

29. Luo, Y., Bernshaw, N. J., Lu, Z. R., Kopecek, J., and Prestwich, G. D. (2002). Targeted delivery of doxorubicin by HPMA copolymer-hyaluronan bioconjugates. Pharm Res 19 (4), 396-402.

30. Luo, Y., Kirker, K. R., and Prestwich, G. D. (2002). Hyaluronic acid hydrogel film: a new biomaterial for drug delivery and wound healing. In *Hyaluronan Volume 2* (Eds. Kennedy, J. F., Phillips, G.O., Williams, P. A., and Hascall, V.C.), Woodhead, Cambridge (UK), 271-276.

31. Picart, C., Mutterer, J., Richert, L., Luo, Y., Prestwich, G. D., Schaaf, P., Voegel, J. C., and Lavalle, P. (2002). Molecular basis for the explanation of the exponential growth of polyelectrolyte multilayers. Proc Natl Acad Sci U S A 99 (20), 12531-12535.

32. Prestwich, G. D., Luo, Y., Kirker, K. R., Ziebell, M. R., and Shelby, J. (2002). Hyaluronan biomaterials for targeted drug delivery and wound healing. In *Hyaluronan Volume 2* (Eds. Kennedy, J. F., Phillips, G.O., Williams, P. A., and Hascall, V.C.), Woodhead, Cambridge (UK), 277-284.

33. Shu, X. Z., Liu, Y., Luo, Y., Roberts, M. C., and Prestwich, G. D. (2002). Disulfide cross-linked hyaluronan hydrogels. Biomacromolecules 3 (6), 1304-1311.

34. Vercruysse, K., Li, H., Luo, Y., and Prestwich, G. (2002). Thermosensitive lanthanide complexes of hyaluronan. Biomacromolecules 3 (4), 639-643.

35. Shu, X. Z., Liu, Y., Palumbo, F., and Prestwich, G. D. (2003). Disulfide-crosslinked hyaluronan-gelatin hydrogel films: a covalent mimic of the extracellular matrix for in vitro cell growth. Biomaterials 24 (21), 3825-3834.

36. Cai, S., Dufner-Beattie, J. L., and Prestwich, G. D. (2004). A selective protein sensor for heparin detection. Anal Biochem 326 (1), 33-41.

37. Chen, Q., Cai, S., Shadrach, K. G., Prestwich, G. D., and Hollyfield, J. G. (2004). Spacrcan binding to hyaluronan and other glycosaminoglycans. Molecular and biochemical studies. J Biol Chem 279 (22), 23142-23150.

38. Kirker, K. R., Luo, Y., Morris, S. E., Shelby, J., and Prestwich, G. D. (2004). Glycosaminoglycan hydrogels as supplemental wound dressings for donor sites. J Burn Care Rehabil 25 (3), 276-286.

39. Li, H., Liu, Y., Shu, X. Z., Gray, S. D., and Prestwich, G. D. (2004). Synthesis and biological evaluation of a cross-linked hyaluronan-mitomycin C hydrogel. Biomacromolecules 5 (3), 895-902.

40. Liu, Y., Shu, X. Z., Gray, S. D., and Prestwich, G. D. (2004). Disulfide-crosslinked hyaluronan-gelatin sponge: growth of fibrous tissue in vivo. J Biomed Mater Res A 68 (1), 142-149.

41. Peattie, R. A., Nayate, A. P., Firpo, M. A., Shelby, J., Fisher, R. J., and Prestwich, G. D. (2004). Stimulation of in vivo angiogenesis by cytokine-loaded hyaluronic acid hydrogel implants. Biomaterials 25 (14), 2789-2798.

42. Pitt, W. G., Morris, R. N., Mason, M. L., Hall, M. W., Luo, Y., and Prestwich, G. D. (2004). Attachment of hyaluronan to metallic surfaces. J Biomed Mater Res 68A (1), 95-106.

43. Richert, L., Lavalle, P., Payan, E., Shu, X. Z., Prestwich, G. D., Stoltz, J. F., Schaaf, P., Voegel, J. C., and Picart, C. (2004). Layer by layer buildup of polysaccharide films: physical chemistry and cellular adhesion aspects. Langmuir 20 (2), 448-458.

44. Shu, X. Z., Ghosh, K., Liu, Y., Palumbo, F. S., Luo, Y., Clark, R. A., and Prestwich, G. D. (2004). Attachment and spreading of fibroblasts on an RGD peptide-modified injectable hyaluronan hydrogel. J Biomed Mater Res A 68 (2), 365-375.

45. Shu, X. Z., Liu, Y., Palumbo, F. S., Luo, Y., and Prestwich, G. D. (2004). In situ crosslinkable hyaluronan hydrogels for tissue engineering. Biomaterials 25 (7-8), 1339-1348.

46. Shu, X. Z., and Prestwich, G. (2004). Therapeutic biomaterials from chemically-modified hyaluronan. In *Chemistry and Biology of Hyaluronan* (Eds. Garg, H. G., and Hales, C. A.), Elsevier, Ltd., Amsterdam (NL), 475-504.

47. Zheng Shu, X., Liu, Y., Palumbo, F. S., Luo, Y., and Prestwich, G. D. (2004). In situ crosslinkable hyaluronan hydrogels for tissue engineering. Biomaterials 25 (7-8), 1339-1348.

48. Ziebell, M. R., and Prestwich, G. D. (2004). Interactions of peptide mimics of hyaluronic acid with the receptor for hyaluronan mediated motility (RHAMM). J Comput Aided Mol Des 18 (10), 597-614.

49. Cai, S., Liu, Y., Zheng Shu, X., and Prestwich, G. D. (2005). Injectable glycosaminoglycan hydrogels for controlled release of human basic fibroblast growth factor. Biomaterials 26 (30), 6054-6067.

50. Chen, Q., Cai, S., Shadrach, K. G., Prestwich, G., and Hollyfield, J. G. (2005). Spacrcan binding to hyaluronan: molecular and biochemical studies. In *Hyaluronan: Structure, Metabolism, Biological Activities, Therapeutic Applications Volume II* (Eds. Balazs, E.A., and Hascall, V.C.), Matrix Biology Institute, Edgewater, NJ (USA), 739-749.

51. Ghosh, K., Shu, X. Z., Mou, R., Lombardi, J., Prestwich, G. D., Rafailovich, M. H., and Clark, R. A. (2005). Rheological characterization of in situ cross-linkable hyaluronan hydrogels. Biomacromolecules 6 (5), 2857-2865.

52. Hansen, J. K., Thibeault, S. L., Walsh, J. F., Shu, X. Z., and Prestwich, G. D. (2005). In vivo engineering of the vocal fold extracellular matrix with injectable hyaluronic acid hydrogels: early effects on tissue repair and biomechanics in a rabbit model. Ann Otol Rhinol Laryngol 114 (9), 662-670.

53. Jiang, D., Liang, J., Fan, J., Yu, S., Chen, S., Luo, Y., Prestwich, G. D., Mascarenhas, M. M., Garg, H. G., Quinn, D. A., Homer, R. J., Goldstein, D. R., Bucala, R., Lee, P. J., Medzhitov, R., and Noble, P. W. (2005). Regulation of lung injury and repair by Toll-like receptors and hyaluronan. Nat Med 11 (11), 1173-1179.

54. Kirker, K. R., Luo, Y., Morris, S. E., Shelby, J., and Prestwich, G. (2005). Glycosaminoglycan hydrogels for wound healing. In *Hyaluronan: Structure, Metabolism, Biological Activities, Therapeutic Applications Volume I* (Eds. Balazs, E.A., and Hascall, V.C.), Matrix Biology Institute, Edgewater, NJ (USA), 397-400.

55. Liu, Y., Li, H., Shu, X. Z., Gray, S. D., and Prestwich, G. D. (2005). Reduction of post-operative adhesions by *in Situ* crosslinked hyaluronan hydrogels. In *Hyaluronan: Structure, Metabolism, Biological Activities, Therapeutic Applications Volume I* (Eds. Balazs, E.A., and Hascall, V.C.), Matrix Biology Institute, Edgewater, NJ (USA), 381-384.

56. Liu, Y., Li, H., Shu, X. Z., Gray, S. D., and Prestwich, G. D. (2005). Crosslinked hyaluronan hydrogels containing mitomycin C reduce postoperative abdominal adhesions. Fertility and Sterility 83 (4, Supplement 1), 1275-1283.

57. Liu, Y., Shu, X. Z., Gray, S. D., and Prestwich, G. D. (2005). Tissue growth in a disulfide-crosslinked hyaluronan-gelatin sponge. In *Hyaluronan:*

Structure, Metabolism, Biological Activities, Therapeutic Applications Volume I (Eds. Balazs, E.A., and Hascall, V.C.), Matrix Biology Institute, Edgewater, NJ (USA), 377-380.

58. Liu, Y., Zheng Shu, X., and Prestwich, G. D. (2005). Biocompatibility and stability of disulfide-crosslinked hyaluronan films. Biomaterials 26 (23), 4737-4746.

59. Mironov, V., Kasyanov, V., Zheng Shu, X., Eisenberg, C., Eisenberg, L., Gonda, S., Trusk, T., Markwald, R. R., and Prestwich, G. D. (2005). Fabrication of tubular tissue constructs by centrifugal casting of cells suspended in an in situ crosslinkable hyaluronan-gelatin hydrogel. Biomaterials 26 (36), 7628-7635.

60. Orlandi, R. R., Li, H., Shu, X. Z., Liu, Y., and Prestwich, G. D. (2005). Preventing ostia closure durign sinus surgery using *in Situ* crosslinked hyaluronan hydrogels. In *Hyaluronan: Structure, Metabolism, Biological Activities, Therapeutic Applications Volume I* (Eds. Balazs, E. A., and Hascall, V.C.), Matrix BIology Institute, Edgewater, NJ (USA), 405-408.

61. Prestwich, G. D., Shu, X. Z., Liu, Y., Kirker, K. R., Li, H., Shelby, J., Morris, S. E., and Gray, S. D. (2005). *In Situ* crosslinkable synthetic extracellular matrices for tissue repair and prevention of surgical adhesions. In *Hyaluronan: Structure, Metabolism, Biological Activities, Therapeutic Applications Volume I* (Eds. Balazs, E.A., and Hascall, V. C.), Matrix Biology Institute, Edgewater, NJ (USA), 409-414.

62. Shu, X. Z., Liu, Y., and Prestwich, G. D. (2005). Injectable, *In Situ*-crosslinkable biomimetic hydrogels for tissue engineering. In *Hyaluronan: Structure, Metabolism, Biological Activities, Therapeutic Applications Volume I* (Eds. Balazs, E.A., and Hascall, V.C.), Matrix Biology Institute, Edgewater, NJ (USA), 415-419.

63. Brown, A. L., Ringuette, M. J., Prestwich, G. D., Bagli, D. J., and Woodhouse, K. A. (2006). Effects of hyaluronan and SPARC on fibroproliferative events assessed in an in vitro bladder acellular matrix model. Biomaterials 27 (20), 3825-3835.

64. Brown, A. L., Srokowski, E. M., Shu, X. Z., Prestwich, G. D., and Woodhouse, K. A. (2006). Development of a model bladder extracellular matrix combining disulfide cross-linked hyaluronan with decellularized bladder tissue. Macromol Biosci 6 (8), 648-657.

65. Duflo, S., Thibeault, S. L., Li, W., Shu, X. Z., and Prestwich, G. (2006). Effect of a synthetic extracellular matrix on vocal fold lamina propria gene expression in early wound healing. Tissue Eng 12 (11), 3201-3207.

66. Duflo, S., Thibeault, S. L., Li, W., Shu, X. Z., and Prestwich, G. D. (2006). Vocal fold tissue repair in vivo using a synthetic extracellular matrix. Tissue Eng 12 (8), 2171-2180.

67. Gajewiak, J., Cai, S., Shu, X. Z., and Prestwich, G. D. (2006). Aminooxy pluronics: synthesis and preparation of glycosaminoglycan adducts. Biomacromolecules 7 (6), 1781-1789.

68. Ghosh, K., Ren, X.-D., Shu, X. Z., Prestwich, G. D., and Clark, R. A. F. (2006). Fibronectin Functional Domains Coupled to Hyaluronan Stimulate Adult Human Dermal Fibroblast Responses Critical for Wound Healing. Tissue Engineering 12 (3), 601-613.

69. Ji, Y., Ghosh, K., Shu, X. Z., Li, B., Sokolov, J. C., Prestwich, G. D., Clark, R. A., and Rafailovich, M. H. (2006). Electrospun three-dimensional hyaluronic acid nanofibrous scaffolds. Biomaterials 27 (20), 3782-3792.

70. Liu, Y., Ahmad, S., Shu, X. Z., Sanders, R. K., Kopesec, S. A., and Prestwich, G. D. (2006). Accelerated repair of cortical bone defects using a synthetic extracellular matrix to deliver human demineralized bone matrix. J Orthop Res 24 (7), 1454-1462.

71. Liu, Y., Shu, X. Z., and Prestwich, G. D. (2006). Osteochondral defect repair with autologous bone marrow-derived mesenchymal stem cells in an injectable, in situ, cross-linked synthetic extracellular matrix. Tissue Eng 12 (12), 3405-3416.

72. Mehra, T. D., Ghosh, K., Shu, X. Z., Prestwich, G. D., and Clark, R. A. (2006). Molecular stenting with a crosslinked hyaluronan derivative inhibits collagen gel contraction. J Invest Dermatol 126 (10), 2202-2209.

73. Park, A. H., Hughes, C. W., Jackson, A., Hunter, L., McGill, L., Simonsen, S. E., Alder, S. C., Shu, X. Z., and Prestwich, G. D. (2006). Crosslinked hydrogels for tympanic membrane repair. Otolaryngol Head Neck Surg 135 (6), 877-883.

74. Peattie, R. A., Rieke, E. R., Hewett, E. M., Fisher, R. J., Shu, X. Z., and Prestwich, G. D. (2006). Dual growth factor-induced angiogenesis in vivo using hyaluronan hydrogel implants. Biomaterials 27, 1868-1875.

75. Pike, D. B., Cai, S., Pomraning, K. R., Firpo, M. A., Fisher, R. J., Shu, X. Z., Prestwich, G. D., and Peattie, R. A. (2006). Heparin-regulated release of growth factors in vitro and angiogenic response in vivo to implanted hyaluronan hydrogels containing VEGF and bFGF. Biomaterials 27 (30), 5242-5251.

76. Prestwich, G. D., Shu, X. Z., Liu, Y., Cai, S., Walsh, J. F., Hughes, C. W., Ahmad, S., Kirker, K. R., Yu, B., Orlandi, R. R., Park, A. H., Thibeault, S. L., Duflo, S., and Smith, M. E. (2006). Injectable synthetic extracellular matrices for tissue engineering and repair. Adv Exp Med Biol 585, 125-133.

77. Proctor, M., Proctor, K., Shu, X. Z., McGill, L. D., Prestwich, G. D., and Orlandi, R. R. (2006). Composition of hyaluronan affects wound healing in the rabbit maxillary sinus. Am J Rhinol 20 (2), 206-211.

78. Riley, C. M., Fuegy, P. W., Firpo, M. A., Zheng Shu, X., Prestwich, G. D., and Peattie, R. A. (2006). Stimulation of in vivo angiogenesis using dual growth factor-loaded crosslinked glycosaminoglycan hydrogels. Biomaterials 27 (35), 5935-5943.

79. Shu, X. Z., Ahmad, S., Liu, Y., and Prestwich, G. D. (2006). Synthesis and evaluation of injectable, in situ crosslinkable synthetic extracellular matrices for tissue engineering. J Biomed Mater Res A 79 (4), 902-912.

80. Sondrup, C., Liu, Y., Shu, X. Z., Prestwich, G. D., and Smith, M. E. (2006). Cross-linked hyaluronan-coated stents in the prevention of airway stenosis. Otolaryngology - Head and Neck Surgery 135 (1), 28-35.

81. Connors, R. C., Muir, J. J., Liu, Y., Reiss, G. R., Kouretas, P. C., Whitten, M. G., Sorenson, T. K., Prestwich, G. D., and Bull, D. A. (2007). Postoperative pericardial adhesion prevention using Carbylan-SX in a rabbit model. J Surg Res 140 (2), 237-242.

82. Flynn, L., Prestwich, G. D., Semple, J. L., and Woodhouse, K. A. (2007). Adipose tissue engineering with naturally derived scaffolds and adipose-derived stem cells. Biomaterials 28 (26), 3834-3842.

83. Horn, E. M., Beaumont, M., Shu, X. Z., Harvey, A., Prestwich, G. D., Horn, K. M., Gibson, A. R., Preul, M. C., and Panitch, A. (2007). Influence of cross-linked hyaluronic acid hydrogels on neurite outgrowth and recovery from spinal cord injury. J Neurosurg Spine 6 (2), 133-140.

84. Liu, Y., Shu, X. Z., and Prestwich, G. D. (2007). Tumor engineering: orthotopic cancer models in mice using cell-loaded, injectable, cross-linked hyaluronan-derived hydrogels. Tissue Eng 13 (5), 1091-1101.

85. Liu, Y., Shu, X. Z., and Prestwich, G. D. (2007). Reduced postoperative intra-abdominal adhesions using Carbylan-SX, a semisynthetic glycosaminoglycan hydrogel. Fertil Steril 87 (4), 940-948.

86. Liu, Y., Skardal, A., Shu, X. Z., and Prestwich, G. D. (2007). Prevention of peritendinous adhesions using a hyaluronan-derived hydrogel film following partial-thickness flexor tendon injury. J Orthop Res.

87. Orlandi, R. R., Shu, X. Z., McGill, L., Petersen, E., and Prestwich, G. D. (2007). Structural variations in a single hyaluronan derivative significantly alter wound-healing effects in the rabbit maxillary sinus. Laryngoscope 117 (7), 1288-1295.

88. Prestwich, G. (2007). Synthetic extracellular matrices for 3-D cell growth: applications in reparative medicine and cell biology. In *Seventh (7th) International Conference on Hyaluronan (Book of Abstracts), Charleston, South Carolina USA, April 22-27* 8.

89. Prestwich, G. (2007). Organ printing. Chem Biol 2, B33-B40.

90. Prestwich, G. D. (2007). Simplifying the extracellular matrix for 3-D cell culture and tissue engineering: a pragmatic approach. J Cell Biochem 101 (6), 1370-1383.

91. Serban, M. A., and Prestwich, G. D. (2007). Synthesis of hyaluronan haloacetates and biology of novel cross-linker-free synthetic extracellular matrix hydrogels. Biomacromolecules 8 (9), 2821-2828.

92. Vanderhooft, J. L., Mann, B. K., and Prestwich, G. D. (2007). Synthesis and characterization of novel thiol-reactive poly(ethylene glycol) cross-linkers for extracellular-matrix-mimetic biomaterials. Biomacromolecules 8 (9), 2883-2889.

93. Flynn, L. E., Prestwich, G. D., Semple, J. L., and Woodhouse, K. A. (2008). Proliferation and differentiation of adipose-derived stem cells on naturally derived scaffolds. Biomaterials 12, 1862-1871.

94. Hosack, L. W., Firpo, M. A., Scott, J. A., Prestwich, G. D., and Peattie, R. A. (2008). Microvascular maturity elicited in tissue treated with cytokine-loaded hyaluronan-based hydrogels. Biomaterials 29 (15), 2336-2347.

95. Peattie, R. A., Yu, B., Cai, S., Pike, D. B., Firpo, M. A., Fisher, R. J., Shu, X. Z., and Prestwich, G. D. (2008). Effect of gelatin on heaparin regulation of cytokine reserach from hyaluronan-based hydrogels. Drug Delivery 15, 363-371.

96. Scaife, C. L., Shea, J. E., Dai, Q., Firpo, M. A., Prestwich, G. D., and Mulvihill, S. J. (2008). Synthetic Extracellular Matrix Enhances Tumor Growth and Metastasis in an Orthotopic Mouse Model of Pancreatic Adenocarcinoma. J Gastrointest Surg 12, 1074-1080.

97. Serban, M. A., Liu, Y., and Prestwich, G. D. (2008). Effects of extracellular matrix analogues on primary human fibroblast behavior. Acta Biomater 4 (1), 67-75.

98. Serban, M. A., and Prestwich, G. D. (2008). Making modular extracellular matrices: solutions for the puzzle. Methods 45, 93-98.

99. Serban, M. A., Yang, G., and Prestwich, G. D. (2008). Synthesis, characterization and chondroprotective properties of a hyaluronan thioethyl ether derivative. Biomaterials 29 (10), 1388-1399.

100. Mironov, V., Kasyanov, V., Markwalkd, R. R., and Prestwich, G. D. (2008). Emergence of solid scaffold-free bioreactor-free and cell-free in vivo tissue engineering: directed tissue assembly by centrifugal casting. Exp Opin Biol Ther 8 (2), 143-152.

101. Turner, W. S., Seagle, C., Galanko, J., Favorov, O., Prestwich, G. D., Macdonald, J. M., and Reid, L. M. (2008). Nuclear magnetic resonance metabolomic footprinting of human hepatic stem cells and hepatoblasts cultured in hyaluronan hydrogels. Stem Cells 26 (6), 1547-1555.

102. Prestwich, G. D., and Kuo, J.-W. (2008). Chemically-modified HA for therapy and regenerative medicine. Current Pharmacaceutical Biotechnology 9 (4), 242-245.

103. Flynn, L., Prestwich, G. D., Semple, J. L., and Woodhouse, K. A. (2008). Adipose tissue engineering *in vivo* with adipose-derived stem cells on naturally derived scaffolds. JBMR (in press).

104. Prestwich, G. D. (2008). Engineering a clinically-useful matrix for cell therapy. Organogenesis (in press).

105. Serban, M. A., Scott, J. A., and Prestwich, G. D. (2008). Use of hyaluronan-derived hydrogels for 3-D cell culture and tumor xenografts. Current Protocols Cell Biol (in press).

John E. Scott (photograph courtesy of J. Scott)

John E. Scott

John E. Scott (b. 1930, Macclesfield, England) received his B.Sc. in Chemistry and Physiology (1951), M.Sc. in Physiology (1953), Ph.D in Chemical Pathology (1956), and was awarded D.Sc. honoris causa (1965) from the University of Manchester. He served in the Royal Air Force as a pilot officer (1956-58), then worked at St. Mary's Hospital in London and at the UK. Medical Research Council Rheumatism Unit (1960-1976). He was visiting professor at four different universities in the United States and Australia for over twenty years. In 1976 he became MRC-funded Professor of Chemical Morphology at Manchester University and held it for twenty years – this was the first ever chair in this field. Since 1996 he has been Emeritus Professor at Manchester University, the first Emeritus who had not previously been a salaried member of staff.

He has received numerous awards and distinctions, among them the Gold Medal of the Biochemical Society of London (1973), the German Robert Feulgen Prize (1986) and the French Barbara Robert Memorial Medal (2000). He is member of several scientific societies and honorary member of five learned societies. He has been on the editorial boards of nine scientific journals. He has published about 260 scientific papers and two books and is also a founding member of the International Society for Hyaluronan Sciences (ISHAS).

Interview[*]

I would like to start by asking you about chemical morphology. You are Professor of Chemical Morphology, which is rather unique.

Chemical morphology, by a quirk of the English language, means both the chemistry of anatomy and the anatomy of chemicals and I believe that you cannot deal with the chemistry of anatomy without knowing about the shape of the chemicals that are involved with building the tissue. What happened was that after spending many years, more than two decades on working out ultra-micro-analytical methods for biopolymers which are present in the connective tissues, I realized that this was not enough. I realized that one needed to know not only how much there was of these molecules but precisely where they were with respect to other molecules, how they were oriented, and what shapes they had. So that was the point at which I looked into the microscopy more and more, finishing up with electron microscopy, to see where these polymers were.

   This was, of course, a realization over a period of years. I was invited back to Manchester, (where I was a student in 1948-56) This happened when the Medical Research Council unit, which I had been at for 16 years, from 1961-1976, closed down. It was the routine practice for the Medical Research Council to give a unit to a very good man and when the man (Eric Byewaters) retired, the unit was disbanded. Professor David Jackson, who was a biochemist in Manchester invited me back there and he asked "what do you want to be professor of"? I thought a little bit and it only took two to three minutes for me (he was sitting opposite to me, like you are now) to say, well, what about Biochemical Morphology? He said fine and then after a while I realized the bio was redundant and it was really chemical

---

[*] This interview was recorded during several sessions in Budapest and Manchester in 2003.

morphology that we were talking about so I reverted to chemical morphology. This was in the Medical School. When David retired, I was invited by the chemistry department to come over to their building. Professor Hamish Sutherland was a good organic chemist there and he appreciated that what I was doing was very relevant to organic chemistry and to polymer chemistry. So when I went over there I became Professor of Chemical Morphology and it's been chemical morphology ever since.

That was 1981, but I have to say that when I started looking into the literature, I found that this term has been used before. The first and earliest use of it I found was by a man called Lansing and I think he was a Canadian. Already back in the 1950s, he used the term chemical morphology without any explanation. I haven't gone back any further than that and I don't know how farther back it goes, but the ideas that I have played about with all my life can be traced back at least to Needham. Joseph Needham published a very, very prescient paper in *Nature* about 1934-35, in which he talked about the necessity for getting chemistry and morphology together. Of course, in 1934, the knowledge of polymers was almost non-existent, so he was asking for something in the future rather than something he could do at that time but he understood absolutely the problem. He could see very clearly that one had to get together the chemistry and morphology in order to make sense of living material. So the ideas go back at least to Joseph Needham and quite possibly before him. The actual term that I have used went back to Lansing, at least, and possibly earlier. But when I came up with it as an idea for my professorship, I hadn't come across it anywhere else; it was Biochemical Morphology to begin with and Chemical Morphology subsequently. As far as I know, I'm the only professor of chemical morphology anywhere and we celebrated the 25th anniversary, if celebration is the right word, the 25th birthday of my chair in 2000. It was from 1976 to 2000, and this happened to coincide with the 150th anniversary of the University of Manchester so we put the two celebrations together.

You mentioned Joseph Needham and the year 1934. That strikes me as a very important year because the first experiment with proteins by X-ray diffraction was done then by J. Desmond Bernal. As Dorothy Hodgkin wrote about it, after the successful experiment, Bernal was wandering all night in Cambridge because he realized that this would be the way to understand the workings of the biological macromolecules. There was also a theoretical biology club to which both Needham and Bernal belonged. Needham must have been a very intellectual person. He was also a famous China scholar.

Yes, he was later. I was an examiner to the University of Hong Kong and I met quite a few Chinese scientists who were actually British but in the sense that they were working in Hong Kong and not in Communist China at that time. They regarded Needham in sort of a God-like way; Needham to them was the man who really shone, he was the great star, he was the man who had shown them as Chinese what the Chinese themselves have done in science and technology. He wrote a treatise in several volumes, but I never actually saw it. But he wrote these treatises in which he laid out all the things Chinese scientists have done, and he was regarded by the Chinese as very, very special. His name was known to people who had never heard of Einstein and Pauling.

I never met him but I had correspondence with him and in a rather tragic kind of way. In the 1980s I published an article in *New Scientist* which was about the basic philosophy of extra-cellular matrix and I don't know how it was that he came to read it, but I got a letter from him, a personal letter from him. He was suffering from a disease of connective tissue, elastic fibers particularly. Of course, he was a very old man by then, and obviously rather sick with this disease, and he wanted to know if I knew of anything that could be done to help the condition of people who suffered from it, and I didn't. But I knew a Hungarian in Paris, Laszlo Robert, who is an expert on elastin and also on aging. So I suggested to Needham to turn to Robert. However, I don't know whether he then wrote to him or not. That was my only contact with him.

In 1989 I published an article in the *Biochemist*, which is the Biochemical Society's journal, not a scientific journal. My article was called "Chemical Morphology, the Shape of Things to Come" (which was a punning crib from H.G. Wells), and I quoted Joseph Needham's comments about chemical morphology or morphology and biochemistry in that article. When I sent it off to the office to edit and print it, I got a call back from one of the staff saying that Joseph Needham had just died. So there's a little footnote to my article saying that 'since this article was written I've heard of the death of Joseph Needham'. Thus, twice he came into my life unfortunately too late, I would have loved to have talked to him, but I didn't.

Although I credit Needham with putting together these ideas of chemistry and morphology in his *Nature* article, I'm doing it differently than I have ever seen it done before. I'd have to say that histology really is based on the assumptions of chemical morphology without any of the data. If we go back through the whole history of microscopy, people have been using techniques which nowadays we would obviously recognize as molecular recognition techniques. They were using stains and colored reagents to try and specifically locate certain kinds of materials in the tissue and they had no idea what these materials were. One of the well springs of my work was to go back over this histology, histo-chemical kind of approach, to try and develop from those the sort of very rough cookbook techniques; to try and get to a position where in the first place the reagent could be recognized as a chemical entity, the process of staining could be described in chemical and physical-chemical terms, and the substrate could be described in chemical and physical-chemical terms. That is the aim of chemical morphology, but that's what these people were trying to do without either knowing what the chemistry of their stains was, or the process of staining involved in terms of binding sites, nor what the nature of the polymers was in the tissue. They had none of that knowledge, but the best of them, and we could talk about people like Paul Ehrlich now, actually came up with the first real scientific idea in the whole of histo-chemistry, and that was the theory of basophilia. He recognized—because he was a good chemist, of course, for his time a superb chemist—that some of the molecules which stained certain items in the tissues, all had the same property of having a positive or negative charge, and the stuff that they stained in the tissue was always stained by members of this group of reagents.

The seven ages of a man (John Scott).[10]

1. Not so much "mewling and puking" as musing and looking (1933).
2. "..unwillingly to school" JS (top right) was a keen cricketer but his parents could not afford the white uniform. The man in the middle was a games master and the other fully clothed boy (top left) was the scorer, King's School (1944).
3. "..the lover, with a woeful ballad to his mistress' eyebrow" (1961) wedding, Lund Sweden.
4. ".. a soldier, jealous in honour... seeking the bubble reputation" Pilot officer in the RAF, Halton (1958).
5. ".. in fair round belly. With eyes severe ...Full of wise saws and modern instances" New professor of Chemical Morphology, Manchester (1980)
6. "Lean and slippered pantaloon, His youthful hose... a world too wide for his shrunk shank" Guest at the Nobel Prize ceremony, outside the Stockholm Town Hall with Prof. Ulf Lindahl (2003).
7. Fortunately NOT "sans teeth, sans eyes, sans taste, sans everything" Passport photograph, 2004.

1   2

---

[10] The quotations are from Jaque's speech in *As You Like It*, Act 2, scene 7 by William Shakespeare "all the world's a stage… etc".

3

4

5

6

7

Basophilia is the attraction for a positively charged reagent, so the things like methylene blue, azure A and so on, which are positively charged dyes, are then attracted to negatively charged substrates in the tissue (such as polysaccharides, nucleic acids and such) that are negatively charged, which, of course, he didn't know much about. But he analyzed what he knew about the phenomenon and said that these reagents have in common the fact that they are bases. They are bases and, of course, you have, conversely, an acidophils, and those were, e.g., sulfuric acid-based dyes, at that time. That was as far as Ehrlich could go, but it was a stupendous step forward, to know that the real attracting force was electrostatic. That's what he was saying but he didn't have the basic physics and chemistry, that wasn't there for him.

Then there was Gustav Mann; he wrote a book about the necessity of good chemistry. I mean, he actually wrote a paragraph that has been quoted and quoted and quoted in review after review, after review, by histochemists.   That paragraph says if you want to get anywhere, your chemistry has got to be good, both on your reagents and your substrates; that was his message. But this was written in about 1905, so he never really had the basis to work on. It wasn't until really much later that those basic ideas of Erlich and Mann and one or two others could be brought into the real world; these were visionary, very farsighted ideas at the time. It wasn't until the understanding of electrolytes and polymers in solution and the knowledge of intermolecular forces, hydrogen bonding, and all that kind of thing, that a coherent picture could be put together.

Even though those ideas have been available for well over fifty years, most people in histochemistry don't want to know them.   They couldn't care less. They are still working in the time where you took a color from a bottle and put it into a solvent, which was completely pragmatic and had no basis of science to enable you to design the package conditions which were applied to the tissue. They maltreat the tissue, extracting it without intending to, putting it through chemical fixative reactions, which completely alter the possible interactions of whatever is in the tissue, and at the end they put it through organic solvents to dehydrate it. Of course, all this collapses the molecules and the structures and so on.

If you were going to be able to correlate what you were doing, based on what other anatomists through the last 150 years had been doing, and pathologists for the last 100 years have been doing, you've got to use the same techniques. That is logic and it is an utterly closed logic. Most of the people who are working in pathology and anatomy are closing off any of those wonderful things which they can do. In my opinion histochemistry is all of biochemistry under the microscope.

We still live in a world of DNA and proteins, and the polysaccharides are in the shadow. Is that right?

Well, I think, I said several times in introductions to my lectures the following: "all the world, and that includes journalists and even politicians, think that life, in the Universe and everything is DNA. But DNA is just a sort of a catalogue of building materials and how you put those materials together to form the house or the building is the next big question". I've been hammering on this for 25 years but I begin to see it being said quite regularly and quite often by other people as well. People are talking about structural biology and in my opinion there is a redundancy here as there is no biology without structure. People are beginning to see now that the way things are put together is somehow implicit in these molecules, because you can't get a molecule to fit together with another molecule if it doesn't want to.

What DNA does is to make sure that the same basic building blocks are available from one generation to the next. The small evolutionary changes can take place on a fairly continuing basis but the functioning 3D structures, which have got to be around for a long time, in some cases, evolved from a testing situation, in which use and function was the thing that decided whether they were going to be with us in the next generation or not. DNA provides the way these things fit together, but after having provided these building blocks, how we use them, how the body, the tissue, the organization uses them is entirely up to evolution to decide. If evolution says no, then that line stops, and it is the way these things fit together that makes the entire story. It's no use producing a brilliantly designed molecule, which has no use.

What codes for the polysaccharides?

This is a question that is interesting to me very much right now, because the answer seems not to be available. What's been happening is that people have rather looked at the end product and not at how it got there, how these things occurred. For instance, there's a calculation I published in *New Scientist* because it's not the kind of calculation which affects basic science too much. Look at the polysaccharides that I'm interested in, the chondroitin sulfates, the keratan sulfates, the dermochondan sulfates and so on. You start with the simplest of the lot and that is hyaluronan; it can be of different molecular sizes but the chemical entity is unique. When you go the next step up, you get to the chondroitin sulfates and then you get an extraordinary increase in complexity, when you introduce that sulfate groups as a substituents on the polymer. In every repeating disaccharide you have two hydroxyl groups on the uronic acid that could be sulfated in principle, and two on the hexosamine ring. That gives you 2x2x2x2 possible disaccharides, i.e., 16 disaccharides. The minimum common size of chain is about 30 disaccharides long, so that gives you 16x16x16x16x16, 30 times over, so we're now talking about astronomical numbers—and that's the simplest of these polysaccharides. Then you move to the next step, that's dermochondran sulfate, the compound that I'm particularly interested in at the moment, there you've got two uronic acids instead of one; iduronic acid and glucuronic acid. So instead of every uronic acid that you had before, you now double the number of possibilities, and if you add to that the fact that each iduronic acid can occur in at least two and possibly three conformations, you can imagine how enormous the number is. The immense amount of information that you have in those molecules is amazing. Chondroitin sulfate has precisely the same amount of information in the disaccharide as the DNA molecule base pair has; so we're talking about a similar level of possible information.

Karl Meyer, who's the real pioneer in this field, said at one time, when DNA was very popular, that there was information in these molecules. But, I think he just threw the idea out. Then Lennart Roden, a Swedish fellow, said, all right, if there's information, then what's the language that this information is in? And the idea then just died. But over the last five to ten years I've got to the point where I think I know what this language is; it's a language of fitting together molecules with steric hindrance on the part of the sulfate ester group. There are basic polymer-polymer interactions which can occur but when you put a sulfate in, they are sterically hindered. If you've got a lot of sulfate groups, then you have increasing electrostatic repulsion of a kind, so the sulfate groups obviously do have a role to play. A role that one could call informational, and by informational I mean pattern recognition; one molecule recognizes another molecule because of its shape.

If we get the right shape and the sulfate isn't there to interfere with things, things happen. I predicted this as early as in the 1990s, when I pointed out that in the case of the 2-fold helical isomers of chondroitin sulfate, the 4-sulfate and the 6-sulfate, the sulfate group of the 6-sulfate is in the plane of the 2-fold helix but spread out on either side of the molecule. The sulfate groups form a kind of line of charge down either side of the molecule, like touch lines down a football pitch, and so it means that the charge is maximally diffused and the planar surfaces of the polysaccharide are not hindered by their presence because they are hooked on the periphery.In the case of chondroitin-4-sulfate the sulphate groups are right down the center line and they are axial so that there is a fairly gross interference with any face to face interaction of the polysaccharide. It can't occur because a sulfate is there so that it prevents it from happening.

I predicted that based on molecular modeling and molecular dynamics calculations. The question we asked was What's chondroitin-6-sulfate going to do when we have chondroitin-6-sulfate in the absence of salt, or in the presence of a screening amount of salt, because in physiological conditions you always have salt present— anything that doesn't contain salt is physiologically irrelevant, it might be nice physical chemistry but it's not relevant to the biology. The computer 'said' the 6-sulfate will not interact with itself to form a stable aggregate in water alone, but when you put in some salt then you've got interactions and this really was what I was looking for. But chondroitin-4-sulfate will never interact with itself, neither in water nor in the presence of salt, and that's what I was hoping would happen. Then we went to our electron microscope, took the chondroitin-6- and the chondroitin-4-sulfate in water and we applied the Paul Mould technique. With this technique you can see the molecules, the shape of them, the size of them, the thickness of them even, but you can only see them if they are forming aggregates because single molecules hardly rise above the background of noise. What we found was that chondroitin-4-sulfate was never visible, even in the presence of a salt. In the case of chondroitin-6-sulfate there was no interaction in water but there was a good interaction in ammonium acetate, which was exactly what was predicted by the computations. We published this in the *European Journal of Biochemistry* in 1992, but I think this was a bit ahead of its time.

Just recently, in 2002, Professor Levick at Imperial College and St. George's Hospital Medical School in London showed precisely what we had been saying, that chondroitin-6-sulfate in the synovial fluid of the knee joints does interact with itself and also with hyaluronan. He showed that in the knee this interaction is very important for allowing the synovial fluid to recycle; in other words, to keep the physiology of the joint in good condition. So the prediction starts with just simple modeling, goes through the computer, through electron microscopy, and finishes in the physiology laboratory at St. George's Hospital Medical School where they do the back-up experiments with viscosimetry and light scattering and then show that physiologically it's all meaningful, which is the way one hopes life would go if it were an ideal world.

This was a kind of background to the question you asked; and that is how you get these structures from DNA; DNA brings forth the protein and the protein brings forth the polysaccharide—and you've got such an immense variety of polysaccharides. I think that at the moment all we can talk about are the general principles, and as I mentioned, the sulfate is the decisive informational tag, which tells the molecules how to behave to a certain extent. But how do those structures actually get made in the cell before they're extruded into the environment, that's a question. I played about with the idea in very crude terms, because you've got to have two molecules coming together if you're going to have a high specificity, then they've got to be complementary shapes and usually that means anti-parallel. You've got waves in 2 dimensions in right angles to each other, you've got due to the shape of the backbone in plan, and you've got the glycosidic bonds in side view. Those things have all got to fit, and the interactions, the hydrogen bonds and so on, have all got to fit. But how you get those molecules out of the cell in exactly the form you want must mean that there is information somewhere; perhaps through templating, so that one molecule acts as a template for the next—but this is only speculation, there's no evidence that I know that this is how it happens.

This templating reminds me of the mad cow disease; one explanation for that is that it spreads through templating without involving nucleic acids. It's very interesting that according to your suggestion, you don't need a nucleic acid for the production of polysaccharides...

No. I think the template concept is an easy one to grab; it's the straw for the drowning man so to speak, because it's such an easy thing to invoke. I'm not against it as a concept, it's the only one in town at the moment, I can't think of an alternative. I'm always a bit cynical with any new idea such as this particular template business. Membranes seem to me to be rather a similar problem; you have a membrane because there was a membrane before that, and there was a membrane before that, and so on, and if you don't pass on the information, which was in an existing membrane you can't make another one.

Yes, but you know about crystallization. It starts if there is nucleation though it doesn't without it.

Absolutely, yes! I couldn't agree more, I agree with you completely. I don't want to talk myself out of what might be the explanation of the phenomenon we're interested in. I just feel that it is like the Darwinian evolutionary theory, it's such a simple hypothesis and it explains so much, and I am so much in love with it as a way of thinking. The template theory, of course, is not on the same global scale as the Darwinian ideas, but it connects an uncomfortably large number of events that might take place. I can't think of any other explanation at the moment, because I can't conceive of how a cell can have an array of enzymes, which are precisely and absolutely in order—after all some of these polysaccharides are of millions of Daltons molecular weight, we're talking of hundreds and hundreds of disaccharides some of which are sulfated and some of which are not—I can't conceive of a line of enzymes along which this is being passed until it comes out with the right structure at the end of it. Nucleic acids don't work like that as far as I know. The problem is to think of a decisive experiment or a decisive argument for saying, yes, this must be so. I don't know one at the moment.

So what makes the variation?

It is the sulfate position, whether they are sulfated or not. If you can get that sequence, you can perhaps then begin to spot whether there are complementary strands in the tissue. At the moment there's a very interesting situation, largely due to the work of Helmut Greiling (in Aachen, Germany). He over many years did some typically thorough German work, first class chemical purifications and characterizations of these polysaccharides, and came up with some quite surprising results that people weren't prepared to accept. One of the things he found was that these molecules were all of the same size; they all had a sharp distribution of molecular size, whereas the molecules you get from chondroitin-4-sulfate had bumpy distributions, sulfates of various ratios. He found this in the cornea of the eye and also in cirrhotic liver. This fits my ideas of a shape module extremely well because one needs to have perfect complementarity; if you have the same length you can imagine these molecules overlapping, the complementary bits overlap without waste, you don't have bits sticking out of the end or they don't have to go hunting for the bit. The fact that this thing fits into a perfect homogenous length is the first step in the argument. After that you need a sequence because we are talking about something like a nucleic acid or a protein; you've got a definite molecular size, if you also have a sequence then you have something like a protein, there is all the information you need. People have begun to make a start on the sequencing but it doesn't interest people at the moment. It's not DNA; it's not molecular biology… Agencies are not interested in funding that kind of work.

This is an interesting question. This area of research seems rather neglected.

Yes. There is a cycle in all subjects; it requires just the right kick start for the next cycle to go up.

What may that kick be? Application?

I suspect it will have to be that. People in the pharmaceutical world are playing about with these polysaccharides in a totally random kind of way and most of the work is not coming out of the West, it's not coming out of what you would call the high-tech countries, places like Britain, the U.S., and Sweden and Germany, where they have rather tough rules about testing protocols. It tends to be coming from the Far East, where they are extracting sulfated polysaccharides from sea cucumbers and things like that, and injecting them into inflamed joints, just to give an example. This under normal circumstances in the West you wouldn't stand a chance of doing. And I suspect that they are causing more pain and stress than there was to begin with, but this is one of the ways that in the past drugs came into use. We don't do that kind of experimentation on human beings anymore.

Do you follow the development of the field? Where is it going?

As a field I'm just restricting myself now to the polysaccharides of connective tissues, which is only one half of my real interest. I started life as a physiologist and I'm interested in function, and function of connective tissues is absolutely bound with structure, which is always the case but it's very clearly so with connective tissues. But concerning the polysaccharide field, that's a very typical thing, like alchemy. For an analogy, why do people climb Mount Everest? Because it's there. Why did people start working on these awful slimy messes? Because they were there. One of the German scientists in the middle of the 19th century said "tierchemie ist schmierchemie" I think that to most organic chemists and inorganic chemists this was the absolute truth. You have these awful slimy mixtures out of tissues, and what could you do with them? That phase lasted for the better part of about a hundred years until the knowledge of polymers and real interactions between molecules and supra-molecular structure began to emerge.

Then they began to have their place in the hierarchy of things. Now we're beginning to get out of that situation because now we can purify it and find out what it is. Now we know what it is, what it is doing, and where it is, and that is the situation we're just beginning to enter now. In that case you can no longer deal only with polysaccharides, you've got to start talking about other things as well. This has always been difficult for scientists and especially for the young scientists to comprehend. What they start working on in their Ph.D., they can't continue working on forever, they've got to do something a bit more broad, the scope's got to be greater.

Earlier in my life, I set up several clubs, one of them was called the Mucopolysaccharide Club and the people in that club didn't want to know anything besides mucopolysaccharides. Then I tried to persuade them to join company with another club, called the Collagen Club, which was about proteins like collagen—these are two types of molecules that you have got in extracellular matrices. But they said: "Collagen? We don't want to know about collagen." And similarly, the collagen people always talked about collagen but with no reference to the proteoglycans; it's not their business, they're not being paid for that, that's the way they came into the field and they were stopping there. Innately conservative, it's a second class mindset to take that kind of view. Of course, there's nothing to stop somebody from staying as a mucopolysaccharide chemist if all they're interested in is mucopolysaccharide chemistry. But if they're interested in it, they can't ignore the fact that you never find mucopolysaccharides in a sort of vein in the ground that you can take out with a pick axe and put pure on a wagon, it's got some relevance to something else, it only exists in relation to something else, it's function can only be a function with that other thing and this is where we're going to now. People are finally beginning to recognize, that yes, interactions between collagen and proteoglycans are the very stuff of our structure and our shape. It has been about 50 years since that idea was first floated and it's only now that people are beginning to pick it up and run with it. And where is it going in the future? Well, if I was to be starting now as a young student, I would want to go into a top class NMR imaging laboratory. I would want to be looking at more precise localization of molecules by NMR. I would go into a department where they put together a kind of multi-discipline, based on NMR and electron microscopy with computers in the background, because that gives you the way in from the textbook chemistry all the way through to almost a clinical function.

Let us talk a little about your background; how you started, etc.

I was born in 1930 in a town called Macclesfield, which is just to the south of Manchester. My family was rather poor; my father was trained as a lathe operator but he had no work because of the Great Depression and was finally employed only digging holes, making a water reservoir for the town where I lived. My parents were very good and worked hard for myself and my two sisters. We went to school in the ordinary Anglican Church schools. The third school I went to was good, and I was very lucky because I met two teachers who took an interest in me personally. One was a man; he was the very first person who showed us a scientific experiment that even now I find surprising, because in such an environment, a church school in a small country town with huge classes, to try to interest them in science at the age between 10 and 12 at that time was a courageous and very farsighted thing. He did a very simple experiment with a flask, which he put some water in and he boiled this water in the flask and he put a stopper on when it took it off the flame; then he took it to the cold water tap and he put it under it and the water inside then boiled. This was magic! He then just said that water boils where there is no air, and I will always remember that. First law I ever came across.

The other teacher was a woman who was very tough. She completely disregarded 49 out of the 50 students and she concentrated on me. She was very open about it, she told them all, if I find anybody who's worth teaching, I'll give them everything and most of you will just go into the mill and will be no use to anybody in the educational sense, and I'm not going to bother you. You stay quiet, you sit still; if you open your mouth I will beat you, and she did that. She was as tough as a Prussian sergeant but she spent time with me and made sure I knew a little bit about other languages, a little bit of mathematics and she pushed me towards a better school, which my parents never would have considered because they simply didn't have the money. She told me, I must try to get a scholarship for the local public school in Macclesfield, which was rather superb. I managed to get there and that's where I was able to follow up what this teacher had started doing, and there I found all these marvelous experiments just waiting to be done.

Then, Mr. Skellam the biology master, Mr. Rawsthorn the chemistry master, Mr. Underwood the physics master, these were the people who really started me off and to whom I owe all the foundations that I had in science. The chemistry teacher, Mr. Rawsthorn, was the man above all who had the power of a magician. He could make a class of 50 or 60 mixed arts and science students take an interest in chemistry. We still don't know how to do it, but this man knew how to do it. That's the background and from that school it was not difficult to go to a university. Many of the students went to Oxford or Cambridge. I didn't have the money to go to a university a distance from my home, Manchester was the nearest great university and I went there. I stayed at home for my first year and travelled every day by train from Macclesfield to Manchester and back in the evening.

I was lucky because the University of Manchester was at one of it's great peaks those days. We had a professor of physics, P. M. S. Blackett, who received the Nobel Prize in Physics in 1948 for his work on cosmic radiations. Tom Kilburn had just built and run his first stored program computer in 1948, which was my first year. We had Alan Turing who was in the mathematics and physics department; at the Chemistry Department Michael Polanyi was Professor of Physical Chemistry; Sir Alexander Todd had been professor there and just left for Cambridge, and the visiting professors included Linus Pauling, Mel Calvin and Paul Flory, all of whom, of course, were Nobel Prize winners. I heard Mel Calvin talk about his photosynthesis work, which was the very first time I had ever heard of the way radioisotopes could be used to track compounds. The great fortune was to be in contact with the physical chemists, as I said that time people like Linus Pauling were habitual visitors to the department. A man named Ernest Warhurst was very close to Linus Pauling, and also to Michael Dewar. Warhurst used to come in fresh from a discussion with Pauling, next door practically, and striding up and down along this long bench and all these ideas were coming out. We had Polanyi in the background with his work on chemical bonding; it was a wonderful background but what I find fascinating now is that nobody seemed to know that this was important, it was just thought routine.

So you just took all of this for granted.

I just took it for granted.   There was no biochemistry course at Manchester at that time; on the other hand, the organic chemists were very strongly into natural products chemistry so they knew the importance of the chemistry of life, so to speak. But there was no organized teaching of biochemistry, so what they did was they built a joint degree with the physiology department in the medical school. The physiology school was superb. They had just discovered a polypeptide hormone, pancreozymin, that time, which was the very first polypeptide hormone for 50 years, only one polypeptide hormone had been known before that and that was secretin. Interestingly, the two schools never ever talked to each other, so the result was that we got the entire chemistry course and we got the entire physiology course. We learned really a lot, we were thrown in at the deep end, and there was never any attempt to water down or dilute or make it easy for us. But that's how we learned.

Summary

Investigations on Hyaluronan

by John E. Scott

Investigations were in several fields:

1. quantitative preparation, purification and analysis of hyaluronan (HA) from tissues etc, based on my discovery of the precipitation reaction of quaternary ammonium salts with polyanions.
2. the elucidation of secondary and tertiary structures of HA in solution using chemical reactions, NMR, electron microscopy and modelling using Courtauld space-filling models and computer simulations.
3. the physiological relevance of these structures in sequestering biological activities and in strepococcal coats. The effect of chemical modifications, free radicals and other physico-chemical agents on the persistence of these structures
4. measurements of elasticity (Young's modulus) of single HA molecules using atomic force spectroscopy.

1. Preparative techniques [1-4][11]

My observation that the precipitation of polyanions with long-chain ammonium salts was quantitative and technically simple at submicrogm to industrial scales led to many new processes and methods in the laboratory and in commerce. It was possible for the first time to obtain pure HA, among many biopolyanions, quickly from a great variety of tissues, usng the critical electrolyte concentration (CEC) methods

---

[11] Numbers in brackets refer to separate Bibliography following this Summary.

which I worked out, coupled with a high temperature papain digestion that released the polyanions from the tissue into solution.

I used it in identifying HA in Heberden's nodes and in its first large scale 'commercial' test. Dennis Lowther, a colleague working in St Mary's Hospital, London, where I was based, identified HA as the intensely viscous component of a mesothelioma fluid from the abdomen of a patient. About two litres a week containing 0.4% HA was being aspirated. Dennis and I thought it worth while trying to purify and sell the HA, which was a very expensive material at that time, on behalf of the patient. I used my papain-cetylpyridinium chloride method with complete success. The patient was out of work and financially embarrassed, resulting in the dispersal of his family who had no place to live. We provided him with a modest income which allowed him to bring them together until he died. Uniquely, he made a living from his tumour. We had to keep the whole thing secret because the firm we dealt with would not have paid good prices if they had known of the scale on which we could work. The market was small and the price was high because the supply was small. Miss Windsor, the Almoner at St. Mary's looked after the financial side. I lost a few night's sleep going to the laboratory in the middle of the night to top up the freeze-dryer with dry ice.

This source of HA was probably the most important in the world for some years. Apart from the commercial side I supplied many scientists with HA for free. My process is still being used globally after almost 50 years

I worked out equations governing the fractionation of polyanions according to their molecular weight using CEC/cetylpyridinium techniques and in collaboration with TC Laurent, proved their validity in the fractionation of HA, *inter alia*.

2. Secondary and tertiary structures in HA solutions [5-20]

The ability to analyse for HA in small tissue samples led to the wish to know where HA and other glycosaminouronans were on a much smaller scale, using light microscopy. I hoped that an established reaction sequence using periodate to oxidise the C2-C3 glycol in the uronate residue followed a by Schiff reaction to demonstrate the aldehydes thus produced might provide a rational basis for this. It was known that the periodate reaction went very slowly and I thought this might be because the strong electrostatic field of the polyanion repelled the periodate anion so that oxidation would be hindered. By adding screening concentrations of electrolyte this was shown to be true, but even so the reaction was still slow, except in the case of dermatan sulphate, in which L-iduronate was oxidised rapidly. I hypothesised that the conformation of glucuronate in HA etc caused the inhibition, but proof could not be obtained at that time (1968) [5-7].

A decade later methylated derivatives of glucuronate became available and I used these to show that glucuronate itself was oxidised rapidly, thus proving that it was the polymer environment which caused the inhibition. Comparison of second order rate constants of periodate oxidation of a range of polymers led to the suggestion that intramolecular H-bnds would prevent access of periodate to the glycol, specifically in the case of HA and chondroitin sulphates [8]. In collaboration with EDT Atkins who had the best X-ray structures from the solid state, it was found that these H-bonds could indeed exist and 4 possible inter-residue H-bonds were identified in HA [10].

The implications for the physiological functions of HA of such a tightly organised secondary structure called for proof that it existed in solution. NMR was reaching the stage at which this question could be tackled and initially in collaboration with B. Casu of Milan who had pioneered the approach Dr Frank Heatley and I assigned the spectrum of the monomers and disaccharide building blocks of HA etc in deuterated dimethyl sulphoxide solution [9, 11, 12]. In this non-protic solvent all hydrogen resonances were visible in principle and it was clear that the original pair of H-bonds hypothesised from the periodate work did exist. With the help of Bill Hull in Karlruhe who had the most advanced NMR machine at the time, clear proof of the others emerged [13] (see Figure 1). Working with H2O/solvent mixtures we showed that a water molecule was an intermediary in the H-bond from the acetamido NH which permitted an adjustment to the structure that allowed for an otherwise anomalous coupling constant [14].

When this structure was modelled using Courtauld space-filling atoms I saw a large hydrophobic patch down the centreline of HA etc, on alternate sides of the molecule, equivalent in size to a C12 fatty acid chain. HA was thus amphipathic and a number of important consequences in physiology and pharmacology were apparent.It explained membrane binding, association of hydrophobic ligands and intermolecular association, as soon became clear [15].

Self-aggregation into meshworks was proven by rotary shadowing of HA deposited on a support and then examined by electron microscopy [16].

A chemically detailed scheme of the way in which HA self-aggregated was based on ^{13}C NMR, which indicated that acetamido NH participated in intermolecular H-bonds. The H-acceptor was the carboxylate group and modification of this by methylation broke up the tertiary structure [20]. Deprotonation of the acetamido group at high pH also broke up the tertiary structure as shown by NMR, thereby explaining a long-standing mystery of how HA could be instantaneously (and reversibly) 'denatured' by exposure to alkaline solutions [23]. Warming broke the intermolecular bonds as shown by ^{13}C NMR, with concomitant falls in the bulk viscosity [23]. Stability was contributed by hydrophobic bonding between molecules. Modelling showed that the tertiary structure was a β-sheet, unique among polysaccharides although common in proteins [20] (see Figure 1).

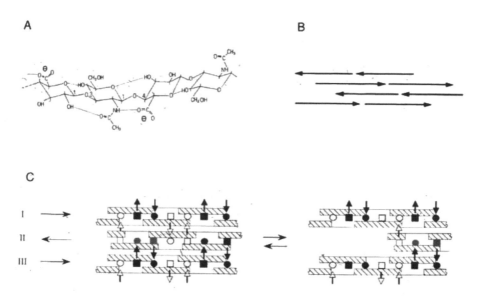

Figure 1. A. Secondary structure of HA as shown by NMR and X-ray crystallography. Dotted lines are H-bonds. Some of these bonds are completed by water and there is a single water molecule interpolated between the acetamido and carboxylate groups in aqueous solution [13,14].
B. Antiparallel alignment of HA molecules providing the basis for meshwork formations of great variety [16], held together as shown in **C** below.
C. Scheme showing interactions between antiparallel HA molecules I, II and III. Cross-hatched blocks are hydrophobic patches positioned to participate in hydrophobic bonding between neighbouring molecules. Arrows represent H-bonds, in front of and behind the plane of the picture. Squares and circles represent acetamido and carboxylate groups respectively [20]. This structure is a β-sheet, the first of its kind to be seen in polysaccharides.
The right hand panel illustrates the breakage of hydrogen- and hydrophobic bonds under tensile stress, reversibly as indicated by the reaction arrows. This endows the meshwork with elasticity [22].

3. Functional and Physiological Relevance of the tertiary structures

Breakdown of the tertiary structure frees the interacting groups to react with other species. A general hypothesis was proposed, that formation of the tertiary structure   hindered the display of activities by the sequestered groups and this phenomenon was suggested to be behind the deactivation of erythrocyte lysis by denatured HA produced by heating and very rapid cooling. It provides an explanation for the difference in behaviour of macromolecular HA compared with HA fragments, as in angiogenesis [23].

HA meshworks were more extensive and complex when formed by HA of high mol. mass rather than with degraded HA. This finding correlated with the extent of protection offered to HA-coated cells subject to free radical attack. High mol. mass HA prevented close approach to the cells of the enzymes forming the OH free radicals more efficiently than low mol. mass HA, presumably by the more coherent meshworks of the former, although both HAs were attacked by OH radicals at the same rate, in terms of second order rate constants [18].

HA meshworks were shown by electron histochemistry to be produced by streptococci as their structured environment, a primitive version of an extracellular matrix. HA in the micrographs appeared to form parallel aggregates of the kind predicted from the 13C NMR data [24].

Physiological significance was demonstrated when *rheo*NMR (in which spectra are obtained while the polymer is under shear stress in a modified Couette viscometer) showed that the tertiary structure disaggregated reversibly under sufficient shearing load [22]. This situation was comparable in terms of shear stress to that experienced by HA in synovial fluid during locomotion, thereby pointing to key molecular mechanisms in joint lubrication.

4. Elasticity in single molecules of HA and in bulk solution

The *rheo*NMR experiments demonstrated that the breakdown of tertiary structures was completely elastic, providing evidence for the hypothesis that such disaggregrations involving self-aggregating glycosaminoglycans could impart reversible deformability to the extracellular matrices of connective tissues (see Figure 1). This was the basis of a sliding filament model.

I realised that there was a need for other smaller scale and less energy-intensive modes within the glycans. I suggested a new possibility, involving changes in conformation in L-iduronate in dermochondan sulphate, which modelling suggested was possible, thereby providing an elastic link in the glycan chain. Direct measurements on single polymer molecules by atomic force spectroscopy proved that this was so. I predicted that glucuronate would not offer this possibility and direct measurements on single molecules of HA and chondroitan sulphate validated this prediction [25].

Nevertheless there is intrinsic although limited elasticity within chemical bonds and we measured the Young's moduli of HA and chondroitan sulphate for the first time, on single molecules [25]. Not for the first time HA provided the prototype of behaviour throughout the whole group of 1e,3e,1,e,4e, glycosaminoglycans, via which to compare and predict patterns of physical, chemical and physiological properties.

Bibliography*

Hyaluronan-Related Publications

1. Scott, J. E. (1955). The reaction of long-chain quaternary ammonium compounds with acidic poysaccharides. Chem and Industry, 16.

2. Scott, J. E. (1960). Aliphatic ammonium salts in the assay of acidic polysaccharides from tissues. In *Methods in Biochemical Analysis* (Ed. Glick, D.), 146-198.

3. Laurent, T. C., and Scott, J. E. (1964). Molecular weight fractionation of polyanions by cetylpyridinium chloride in salt solutions. Nature 202 (4933), 661-664.

4. Begg, M., and Scott, J. E. (1966). Hyaluronic acid and protein in simple ganglia and Heberden's nodes. Ann Rheum Dis 25, 145-148.

5. Scott, J. E., and Harbinson, R. J. (1968). Periodate oxidation of acid polysaccharides inhibition by the electrostatic field of the substrate. Histochemie 14 (3), 215-220.

6. Scott, J. (1968). Periodate oxidation, pK_a and conformation of hexuronic acids in polyuronides and mucopolysaccharides. Biochim Biophys Acta 170, 471-473.

7. Scott, J. E., and Harbinson, R. J. (1969). Periodate oxidation of acid mucopolysaccharides. 11. Rates of oxidation of uronica acids in polyuronides and acid mucopolysacchardies. Hisatochemie 19, 155-161.

8. Scott, J. E., and Tigwell, M. J. (1978). Periodate oxidation and the shapes of glycosaminoglycuronans in solution. Biochem J 173, 103-114.

9. Heatley, F., Scott, J. E., and Casu, B. (1979). [1]H-N.M.R. spectra of glycosaminoglycan monomers and dimers in solution in methyl sulphoxide and water. Carbohydrate Res 72, 13-23.

10. Atkins, E. D. T., Meader, D., and Scott, J. E. (1980). Model for hyaluronic acid incorporating four intramolecular hydrogen bonds. Int J Biol Macromol 2, 318-319.

11. Scott, J. E., Heatley, F., Moorcroft, D., and Olavesen, A. H. (1981). Secondary Structures of Hyaluronate and Chondroitin Sulphates. Biochem J 199, 829-832.

12. Heatley, F., Scott, J. E., Jeanloz, R. W., and Walker-Nasir, E. (1982). Secondary structure in glycosaminoglycans: N.M.R. spectra in dimethyl sulphoxide of disaccharides related to hyaluronic acid and chondroitin sulphate. Carbohydrate Res 99, 1-11.

---

* Provided by the interviewee.

13. Scott, J. E., Heatley, F., and Hull, W. E. (1984). Secondary structure of hyaluronate in solution: A H-n.m.r. investigation at 300 and 500 MHz in [2H6] dimethyl sulfoxide solution. Biochem J 220, 197-205.

14. Heatley, F., and Scott, J. E. (1988). A water molecule participates in the secondary structure of hyaluronan. Biochem J 254, 489-493.

15. Scott, J. E. (1989). Secondary structures in hyaluronan solutions: chemical and biological implications. In *The biology of hyaluronan CIBA Foundation Symposium* (Eds. Evered, D. , and Whelan, J.), John Wiley & Sons Ltd., Chichester, UK, 6-20.

16. Scott, J. E., Cummings, C., Brass, A., and Chen, Y. (1991). Secondary and tertiary structures of hyaluronan in aqueous solution, investigated by rotary shadowing-electron microscopy and computer simulation. Biochem J 274, 699-705.

17. Mikelsaar, R.-H., and Scott, J. E. (1994). Molecular modelling of secondary and tertiary structures of hyaluronan, compared with electron microscopy and NMR data. Possible sheets and tubular structures in aqueous solution. Glycoconjugate J 11, 65-71.

18. Presti, D., and Scott, J. E. (1994). Hyaluronan-mediated protective effect against cell damage caused by enzymatically produced hydroxyl (OH) radicals is dependent on hyaluronan molecular mass. Cell Biochem Function 12, 281-288.

19. Scott, J. E. (1998). Chemical morphology of hyaluronan. In *The Chemistry, Biology and Medical Applications of Hyaluronan and its Derivatives* (Ed. Laurent, T. C.), Portland Press Ltd., London, 7-15.

20. Scott, J. E., and Heatley, F. (1999). Hyaluronan forms specific stable tertiary structures in aqueous solution: A ^{13}C NMR study. Proc Natl Acad Sci USA 96 (9), 4850-4855.

21. Scott, J. E. (2000). Secondary and tertiary structures in solutions of hyaluronan and related "shape module" anionic glycosaminoglycans. In *New Frontiers in Medical Sciences: Redefining Hyaluronan (Proceedings of the Symposium held in Padua, Italy, 17-19 June 1999)* (Eds. Abatangelo, G. , and Weigel, P.), Elsevier, Amsterdam, The Netherlands, 11-18.

22. Fischer, E., Callaghan, P. T., Heatley, F., and Scott, J. E. (2002). Shear flow affects secondary and tertiary structures in hyaluronan solution as shown by *rheo*-NMR. J Molecular Structures 602-603, 303-311.

23. Scott, J. E., and Heatley, F. (2002). Biological properties of hyaluronan in aqueous solution are controlled and sequestered by reversible tertiary structures, defined by NMR spectroscopy. Biomacromolecules 3, 547-553.

24. Scott, J. E., Thomlinson, A. M., and Prehm, P. (2003). Supramolecular organization in streptococcal pericellular capsules is based on hyaluronan tertiary structures. Exp Cell Res 285 (1), 1-8.

25. Haverkamp, R. G., Williams, M. A., and Scott, J. E. (2005). Stretching single molecules of connective tissue glycans to characterize their shape-maintaining elasticity. Biomacromolecules 6 (3), 1816-1818.

Robert Stern, 2003 (photograph by I. Hargittai)

Robert Stern

Robert Stern (b. 1936, Bad Kreuznach, Germany) received his B.A. in Biochemical Sciences at Harvard College, Cambridge, MA (1957) and his MD at the University of Washington, Seattle (1962). He obtained residency training in Pathology at the National Cancer Institute of NIH in Bethesda, Maryland, and was a research scientist there until 1976. Since 1977 he has been a member of the Pathology Department of the University of California at San Francisco, for the past 21 years as Professor. He is a board-certified Anatomic Pathologist. He has received numerous awards and fellowships and is member of many scientific societies,and is a founding member of the International Society for Hyaluronan Sciences (ISHAS).

Interview*

Something about your family background...

I was born in Germany in 1936, to a Jewish family in the Rhineland.
We left Germany in 1938, just in time, and came to the U.S. We left
with absolutely nothing, the three of us, my parents and myself. We
took the train to Paris, on to Le Havre, and by the ship "Manhattan"
we arrived in New York in April 1938, taking another train across the
country to Seattle, Washington. I grew up in Seattle. My father had
been a butcher, and continued in the same trade. Needless to say we
were very poor. We came with no language, no real family, no friends,
like all immigrants, they did what they needed to do in order to survive.

Your parents had some family in the U.S.?

Yes, but they were very distant relatives, in Seattle. My parents had to
go there because our relatives were responsible for them. My father
worked for the Armour Packing Company. He stripped hides from
cattle, earning 25 cents per hide.

I learned English before my parents did. So that strange
situation existed in which the child functions as the parent, because
they had a harder time with the language. My father and mother had
gone to school only until they were 11 or 12 years old, which was also
very typical in a farming community at that time in Germany.

I went to high school in Seattle and then to study at Harvard
College. There we actually had an opportunity to do research, as
undergraduates. I worked in a laboratory in order to write an honors
thesis. So I got started there in Paul Zamecnik's and Robert Loftfield's
laboratories. They had discovered soluble RNA, which later became

---

* This interview was recorded during the second meeting "Conversations on
Hyaluronan" in St. Tropez, June 2003.

A family photo from just before the time when Robert Stern and his parents left Germany in the spring of 1938. Robert sits on his grandmother's lap. His mother stands directly behind him, and his father is the third from the right. His grandfather is second from the left. Besides Robert and his parents, all the others were killed in Theresienstadt or in Auschwitz. Robert Stern counts the Holocaust as the defining event of his life.

tRNA. Mahlon Hoagland was a student at Harvard Medical School who took time off because of illness, probably TB, and discovered soluble RNA, a low molecular weight RNA important for *in vitro* protein synthesis.

That was an area of biology that was just beginning to evolve. It was at the Huntington Laboratories of the Massachusetts General Hospital where I did my research. Because it was a medical school and a hospital, they felt they had an obligation to work with animal cells. In fact, Joseph Aub, a very distinguished cancer physician, today we would call an Oncologist, made only this one request of his research team, that they work on animal cells. Bacteria don't get cancer. We worked with Ehrlich ascites tumor cells. We prepared ribosomes, polysomes, and soluble RNA from that source.

Scientists elsewhere then started working in the *E. coli* system, in which the rate of protein synthesis is much much slower. But because we were obliged to work on an animal system, Zamecnik, Hoagland, and that group missed a great opportunity, to probably break the genetic code. If they had done what they really felt they ought to do, they would have broken the genetic code. In fact they taught the NIH team headed by Marshall Nirenberg how to prepare polysomes. But because Zamecnik's group was obliged to work on animal systems, they had to bypass the opportunity completely. And that happened in the early 1960s. The polyU-dependent protein synthesizing system, which generated poly-phenylalanine, was the experiment that led Marshall Nirenberg to the deciphering of the genetic code. But those kinds of things were already being thought about a few years earlier, several years before, at the Huntington Laboratories of MGH. So this one concession to Joseph Aub, needing to pay homage to some absurd preconceived dogma, prevented these people from doing the key experiments that no doubt would have gotten them the Nobel Prize.

I think what this indicates is that if you've got able people, let them do what they feel they have to do, without preconceived notions about what ought to be done. What this does is smother the creative process. You lose out when pure free unbridled unfettered thought is stifled and must instead serve and ratify some preconceived dogma. Free thought is the reason that the institution of the University has flourished in Western civilization, and has lead to so many break-throughs. It is one of the reasons for the triumph of the West.

One of the definitions of a good education is the exposure to greatness. And that is what makes Harvard such a fine institution. At the Huntington Labs and at the Mass. General at that time, there was Fritz Lipmann up one floor, also a German Jewish refugee, Jerome Gross, Herman Kalckar, and on the Harvard campus, in Biochemistry, John Edsall, Konrad Bloch, George Wald, George Kistiakowski; an array of talent that staggers the imagination, and I had lectures from each one of these men. I was incredibly privileged, which I can appreciate today much more than I could then. In fact, I had no concept of what an astounding environment this was.

Don't you think that you should have stayed at Harvard?

I applied, but I wasn't accepted to the medical school. I would have stayed there, had I been admitted. It would have been quite expensive for my parents, but somehow, it could have been managed. So I went to medical school back in Seattle, at the University of Washington, which was a great experience. It was a relatively new school with a brilliant faculty, a very inspirational faculty. There I started doing serious research. I had been admitted to Albert Einstein in New York as well, at that time also a new medical school; but going home seemed a reasonable thing to do, so I ended up at the University of Washington.

It was not as expensive as Harvard?

No. The University of Washington is a state institution. At that time I was also toying with the idea of getting a Ph.D. However, I think an MD was the wiser choice. I think Medicine is the best background in general biology today. It's unfortunate that for most students, in getting their Ph.D.s, they get trained so narrowly that there's a danger that they're going to become outmoded in no time. For instance, the people that got trained to become gene jockeys, everything that they learned to do, you can now perform by buying a kit. And unless they are brilliant, they have a hard time getting key academic jobs. But in getting a broad education as you do in Medicine, you know what the big questions are. You may not be able to answer them, but you can hire people who know how to answer them. In Medicine you get a broad perspective on problems in biology. So I would recommend that people who are interested in biology get a medical background. It's one of the best ways of functioning properly in biology, in being able to ask the big questions.

There are other opinions that medical doctors don't learn how to think.

I disagree. If you're smart enough, you'll figure it out. The problem is you need very thorough training as well, I'd say at least 4–5 years of post-doctoral experience to be competitive today. When I started you didn't really need that. You could get away with doing what you wanted to do. I don't think I could have survived in the current market.

So, you got your MD at the University of Washington?

Yes. I started doing research in the laboratory of Ed Krebs and Edmund Fisher [both future Nobel laureates], working on phosphorylase and glycogen metabolism.

Tell us more about that.

At the University of Washington, in Seattle, Hans Neurath was the chairman of the Biochemistry Department. He was Viennese, and also an immigrant. Hans Neurath was the founder of the journal *Biochemistry*, a very good scientist and a very good administrator. And he knew how to hire very good people. That was when the medical school was being started and the array of talent at the University of Washington at that time was really impressive. He hired Fisher and Krebs and other people such as, Donald Hannahan who made his name in lipid biochemistry, and Frank Huennekens, in carbon metabolism. He knew how to choose good people.

My research, as a medical student, was mostly done during summers. So I got into biochemistry and I think most research today is some aspect of biochemistry although the molecular biologists won't admit it. But they all use biochemical techniques essentially.

Where are you now?

I'm at the University of California at San Francisco, in the Department of Pathology. I got training in pathology at the National Cancer Institute of the NIH. Here is another statement grandiose, and only partly correct. I think there is a need for specialty training in medicine to really travel first class. You have to be recognized as a Pathologist or as an Internist or as an Endocrinologist, in order to command respect in the field.

You have to make your name somewhere...

Exactly. And you need to have credibility in the field and people need to come to you for opinions that matter. So I got training in Anatomic Pathology. Today, I am a board-certified pathologist and practice diagnostic pathology, participating in the teaching and diagnostic services of the University, and also have a research laboratory. And what's nice is that they all balance each other. What I do in research has repercussions in diagnostic techniques in immuno-histochemistry and in service Pathology. I can give you one example. I have always had an interest in cancer, particularly breast cancer. Very recently it's been observed that there are stem cells in malignancies, and progression occurs because of these stem cells. Probably all cancers have stem cells, though this has not been shown unequivocally. The lesion in malignancy probably arises from cancer stem cells. If you look at cancer tissue under the microscope, most of the cells that you see have such pleomorphism and bizarre chromatin configurations that such cells could not possibly divide, and are probably on their way out.

What's been shown with stem cells in cancer biology is that if you disperse these cells and put them through flow cytometry, a very minor fraction, not more than 0.1 % are actual cancer stem cells, 99% are not. If you take 100 stem cells, and you place them into an immuno-deficient mouse, a skid mouse, you get a tumor. If you take tens of thousands of the other cells, you get nothing. This means that the entire paradigm of how you treat a malignancy has changed. Your chemotherapy and radiation have to be directed at the stem cells, not at the mass of the tumor. Even though the mass of the tumor will shrink, there will be a recurrence unless the cancer stem cells are destroyed.

But how can you differentiate?

They have specific receptors and other surface markers, but we still don't know the identity of most of those. But by flow cytometry you can separate cells on the basis of receptor binding. Ironically among the receptors is CD44, which is a receptor for hyaluronan. So we've come all the way around. We couldn't have predicted that.

But to be successful, you have to maintain a focus in one single area. If you try to become an expert in two things, you're going to miss out on both. I tell my students to focus on a single grain of sand, and very very slowly increase that focus. The biological systems are so incredibly clever. Science and biology are so subtle and so smart that you've got to focus on one thing. So I have had an interest for the past 10 years in hyaluronan and have worked very hard. It has been a very productive period, but hyaluronan really hasn't made the mainstream yet. Even now, it is taking time to be recognized. We feel we're making progress, and it may start to become recognized as an important area.

In biology?

Yes, hyaluronan is about to take off in importance, we hope.

Your research made the mainstream in hyaluronan research and hyaluronan research is still waiting to make the mainstream in biology.

It may be going to come. It's a prediction. It's got some of the attributes of a growth industry. That area if science has gotten a very elegant name now, "glycobiology." The techniques were not there when we started. We had to invent the techniques to pursue it. For example, we had to develop the enzyme assays in order to follow the enzyme activities.

This is following in the footsteps of those working in carbohydrate chemistry. This reached its zenith perhaps in the 1950s and 1960s in places like the Cori laboratory. Ed Krebs, who was my mentor at the University of Washington, started there. So did Arthur Kornberg. He also started in the Cori laboratory. In fact many people did. And they were very committed to one small area, which was not fashionable at the time, and much of carbohydrate chemistry came from that laboratory and of course from Germany, from Meyerhof, Krebs, Embden, and Warburg. This coalesced and came to some kind of fruition, and then slowed down and virtually stopped. There was a hiatus of maybe 20 or 30 years and now glycobiology is picking up the kernels from that carbohydrate research and is running with it. It's virtually an untouched field. The assays now are all micro-assays, Elisa plates if you have antibodies, or binding proteins. In fact, you couldn't use the assays that were developed by the Coris. Those were based on spectrophotometry, on changes in absorption at a particular wavelength of light.

Those are the classical techniques. You probably remember the old fashioned colorimeters. But you needed 2ml or 5ml of a solution for colorimeters, for enzyme incubation mixtures, for doing column fractionation work. You can't afford or you can't obtain such volumes of materials now. You need microliters. So now we have techniques that let you look at a microliter to detect activity or even a dilution of a microliter. That's the way it has to go because you're dealing with small amounts of material when you're dealing with cultured cells. You don't have whole tissues to grind, as you used then. So it's a matter of turning to micro-techniques, and those are now available.

The area of hyaluronan that I focused on was one that was developed because of a lecture I attended that Bryan Toole gave at the NIH. After medical school I went to the NIH and worked there for two years, in the laboratory of Alan Mehler. He was also an enzymologist, and a product of the Cori laboratory at Washington University in St. Louis.

Then I went to Israel for two years as a post doc, at the Weizmann Institute in Rehovoth, in Uri Littauer's laboratory. There I learned how to deal with RNA. After this time, I came back to the NIH and continued research. Ten years later I got my 10-year pin. I looked at it, and said to myself, if I stay here one more day I'm going to be waiting to retire, because you can retire after 20 years with the government. And to sit in a place because you're waiting to retire feels like a living death. I knew I had to get out of there. So I applied for an academic position at various places, Seattle, San Francisco, Los

Angeles, because I wanted to go back to the west coast where I had family and parents. And finally I ended up in San Francisco.

What was the motivation for you becoming a scientist?

Curiosity, just insatiable curiosity. And growing up in a household where people worked very hard and didn't have time for their children, I had to find ways of amusing and entertaining myself. One of my weaknesses, or perhaps it is a strength, is that I abhor boredom. I can't tolerate being bored. I constantly need to have some kind of stimulation. And I've learned how to stimulate myself. I read voraciously and when I was young, I read adventure books because it was very exciting, authors such as Richard Halliburton. He wrote *The Book of Marvels*, my favorite book as a young child. He was a person who explored various parts of the world, and traveled in very exotic places. I quickly figured out how to have a career in which every day is different. That would be science. Even as a physician after you've seen 20 or 30 sore throats there's a limited number of things you can see. But in science every day is different.

How did you get started in the hyaluronan field?

As I mentioned before, I went to a seminar at NIH by Bryan Toole and that was the turning point for me. He is one of the founders of today's hyaluronan biology. I remember a slide that he showed at that time. There is, in early embryology, a lot of hyaluronan, when cells are undifferentiated, when they have to proliferate and to move about. They are called pluripotential cells, which is another way of saying stem cells in a way, but that's not entirely accurate. They then have to commit to a program of differentiation. In order to do that, they have to lose their hyaluronan coat. The hyaluronan instructs the cell to remain pluripotent, to remain undifferentiated. Once the hyaluronan is removed or degraded, cells become committed to that program of differentiation. It's an irreversible step. But to do that, you have to get rid of the hyaluronan. The way to remove the hyaluronan is with an enzyme called hyaluronidase. It specifically degrades the hyaluronan. I thought to myself, there has to be something, some intelligence, some signal, that controls the transition from one to the other. Bryan Toole's lecture at that time, for me, was a scientific epiphany.

The somatic hyaluronidases had not been purified. Nobody knew anything about them, only that they existed. They were shown to exist during that golden age of carbohydrate chemistry. You could show that there was something in circulation in the blood stream that degraded hyaluronan but nobody could purify it. Remember, I come from a background of enzymology from the Fisher and Krebs lab, and I knew what proteins were. I knew what enzymes were. Ed Krebs comes from the Cori laboratory so there is a real tradition. I consider myself a 3rd or 4th generation. I knew what a column was, I knew that you put the protein on the top and it comes out the bottom.

There were many clinicians at the time who didn't know that, which is the working end of how to do protein fractionation, to look for protein profiles and for enzymatic activity and what specific activity meant. You constantly want to increase specific activity. You want lots of activity and very little protein until eventually you get one band of protein on a gel. At that time there weren't even gels. But I knew how to do those sorts of things. So I thought to myself, this is a perfect opportunity to look for the hyaluronidases, the enzymes that make the transition from the undifferentiated to the differentiated state. That is the critical part of the program that commits stem cells to undergo differentiation.

This took us quite a few years. We started with liver, and it was a big mess because the liver is a big protein factory, literally a bag with thousands of proteins. There were just too many proteins. So we then took a strategic step backwards, and started looking at plasma. We started with outdated plasma from the Blood Bank. It took us 3–4 years to purify hyaluronidase from plasma to a single band so that we could sequence it. And the secret was to have the constant presence of detergents and protease inhibitors through all the steps in purification. All the buffers had to contain detergent and all of the buffers had to have protease inhibitors, which fortunately didn't inhibit the enzyme activity we were measuring. We had to choose an inhibitor cocktail that didn't interfere with the assay, with the ELISA assay that we had developed for hyaluronidase activity, so that we could do a rapid assay. If you have a rapid assay for an enzyme, there is nothing you cannot do. But if you have a slow sluggish assay, there is nothing you can do. So the point was to develop a rapid assay and to figure out what the conditions are that an enzyme likes, that is, the conditions under which enzyme activity survives *in vitro*.

Arthur Kornberg states this very well. He states that every enzyme has its own personality. You have to know whether it tolerates being frozen and thawed, what pH it likes, what salt concentrations, what cations it is comfortable with, and how it survives freezing and thawing on storage. Once you know that, then you know what your limitations are and you formulate your purification scheme, keeping in mind the personality of the enzyme, what it likes and what it doesn't like. Proteins denature, curdle, turn into cottage cheese when they are in an environment they don't like. So we ended up with a pure protein, the first hyaluronidase to be isolated from somatic tissues.

This was a protein that we could sequence. And at that time the human genome project was going on, and there was also something called ESTs, the Express Sequence Tag Data Bank. We sequenced a tryptic N-terminal fragment and an internal tryptic fragment. We put that into the data bank and out came a family of 6 enzymes.

Suddenly we were very rich. We had more than we could possibly do. It was an enzyme family that was not known previously. It had probably started out in evolution originally with one protein sequence, which then underwent two duplication events. Then you had three. This was followed by *en masse* duplication, from three to six. And each one of the enzymes from these sequences has its own character and personality. But they're all hyaluronidases or hyaluronidase-like sequences. So that's where we are today. We've become the world experts in hyaluronidase biology, in those enzymes that degrade hyaluronan, the substrate to which Bandi—Endre A. Balazs—has devoted his entire life. We have the expertise on how hyaluronan is recognized and degraded. This is an important part of the biology of hyaluronan.

What is your assessment of the hyaluronan field; about how it developed? What would be, in your opinion, the most important turning point or can you think about anything that was critical historically?

Well, it came from connective tissue biology, which then became extracellular matrix biology and now it's beginning to come into the mainstream. I think hyaluronan has been on the shirttails of that movement. By itself it has always been marginal, but now because of the efforts of a number of very gifted people it's going to become mainstream, now that it's recognized to be involved in stem cell biology, in differentiation, and in malignancy. There are just so many biological phenomena in which hyaluronan is involved, that's becoming more widely known.

Nucleic acids used to be considered to be a very dull field, prior to the Watson–Crick model and before the genetic code was broken. Now if there is anything duller, it's polysaccharides. They are very monotonous as polymer molecules.

How can there be information in such polymers?

There are several answers. As it changes size it changes conformation and it changes the ability to interact with very informational protein molecules. And it's the proteins that are associated with hyaluronan that give it biological significance. I think the hyaluronan binding proteins are one of the locks to unlock the mystery. To understand these binding proteins, where they are, where they are located, how they are informational, where do the instructions come from, what binding proteins have to occur at a particular time. That's just putting the question one step further back. But it's a combination of hyaluronan and its binding proteins that make it informational.

It is also intrinsic to the molecule, in terms of the size and the conditions in which it is found, which pH, salt concentrations, what cations it has been exposed to, and its history, where it has been previously. There are certain conformations that it can take only under certain conditions. But if it has already been through some other phase, it may not be able to reach that new conformation. So that is physical chemistry, viscometry, all the work that's been done on the physical chemistry of the molecule are going to interact now with the pure protein and carbohydrate chemistry.

Hyaluronan has also been studied morphologically. You can stain for it in tissue sections so there is a natural connection. It's not only an abstract biochemical hypothesis. You can see the molecule and look at its distribution and deposition in normal and pathologic tissues, which is a real advantage. Here it is and there it isn't.

Unfortunately, so far there has been very little support for this field. Many of us at this meeting have trouble getting our grants funded. In fact our grants are constantly being rejected. We are the poor starving orphans in the storm, because we can't get our grants funded. The NIH is a very conservative institution and it is not going to go out on a limb to support things about which there isn't a certain amount of certainty. Even though it doesn't admit to that. But it is obvious, if you look at the pattern. The NIH doesn't take chances very well. And with the hyaluronan molecule it's always been marginal, and now that it's involved in stem cell biology maybe they'll wake up to the fact that glycoproteins and glycobiology are important areas. As Harold Varmus, the head of the NIH says, NIH is equipped to support good research, but not great research.

My impression has been that organic chemists get very good support from NIH for very fundamental research.

But biology is different. It's not as linear as organic chemistry. It is difficult to understand what NHI's mandate is, or perhaps the mandate keeps changing. I was part of a Program Project in breast cancer and I think there were four or five projects, four of which were very pedestrian and were funded, and mine was thrown out. Each of the hypotheses and specific aims that I had proposed has turned out to be correct. Ours was the most imaginative and innovative proposal, and it was singled out for elimination.

What you have told me about the possible relationship between hyaluronan and breast cancer sounds tremendously important.

But this happened seven years ago and it was not recognized at that time. It turned out that we have been vindicated, but we have been struggling for the last several years to stay alive, to keep the laboratory going, because they didn't know then what we know now. That is always the case, but the NIH team was not willing to take a chance, and not willing to take a leap of faith even though we had data to support what we suggested. At that time we said that CD44 was important and that its isoforms were even more important, and they threw it out and said that's not the way to do science.

Do you currently have support?

I have support from a grant that I'm not interested in. And the grant that I would have embraced more enthusiastically was not awarded. So you end up doing things you don't want to do. But you go along anyway. I am going into an area that is not very interesting, to do experiments that I'm not as fascinated by, and that I am not very good at doing. But it pays the bills.

How large is your group?

Right now we are down to two and it has never been larger than three or four people. In addition to research, I also have clinical and teaching responsibility. That's something of a protective barrier that many of the people in basic sciences don't have. They are on soft money, which means their salary has to come from grants. My salary is guaranteed because I perform these other functions. The reason that medical schools exist, such as in the University of California system, is because the state legislature must provide physicians for the State of California; they have to support medical schools. So the purpose of our existence is to teach medical students, and teach them how to become doctors. That is part of my job.

I meant to ask you, how do you feel about this project of creating an encyclopedic resource of hyaluronan science?

I'm enthusiastic about it. As I said, hyaluronan is going to continue to become a growth industry. But the field is still small enough currently that it is still possible to go back and to cover the literature in it's entirety; every article that has ever been published with hyaluronan in the title. We are planning to look and read and comment on how each article fits into the large picture. There are very few fields in biology in which you can do that. You can still do that with hyaluronan. I would suspect that in about 5 or 6 years, that will no longer be possible. And if you look up in PubMed, do a Medline search and look under p53, a protein very much involved in tumor biology, you will find something like 53,000 references, or MMT, matrix metalloproteinases, 14,000 references are available on-line, or integrins. But if you look up hyaluronan or hyaluronidases it's still a reasonable number of citations.

Do you think it can serve as a model for others?

Exactly, not only as a model for what should have been done, but that is still not too late to do now. In other words, we expect many people to come into the field in the near future. However, they will be able to use this library and ask important questions. We are also going to write position papers and document what we think are the important questions that are left to be answered.

    Normally a person has to read in an area in a very amorphous fashion. It's kind of hit or miss, to find that one paragraph that's going to resonate in terms of what one wants to do. In that very Socratic manner, what do you want to know, why do you want to know it, and what are you going to do with it once you know it. Those are important questions, and no experiment is a dead end. You answer a question because it permits you to ask an even better question. You have to know what that next question is before you start the first one. Otherwise you have no business doing it. And in hyaluronan, it's still possible to do that because it's a field that's still in its infancy. You can review the entire literature and find out what it is that you want to know, and ask why you want to know it.

In the more mature fields, it is difficult for young people to get oriented.   The big questions have often been addressed.   But glycobiology, and particularly hyaluronan are not like that. They have not been fully exploited. And my impression is that with a person like Bandi, not only with his personality but with his financial backing also, you can facilitate exploration of the field, and project into the future. That, I think is the key point. That is what it is all about here in St. Tropez. Without this, it's unlikely to happen.

This is a paradigm of how science in the future could be supported. It is a paradigm, and perhaps an unrealistic one. But I could give you an example, and I think examples are the best way to understand it. If you take an animal, a rat or a mouse, and you clamp the arteries to the liver, the level of hyaluronan in the bloodstream goes up instantly to a very high level. This means the liver is very involved in hyaluronan degradation. If you clamp the renal arteries, the same thing happens. Now we can begin to know why the liver or how the liver degrades hyaluronan. There's a man here by the name of Paul Weigel. He is the man who discovered, characterized, isolated, and sequenced the receptors for the uptake of hyaluronan in the liver. So in the liver system we now can begin to understand how that catabolism occurs.

But the same thing happens in the kidney. However, it is a total black box. We don't know how hyaluronan is taken up in the kidney, how it's done, what cells are involved, what renal pathology is associated with abnormalities, or what happens in the urine, where huge amounts of hyaluronidase enzyme are found. But a person who looks at this library will quickly be able to identify that question. That would be an ideal area for someone interested in renal disease.

Now for the sake of argument, you said you are writing position papers; otherwise you are wandering the literature to find the important paradigms and so on. How much does your bias or the bias of this group will influence the outcome?

Oh tremendously. And I suspect that in five years people will be laughing at us. Isn't it ridiculous what they used to think in those days? It will be completely absurd. I don't think that's a problem, however.

You have to start by making a statement, a statement that can be tested. And yet you have to be secure enough, or you should not be so insecure that you're afraid to be laughed at.

It's wonderful that you're saying this. Of course, this is a danger.

And we will be laughed at. If you read the discussions of papers that were published 10 or 20 years ago, they're ludicrous. We shouldn't even write Discussions in our papers. But you write them for people to think about. It's the data that's important, but you also have to position that data within the context of what is known and available. A scientist shouldn't be afraid to be laughed at. And at some point you have to take a position, the right moment never comes.

This is a wonderful experiment, especially if you consider it an experiment and not a final product.

Well, the people who are involved in hyaluronan are very excited by it. And it has been good to us, not financially, but scientifically. It's been highly productive. Everything you turn to is new.

Do you plan to continue the workshop?

If I'm invited, it's by invitation only. As long as I can convince Bandi that what I'm doing is reasonably important, then I'll be invited back. But next year is going to be clinical and whole body situations. It started off with the physical chemistry, then the biochemistry. It's a logical progression. It then goes on to the clinical relevance. I'm the only person here that has clinical responsibility at the moment. Bandi is an MD, Torvard Laurent is an MD, but they haven't seen patients in years. And I deal with clinical problems on a daily basis. So I manage to straddle both worlds.

Already with Bandi I'm going to have major fights. I think that the questions and I hope he reads this, unless the questions are addressed in relation to clinical disciplines, things for the orthopedist, things for people in Ob/Gyn, Rheumatology, Dermatology,

Endocrinology, that's the way to group information into piles. He wants to do it by disease, and that's a hair-brained way to do it. It won't work, and the clinicians who should be reading this overview, these position statements, are not going to approach it because they don't think in terms of disease process. They think in terms of their own discipline. Clinicians and clinician-scientists have very little spare time. You have to use existing mechanisms to get their attention. "Hyaluronan and Disease" won't sell. Bur 'Hyaluronan in Dermatology" or 'Hyaluronan in Disorders of the G.I.-tract" will sell.

I don't think it will work his way. Because there are many important things that have to do with hyaluronan metabolism that have nothing to do with disease, I'll give you one example for those that understand this kind of thing. There is something called ADH or antidiuretic hormone, which works in the kidney to concentrate urine. This ensures that you don't become severely dehydrated when you're water deprived, as in a hot desert situation. ADH is the mechanism for doing that. It's hyaluronan-related, which I won't go into.

There is a problem in women in labor who are getting what we call a pitocin drip. It speeds up delivery, to make it go faster. Vasopressin, oxytocin, and ADH are practically identical. They're from the posterior pituitary. They're peptides that are 85-90% identical. Women who are in labor who are getting the pitocin drip often get water logged. They are getting an ADH effect from their pitocin. Those 2 things are connected. Now that's not a disease process. It is a clinical observation. When you give a woman a pitocin drip to stimulate labor and antidiuresis are not obviously connected. Neither of those is disease related. So where is that going to fit into Bandi's profile? It'll be ignored, but they're both very important hyaluronan-related phenomena. And I'm going to try to convince him. And I'll write him letters about why I think the disease approach is wrong headed. We already had an argument yesterday, and of course Bandi is a very determined person. He's very good at getting done what he wants done and with such gracious hospitality it's very hard to say no. It's very hard to argue with him, but I'm going to argue with him because I think that's my obligation.

He's a very gifted individual, and a very generous person, but you have to stand up to him if you have a position that you think is right. I admire his style it's very effective obviously. And I admire him tremendously. But one has to know where to draw the line. It's a matter of integrity. But it is also the male instinct. Testosterone does funny things to the brain. Women in science would handle these arguments differently. But their way is more effective under some circumstances. You need both.

Bandi enjoys what he does. He wouldn't look so good unless he really enjoyed what he does. He enjoys every minute. It's wonderful to be around him, you absorb the energy. He really is a role model for scientists. And he had an academic career that was enormously successful but was not recognized. Columbia had him. He was at Harvard, at the Massachusetts General Hospital, and he started eye research there. They didn't realize what a jewel they had and I think they were probably I would think or suspect, jealous. So they pushed him out instead of taking advantage of him

Karl Meyer was another pioneer in hyaluronan research. He also was a very gifted biochemist, obviously. His papers describing hyaluronan are magnificent in their clarity and the precision and the carefulness in which they were done. But Columbia treated him very shabbily. He eventually left Columbia.

Bibliography*

Hyaluronan-Related Publications

1. Decker, M., Chiu, E. S., Dollbaum, C., Moiin, A., Hall, J., Spendlove, R., Longaker, M. T., and Stern, R. (1989). Hyaluronic acid-stimulating activity in sera from the bovine fetus and from breast cancer patients. Cancer Res 49, 3499-3505.

2. Longaker, M. T., Chiu, E. S., Harrison, M. R., Crombleholme, T. M., Langer, J. C., Duncan, B. W., Adzick, N. S., Verrier, E. D., and Stern, R. (1989). Studies in fetal wound healing. IV. Hyaluronic acid-stimulating activity distinguishes fetal would fluid from adult wound fluid. Ann Surg 210 (5), 667-672.

3. Longaker, M. T., Harrison, M. R., Crombleholme, T. M., Langer, J. C., Decker, M., Verrier, E. D., Spendlove, R., and Stern, R. (1989). Studies in fetal wound healing. I. A factor in fetal serum that stimulates deposition of hyaluronic acid. J Pediatric Surg 24 (8), 789-792.

4. Longaker, M. T., Harrison, M. R., Langer, J. C., Crombleholme, T. M., Verrier, E. D., Spendlove, R., and Stern, R. (1989). Studies in fetal wound healing: II. A fetal environment accelerates fibroblast migration in vitro. J Pediatr Surg 24 (8), 793-797; discussion 798.

5. Chiu, E. S., Longaker, M. T., Adzick, N. S., Stern, M., Harrison, M. R., and Stern, R. (1990). Hyaluronc acid patterns in fetal and adult wound fluid. Surg Forum 41, 636-639.

6. Huey, G., Moiin, A., and Stern, R. (1990). Levels of [3H] glucosamine incorporation into hyaluronan acid by fibroblasts is modulated by culture conditions. Matrix 10, 75-83.

7. Huey, G., Stair, S., and Stern, R. (1990). Hyaluronic acid determinations: optimizing assay parameters. Matrix 10 (2), 67-74.

8. Kao, J., Huey, G., Kao, R., and Stern, R. (1990). Ascorbic acid stimulates production of gyycosaminoglycans in cultured fibroblasts. Exp Mol Pathol 53, 1-10.

---

* Provided by the interviewee.

9. Lien, Y. H., Fu, J., Rucker, R. B., Scheck, M., Abbott, U., and Stern, R. (1990). Collagen, proteoglycan and hyaluronidase activity in cultures from normal and scoliotic chicken fibroblasts. Biochimica et Biophysica Acta 1034, 318-325.

10. Longaker, M. T., Adzick, N. S., Hall, J. L., Stair, S. E., Cromnbleholme, T. M., Duncan, B. W., Bradley, S. M., Harrison, M. R., and Stern, R. (1990). Studies in fetal wound healing: VII. Fetal wound healing may be modulated by hyaluronic acid stimulating activity in amniotic fluid. J Pediatric Surg 25 (4), 430-433.

11. Longaker, M. T., Adzick, N. S., Sadigh, D., Hendin, B., Stair, S. E., Duncan, B. W., Harrison, M. R., Spendlove, R., and Stern, R. (1990). Hyaluronic acid-stimulating activity in the pathophysiology of Wilms' tumors. J Natl Cancer Inst 82 (2), 135-139.

12. Longaker, M. T., Scott Adzick, N., Harrison, M. R., and Stern, R. (1990). To the editor. A new tumor marker for Wilm's tumor called hyaluronic acid-stimulating activity (HASA). Journal of Pediatric Surgery 25 (9), 1015.

13. Longaker, M. T., and Stern, R. (1990). Wound environment: parallels between healing and tumorigenesis. Surgery 107 (6), 715.

14. Longaker, M. T., Whitby, D. J., Adzick, N. S., Crombleholme, T. M., Langer, J. C., Duncan, B. W., Bradley, S. M., Stern, R., Ferguson, M. W., and Harrison, M. R. (1990). Studies in fetal wound healing, VI. Second and early third trimester fetal wounds demonstrate rapid collagen deposition without scar formation. J Pediatr Surg 25 (1), 63-68; discussion 68-69.

15. Stern, M., Longaker, M. T., Adzick, N. S., Harrison, M. R., and Stern, R. (1990). A new tumor marker for Wilm's tumor called hyaluronic acid-stimulating activity (HASA). J Pediatr Surg 25, 1015.

16. Hendin, B. N., Longaker, M. T., Finkbeiner, W. E., Roberts, L. J., and Stern, R. (1991). Hyaluronic acid deposition in cardiac myxomas: Localization using a hyaluronate-specific binding protein. Am J Cardiovasc Pathol 3, 209-215.

17. Longaker, M. T., Chiu, E. S., Adzick, N. S., Stern, M., Harrison, M. R., and Stern, R. (1991). Studies in fetal wound healing. V. A prolonged presence of hyaluronic acid characterizes fetal wound fluid. Ann Sug 213, 292-296.

18. Longaker, M. T., Chiu, E. S., Hendin, B., Finkbeiner, W. E., and Stern, R. (1991). Hyaluronic acid in a cardiac myxoma: a biochemical and histological analysis. Virchows Arch A Pathol Anat Histopathol 418 (5), 435-437.

19. Smith, H. S., Stern, R., Liu, E., and Benz, C. (1991). Early and late events in the development of human breast cancer. Basic Life Sci 57, 329-337; discussion 337-340.

20. Smith, H. S., Stern, R., Liu, E., and Benz, C. (1991). Early and late events in the development of human breast cancer. In *The Boundaries Between Promotion*

and Progression During Carcinogenesis Basic Life Sciences Volume 57 (Eds. Liotta, L. A., Sudilovsky, O. , and Pitot, H. C.), Plenum Press, New York, NY (US), 329-340.

21. Stern, M., Longaker, M. T., Adzick, N. S., Harrison, M. R., and Stern, R. (1991). Hyaluronidase levels in urine from Wilms' tumor patients. J Natl Cancer Inst 83 (21), 1569-1574.

22. Stern, M. l., Longaker, M. T., and Stern, R. (1991). Hyaluronic acid and its modulatoin in fetal and adult wound healing. In *Fetal Wound Healing* (Eds. Adzick, N. S., and Longaker, M. T.), Elsevier, New York, NY (US), 189-198.

23. Byl, N. B., McKenzie, A. L., Longaker, M. T., West, J., and Stern, R. (1992). Application of hyaluronic acid enhances early healing incisional wounds. Eur J Phy Med Rehab 2, 184-187.

24. Gross-Jendroska, M., Lui, G. M., Song, M. K., and Stern, R. (1992). Retinal pigment epithelium-stromal interactions modulate hyaluronic acid deposition. Invest Ophthalmol Vis Sci 33 (12), 3394-3399.

25. Guntenhöner, M. W., Pogrel, M. A., and Stern, R. (1992). A substrate-gel assay for hyaluronidase activity. Matrix 12, 388-396.

26. Lorenz, H. P., Adzick, N. S., Longaker, M. T., and Stern, R. (1992). Scarless wound repair: A Review. In *Advances in Plastic and Reconstructive Surgery Volume IX* (Ed. Habal, M. B.), Mosby Yearbook, Philadelphia, PA (USA), 83-101.

27. Stern, M., Schmidt, B. L., Dodson, T., Stern, R., and Kaban, L. (1992). Fetal cleft lip repair in rabbits: histology and role of hyaluronic acid. J Oral Maxillofac Surg 50 (3), 263-268; discussion 269.

28. Stern, M., and Stern, R. (1992). An ELISA-like assay for hyaluronidase and hyaluronidase inhibitors. Matrix 12, 397-403.

29. Stern, M., and Stern, R. (1992). A collagenous sequence in a prokaryotic hyaluronidase. Mol Biol Evol 9 (6), 1179-1180.

30. Afify, A. M., Stern, M., Guntenhöner, M., and Stern, R. (1993). Purification and characterization of human serum hyaluronidase. Arch Biochem Biophys 305 (2), 434-441.

31. Byl, N. N., McKenzie, A. L., West, J., Stern, M., Holliday, B., Stern, R., and Wong, T. (1993). Amniotic fluid enhances wound healing: A randomized controlled three week trial in mini Yucatan pigs. Eur J Phys Med Rehab 3, 105-113.

32. Estes, J. M., Adzick, N. S., Harrison, M. R., Longaker, M. T., Stern, R., and Krummel, T. (1993). Hyaluronate metabolism undergoes an ontogenic transition during fetal development: Implications for scar-free wound healing. J Pediatr Surg 28 (10), 1227-1231.

33. Pogrel, M. A., Pham, H. D., Guntenhoner, M., and Stern, R. (1993). Profile of hyaluronidase activity distinguishes carbon dioxide laser from scalpel wound healing. Ann Surg 217 (2), 196-200.

34. Suman, V. J., Tazelaar, H. D., Bailey, K., Melton, J., Longaker, M. T., Stern, R., and Finkbeiner, W. E. (1993). Are patients with neoplasia at an increased risk for cardiac myxomas? Hum Pathol 24 (9), 1008-1011.

35. Tate, D. J., Jr., Oliver, P. D., Miceli, M. V., Stern, R., Shuster, S., and Newsome, D. A. (1993). Age-dependent change in the hyaluronic acid content of the human chorioretinal complex. Arch Ophthalmol 111 (7), 963-967.

36. Meyer, L., and Stern, R. (1994). Age-dependent changes of hyaluronan in human skin. J Invest Dermatol 102 (3), 385-389.

37. Zhu, L., Hope, T. J., Hall, J., Davies, A., Stern, M., Muller-Everhard, U., Stern, R., and Parslow, T. G. (1994). Molecular cloning of a mammalian hyaluronidase reveals identity with hemopexin, a serum heme-binding protein. J Biol Chem 269 (51), 32092-32097.

38. Guntenhoner, M. W., Pogrel, M. A., Pham, H. D., and Stern, R. (1995). Wundheilung-substrat-gelgelelektrophorese zur hyaluronidase-akitivitatsbuestimmung. Dtsch Zahnaerztl Z 50, 88-90.

39. Lin, R. Y., Argenta, P. A., Sullivan, K., Stern, R., and Adzick, N. (1995). Urinary hyaluronic acid is a Wilms' tumor marker. J Pediatr Surg 30 (2), 304-308.

40. Savani, R. C., Wang, C., Yang, B., Zhang, S., Kinsella, M. G., Wight, T. N., Stern, R., Nance, D. M., and Turley, E. A. (1995). Migration of bovine aortic smooth muscle cells after wounding injury. The role of hyaluronan and RHAMM. J Clin Invest 95 (3), 1158-1168.

41. Byl, N. N., Hill-Toulouse, L., Stitton, P., Hall, J., and Stern, R. (1996). Effects of ultrasound on the orientation of fibroblasts: An in-vitro study. Eur J Phy Med Rehab 6, 180-184.

42. Cohen, A. M., Hodak, E., David, M., Mittelman, M., Gal, R., and Stern, R. (1996). Beneficial effect of granulocyte-colony stimulating factor in scleromyxoedema associated with severe idiopathic neutropenia. Br J Dermatol 135 (4), 626-629.

43. Frost, G. I., Csóka, B., and Stern, R. (1996). The hyaluronidases: A chemical, biological and clinical overview. Trends in Glycoscience Glycotechnol 8 (44), 419-434.

44. Goshen, R., Ariel, I., Shuster, S., Hochberg, A., Vlodavsky, I., de Groot, N., Ben-Rafael, Z., and Stern, R. (1996). Hyaluronan, CD44 and its variant exons in human trophoblast invasion and placental angiogenesis. Mol Hum Reprod 2 (9), 685-691.

45. Hrkal, Z., Kuzelova, K., Muller-Eberhard, U., and Stern, R. (1996). Hyaluronan-binding properties of human serum hemopexin. FEBS Lett 383 (1-2), 72-74.

46. Pogrel, M. A., Lowe, M. A., and Stern, R. (1996). Hyaluronan (hyaluronic acid) in human saliva. Arch Oral Biol 41 (7), 667-671.

47. Schwartz, D. M., Shuster, S., Jumper, M. D., Chang, A., and Stern, R. (1996). Human vitreous hyaluronidase: isolation and characterization. Curr Eye Res 15 (12), 1156-1162.

48. Stern, R. (1996). Cardiac myxomas. N Engl J Med 334 (21), 1408; author reply 1408-1409.

49. Csoka, T. B., Frost, G. I., and Stern, R. (1997). Hyaluronidases in tissue invasion. Invasion Metastasis 17 (6), 297-311.

50. Csoka, T. B., Frost, G. I., Wong, T., Stern, R., and Csoka, A. B. (1997). Purification and microsequencing of hyaluronidase isozymes from human urine. FEBS Lett 417 (3), 307-310.

51. Equi, R. A., Jumper, M., Cha, C.-J., Stern, R., and Schwartz, D. M. (1997). Hyaluronan polymer size modulates intraocular pressure. J Ocular Pharmacol Therapeutics 13 (4), 289-295.

52. Frost, G., and Stern, R. (1997). A microtiter-based assay for hyaluronidase activity not requiring specialized reagents. Anal Biochem 251 (1), 263-269.

53. Frost, G. I., Csoka, T. B., Wong, T., Stern, R., and Csoka, A. B. (1997). Purification, cloning, and expression of human plasma hyaluronidase. Biochem Biophys Res Commun 236 (1), 10-15.

54. Gakunga, P., Frost, G., Shuster, S., Cunha, G., Formby, B., and Stern, R. (1997). Hyaluronan is a prerequisite for ductal branching morphogenesis. Development 124 (20), 3987-3997.

55. Jumper, J. M., Chang, D. F., Hoyt, C. S., Hall, J. L., Stern, R., and Schwartz, D. M. (1997). Aqueous hyaluronic acid concentration: comparison in pediatric and adult patients. Curr Eye Res 16 (10), 1069-1071.

56. Lerner, L. E., Polansky, J. R., Howes, E. L., and Stern, R. (1997). Hyaluronan in the human trabecular meshwork. Invest Ophthalmol Vis Sci 38 (6), 1222-1228.

57. Lin, W., Shuster, S., Maibach, H. I., and Stern, R. (1997). Patterns of hyaluronan staining are modified by fixation techniques. J Histochem Cytochem 45 (8), 1157-1163.

58. Schwartz, D. M., Jumper, M. D., Lui, G. M., Dang, S., Schuster, S., and Stern, R. (1997). Corneal endothelial hyaluronidase: a role in anterior chamber hyaluronic acid catabolism. Cornea 16 (2), 188-191.

59. Afify, A. M., Stern, R., Jobes, G., Bailey, J. L., and Werness, B. A. (1998). Differential expression of CD44 and hyaluronic acid in malignant

mesotheliomas, adenocarcinomas, and reactive meothelial hyperplasias. Applied Immunohistochemistry 6 (1), 11-15.

60. Csoka, A. B., Frost, G. I., Heng, H. H., Scherer, S. W., Mohapatra, G., Stern, R., and Csoka, T. B. (1998). The hyaluronidase gene HYAL1 maps to chromosome 3p21.2-p21.3 in human and 9F1-F2 in mouse, a conserved candidate tumor suppressor locus. Genomics 48 (1), 63-70.

61. Formby, B., and Stern, R. (1998). Phosphorylation stabilizes alternatively spliced CD44 mRNA transcripts in breast cancer cells: inhibition by antisense complementary to casein kinase II mRNA. Mol Cell Biochem 187 (1-2), 23-31.

62. Jumper, M. D., Stern, R., Lui, G. M., Formby, B., and Schwartz, D. M. (1998). Expression of CD44 isoforms in cultured human trabecular meshwork cells. Ophthalmic Res 30 (5), 314-320.

63. Lerner, L. E., Schwartz, D. M., Hwang, D. G., Howes, E. L., and Stern, R. (1998). Hyaluronan and CD44 in the human cornea and limbal conjunctiva. Exp Eye Res 67 (4), 481-484.

64. Pogrel, M. A., Lowe, M. A., and Stern, R. (1998). Hyaluronases in human saliva. Int J Oral Biol 23 (2), 111-118.

65. Stern, R., Frost, G., Shuster, S., Shuster, V., Hall, J., Wong, T., and Gakunga, P. (1998). Hyaluronic acid and skin: an expanding biological universe. Cosmetics Toiletries 113, 43-48.

66. Wang, C., Thor, A., Moore II, D., Zhao, Y., Kerschmann, R., Stern, R., Watson, P., and Turley, E. (1998). The overexpression of RHAMM, a hyaluronan-binding protein that regulates ras signaling, correlates with overexpression of mitogen-activated protein kinase and Is a significant parameter in breast cancer progression. Clinical Cancer Research 4 (3), 567-576.

67. Xing, R., Regezi, J. A., Stern, M., Shuster, S., and Stern, R. (1998). Hyaluronan and CD44 expression in minor salivary gland tumors. Oral Dis 4 (4), 241-247.

68. Csoka, A. B., Scherer, S. W., and Stern, R. (1999). Expression analysis of six paralogous human hyaluronidase genes clustered on chromosomes 3p21 and 7q31. Genomics 60 (3), 356-361.

69. Csoka, T. B., and Stern, R. (1999). Human hyaluronidases map to a candidate tumor suppressor locus. Proc Indian Acad Sci 1111, 275-281.

70. Duncan, K. G., Jumper, M. D., Ribeiro, R. C., Bailey, K. R., Yen, P. M., Sugawara, A., Patel, A., Stern, R., Chin, W. W., Baxter, J. D., and Schwartz, D. M. (1999). Human trabecular meshwork cells as a thyroid hormone target tissue: presence of functional thyroid hormone receptors. Graefes Arch Clin Exp Ophthalmol 237 (3), 231-240.

71. Namba, R. S., Shuster, S., Tucker, P., and Stern, R. (1999). Localization of hyaluronan in pseudocapsule from total hip arthroplasty. Clin Orthop Relat Res (363), 158-162.

72. Pogrel, M. A., Low, M. A., and Stern, R. (1999). The hyaluronidase inhibitors in human saliva: partial charactrization and possible functions. Int J Oral Biol 24 (2), 75-80.

73. Stair-Nawy, S., Csóka, T. B., and Stern, R. (1999). Hyaluronidase expression in human skin fibroblasts. Biochem Biophys Res Commun 266, 268-273.

74. Frost, G. I., Mohapatra, G., Wong, T. M., Csoka, A. B., Gray, J. W., and Stern, R. (2000). HYAL1LUCA-1, a candidate tumor suppressor gene on chromosome 3p21.3, is inactivated in head and neck squamous cell carcinomas by aberrant splicing of pre-mRNA. Oncogene 19 (7), 870-877.

75. Laugier, J. P., Shuster, S., Rosdy, M., Csoka, A. B., Stern, R., and Maibach, H. I. (2000). Topical hyaluronidase decreases hyaluronic acid and CD44 in human skin and in reconstituted human epidermis: evidence that hyaluronidase can permeate the stratum corneum. Br J Dermatol 142 (2), 226-233.

76. Meyer, L. J., Russell, S. B., Russell, J. D., Trupin, J. S., Egbert, B. M., Shuster, S., and Stern, R. (2000). Reduced hyaluronan in keloid tissue and cultured keloid fibroblasts. J Invest Dermatol 114 (5), 953-959.

77. Mio, K., Carrette, O., Maibach, H. I., and Stern, R. (2000). Evidence that the serum inhibitor of hyaluronidase may be a member of the inter-alpha-inhibitor family. J Biol Chem 275 (42), 32413-32421.

78. Mio, K., and Stern, R. (2000). Reverse hyaluronan substrate gel zymography procedure for the detection of hyaluronidase inhibitors. Glycoconj J 17 (11), 761-766.

79. Neudecker, B., Csoka, A. B., Stair-Nawy, S., Mio, K., Mailbach, H. I., and Stern, R. (2000). Hyaluonan, the natural skin moisturizer. In *Cosmeceuticals* (Eds. Elsner, P. , and Maibach, H.), Marcel Dekker Press, Inc., New York, NY (US), 319-355.

80. Neudecker, B. A., Csóka, A. B., Nawy, S. S., Mailbach, H. I., and Stern, R. (2000). Hyaluronan: Biology, pathology and pharmacology. Cosmetics Toiletries 115 (11), 43-57.

81. Neudecker, B. A., Csóka, A. B., Nawy, S. S., Mailbach, H. I., and Stern, R. (2000). Hyaluronan: history and biochemistry. Cosmetics Toiletries 115 (9), 36-43.

82. Nickel, R., Stern, R., and Leippe, M. (2000). Evidence that hyaluronidase is not involved in tissue invasion of the protozoan *Entmeba histolytica*. Infect Immun 68, 3053-3055.

83. Pogrel, M. A., Low, M. A., Stern, R., and Schmidt, B. L. (2000). The molecular weight of hyaluronan in parotid and mixed human saliva. Int J Oral Biol 25 (1), 13-16.

84. Savani, R. C., Hou, G., Liu, P., Wang, C., Simons, E., Grimm, P. C., Stern, R., Greenberg, A. H., DeLisser, H. M., and Khalil, N. (2000). A role for hyaluronan in macrophage accumulation and collagen deposition after bleomycin-induced lung injury. Am J Respir Cell Mol Biol 23 (4), 475-484.

85. Stern, R. (2000). Mammalian hyaluronidases. In *Glycoforum Hyaluronan Today*. (Eds. Hascall, V.C. and Yanagishita, M.) (Seikagaku Corporation Glycoforum) (Accessed   at http://www.glycoforum.gr.jp/science/hyaluronan/HA15/HA15E.html) Tokyo (JP).

86. Weiss, L., Slavin, S., Reich, S., Cohen, P., Shuster, S., Stern, R., Kaganovsky, E., Okon, E., Rubinstein, A. M., and Naor, D. (2000). Induction of resistance to diabetes in non-obese diabetic mice by targeting CD44 with a specific monoclonal antibody. Proc Natl Acad Sci U S A 97 (1), 285-290.

87. Csoka, A. B., Frost, G. I., and Stern, R. (2001). The six hyaluronidase-like genes in the human and mouse genomes. Matrix Biol 20 (8), 499-508.

88. Levin, C., Zhai, H., Bashir, S., Chew, A.-L., Stern, R., and Maibach, H. (2001). Efficacy of corticosteriods in acute experimental irritant contat dermatitis. Skin Research & Technology 7, 214-218.

89. Lin, G., and Stern, R. (2001). Plasma hyaluronidase (Hyal-1) promotes tumor cell cycling. Cancer Letters 163, 95-101.

90. Mio, K., Csoka, A. B., Nawy, S. S., and Stern, R. (2001). Detecting hyaluronidase and hyaluronidase inhibitors. Hyaluronan-substrate gel and - inverse substrate gel techniques. In *Methods in Molecular Biology Volume 171: Proteoglycan Protocols* (Ed. Iozzo, R. V.), Humana Press, Totowa, NJ (USA), 391-397.

91. Salamonsen, L. A., Shuster, S., and Stern, R. (2001). Distribution of hyaluronan in human endometrium across the menstrual cycle. Implications for implantation and menstruation. Cell Tissue Res 306 (2), 335-340.

92. Stair-Nawy, S., Csoka, A. B., Mio, K., and Stern, R. (2001). Hyaluronidase activity and hyaluronidase inhibitors. Assay using a microtiter-based system. In *Methods in Molecular Biology Volume 171: Proteoglycan Protocols* (Ed. Iozzo, R. V.), Humana Press, Totowa, NJ (USA), 383-389.

93. Stern, R. (2001). Minireview on the mammalian hyaluronidases: introductory remarks. Matrix Biol 20, 497-508.

94. Stern, R., Shuster, S., Wiley, T. S., and Formby, B. (2001). Hyaluronidase can modulate expression of CD44. Exp Cell Res 266, 167-176.

95. Csoka, A. B., and Stern, R. (2002). Mammalian hyaluronidases. In *Encyclopedia of Molecular Medicine* (Ed. Creighton, T. E.), John Wiley & Sons, New York, NY (US), 37494-37496.

96. Mio, K., and Stern, R. (2002). Inhibitors of the hyaluronidases. Matrix Biol 21 (1), 31-37.

97. Nicoll, S. B., Barak, O., Csóka, A. B., Bhatnagar, R. S., and Stern, R. (2002). Hyaluronidases and CD44 undergo differntial modulation during chondrogenesis. Biochem Biophys Res Commun 292, 819-825.

98. Shuster, S., Frost, G. I., Csoka, A. B., Formby, B., and Stern, R. (2002). Hyaluronidase reduces human breast cancer xenografts in SCID mice. Int J Cancer 102 (2), 192-197.

99. Stair-Nawy, S., Carlson, K. W., Shuster, S., Wei, E. T., and Stern, R. (2002). Mystixin peptides reduce hyaluronan deposition and edema formation. Eur J Pharmacol 450 (3), 291-296.

100. Stern, R. (2002). Book review: The Chemistry, Biology and Medical Applications of Hyaluronan and its Derivatives edited by T. C. Laurent. Quarterly Review of Biology.

101. Stern, R., Shuster, S., Neudecker, B. A., and Formby, B. (2002). Lactate stimulates fibroblast expression of hyaluronan and CD44: the Warburg effect revisited. Exp Cell Res 276 (1), 24-31.

102. Formby, B., and Stern, R. (2003). Lactate-sensitive response elements in genes involved in hyaluronan catabolism. Biochem Biophys Res Commun 305 (1), 203-208.

103. Pogrel, M. A., Low, M., and Stern, R. (2003). Hyaluronan (hyaluronic acid) and its regulation in human saliva by hyaluronidase and its inhibitors. J Oral Sci 45, 85-91.

104. Stern, R. (2003). Devising a pathway for hyaluronan catabolism. Are we there yet? Glycobiology 13 (12), 105R-115R.

105. Bourguignon, L. Y., Singleton, P. A., Diedrich, F., Stern, R., and Gilad, E. (2004). CD44 interaction with Na+-H+ exchanger (NHE1) creates acidic microenvironments leading to hyaluronidase-2 and cathepsin B activation and breast tumor cell invasion. J Biol Chem 279 (26), 26991-27007.

106. George, J., and Stern, R. (2004). Serum hyaluronan and hyaluronidase: very early markers of toxic liver injury. Clin Chim Acta 348 (1-2), 189-197.

107. Neudecker, B. A., Stern, R., and Connolly, M. K. (2004). Aberrant serum hyaluronan and hyaluronidase levels in scleroderma. Br J Dermatol 150 (3), 469-476.

108. Stern, R. (2004). Hyaluronan catabolism: a new metabolic pathway. Eur J Cell Biol 83 (7), 317-325.

109. Stern, R. (2004). Hyaluronan degradation in tumor growth and metastasis. Trends Glycoscience Glycotechnol 16 (89), 171-185.

110. Stern, R. (2004). Update on the mammalian hyaluronidases. In *Glycoforum Hyaluronan Today.* (Eds. Hascall, V.C. and Yanagishita, M.) (Seikagaku Corporation   Glycoforum)   (Accessed   at http://www.glycoforum.gr.jp/science/hyaluronan/HA15a/HA15aE.html) Tokyo (JP).

111. Udabage, L., Brownlee, G. R., Stern, R., and Brown, T. J. (2004). Inhibition of hyaluronan degradation by dextran sulphate facilitates characterisation of hyaluronan synthesis: an in vitro and in vivo study. Glycoconj J 20 (7-8), 461-471.

112. Afify, A. M., Craig, S., Paulino, A. F., and Stern, R. (2005). Expression of hyaluronic acid and its receptors, CD44s and CD44v6, in normal, hyperplastic, and neoplastic endometrium. Ann Diagn Pathol 9 (6), 312-318.

113. Afify, A. M., Stern, R., and Michael, C. W. (2005). Differentiation of mesothelioma from adenocarcinoma in serous effusions: the role of hyaluronic acid and CD44 localization. Diagn Cytopathol 32 (3), 145-150.

114. Bashir, S. J., Dreher, F., Chew, A. L., Zhai, H., Levin, C., Stern, R., and Maibach, H. I. (2005). Cutaneous bioassay of salicylic acid as a keratolytic. Int J Pharm 292 (1-2), 187-194.

115. Jedrzejas, M. J., and Stern, R. (2005). Structures of vertebrate hyaluronidases and their unique enzymatric mechanism of hydrolysis. Proteins 61 (2), 227-238.

116. Neudecker, B., Maibach, H., and Stern, R. (2005). Hyaluronan, the natural skin moisturizer. In *Cosmeceuticals 2nd Edition* (Eds. Elsner, P. , and Maibach, H.), Marcel Dekker Press, Inc., New York, NY (US).

117. Neudecker, B. A., Stern, R., Mark, L. A., and Steinberg, S. (2005). Scleromyxedema-like lesions of patients in renal failure contain hyaluronan: a possible pathophysiological mechanism. J Cutan Pathol 32 (9), 612-615.

118. Shiftan, L., Israely, T., Cohen, M., Frydman, V., Dafni, H., Stern, R., and Neeman, M. (2005). Magnetic resonance imaging visualization of hyaluronidase in ovarian carcinoma. Cancer Res 65 (22), 10316-10323.

119. Soltes, L., Stankovska, M., Kogan, G., Gemeiner, P., and Stern, R. (2005). Contribution of oxidative-reductive reactions to high-molecular-weight hyaluronan catabolism. Chem Biodivers 2 (9), 1242-1245.

120. Stern, R. (2005). Devising a pathway for hyaluronan catabolism: how the goo gets cut. In *Hyaluronan: Structure, Metabolism, Biological Activities, Therapeutic Applications Volume I* (Eds. Balazs, E. A. , and Hascall, V. C.), Matrix Biology Institute, Edgewater, NJ (USA), 257-266.

121. Stern, R. (2005). Hyaluronan: Key to skin moisturizers. In *Dry Skin and Moisturizers: Chemistry and Function 2nd Edition* (Eds. Loden, M. , and Maibach, H.), CRC Press, Boca Raton, FL (USA), 245-278.

122. Wisniewski, H. G., Sweet, M. H., and Stern, R. (2005). An assay for bacterial and eukaryotic chondroitinases using a chondroitin sulfate-binding protein. Anal Biochem 347 (1), 42-48.

123. Stern, R., Asari, A. A., and Sugahara, K. N. (2006). Hyaluronan fragments: an information-rich system. Eur J Cell Biol 85 (8), 699-715.

124. Stern, R., and Jedrzejas, M. J. (2006). Hyaluronidases: Their Genomics, Structures, and Mechanisms of Action. Chem Rev 106 (3), 818-839.

125. Sugahara, K. N., Hirata, T., Hayasaka, H., Stern, R., Murai, T., and Miyasaka, M. (2006). Tumor cells enhance their own CD44 cleavage and motility by generating hyaluronan fragments. J Biol Chem 281 (9), 5861-5868.

126. Kogan, G., Soltes, L., Stern, R., and Gemeiner, P. (2007). Hyaluronic acid: a natural biopolymer with a broad range of biomedical and industrial applications. Biotechnol Lett 29 (1), 17-25.

127. Neudecker, J., Neudecker, B. A., Raue, W., Stern, R., and Schwenk, W. (2007). Hyaluronan levels during laparoscopic versus colonic resections. J Endosc 22, 660-663.

128. Stern, R. (2007). Complicated hyaluronan patterns in skin: enlightenment by UVB? J Invest Dermatol 127 (3), 512-513.

129. Stern, R., Kogan, G., Jedrzejas, M. J., and Soltes, L. (2007). The many ways to cleave hyaluronan. Biotechnol Adv 25 (6), 537-557.

130. Kogan, G., Soltes, L., Stern, R., and Mendichi, R. (2007). Hyaluronic acid: A biopolymer with versatile physico-chemical and biological properties. In *Polymer Yearbook Volume 22* (Eds. Ballada, A. , and Zaikov, G. E.), Nova Science Publishers, New York, NY (US) (in press).

131. Kogan, G., Soltes, L., Stern, R., Schiller, J., and Mendichi, R. (2008). Hyaluronic acid: its functions and degradation in *in vivo* systems. In *Studies in Natural Product Chemistry Volume 35* (Ed. Atta-ur-Rahman), Elsevier, Amsteram (The Netherlands).

132. Martin, D. C., Atmuri, V., Hemming, R. J., Mort, J. S., Farley, J. M., J.S., Byers, S., Plaas, A., Hombach, S., and Stern, R. (2008). A mouse model of human *Mucopolysaccharidosis IX* exhibits osteoarthritis. Human Molecular Genetics.

133. Stern, R. (2008). Association between cancer and "acid mucopolysaccharides": An old concept comes of age, finally. In *Hyaluronan and Cancer* (Ed. Stern, R.), Elsevier, Amsteram (The Netherlands).

134. Stern, R., and Maibach, H. I. (2008). Hyaluronan in skin: aspects of aging and its pharmacologic modulation. Clin Dermatol 26 (2), 106-122.

Markku I. Tammi, 2007 (photograph by M. Hargittai)

Markku I. Tammi

Markku Tammi (b. 1949 in Turku, Finland) is Professor of Anatomy at the University of Kuopio, Finland. He received his MD (1975) and his Ph.D. degrees (1979) at the University of Turku. Since 1981 he has been at the University of Kuopio, except for his postdoctoral years (1984–1986) at the University of California, Berkeley and a sabbatical at the Cleveland Clinic (1994–1996). He is Head of the Anatomy Section of the Department of Biomedicine at the University of Kuopio and Director of the Finnish National Glycoscience Graduate School. Dr. Tammi is member of the Finnish Medical Association, and other learned societies.

Interview*

Please tell me something about your background and schooling.

I was born in Turku, Finland, in a working-class family and went through the regular schools. After that I went to medical school in Turku and during my medical studies I got interested in science. As it happened, I had to wait for half a year to get to the clinic and thus I went, as a technician, to a person who did research on vessel wall glycosaminoglycans. I set up an assay method for this and I had my very first paper on that topic, while waiting for the possibility to do my clinical training. Later on I had teaching positions at the Department of Medical Biochemistry, so I actually worked through the rest of my study period until I finished medical school. After a couple of years I completed my thesis; that was also on arterial wall glycosaminoglycans in atherogenesis. My supervisor was a clinician, so I more or less had to work on my own in the lab during that period. Then I met Raija and as we are both nature lovers, we decided that we would like to raise our children somewhere outside of a city. We sat down and studied the map of Finland to find out where we would like to live. Just by about that time, they built a new university in Kuopio, which is about 300 miles north from the southern coast, a small city. We decided to move there; we bought a house on an island close to Kuopio so that we could commute from home and live in the countryside and work at a university at the same time. We did that in 1979 and since then we have been living on that island, except that we had two two-year breaks abroad.

How do you commute?

---

* This interview was recorded during the Hyaluronan Meeting in Charleston, South Carolina, April 2007.

By car. It is about 32 km, and there is a ferry from the island to the mainland. But in wintertime, when the lake is frozen, we drive across and then it is a lot shorter—only about 8 km to drive to the university from home.

You actually drive across the ice?

Yes, yes. We didn't actually have a car in the beginning, so we took a bus in the summertime; in winter I was biking across the ice and Raija was using sleds to get to the other side of the lake. It is an about 2 km wide lake so that was fairly reasonable.

That sounds quite romantic. Did it ever happen that because of bad weather you couldn't go?

Oh yes, in the blizzard it sometimes happened that we were driving there and you could not see where you should go because the wind and the snow wiped away the road. So you just had to drive to the expected direction and hope that you hit the shoreline at the place where the road goes into the city. You could not stop either because if you stop you were stuck in the snow; that was fun in a way.

Have you ever got lost – I mean driving in circles on the lake?

No, no. It once happened though that we dropped into the ice. It was late April and the kids were waiting at home and we thought that well, this last time we drive across the lake so that the pizza doesn't get too cold, and that is what we did. Unfortunately, during the day the ice had melted in the shoreline so that our car dropped there. We had to walk the rest and get our neighbor with a tractor to get the car out of the lake.

What made you originally think about going to medical school?

Well, I guess many of my friends went there. I knew that I wanted to do science, but people said that you can also do science at med school even if you are an MD. The alternative was biochemistry, so I decided rather to go to med school. In fact, at that time it was very common that medical doctors remained in basic sciences and became teachers there. The salary difference between clinicians and basic scientists was not as big as it is nowadays. There was a certain safety feature in this, because you could be sure you would have a profession that you can live on.

You said earlier that already as a medical student you started to work with polysaccharides. When did hyaluronan studies start in Finland? Who was the one who started that line of research?

It was my supervisor, Dr. Pentti Seppälä. He had studied synovial fluid hyaluronan at his time and he had spent time in the laboratories of both Endre Balazs and Torvard Laurent. But during the time I was working on my thesis, hyaluronan was just one of the topics we studied. After we moved to Kuopio, I worked with professor Heikki Helminen on articular cartilage problems, there, again, hyaluronan was not the main theme. Actually, it was Raija's project that brought my attention to hyaluronan originally. She had studied skin in Turku and she continued that in Kuopio as well. One day she said that she would start to study hyaluronan in skin. After that we collaborated for a while; I was still involved in the cartilage research but when we went to Cleveland to Dr. Hascall's laboratory during our sabbatical between 1994 and 1996, there we both worked on hyaluronan-related topics; started with the skin and then continued also on cancer.

Were you married by that time?

Yes. We were married already during medical school years, actually our son was born when we were in the fourth year of our studies there.

How does it work from your perspective, working together in a group with your spouse?

Very well for me.

Raija Tammi, Vanya Jordan and Vince Hascall on a hike in Lapland, 2000
(photograph courtesy of M. Tammi)

I understand that. But how do the others in the lab look at it? Is there any jealousy or resentment?

I have not really noticed that sort of thing. I don't know what they think, and I do not care either. If you are really interested in science, it is so nice to have somebody who you can discuss all your ideas and new results with. When we have the half an hour drive back home, we often have very good discussions and do some planning ahead – that is often the best part of the day.

Again, from your perspective, has it ever occurred to you that some of her results might be looked at with the thought that they were in fact yours and she just participated in it? Or the other way around?

Yes, of course. I have to say that she has been really the sort of progenitor of the research in our lab because I have been involved in all sorts of administration and similar things. Moreover, people by tradition tend to give more honor for somebody who is a head of the department like me, so we always have to correct that and try to get it straight. We have to explain that it was really her result.

Are you the head of the laboratory?

Yes, the Department of Anatomy. My wife is also a professor at the department and there are two more professors and other staff members.

What are the current research directions in your laboratory?

We continue on the regulation of hyaluronan synthesis, this involves kinase cascades, transcription factors, response elements on HAS gene promoters, and very recently role of the HAS substrates UDP−GlcA and UDP−GlcNAc. We are also interested in the regulation that probably occurs in intracellular trafficing of Has in the ER − Golgi − plasma membrane − endocytic vesicle route. The cell biological effects of hyaluronan synthesis in different cells are studied using inhibitors. In the department, research on articular cartilage research that I started long ago, is also continuing. Professor Mikko Lammi and Assistant Professor Virpi Tiitu are conducting mesenchymal stem cell research and studies on articular cartilage, in particular their applications for cartilage defect repair.

Where do you get your funding from? Also, I wonder, do you have the same possibilities as people at a big university, say, the University of Helsinki, have?

The University of Helsinki is very rich and they can get new equipment more easily, so I would say that the infrastructure there is stronger than in Kuopio. On the other hand, in Kuopio, we have the tradition of sharing everything, so if somebody acquires a certain equipment in the campus, there is an agreement that we all can use. As to the funding; we get that from the Finnish Academy of Sciences and there they try to be objective. They try to evaluate the requests based on the quality of the research. This means that if we do high-level research, the funding is good. We have been fortunate in our group in that we have five lower teacher positions and our graduate students can work in those positions so we do not need that much money from other sources to hire people. We have a couple of funds to get money for consumables and that sort of thing but most of our people have positions for a five-year term that they need to renew and it is expected that during that five years they finish their graduate studies and have their thesis ready.

How expensive is the research that you do?

I don't consider it very expensive. Of course, we need new antibodies quite a lot, we need tissue culture ware and sometimes we need radioisotopes and general chemicals. We also have important instruments such as a real time PCR and confocal microscope for live cells; we have chromatographic equipments that are old but they are working well. So we do not have problem with that.

You said you spent two years in Dr. Hascall's laboratory, so you can compare research in the United States and in your university. Is it just as easy or just as difficult there as here?

I think that it depends on the person. Actually, there is a difference between the two setups and that is in favor of Finland. We have technical personnel to take care of the dish washing and making the basic solutions and even some experiments, basic cell culture experiments and there is no such thing in Dr. Hascall's laboratory. In Finland, these are budget-funded positions. Of course, we may not have all the very specific instruments—but I feel that it is as easy in Finland as in America. There was, in fact, one difference very much in favor of the U.S. In America, the spirit of the people in the lab was much better; they were excited about their research, they discussed it often, they worked longer hours.

Do people keep office hours even in research in Finland?

It looks like that. We have a professor from Germany in the neighboring Department of Biochemistry and he calls it the "four-o'clock disease" because his graduate students leave at four; they have to go home because they have to get their kids out of daycare or for some other reason.

Do you have cooperation with people from other countries?

Yes, we do. For instance, we exchange plasmids with Dr. Toole's laboratory. Then I can send people working in Dr. Hascall's laboratory; actually three or four of them have gone there for a couple of months to learn things. We have joint research papers on certain issues. We also have collaboration in Europe; we share ideas and reagents with people like Alberto Passi's laboratory at the University of Insubria in Italy, Paraskevi Heldin in Uppsala, Sweden, Tony Day at Manchester University and David Jackson at Oxford University in the UK.

How about competition with people in the same field?

I don't want to compete.

You don't feel that there is any competition, when people work on the same or similar topics? Does not it matter who publishes the results first?

I don't experience it like that. I simply cannot imagine that I would not share any information that I know or give advice that I feel somebody needs just so that I could publish earlier. There has not been that sort of spirit in this field, I don't know what it is in other fields.

This is a special scientific field in that beside fundamental research, you can also work on topics that are very close to application. The question of competition must come up there. Have you been involved with that kind or research?

No. The only thing is that we have done certain small services to certain companies. If they want some analyses that nobody else can do, we do it for a small fee. We got some money for our basic research through that but it was not much. We have also done work for the clinicians in our university since we have good probes for hyaluronan. For example, we have stained their sections from cancer samples—but that is something that we don't consider our main field.

Talking about cancer: do you think that if the role of hyaluronan in cancer will be better understood it may eventually lead to ways of fighting cancer?

I think, it could be one tool. I don't think it alone provides an answer but combined with other means. There are always new results coming up that find the weak points of cancers and I think this is one of them. Just inhibiting hyaluronan synthesis would be profitable in some cancers and there are actually some ways to do that already in animal experiments. I don't know if those hyaluronan synthesis inhibitors will ever come to the market but there are others and perhaps we can work on new compounds.

Have you been involved with this kind of research?

We have actually some inhibitors but we don't do them in cancer we just do cell culture experiments.

What do you consider your most important result so far in science?

I think it is very fascinating that we discovered this new "organelle," these microvilli seem to be the main site of hyaluronan synthesis.

And what was the greatest challenge in your scientific life?

Perhaps it is that I was so shy that I didn't contact people that I should have contacted early enough.

For suggestions or cooperation?

Both.

Who are these people you referred to here?

Torvard Laurent and Vincent Hascall.

What do you consider as the most promising in the hyaluronan research field?

I think, considering the medical applications, it might be inflammation in various forms. There is so much interesting and important stuff coming up all the time that there must be some applications very soon.

Is there anything else you feel should have been discussed in this interview?

I don't know, I'm fairly happy about this.

Bibliography*

Hyaluronan-Related Publications

1. Saarni, H., and Tammi, M. (1977). Rapid method for separation and assay of radiolabeled mucopolysaccharides from cell culture medium. Anal Biochem 81, 40-46.

2. Saarni, H., Tammi, M., and Vuorio, E. (1977). Effects of cortisol on glycosaminoglycans synthesized by normal and rheumatoid synovial fibroblasts in vitro. Scand J Rheum 6, 222-224.

3. Saarni, H., and Tammi, M. (1978). Time and concentration dependence of the action of cortisol on fibroblasts in vitro. Biochim Biophys Acta 540, 117-126.

4. Saarni, H., Tammi, M., and Doherty, N. S. (1978). Decreased hyaluronic acid synthesis, a sensitive indicator of cortisol action on fibroblast. J Pharm Pharmacol 30 (3), 200-201.

5. Larjava, H., Saarni, H., Tammi, M., Penttinen, R., and Ronnemaa, T. (1980). Cortisol decreases the synthesis of hyaluronic acid by human aortic smooth muscle cells in culture. Atherosclerosis 35 (2), 135-143.

6. Saarni, H., Tammi, M., Vuorio, E., and Penttinen, R. (1980). Distribution of glycosaminoglycans in rheumatoid cultures and effects of cortisol on it. Scand J Rheumatol 9 (1), 11-16.

7. Tammi, R. and Tammi, M. (1986). Influence of retinoic acid on the ultrastructure and hyaluronic acid synthesis of adult human epidermis in whole skin organ culture. J Cell Physiol 126, 389-398.

8. Tammi, R., Ripellino, J. A., Margolis, R. U., and Tammi, M. (1988). Localization of epidermal hyaluronic acid using the hyaluronate binding region of cartilage proteoglycan as a specific probe. J Invest Dermatol 90, 412-414.

---

* Provided by the interviewee.

9.   Tammi, R., Rippelino, J., Margolis, R. U., Maibach, H. I., and Tammi, M.
      (1989). Hyaluronate accumulation in human epidermis treated with retinoic
      acid in skin organ culture. Soc Invest Dermatol 92, 326-332.

10.   Tammi, R., Tammi, M., Hakkinen, L., and Larjava, H. (1990).
      Histochemical localization of hyaluronate in human oral epithelium using a
      specific hyaluronate-binding probe. Arch Oral Biol 35 (3), 219-224.

11.   Tammi, R., Saamanen, A. M., Maibach, H. I., and Tammi, M. (1991).
      Degradation of newly synthesized high molecular mass hyaluronan in the
      epidermal and dermal compartments of human skin in organ culture. Soc
      Invest Dermatol 97 (1), 126-130.

12.   Tammi, R., and Tammi, M. (1991). Correlations between hyaluronan and
      epidermal proliferation as studied by [3H]glucosamine and [3H]thymidine
      incorporations and staining of hyaluronan on mitotic keratinocytes. Exp
      Cell Res 195 (2), 524-527.

13.   Wang, C., Tammi, M., and Tammi, R. (1992). Distribution of hyaluronan
      and its CD44 receptor in the epithelia of human skin appendages.
      Histochemistry 98 (2), 105-112.

14.   Ågren, U. M., Tammi, R., and Tammi, M. (1994). A dot-blot assay of
      metabolically radiolabeled hyaluronan. Anal Biochem 217, 311-315.

15.   Tammi, M., Savolainen, S., Wang, C., Parkkinen, J. J., Lammi, M. J., Ågren,
      U., Hakkinen, T., Inkinen, R., and Tammi, R. (1994). Distribution of
      hyaluronan in articular cartilage as probed by a biotinylated binding region
      link protein complex of aggrecan. Trans Orthop Res Soc 19, 399.

16.   Tammi, R., Ågren, U. M., Tuhkanen, A. L., and Tammi, M. (1994).
      Hyaluronan metabolism in skin.   Invited Review. Prog Histochem
      Cytochem 29 (2), 1-81.

17.   Tammi, R., Paukkonen, K., Wang, C., Horsmanheimo, M., and Tammi, M.
      (1994). Hyaluronan and CD44 in psoriatic skin. Intense staining for and
      hyaluronan on dermal loops and reduced expression of CD44 and
      hyaluronan in keratinocyte-leukocyte interfaces. Arch Dermatol Res 286
      (1), 21-29.

18.   Tammi, R., Ronkko, S., Ågren, U. M., and Tammi, M. (1994). Distribution
      of hyaluronan in bull reproductive organs. J Histochem Cytochem 42 (11),
      1479-1486.

19.   Ågren, U. M., Tammi, M., and Tammi, R. (1995). Hydrocortisone
      regulation of hyaluronan metabolism in human skin organ culture. J Cell
      Physiol 164, 240-248.

20.   Tammi, R., Tuhkanen, A.-L., Ågren, U., and Tammi, M. (1995). Whole
      skin organ culture as a tool to study hyaluronan and proteoglycan

metabolism. In *Dermatological Research Techniques* (Ed. Mailbach, H. I.), CRC Press, Boca Raton, FL (USA), 91-111.

21. Haapala, J., Lammi, M. J., Inkinen, R., Parkkinen, J. J., Ågren, U. M., Arokoski, J., Kiviranta, I., Helminen, H. J., and Tammi, M. I. (1996). Coordinated regulation of hyaluronan and aggrecan content in the articular cartilage of immobilized and exercised dogs. J Rheumatol 23 (9), 1586-1593.

22. Noonan, K. J., Stevens, J. W., Tammi, R., Tammi, M., Hernandez, J. A., and Midura, R. J. (1996). Spatial distribution of CD44 and hyaluronan in the proximal tibia of the growing rat. J Orthop Res 14 (4), 573-581.

23. Parkkinen, J. J., Hakkinen, T. P., Savolainen, S., Wang, C., Tammi, R., Ågren, U., Lammi, M. J., Arokoski, J., Helminen, H. J., and Tammi, M. I. (1996). Distribution of hyaluronan in articular cartilage as probed by a biotinylated binding region of aggrecan. Histochem Cell Biol 105, 187-194.

24. Stevens, J.W., Noonan, K.J., Bosch, P.P., Rapp, T.B., Martin, J.A., Kurriger, G.L., Maynard, J.A., Daniels, K.J., Solursh, M., Tammi, R., Tammi, M, and Midura, R.J. (1996). CD44 in growing normal and neoplastic rat cartilage. Ann NY Acad Sci 785, 333-336.

25. Wang, C., Tammi, M., Guo, H., and Tammi, R. (1996). Hyaluronan distribution in the normal epithelium of esophagus, stomach, and colon and their cancers. Am J Pathol 148 (6), 1861-1869.

26. Ågren, U. M., Tammi, M., Ryynanen, M., and Tammi, R. (1997). Developmentally programmed expression of hyaluronan in human skin and its appendages. J Invest Dermatol 109 (2), 219-224.

27. Ågren, U. M., Tammi, R. H., and Tammi, M. I. (1997). Reactive oxygen species contribute to epidermal hyaluronan catabolism in human skin organ culture. Free Radic Biol Med 23 (7), 996-1001.

28. Tuhkanen, A. L., Tammi, M., and Tammi, R. (1997). CD44 substituted with heparan sulfate and endo-beta-galactosidase-sensitive oligosaccharides: a major proteoglycan in adult human epidermis. J Invest Dermatol 109 (2), 213-218.

29. Weigel, P., Hascall, V., and Tammi, M. (1997). Minireview. Hyaluronan synthases. J Biol Chem 272 (22), 13997-14000.

30. Hascall, V. C., Fulop, C., Salustri, A., Goodstone, N. J., Calabro, A., Hogg, M., Tammi, R., Tammi, M., and MacCallum, D. (1998). Metabolism of hylauronan. In *The Chemistry, Biology and Medical Applications of Hyaluronan and its Derivatives Proceedings of the Wenner-Gren Foundation International Symposium held in honor of Endre A Balazs, Stockholm, Sweden, September 18-21, 1996* (Ed. Laurent, T. C.), Portland Press Ltd., London (UK), 67-76.

31. Hollyfield, J. G., Rayborn, M. E., Tammi, M., and Tammi, R. (1998). Hyaluronan in the interphotorecpetor matrix of the eye: species differences in content, distribution, ligand binding and degradation. Exp Eye Res 66, 241-248.

32. Pirinen, R. T., Tammi, R. H., Tammi, M. I., Paakko, P. K., Parkkinen, J. J., Ågren, U. M., Johansson, R. T., Viren, M. M., Tormanen, U., Soini, Y. M., and Kosma, V. M. (1998). Expression of hyaluronan in normal and dysplastic bronchial epithelium and in squamous cell carcinoma of the lung. Int J Cancer 79 (3), 251-255.

33. Ropponen, K., Tammi, M., Parkkinen, J., Eskelinen, M., Tammi, R., Lipponen, P., Ågren, U., Alhava, E., and Kosma, V. M. (1998). Tumor cell-associated hyaluronan as an unfavorable prognostic factor in colorectal cancer. Cancer Res 58 (2), 342-347.

34. Tammi, R., MacCallum, D., Hascall, V. C., Pienimäki, J.-P., Hyttinen, M., and Tammi, M. (1998). Hyaluronan bound to CD44 on keratinocytes is displaced by hyaluronan decasaccharides and not hexasaccharides. J Biol Chem 273 (44), 28878-28888.

35. Tammi, R., and Tammi, M. (1998). Hyaluronan in the epidermis. In *Glycoforum. Hyaluronan Today.* (Eds. Hascall, V.C. and Yanagishita, M.)(Seikagaku Corporation Glycoforum) (Accessed at http://www.glycoforum.gr.jp/science/hyaluronan/HA04 /HA04E.html) (June 15, 1998), Tokyo (JP).

36. Tuhkanen, A.-L., Tammi, M., Peltarri, A., Ågren, U. M., and Tammi, R. (1998). Ultrastructural analysis of human epidermal CD44 reveals preferential distribution on plasma membrane domains facing the hyaluronan-rich matrix pouches. J Histochem Cytochem 46 (2), 241-248.

37. Hirvikoski, P., Tammi, R., Kumpulainen, E., Virtaniemi, J., Parkkinen, J. J., Tammi, M., Johansson, R., Ågren, U., Karhunen, J., and Kosma, V.-M. (1999). Irregular expression of hyaluronan and its CD44 receptor is associated with metastatic phenotype in laryngeal squamous cell carcinoma. Virchows Arch 434, 37-44.

38. Inkinen, R. I., Lammi, M. J., Ågren, U., Tammi, R., Puustjarvi, K., and Tammi, M. I. (1999). Hyaluronan distribution in the human and canine intervertebral disc and cartilage endplate. Histochem J 31 (9), 579-587.

39. Setala, L. P., Tammi, M. I., Tammi, R. H., Eskelinen, M. J., Lipponen, P. K., Agren, U. M., Parkkinen, J., Alhava, E. M., and Kosma, V. M. (1999). Hyaluronan expression in gastric cancer cells is associated with local and nodal spread and reduced survival rate. Br J Cancer 79 (7-8), 1133-1138.

40. Tuhkanen, A. L., Ågren, U. M., Tammi, M. I., and Tammi, R. H. (1999). CD44 expression marks the onset of keratinocyte stratification and mesenchymal maturation into fibrous dermis in fetal human skin. J Histochem Cytochem 47 (12), 1617-1624.

41. Anttila, M. A., Tammi, R. H., Tammi, M. I., Syrjänen, K. J., Saarikoski, S. V., and Kosma, V.-M. (2000). High levels of stromal hyaluronan predict poor disease outcome in epithelial ovarian cancer. Cancer Res 60, 150-155.

42. Auvinen, P., Tammi, R., Parkkinen, J., Tammi, M., Ågren, U., Johansson, R., Hirvikoski, P., Eskelinen, M., and Kosma, V.-M. (2000). Hyaluronan in peritumoral stroma and malignant cells associates with breast cancer spreading and predicts patient survival. Am J Pathol 156, 529-536.

43. Calabro, A., Benavides, M., Tammi, M., Hascall, V. C., and Midura, R. J. (2000). Microanalysis of enzyme digests of hyaluronan and chondroitin/dermatan sulfate by fluorophore-assisted carbohydrate electrophoresis (FACE). Glycobiology 10 (3), 273-281.

44. Felszeghy, S., Hyttinen, M., Tammi, R., Tammi, M., and Modis, L. (2000). Quantitative image analysis of hyaluronan expression in human tooth germs. Eur J Oral Sci 108 (4), 320-326.

45. Hascall, V. C., Tammi, R., Tammi, M., Hunziker, E., and MacCallum, D. K. (2000). Does keratinocyte hyaluronan determine the volume of extracellular space in the epidermis? In *New Frontiers in Medical Sciences: Redefining Hyaluronan (Proceedings of the Symposium held in Padua, Italy, 17-19 June 1999)* (Eds. Abatangelo, G. , and Weigel, P.), Elsevier, Amsterdam, 31-40.

46. Karjalainen, J. M., Tammi, R. H., Tammi, M. I., Eskelinen, M. J., Ågren, U., Parkkinen, J. J., Alhava, E. M., and Kosma, V.-M. (2000). Reduced level of CD44 and hyaluronan associated with unfavorable prognosis in clinical stage I cutaneous melanoma. Am J Pathol 157 (3), 957-965.

47. Lesley, J., Hascall, V. C., Tammi, M., and Hyman, R. (2000). Hyaluronan binding by cell surface CD44. J Biol Chem 275 (35), 26967-26975.

48. Tammi, R. H., Tammi, M. I., Hascall, V. C., Hogg, M., Pasonen, S., and MacCallum, D. K. (2000). A preformed basallamina laters the metabolism and distribution of hyaluronan in epidermal keratinocyte "organotypic" cultures grown on collagen matrices. Histochem Cell Biol 113, 265-277.

49. Felszeghy, S., Modis, L., Tammi, M., and Tammi, R. (2001). The distribution pattern of the hyaluronan receptor CD44 during human tooth development. Arch Oral Biol 46 (10), 939-945.

50. Konttinen, Y. T., Li, T. F., Mandelin, J., Ainola, M., Lassus, J., Virtanen, I., Santavirta, S., Tammi, M., and Tammi, R. (2001). Hyaluronan synthases,

hyaluronan, and its CD44 receptor in tissue around loosened total hip prostheses. J Pathol 194 (3), 384-390.

51. Lipponen, P., Aaltomaa, S., Tammi, R., Tammi, M., Ågren, U., and Kosma, V.-M. (2001). High stromal hyaluronan level is associated with poor differentiation and metastasis in prostrate cancer. Eur J Cancer 37, 849-856.

52. Pienimäki, J.-P., Rilla, K., Fülöp, C., Sironen, R. K., Karvinen, S., Pasonen, S., Lammi, M. J., Tammi, R., Hascall, V. C., and Tammi, M. (2001). Epidermal growth factor activates hyaluronan synthase 2 (Has2) in epidermal keratinocytes and increases pericellular and intracellular hyaluronan. J Biol Chem 276, 20428-20435.

53. Pirinen, R., Tammi, R., Tammi, M., Hirvikoski, P., Parkkinen, J. J., Johansson, R., Böhm, J., Hollmén, S., and Kosma, V.-M. (2001). Prognostic value of hyaluronan expression in non-small cell lung cancer: increased stromal expression indicates unfavorable outcome in patients with adenocarcinoma. Int J Cancer 95, 12-17.

54. Ruponen, M., Ronkko, S., Honkakoski, P., Pelkonen, J., Tammi, M., and Urtti, A. (2001). Extracellular glycosaminoglycans modify cellular trafficking of lipoplexes and polyplexes. J Biol Chem 276 (36), 33875-33880.

55. Setala, L., Lipponen, P., Tammi, R., Tammi, M., Eskelinen, M., Alhava, E., and Kosma, V. M. (2001). Expression of CD44 and its variant isoform v3 has no prognostic value in gastric cancer. Histopathology 38 (1), 13-20.

56. Tammi, R., Rilla, K., Pienimäki, J.-P., MacCallum, D. K., Hogg, M., Luukkonen, M., Hascall, V. C., and Tammi, M. (2001). Hyaluronan enters keratinocytes by a novel endocytic route for catabolism. J Biol Chem 276 (37), 35111-35122.

57. Aaltomaa, S., Lipponen, P., Tammi, R., Tammi, M., Viitanen, J., Kankkunen, J. P., and Kosma, V. M. (2002). Strong Stromal Hyaluronan Expression Is Associated with PSA Recurrence in Local Prostate Cancer. Urol Int 69 (4), 266-272.

58. Böhm, J., Niskanen, L., Tammi, R., Tammi, M., Eskelinen, M., Pirinen, R., Hollmen, S., Alhava, E., and Kosma, V. M. (2002). Hyaluronan expression in differentiated thyroid carcinoma. J Pathol 196 (2), 180-185.

59. Hiltunen, E. L., Anttila, M., Kultti, A., Ropponen, K., Penttinen, J., Yliskoski, M., Kuronen, A. T., Juhola, M., Tammi, R., Tammi, M., and Kosma, V. M. (2002). Elevated hyaluronan concentration without hyaluronidase activation in malignant epithelial ovarian tumors. Cancer Res 62 (22), 6410-6413.

60. Karvinen, S., Tammi, M., and Tammi, R. (2002). Effects of KGF and TGF-b on Hyaluronan synthesis and distribution in extra-, peri, and intracellular compartments of epidermal kerationocytes. In *Hyaluronan Volume 1* (Eds. Kennedy, J. F., Phillips, G. O., Williams, P. A., and Hascall, V. C.), Woodhead, Cambridge, UK, 545-550.

61. Melrose, J., Tammi, M., and Smith, S. (2002). Visualisation of hyaluronan and hyaluronan-binding proteins within ovine vertebral cartilages using biotinylated aggrecan G1-link complex and biotinylated hyaluronan oligosaccharides. Histochem Cell Biol 117, 327-333.

62. Pasonen-Seppanen, S., Tammi, R., Tammi, M., Hogg, M., Hascall, V. C., and MacCallum, D. K. (2002). Hyaluronan metabolism and distribution in stratified differentiated cultures of epidermal keratinocytes. In *Hyaluronan Volume 1* (Eds. Kennedy, J. F., Phillips, G. O., Williams, P. A., and Hascall, V. C.), Woodhead, Cambridge, UK, 511-516.

63. Rilla, K., Lammi, M. J., Sironen, R. K., Hascall, V. C., Midura, R. J., Tammi, M., and Tammi, R. (2002). Hyaluronan synthase 2 (HAS2) regulates migration of epidermal kerationocytes. In *Hyaluronan Volume 1* (Eds. Kennedy, J. F., Phillips, G. O., Williams, P. A., and Hascall, V. C.), Woodhead, Cambridge, UK, 557-560.

64. Rilla, K., Lammi, M. J., Sironen, R. K., Törrönen, K., Luukkonen, M., Hascall, V. C., Midura, R. J., Hyttinen, M., Pelkonen, J., Tammi, M., and Tammi, R. (2002). Changed lamellipodial extension, adhesion plaques and migratin in epidermal keratinocytes containing constitutively expressed sense and antisense *hyaluronan synthase 2 (Has2)* genes. J Cell Sci 115, 3633-3643.

65. Tammi, M., Pienimäki, J. P., Rilla, K., Fülöp, C., Lammi, M. J., Sironen, R. K., Midura, R., Hascall, V. C., Luukkonen, M., Törrönen, K., Lehto, T., and Tammi, R. (2002). EGF regulates HAS2 expression controls epidermal thickness and stimulates kerationocyte migration. In *Hyaluronan Volume 1* (Eds. Kennedy, J. F., Phillips, G. O., Williams, P. A., and Hascall, V. C.), Woodhead, Cambridge, UK, 561-570.

66. Tammi, M. I., Day, A. J., and Turley, E., A. (2002). Hyaluronan and homeostatis: a balancing act. J Biol Chem 277 (7), 4581-4584.

67. Tammi, R., Rilla, K., Pienimäki, J. P., Hogg, M., MacCallum, D. K., Hascall, V. C., and Tammi, M. (2002). Intracellular hyaluronan in epidermal keratinocytes. In *Hyaluronan Volume 1* (Eds. Kennedy, J. F., Phillips, G. O., Williams, P. A., and Hascall, V. C.), Woodhead, Cambridge, UK, 517-524.

68. Toole, B. P., Wight, T. N., and Tammi, M. I. (2002). Hyaluronan -cell interactions in cancer and vascular disease. J Biol Chem 277 (7), 4593-4596.

69. Torronen, K., Yabal, M., Rilla, K., Kaarniranta, K., Tammi, R., Lammi, M. J., and Tammi, M. (2002). Hyaluronan stimulates kerationocyte migration and activates the transcription factor AP-1 in keratinocytes. In *Hyaluronan Volume 1* (Eds. Kennedy, J. F., Phillips, G. O., Williams, P. A., and Hascall, V. C.), Woodhead, Cambridge, UK, 551-556.

70. Karvinen, S., Kosma, V. M., Tammi, M. I., and Tammi, R. (2003). Hyaluronan, CD44 and versican in epidermal keratinocyte tumours. Brit J Dermatol 148, 86-94.

71. Karvinen, S., Pasonen-Seppanen, S., Hyttinen, J. M., Pienimaki, J. P., Torronen, K., Jokela, T. A., Tammi, M. I., and Tammi, R. (2003). Keratinocyte growth factor stimulates migration and hyaluronan synthesis in the epidermis by activation of keratinocyte hyaluronan synthases 2 and 3. J Biol Chem 278 (49), 49495-49504.

72. Marjukka Suhonen, T., Pasonen-Seppanen, S., Kirjavainen, M., Tammi, M., Tammi, R., and Urtti, A. (2003). Epidermal cell culture model derived from rat keratinocytes with permeability characteristics comparable to human cadaver skin. Eur J Pharm Sci 20 (1), 107-113.

73. Midura, R. J., Su, X., Morcuende, J. A., Tammi, M., and Tammi, R. (2003). Parathyroid hormone rapidly stimulates hyaluronan synthesis by periosteal osteoblasts in the tibial diaphysis of the growing rat. J Biol Chem 278 (51), 51462-51468.

74. Pasonen-Seppanen, S., Karvinen, S., Torronen, K., Hyttinen, J. M., Jokela, T., Lammi, M. J., Tammi, M. I., and Tammi, R. (2003). EGF upregulates, whereas TGF-beta downregulates, the hyaluronan synthases Has2 and Has3 in organotypic keratinocyte cultures: correlations with epidermal proliferation and differentiation. J Invest Dermatol 120 (6), 1038-1044.

75. Sillanpää, S., Anttila, M. A., Voutilainen, K., Tammi, R. H., Tammi, M. I., Saarikoski, S. V., and Kosma, V. M. (2003). CD44 expression indicates favorable prognosis in epithelial ovarian cancer. Clin Cancer Res 9 (14), 5318-5324.

76. Voutilainen, K., Anttila, M. A., Sillanpää, S., Tammi, R., Tammi, M., Saarkoski, S., and Kosma, V.-.-M. (2003). Versican in epithelial ovariana cancer: Relation to hyaluornan, clinicopathologic factors and prognosis. Int J Cancer 107, 359-364.

77. Kosunen, A., Ropponen, K., Kellokoski, J., Pukkila, M., Virtaniemi, J., Valtonen, H., Kumpulainen, E., Johansson, R., Tammi, R., Tammi, M.,

Nuutinen, J., and Kosma, V. M. (2004). Reduced expression of hyaluronan is a strong indicator of poor survival in oral squamous cell carcinoma. Oral Oncol 40 (3), 257-263.

78. Rilla, K., Pasonen-Seppanen, S., Rieppo, J., Tammi, M., and Tammi, R. (2004). The hyaluronan synthesis inhibitor 4-methylumbelliferone prevents keratinocyte activation and epidermal hyperproliferation induced by epidermal growth factor. J Invest Dermatol 123 (4), 708-714.

79. Suwiwat, S., Ricciardelli, C., Tammi, R., Tammi, M., Auvinen, P., Kosma, V. M., LeBaron, R. G., Raymond, W. A., Tilley, W. D., and Horsfall, D. J. (2004). Expression of extracellular matrix components versican, chondroitin sulfate, tenascin, and hyaluronan, and their association with disease outcome in node-negative breast cancer. Clin Cancer Res 10 (7), 2491-2498.

80. Tammi, R. H., and Tammi, M. (2004). Hyaluronan in the epidermis and other epithelial tissues. In *Chemistry and Biology of Hyaluronan* (Eds. Garg, H. G. , and Hales, C. A.), Elsevier, Ltd., Amsterdam, 395-413.

81. Teriete, P., Banerji, S., Noble, M., Blundell, C. D., Wright, A. J., Pickford, A. R., Lowe, E., Mahoney, D. J., Tammi, M. I., Kahmann, J. D., Campbell, I. D., Day, A. J., and Jackson, D. G. (2004). Structure of the regulatory hyaluronan binding domain in the inflammatory leukocyte homing receptor CD44. Mol Cell 13 (4), 483-496.

82. Auvinen, P., Tammi, R., Tammi, M., Johansson, R., and Kosma, V.-M. (2005). Expression of CD44s, CD44v3 and CD44v6 in benign and malignant breast lesions: correlation and colocalization with hyaluronan. Histopathology 47 (4), 420-428.

83. Kemppainen, T., Tammi, R., Tammi, M., Ågren, U., Julkunen, R., Bohm, J., Uusitupa, M., and Kosma, V. M. (2005). Elevated expression of hyaluronan and its CD44 receptor in the duodenal mucosa of coeliac patients. Histopathology 46 (1), 64-72.

84. Kultti, A., Rilla, K., Törrönen, K., McDonald, J. A., Tammi, R., and Tammi, M. (2005). 4-methylumbelliferone inhibits hyaluronan synthesis, proliferation and migration by suppresssing hyaluronan synthase 2 and 32 messenger RNA levels in breast cancer cells. In *Hyaluronan: Structure, Metabolism, Biological Activities, Therapeutic Applications Volume I* (Eds. Balazs, E. A. , and Hascall, V. C.), Matrix Biology Institute, Edgewater, NJ (USA), 283-287.

85. Rilla, K., Siiskonen, H., Spicer, A. P., Hyttinen, J. M., Tammi, M. I., and Tammi, R. H. (2005). Plasma membrane residence of hyaluronan synthase is coupled to its enzymatic activity. J Biol Chem 280 (36), 31890-31897.

86. Saavalainen, K., Pasonen-Seppanen, S., Dunlop, T. W., Tammi, R., Tammi, M. I., and Carlberg, C. (2005). The human hyaluronan synthase 2 gene is a primary retinoic acid and epidermal growth factor responding gene. J Biol Chem 280 (15), 14636-14644.

87. Tammi, R., Pasonen-Seppanen, S., Kolehmainen, E., and Tammi, M. (2005). Hyaluronan synthase induction and hyaluronan accumulation in mouse epidermis following skin injury. J Invest Dermatol 124 (5), 898-905.

88. Tammi, R. H., Pasonen-Seppanen, S., Kultti, A., Hyttinen, J. M., MacCallum, D., Hascall, V. C., and Tammi, M. I. (2005). Hyaluronan degradation in epidermis. In *Hyaluronan: Structure, Metabolism, Biological Activities, Therapeutic Applications Volume I* (Eds. Balazs, E. A. , and Hascall, V. C.), Matrix Biology Institute, Edgewater, NJ (USA), 241-245.

89. Kultti, A., Rilla, K., Tiihonen, R., Spicer, A. P., Tammi, R. H., and Tammi, M. I. (2006). Hyaluronan synthesis induces microvillus-like cell surface protrusions. J Biol Chem 281 (23), 15821-15828.

90. Evanko, S. P., Tammi, M. I., Tammi, R. H., and Wight, T. N. (2007). Hyaluronan-dependent pericellular matrix. Adv Drug Deliv Rev 59 (13), 1351-1365.

91. Karihtala, P., Soini, Y., Auvinen, P., Tammi, R., Tammi, M., and Kosma, V. M. (2007). Hyaluronan in breast cancer: correlations with nitric oxide synthases and tyrosine nitrosylation. J Histochem Cytochem 55 (12), 1191-1198.

92. Mannisto, M., Reinisalo, M., Ruponen, M., Honkakoski, P., Tammi, M., and Urtti, A. (2007). Polyplex-mediated gene transfer and cell cycle: effect of carrier on cellular uptake and intracellular kinetics, and significance of glycosaminoglycans. J Gene Med 9 (6), 479-487.

93. Palyi-Krekk, Z., Barok, M., Isola, J., Tammi, M., Szollo si, J., and Nagy, P. (2007). Hyaluronan-induced masking of ErbB2 and CD44-enhanced trastuzumab internalisation in trastuzumab resistant breast cancer. Eur J Cancer 43 (16), 2423-2433.

94. Saavalainen, K., Tammi, M. I., Bowen, T., Schmitz, M. L., and Carlberg, C. (2007). Integration of the activation of the human hyaluronan synthase 2 gene promoter by common cofactors of the transcription factors retinoic acid receptor and nuclear factor kappaB. J Biol Chem 282 (15), 11530-11539.

95. Jokela, T. A., Jauhiainen, M., Auriola, S., Kauhanen, M., Tiihonen, R., Tammi, M. I., and Tammi, R. H. (2008). Mannose inhibits hyaluronan synthesis by down-regulation of the cellular pool of UDP-N-acetylhexosamines. J Biol Chem 283 (12), 7666-7673.

96. Pasonen-Seppanen, S. M., Maytin, E. V., Torronen, K. J., Hyttinen, J. M. T., Hascall, V. C., MacCallum, D. K., Kultti, A. H., Jokela, T. A., Tammi, M. I., and Tammi, R. H. (2008). All-trans Retinoic Acid-Induced Hyaluronan Production and Hyperplasia Are Partly Mediated by EGFR Signaling in Epidermal Keratinocytes. J Invest Dermatol 128 (4), 797-807.

97. Tammi, R. H., Kultti, A. H., Kosma, V. M., Pirinen, R., Auvinen, P., and Tammi, M. I. (2008). Hyaluronan in human tumors: importance of stromal and cancer cell-associated hyaluronan. Seminars Cancer Biology 18, 288-295.

98. Jokela, T., Lindgren, A., Rilla, K., Maytin, E., Hascall, V. C., Tammi, R. H., and Tammi, M. I. (2008). Induction of hyaluronan cables and monocyte adherence in epidermal keratinocytes. Connect Tissue Res 49(3), 115-119.

99. Nykopp, T. K., Sironen, R., Tammi, M. I., Tammi, R. H., Ropponen, K., Kosma, V.-M., and Anttila, M. Increased accumulation of hyaluronan in serious ovarian carcinoma correlates with decreased expression of HYAL1 hyaluronidase. (Submitted for publication).

100. Rilla, K., Kultti, A., Tammi, M. and Tammi, R. (2008). Pericellular hyaluronan coat visualized in live cells with a fluorescent probel is scaffolded by plasma membrane protrusions. J Histochem Cytochem June 23 (Epub ahead of print).

101. Hartmann-Petersen, S., Tammi, R.H., Tammi, M.I. and Kosma, V.M. Depletion of cell surface CD44 in non-melanoma skin tumors is associated with increased expression of MMP-7. Brit J Dermatol (in press).

102. Tammi, R.H., Kultti, A., Kosma, V. M., Pirinen, R., Auvinen, P., and Tammi, M.I. (2008). Hyaluronan in human tumors: importance of stromal and cancer cell-associated hyaluronan. In *Hyaluronan and Cancer* (Ed. Stern, R.) Elsevier, Amsterdam, The Netherlands (in press).

Raija Tammi, 2007 (photograph by M. Hargittai)

Raija H. Tammi

Raija Tammi (b. 1949, Iisalmi, Finland) is Professor at the Department of Biomedicine and Anatomy, University of Kuopio, Finland. She received her MD degree (1975) and Ph.D. of Medical Science (1981) at the University of Turku Medical School. She spent her postdoctoral years at the University of California Medical School in San Francisco (1984-1986) and has been at the University of Kuopio since 1979. Dr. Tammi is a member of the Finnish Medical Association and other learned societies. She is Member of the Editorial Board of the *Journal of Biological Chemistry*.

Interview*

What made you interested in medicine or science?

When I was in school, I was mostly interested in history and I thought that I should go to university to study history. But then my brother, who was an MD, told me that it would be much better to go to medical school. I started to think about this and I realized that he was probably right, so I went to the tests and I passed. But I was always more interested in a research-oriented work than in practicing medicine so I tried to find a job where I could do research.

If you were more interested in research why didn't you go to study biology, chemistry, or biochemistry?

Well, this is a good question. But at that time in Finland it was a tradition that people went to the medical school even if they were interested in doing research later; that was a traditional way to do in Finland at that time.

Tell me something about your background, parents, schooling.

I had a very large family, six brothers and six sisters. This was not so uncommon at that time in Finland; there were many large families and I guess it was somewhat influenced by the religious believes of my parents. They are Lutherans but in a special revival movement.

Where did you live?

---

* This interview was recorded during the Hyaluronan Meeting in Charleston, South Carolina, April 2007.

I lived in a very small place; actually in the countryside close to a very small town called Iisalmi. It is in the middle of Finland about 500 km north of Helsinki. My father was a farmer and my mother was taking care of the family.

What did your parents think about you becoming a medical doctor?

Actually my father had died by that time but my mother was very happy and proud, of course. In fact, several of my siblings went to the medical profession, either as a doctor, a dentist, or a nurse. Others continued the family tradition and became farmers.

I went to medical school at the University of Turku in 1969. Already while being a medical student, I started lab work in one laboratory and then, after finishing the medical school, I went to do a Ph.D. This was at the Department of Anatomy of the University of Turku. It was there that I met Markku, my husband and we got married while I was still a student. Eventually, we moved to the University of Kuopio and I got a position as a lecturer there. I was teaching anatomy and I also continued my research.

What was your Ph.D. topic?

It was the skin and the influences of steroid hormones on differentiation and proliferation of epidermis.

How and when did you start doing hyaluronan research?

In fact, I already wanted to do research on hyaluronan during my Ph.D. studies, I was interested in its role in skin, but my supervisor thought that I should do something that he was interested in; so I did the work on steroid hormones and epidermal differentiation. But after I had finished my Ph.D., I decided to go to hyaluronic acid research and that was partly because of Markku. He was doing research in connective tissue and glycosaminoglycans at that time. This was around 1983 or so.

I found in the literature that retinoic acid and vitamin A influenced very much epidermal morphology and caused some changes there. I thought that those morphological changes were probably related to hyaluronan metabolism and then I tried to start to test the influence of retinoic acid on hyaluronan metabolism in epidermis and in skin. I did experiments using human skin organ culture model at that time and could show that retinoic acid indeed increased hyaluronan synthesis and resulted in increased amounts of hyaluronan in the epidermis. So this is how this project started.

Did you have any contacts with other groups in the world who did hyaluronan research?

Not at that time. Later I went to the Medical School of the University of California in San Francisco in 1984, and continued the retinoic acid project there, but I did that by myself and did not have any contacts with people there. Later, we also had hyaluronan-related scientific collaboration with some colleagues in Hungary at the University of Debrecen with Professor Laszlo Modis.

How did you get to San Francisco?

It was an invitation for me by Dr. Howard Maibach from the University of California, I was a postdoc there. He was interested in the organ culture model that I had developed during my Ph.D. studies; he wanted to use that model for testing drugs. So I did that work for him and continued my own work on hyaluronan metabolism during that time.

Did you go together with your husband?

My husband went to the University of California at Berkeley and he did work there with Dr. Clinton Ballou.

Do you have children?

We have two children, our son Tuomas was born in 1974 and our daughter Eeva was born in 1979. They also came with us to the U.S., of course; our son went to school and our daughter went to kindergarten. We spent there two years.

Could you please elaborate a little bit on your further research?

After returning back from San Francisco, I continued to study hyaluronic acid in epidermis and characterized epidermal hyaluronan metabolism. I checked the size of hyaluronan in epidermis and the degradation rate. Using HABR I studied hyaluronan localization in epidermis. I also spent some time to develop our own HABR probe; how to purify the protein and label it with biotin. We have prepared a number of batches of the probe using that protocol. Actually, that turned out to be a good idea because it was difficult to get the probe at that time and even later the commercial sources have not always been available. We used it to characterize hyaluronan distribution in various normal tissues like oral epithelium and reproductive organs and correlated it with the postulated receptor CD44. Later we used the probe on clinical materials mainly to characterize hyaluronan in tumors but also in inflamed tissues like psoriatic skin and inflamed intestine. During the sabbatical leave in Cleveland in Dr. Hascall's laboratory I learned to make 3D organotypic skin equivalents, which has helped us to study hyaluronan metabolism under conditions that resemble normal physiological conditions. We have later used that to study the effects of growth factors on HAS and hyaluronan expressions and correlated that to epidermal growth and differentiation.

How large is your group?

At the moment we have five people working full time and then we have students who work half time.

Do you have a different group from your husband?

No, actually we are sharing, some people are working for both of us, he takes care of some aspects and I take care of other respects. He is supervising the biochemistry and is responsible for the biochemical methods and I am responsible for the microscopy work. We also have collaboration with people in pathology and the clinical departments. This is because we have studied tumor materials on patients.

Would you mind telling me a little about this work?

We have stained different tumors for hyaluronic acid and CD44 and characterized hyaluronan distribution in these tumors. We have also looked at the question, how the amount of hyaluronan correlates with the tumor stage differentiation and the prognosis of the patients. We have found that the amount of hyaluronan usually increases when the tumors dedifferentiate and the tumor grade is high. We see that often, the more hyaluronan the patients have the worse the prognosis is. In breast, ovarian and prostate cancer hyaluronan accumulates mainly in the tumor stroma while in colon cancer and gastric cancer it is found around the tumor cells. However, the tumors originating from stratified epithelia like skin epidermis, esophagus or oral epithelium show a biphasic response so that in early stage hyaluronan is increased on the tumor cells while in the most aggressive tumors the expression of hyaluronan and its receptor CD44 tend to diminish.

It may be terribly naïve to ask but would it be possible to look into the question that if you somehow could decrease the amount of hyaluronan in these situations that might help to get the tumor die?

Well, that is a very important question. We have not done such experiments by ourselves, but there are some reports on experimental animal models suggesting that there might be drugs which decrease the hyaluronan production and influence the tumor progression. There have been some melanoma models showing that kind of effect. So our long term plan is that we might do some work along this line, but we have not done yet. We have started to develop new 3D organotypic culture models for melanomas and squamous cell carcinomas to study cell-cell interactions and the role of hyaluronan and hyaluronan synthesis inhibitors for the growth and invasion of the cancer cells and stromal fibroblasts. We will use confocal imaging of live cells in these models. It will be interesting to know whether invading cells form HAS-associated microvilli or hyaluronan cables.

It seems that the interest in hyaluronan or the extracellular matrix in general has increased in recent years.

Yes, this field has been expanding very much. Ten years ago there were only few people working in this field but nowadays there are so many and the number of papers in the literature is huge. Definitely, there is growing interest in this topic.

There is also another side to this research. You said that you are interested in basic research. On the other hand, this is a field where applications might be very close to basic research. I am thinking, for example, of pharmaceutical products. Have you been interested in this?

We have been thinking about this a little, but we have not done anything about it. We found a compound which could be used to decrease hyaluronan synthesis in cell culture and we thought that that might be a candidate for that kind of work but we have not proceeded with it. After all, we are a small group and one has to think how much one can do.

I would like to hear a little about science in general in Finland. How is it funded?

The research money in Finland is rather limited; we do not have very big grants and the system has been changing during the past 15 years. Previously the university was able to give more money for research, so that we could buy at least something with the university money but nowadays we have to get grants to support all the research.

Where do the salaries come from, the university or grants?

At the moment we have salaries for some of the people from the university and those people have to teach in return; some other people get their salaries from the grants. These are grants similar to the NSF or NIH grants in the US.

How much of your time do you have to spend on teaching?

I guess, it is about 40%. I teach gross anatomy, muscles and bones and things like that.

Hyaluronan research started very early in Sweden mostly in Stockholm and in Uppsala, do you have any connection with them?

We have been collaborating a little with Dr. Heldin in Uppsala and know Dr. Laurent but that's all. Actually the connection of Finnish hyaluronan research is connected to Torvard Laurent; the person who was Markku's supervisor had been working with Endre Balazs and Torvard Laurent. I guess that the hyaluronan research started around the 1960s in Finland.

There is another topic I am interested in and that is women's possibilities and their role in science. Are men and women really equal in Finland?

Well, in principle we are equal and nowadays the majority of students in universities are women. In the medical school it is sometimes 70 − 65% women and that is very good. But if you consider the higher levels, it is not so; there it is still difficult for women. All the practical reasons, like getting married, having children, and taking care of the family delays your progress. According to our system, you have to get certain recognition by a certain age; otherwise you will have difficulties with the granting agencies. So for women who want to stay home or work half-time earlier, this is a problem. Yes, I think that for women it is still more difficult to proceed in their career than for men. I guess that is going to change with time, at least I hope so.

Markku and Raija Tammi on a plantation tour during the hyaluronan conference in Charleston, North Carolina, 2007 (photograph by M. Hargittai)

Is it general that women work in Finland?

Yes. Most women work. It started, I think, around the 1960s. So when I started to go to medical school, it was quite natural for a girl to study and learn a profession.

You are in the same group with your husband; does that provide some difficulties?

We work very well together, I guess.

I'm not thinking of how it works between the two of you but about how others look at it.

Well, I think that it happens sometimes that people have difficulties accepting that we are both equal and contribute to the science and to the results equally. I think that these people are suspicious about what we achieve. I sometimes feel that it would have been easier for me if I had had my separate career, but on the other hand I really have enjoyed working in this project and working together with my husband.

What do your children do?

Our son studied computer science and he works for Nokia in Helsinki, he is 32 years old and he is married. Our daughter is still studying at the university; she's doing handicraft studies.

How do you see the future of hyaluronan science?

That is an interesting question. I have not thought about it much but I think that the basic science is very interesting and continues to be so. There are also many ideas, new ideas now, some of which are quite confusing; take for example, signaling, or what really is going on in regulation of cellular functions. There are so many suggestions that lead to different directions. But I hope that they will be worked out in the future. There are also the practical uses for hyaluronan research and I hope that there will be serious medical clinical applications. They were talking this morning about the role of hyaluronan in brain tumors. I hope very much that they will find something important there; this work is close to our work on hyaluronan in cancer. There are also other applications using hyaluronan in cosmetics and many other things, like relieving joint pain or using hyaluronan as a carrier for drugs.

Anything else you would like to add?

I don't think so.

Summary of the work of Markku and Raija Tammi

by Markku Tammi

Perhaps the single most impressive line of research Raija and I have done is the discovery of hyaluronan abundance in human skin epidermis, and characterizing its regulation and functions. Hyaluronan was previously considered a connective tissue component, with little occurrence or function in mature epithelia like epidermis. During the years we have worked on epidermal hyaluronan, its synthesis, content and metabolism were shown to be tightly regulated by hormones, growth factors and cytokines, with dramatic changes that contribute to keratinocyte migration, proliferation and differentiation. In skin irritation and wound healing Has2 and Has3 are upregulated, resulting in severalfold increase in epidermal hyaluronan. Skin squamous cell cancers and psoriasis also present distincts changes in hyaluronan content and distribution. Inhibiting hyaluronan synthesis calms down epidermal activation.

An important factor in our research has been the purification and labeling of the aggrecan G1 domain-link protein complex, a specific probe for hyaluronan, a procedure developed by Raija. The probe worked well on paraffin-embedded tissue sections, and we first noticed that healthy single layered epithelia express little if any hyaluronan, while as a rule the lower layers but not terminally differentiated, stained for hyaluronan. We then checked cancer specimen and noted from the first samples of colon cancers in 1998 that the simple epithelia that had undergone malignant transformation expressed hyaluronan. Most interestingly, the expression level of hyaluronan showed a strong negative correlation with the survival rate of the patients. The studies were then expanded to other common malignant tumors, with the results that cell associated hyaluronan, or that in the peritumoral stroma had a strong influence on the prognosis of the diseases. This set of papers has encouraged a number of experimental studies in several groups, confirming the promotive influence of hyaluronan on cancer growth and spreading, and exploring the mechanisms involved.

A few years ago we made by chance a finding that turned out to be quite exciting in many ways. When Dr. Kirsi Rilla had transfected GFP-HAS2 or GFP-HAS3 to cell cultures, the GFP signal looked peculiar with thin extensions protruding to all directions, making the cell look like a hedgehog. Further experimentation revealed that cells transfected with enzymatically inactive GFP-HAS had no such microvilli, indeed inactive GFP-HAS did not even reside in plasma membrane. The microvilli collapsed upon treatment with hyaluronidase, and gradually withered by depletion of the UDP-sugar precursors required for hyaluronan synthesis. We have later shown that similar HAS-enriched, hyaluronan covered microvilli exist in non-transfected cells spontaneously producing large quantities of hyaluronan. The novelties from these data include i) HAS does not get to, or stay in plasma membrane unless it can produce hyaluronan; ii) hyaluronan synthesis induces or supports plasma membrane extensions; iii) high volume hyaluronan synthesis requires extended plasma membrane, like that in microvilli; iv) the microvilli form the scaffold in the several micrometers thick "hyaluronan coat", a hyaluronidase sensitive exclusion space around hyaluronan producing cells, demonstrated by particles allowed to sediment on sparse cell cultures. With GFP-HAS we also showed that HAS travels from ER to Golgi to plasma membrane to endocytic vesicles with a kinetics supporting a previous proposal that one HAS protein produces on the average one hyaluronan chain.

The most recent focus of our research has been on the regulation of hyaluronan synthesis exerted by its building blocks UDP-GlcUA and UDP-GlcNAc. We showed that depletion of UDP-GlcUA through conjugation to 4-methylumbelliferone is associated to hyaluronan synthesis inhibition, as suggested previously. However, we found that even a moderate reduction of UDP-GlcNAc by incubation with mannose inhibits hyaluronan synthesis despite the high cellular concentration of this nucleotide sugar. It is obvious that membrane transporters that pump the nucleotide sugars into Golgi apparatus may in conditions of low supply leave HAS, dependent on the cytosolic pool, missing these critical substrates. In contrast, an elevated cellular UDP-GlcNAc pool, created by incubation with glucosamine, increases hyaluronan synthesis. These findings suggest that UDP-GlcNAc content, regulated by the cellular energy state and glucose level, may have unexpected and important effects on hyaluronan synthesis.

Bibliography*

Hyaluronan-Related Publications

1. Tammi, R., and Tammi, M. (1986). Influence of retinoic acid on the ultrastructure and hyaluronic acid synthesis of adult human epidermis in whole skin organ culture. J Cell Physiol 126, 389-398.

2. Tammi, R., and Tammi, M. (1987). Epidermaaliset glykosaminoglykaanit. Solubiology 4, 15-20.

3. Tammi, R. H., Hyyryläinen, A. M. H., Maibach, H. I., and Tammi, M. I. (1987). Ultrastructural localization of keratinocyte surface associated heparan sulphate proteoglycans in human epidermis. Histochemistry 87, 249-250.

4. Tammi, R., Ripellino, J. A., Margolis, R. U., and Tammi, M. (1988). Localization of epidermal hyaluronic acid using the hyaluronate binding region of cartilage proteoglycan as a specific probe. J Invest Dermatol 90, 412-414.

5. Tammi, R., Rippelino, J., Margolis, R. U., Maibach, H. I., and Tammi, M. (1989). Hyaluronate accumulation in human epidermis treated with retinoic acid in skin organ culture. Soc Invest Dermatol 92, 326-332.

6. Tammi, R., Tammi, M., Hakkinen, L., and Larjava, H. (1990). Histochemical localization of hyaluronate in human oral epithelium using a specific hyaluronate-binding probe. Arch Oral Biol 35 (3), 219-224.

7. Tammi, R. et al. (1990). Hyaluronate accumulation in human epidermis treated with retinoic acid in skin organ culture. Dermatol Digest 1, 16-17.

8. Tammi, R., Saamanen, A. M., Maibach, H. I., and Tammi, M. (1991). Degradation of newly synthesized high molecular mass hyaluronan in the epidermal and dermal compartments of human skin in organ culture. Soc Invest Dermatol 97 (1), 126-130.

9. Tammi, R., and Tammi, M. (1991). Correlations between hyaluronan and epidermal proliferation as studied by [3H]glucosamine and [3H]thymidine incorporations and staining of hyaluronan on mitotic keratinocytes. Exp Cell Res 195 (2), 524-527.

---

* Provided by the interviewee.

10. Martikainen, A. L., Tammi, M., and Tammi, R. (1992). Proteoglycans synthesized by adult human epidermis in whole skin organ culture. J Invest Dermatol 99 (5), 623-628.

11. Wang, C., Tammi, M., and Tammi, R. (1992). Distribution of hyaluronan and its CD44 receptor in the epithelia of human skin appendages. Histochemistry 98 (2), 105-112.

12. Ågren, U. M., Tammi, R., and Tammi, M. (1994). A dot-blot assay of metabolically radiolabeled hyaluronan. Anal Biochem 217, 311-315.

13. Tammi, M., Savolainen, S., Wang, C., Parkkinen, J. J., Lammi, M. J., Ågren, U., Hakkinen, T., Inkinen, R., and Tammi, R. (1994). Distribution of hyaluronan in articular cartilage as probed by a biotinylated binding region link protein complex of aggrecan. Trans Orthop Res Soc 19, 399.

14. Tammi, R., Ågren, U. M., Tuhkanen, A. L., and Tammi, M. (1994). Hyaluronan metabolism in skin. Invited Review. Prog Histochem Cytochem 29 (2), 1-81.

15. Tammi, R., Paukkonen, K., Wang, C., Horsmanheimo, M., and Tammi, M. (1994). Hyaluronan and CD44 in psoriatic skin. Intense staining for and hyaluronan on dermal loops and reduced expression of CD44 and hyaluronan in keratinocyte-leukocyte interfaces. Arch Dermatol Res 286 (1), 21-29.

16. Tammi, R., Ronkko, S., Ågren, U. M., and Tammi, M. (1994). Distribution of hyaluronan in bull reproductive organs. J Histochem Cytochem 42 (11), 1479-1486.

17. Ågren, U. M., Tammi, M., and Tammi, R. (1995). Hydrocortisone regulation of hyaluronan metabolism in human skin organ culture. J Cell Physiol 164, 240-248.

18. Oksala, O., Salo, T., Tammi, R., Hakkinen, L., Jalkanen, M., Inki, P., and Larjava, H. (1995). Expression of proteoglycans and hyaluronan during wound healing. J Histol Cytochem 43 (2), 125-135.

19. Noonan, K. J., Stevens, J. W., Tammi, R., Tammi, M., Hernandez, J. A., and Midura, R. J. (1996). Spatial distribution of CD44 and hyaluronan in the proximal tibia of the growing rat. J Orthop Res 14 (4), 573-581.

20. Parkkinen, J. J., Hakkinen, T. P., Savolainen, S., Wang, C., Tammi, R., Ågren, U., Lammi, M. J., Arokoski, J., Helminen, H. J., and Tammi, M. I. (1996). Distribution of hyaluronan in articular cartilage as probed by a biotinylated binding region of aggrecan. Histochem Cell Biol 105, 187-194.

21. Stevens, J. W., Noonan, K. J., Bosch, P. P., Rapp, T. B., Martin, J. A., Kurriger, G. L., Maynard, J. A., Daniels, K. J., Solursh, M., Tammi, R., Tammi, M., and Midura, R. J. (1996). CD44 in growing normal and neooplsatic rat cartilage. Ann N Y Acad Sci 785, 333-336.

22. Wang, C., Tammi, M., Guo, H., and Tammi, R. (1996). Hyaluronan distribution in the normal epithelium of esophagus, stomach, and colon and their cancers. Am J Pathol 148 (6), 1861-1869.

23. Ågren, U. M., Tammi, M., Ryynanen, M., and Tammi, R. (1997). Developmentally programmed expression of hyaluronan in human skin and its appendages. J Invest Dermatol 109 (2), 219-224.

24. Ågren, U. M., Tammi, R. H., and Tammi, M. I. (1997). Reactive oxygen species contribute to epidermal hyaluronan catabolism in human skin organ culture. Free Radic Biol Med 23 (7), 996-1001.

25. Auvinen, P. K., Parkkinen, J. J., Johansson, R. T., Ågren, U. M., Tammi, R. H., Eskelinen, M. J., and Kosma, V. M. (1997). Expression of hyaluronan in benign and malignant breast lesions. Int J Cancer 74 (5), 477-481.

26. Hollyfield, J. G., Rayborn, M. E., and Tammi, R. (1997). Hyaluronan localization in tissues of the mouse posterior eye wall: absence in the interphotoreceptor matrix. Exp Eye Res 65, 603-608.

27. Hascall, V. C., Fulop, C., Salustri, A., Goodstone, N. J., Calabro, A., Hogg, M., Tammi, R., Tammi, M., and MacCallum, D. (1998). Metabolism of hylauronan. In *The Chemistry, Biology and Medical Applications of Hyaluronan and its Derivatives Proceedings of the Wenner-Gren Foundation International Symposium held in honor of Endre A Balazs, Stockholm, Sweden, September 18-21, 1996* (Ed. Laurent, T. C.), Portland Press Ltd., London (UK), 67-76.

28. Hollyfield, J. G., Rayborn, M. E., Tammi, M., and Tammi, R. (1998). Hyaluronan in the interphotorecpetor matrix of the eye: species differences in content, distribution, ligand binding and degradation. Exp Eye Res 66, 241-248.

29. Pirinen, R. T., Tammi, R. H., Tammi, M. I., Paakko, P. K., Parkkinen, J. J., Ågren, U. M., Johansson, R. T., Viren, M. M., Tormanen, U., Soini, Y. M., and Kosma, V. M. (1998). Expression of hyaluronan in normal and dysplastic bronchial epithelium and in squamous cell carcinoma of the lung. Int J Cancer 79 (3), 251-255.

30. Ropponen, K., Tammi, M., Parkkinen, J., Eskelinen, M., Tammi, R., Lipponen, P., Ågren, U., Alhava, E., and Kosma, V. M. (1998). Tumor cell-associated hyaluronan as an unfavorable prognostic factor in colorectal cancer. Cancer Res 58 (2), 342-347.

31. Tammi, R. and Tammi, M. (1998). Hyaluronan in the epidermis. In *Glycoforum. Hyaluronan Today.* (Eds. Hascall, V. C., and Yanagishita, M.) (Seikagaku Corporation Glycoforum) (Accessed at http://www.glycoforum.gr.jp/science/hyaluronan/HA04/HA04E.html) (June 15, 1998), Tokyo (JP).

32. Tammi, R., MacCallum, D., Hascall, V. C., Pienimäki, J.-P., Hyttinen, M., and Tammi, M. (1998). Hyaluronan bound to CD44 on keratinocytes is displaced by

hyaluronan decasaccharides and not hexasaccharides. J Biol Chem 273 (44), 28878-28888.

33. Tuhkanen, A.-L., Tammi, M., Peltarri, A., Ågren, U. M., and Tammi, R. (1998). Ultrastructural analysis of human epidermal CD44 reveals preferential distribution on plasma membrane domains facing the hyaluronan-rich matrix pouches. J Histochem Cytochem 46 (2), 241-248.

34. Banerji, S. D., Ni, J., Wang, S., Clasper, S., Su, J.-L., Tammi, R., Jones, M., and Jackson, D. G. (1999). LYVE-1, a new homologue of the CD44 glycoprotein, is a lymph-specific receptor for hyaluronan. J Cell Biol 144 (4), 789-801.

35. Hirvikoski, P., Tammi, R., Kumpulainen, E., Virtaniemi, J., Parkkinen, J. J., Tammi, M., Johansson, R., Ågren, U., Karhunen, J., and Kosma, V.-M. (1999). Irregular expression of hyaluronan and its CD44 receptor is associated with metastatic phenotype in laryngeal squamous cell carcinoma. Virchows Arch 434, 37-44.

36. Inkinen, R. I., Lammi, M. J., Ågren, U., Tammi, R., Puustjarvi, K., and Tammi, M. I. (1999). Hyaluronan distribution in the human and canine intervertebral disc and cartilage endplate. Histochem J 31 (9), 579-587.

37. Setälä, L. P., Tammi, R. H., Eskelinen, M. J., Lipponen, P. K., Ågren, U. M., Parkinnen, J., Alhava, E. M., and Kosma, V.-M. (1999). Hyaluronan expression in gastric cancer cells is associated with local and nodal spread and reduced survival rate. Brit J Cancer 79 (7/8), 1133-1138.

38. Anttila, M. A., Tammi, R. H., Tammi, M. I., Syrjänen, K. J., Saarikoski, S. V., and Kosma, V.-M. (2000). High levels of stromal hyaluronan predict poor disease outcome in epithelial ovarian cancer. Cancer Res 60, 150-155.

39. Auvinen, P., Tammi, R., Parkkinen, J., Tammi, M., Ågren, U., Johansson, R., Hirvikoski, P., Eskelinen, M., and Kosma, V.-M. (2000). Hyaluronan in peritumoral stroma and malignant cells associates with breast cancer spreading and predicts patient survival. Am J Pathol 156, 529-536.

40. Felszeghy, S., Hyttinen, M., Tammi, R., Tammi, M., and Modis, L. (2000). Quantitative image analysis of hyaluronan expression in human tooth germs. Eur J Oral Sci 108 (4), 320-326.

41. Hascall, V. C., Tammi, R., Tammi, M., Hunziker, E., and MacCallum, D. K. (2000). Does keratinocyte hyaluronan determine the volume of extracellular space in the epidermis? In *New Frontiers in Medical Sciences: Redefining Hyaluronan (Proceedings of the Symposium held in Padua, Italy, 17-19 June 1999)* (Eds. Abatangelo, G., and Weigel, P.), Elsevier, Amsterdam, 31-40.

42. Karjalainen, J. M., Tammi, R. H., Tammi, M. I., Eskelinen, M. J., Ågren, U., Parkkinen, J. J., Alhava, E. M., and Kosma, V.-M. (2000). Reduced level of CD44 and hyaluronan associated with unfavorable prognosis in clinical stage I cutaneous melanoma. Am J Pathol 157 (3), 957-965.

43. Tammi, R. H., Tammi, M. I., Hascall, V. C., Hogg, M., Pasonen, S., and MacCallum, D. K. (2000). A preformed basallamina laters the metabolism and distribution of hyaluronan in epidermal keratinocyte "organotypic" cultures grown on collagen matrices. Histochem Cell Biol 113, 265-277.

44. Felszeghy, S., Modis, L., Tammi, M., and Tammi, R. (2001). The distribution pattern of the hyaluronan receptor CD44 during human tooth development. Arch Oral Biol 46 (10), 939-945.

45. Konttinen, Y. T., Li, T. F., Mandelin, J., Ainola, M., Lassus, J., Virtanen, I., Santavirta, S., Tammi, M., and Tammi, R. (2001). Hyaluronan synthases, hyaluronan, and its CD44 receptor in tissue around loosened total hip prostheses. J Pathol 194 (3), 384-390.

46. Lammi, P. E., M.J., L., Tammi, R. H., Helminen, H. J., and Espanha, M. M. (2001). Strong hyaluronan expression in the full-thickness rat articular cartilage repair tissue. Histochem Cell Biol 115, 301-308.

47. Lipponen, P., Aaltomaa, S., Tammi, R., Tammi, M., Ågren, U., and Kosma, V.-M. (2001). High stromal hyaluronan level is associated with poor differentiation and metastasis in prostrate cancer. Eur J Cancer 37, 849-856.

48. Pienimäki, J.-P., Rilla, K., Fülöp, C., Sironen, R. K., Karvinen, S., Pasonen, S., Lammi, M. J., Tammi, R., Hascall, V. C., and Tammi, M. (2001). Epidermal growth factor activates hyaluronan synthase 2 (Has2) in epidermal keratinocytes and increases pericellular and intracellular hyaluronan. J Biol Chem 276, 20428-20435.

49. Pirinen, R., Tammi, R., Tammi, M., Hirvikoski, P., Parkkinen, J. J., Johansson, R., Böhm, J., Hollmén, S., and Kosma, V.-M. (2001). Prognostic value of hyaluronan expression in non-small cell lung cancer: increased stromal expression indicates unfavorable outcome in patients with adenocarcinoma. Int J Cancer 95, 12-17.

50. Tammi, R., Rilla, K., Pienimäki, J.-P., MacCallum, D. K., Hogg, M., Luukkonen, M., Hascall, V. C., and Tammi, M. (2001). Hyaluronan enters keratinocytes by a novel endocytic route for catabolism. J Biol Chem 276 (37), 35111-35122.

51. Aaltomaa, S., Lipponen, P., Tammi, R., Tammi, M., Viitanen, J., Kankkunen, J. P., and Kosma, V. M. (2002). Strong Stromal Hyaluronan Expression Is Associated with PSA Recurrence in Local Prostate Cancer. Urol Int 69 (4), 266-272.

52. Böhm, J., Niskanen, L., Tammi, R., Tammi, M., Eskelinen, M., Pirinen, R., Hollmen, S., Alhava, E., and Kosma, V. M. (2002). Hyaluronan expression in differentiated thyroid carcinoma. J Pathol 196 (2), 180-185.

53. Hiltunen, E. L., Anttila, M., Kultti, A., Ropponen, K., Penttinen, J., Yliskoski, M., Kuronen, A. T., Juhola, M., Tammi, R., Tammi, M., and Kosma, V. M. (2002). Elevated hyaluronan concentration without hyaluronidase activation in malignant epithelial ovarian tumors. Cancer Res 62 (22), 6410-6413.

54. Karvinen, S., Tammi, M., and Tammi, R. (2002). Effects of KGF and TGF-b on Hyaluronan synthesis and distribution in extra-, peri, and intra-cellular compartments of epidermal kerationocytes. In *Hyaluronan Volume 1* (Eds. Kennedy, J. F., Phillips, G.O., Williams, P. A., and Hascall, V. C.), Woodhead, Cambridge (UK), 545-550.

55. Pasonen-Seppanen, S., Tammi, R., Tammi, M., Hogg, M., Hascall, V. C., and MacCallum, D. K. (2002). Hyaluronan metabolism and distribution in stratified differentiated cultures of epidermal keratinocytes. In *Hyaluronan. Volume 1* (Eds. Kennedy, J. F., Phillips, G. O., Williams, P. A. , and Hascall, V. C.), Woodhead, Cambridge (UK), 511-516.

56. Rilla, K., Lammi, M. J., Sironen, R. K., Hascall, V. C., Midura, R. J., Tammi, M., and Tammi, R. (2002). Hyaluronan synthase 2 (HAS2) regulates migration of epidermal kerationocytes. In *Hyaluronan. Volume 1* (Eds. Kennedy, J. F., Phillips, G. O., Williams, P. A., and Hascall, V. C.), Woodhead, Cambridge (UK), 557-560.

57. Rilla, K., Lammi, M. J., Sironen, R. K., Törrönen, K., Luukkonen, M., Hascall, V. C., Midura, R. J., Hyttinen, M., Pelkonen, J., Tammi, M., and Tammi, R. (2002). Changed lamellipodial extension, adhesion plaques and migratin in epidermal keratinocytes containing constitutively expressed sense and antisense *hyaluronan synthase 2 (Has2)* genes. J Cell Sci 115, 3633-3643.

58. Tammi, M., Pienimäki, J. P., Rilla, K., Fülöp, C., Lammi, M. J., Sironen, R. K., Midura, R., Hascall, V. C., Luukkonen, M., Törrönen, K., Lehto, T., and Tammi, R. (2002). EGF regulates HAS2 expression controls epidermal thickness and stimulates kerationocyte migration. In *Hyaluronan Volume 1* (Eds. Kennedy, J. F., Phillips, G. O., Williams, P. A., and Hascall, V. C.), Woodhead, Cambridge (UK), 561-570.

59. Tammi, R., Rilla, K., Pienimäki, J. P., Hogg, M., MacCallum, D. K., Hascall, V. C., and Tammi, M. (2002). Intracellular hyaluronan in epidermal keratinocytes. In *Hyaluronan. Volume 1* (Eds. Kennedy, J. F., Phillips, G. O., Williams, P. A. , and Hascall, V. C.), Woodhead, Cambridge (UK), 517-524.

60. Torronen, K., Yabal, M., Rilla, K., Kaarniranta, K., Tammi, R., Lammi, M. J., and Tammi, M. (2002). Hyaluronan stimulates kerationocyte migration and activates the transcription factor AP-1 in keratinocytes. In *Hyaluronan Volume 1* (Eds. Kennedy, J. F., Phillips, G. O., Williams, P. A., and Hascall, V. C.), Woodhead, Cambridge (UK), 551-556.

61. Karvinen, S., Kosma, V. M., Tammi, M. I., and Tammi, R. (2003). Hyaluronan, CD44 and versican in epidermal keratinocyte tumours. Brit J Dermatol 148, 86-94.

62. Karvinen, S., Pasonen-Seppanen, S., Hyttinen, J. M., Pienimaki, J. P., Torronen, K., Jokela, T. A., Tammi, M. I., and Tammi, R. (2003). Keratinocyte growth factor stimulates migration and hyaluronan synthesis in the epidermis by

activation of keratinocyte hyaluronan synthases 2 and 3. J Biol Chem 278 (49), 49495-49504.

63. Midura, R. J., Su, X., Morcuende, J. A., Tammi, M., and Tammi, R. (2003). Parathyroid hormone rapidly stimulates hyaluronan synthesis by periosteal osteoblasts in the tibial diaphysis of the growing rat. J Biol Chem 278 (51), 51462-51468.

64. Pasonen-Seppanen, S., Karvinen, S., Torronen, K., Hyttinen, J. M., Jokela, T., Lammi, M. J., Tammi, M. I., and Tammi, R. (2003). EGF upregulates, whereas TGF-beta downregulates, the hyaluronan synthases Has2 and Has3 in organotypic keratinocyte cultures: correlations with epidermal proliferation and differentiation. J Invest Dermatol 120 (6), 1038-1044.

65. Sillanpaa, S., Anttila, M. A., Voutilainen, K., Tammi, R. H., Tammi, M. I., Saarikoski, S. V., and Kosma, V. M. (2003). CD44 expression indicates favorable prognosis in epithelial ovarian cancer. Clin Cancer Res 9 (14), 5318-5324.

66. Voutilainen, K., Anttila, M. A., Sillanpää, S., Tammi, R., Tammi, M., Saarkoski, S., and Kosma, V.-.-M. (2003). Versican in epithelial ovariana cancer: Relation to hyaluornan, clinicopathologic factors and prognosis. Int J Cancer 107, 359-364.

67. Kosunen, A., Ropponen, K., Kellokoski, J., Pukkila, M., Virtaniemi, J., Valtonen, H., Kumpulainen, E., Johansson, R., Tammi, R., Tammi, M., Nuutinen, J., and Kosma, V. M. (2004). Reduced expression of hyaluronan is a strong indicator of poor survival in oral squamous cell carcinoma. Oral Oncol 40 (3), 257-263.

68. Rilla, K., Pasonen-Seppanen, S., Rieppo, J., Tammi, M., and Tammi, R. (2004). The hyaluronan synthesis inhibitor 4-methylumbelliferone prevents keratinocyte activation and epidermal hyperproliferation induced by epidermal growth factor. J Invest Dermatol 123 (4), 708-714.

69. Suwiwat, S., Ricciardelli, C., Tammi, R., Tammi, M., Auvinen, P., Kosma, V. M., LeBaron, R. G., Raymond, W. A., Tilley, W. D., and Horsfall, D. J. (2004). Expression of extracellular matrix components versican, chondroitin sulfate, tenascin, and hyaluronan, and their association with disease outcome in node-negative breast cancer. Clin Cancer Res 10 (7), 2491-2498.

70. Tammi, R. H., and Tammi, M. (2004). Hyaluronan in the epidermis and other epithelial tissues. In *Chemistry and Biology of Hyaluronan* (Eds. Garg, H. G. , and Hales, C. A.), Elsevier, Ltd., Amsterdam, 395-413.

71. Tuhkanen, H., Anttila, M., Kosma, V. M., Yla-Herttuala, S., Heinonen, S., Kuronen, A., Juhola, M., Tammi, R., Tammi, M., and Mannermaa, A. (2004). Genetic alterations in the peritumoral stromal cells of malignant and borderline epithelial ovarian tumors as indicated by allelic imbalance on chromosome 3p. Int J Cancer 109 (2), 247-252.

72. Edward, M., Gillan, C., Micha, D., and Tammi, R. H. (2005). Tumour regulation of fibroblast hyaluronan expression: a mechanism to facilitate tumour growth and invasion. Carcinogenesis 26 (7), 1215-1223.

73. Kemppainen, T., Tammi, R., Tammi, M., Ågren, U., Julkunen, R., Bohm, J., Uusitupa, M., and Kosma, V. M. (2005). Elevated expression of hyaluronan and its CD44 receptor in the duodenal mucosa of coeliac patients. Histopathology 46 (1), 64-72.

74. Klekner, A., Felszeghy, S., Tammi, R., Tammi, M., Csecsei, G., and Modis, L. (2005). Quantitative determination of hyaluronan content in cerebral aneurysms by digital densitometry. Zentralbl Neurochir 66 (4), 207-212.

75. Kultti, A., Rilla, K., Törrönen, K., McDonald, J. A., Tammi, R., and Tammi, M. (2005). 4-methylumbelliferone inhibits hyaluronan synthesis, proliferation and migration by suppresssing hyaluronan synthase 2 and 32 messenger RNA levels in breast cancer cells. In *Hyaluronan: Structure, Metabolism, Biological Activities, Therapeutic Applications Volume I* (Eds. Balazs, E. A. , and Hascall, V. C.), Matrix Biology Institute, Edgewater, NJ (USA), 283-287.

76. Pasonen-Seppänen, S., Hyttinen, J. M., Kolehmainen, E., Tammi, M., and Tammi, R. (2005). Wounding-induced upregulation of Has2/Has3 expression and hyaluronan synthesis in adult mouse epidermis correlatees with keratinocyte migration and proliferation. In *Hyaluronan: Structure, Metabolism, Biological Activities, Therapeutic Applications Volume II* (Eds. Balazs, E. A. , and Hascall, V. C.), Matrix Biology Institute, Edgewater, NJ (USA), 561-564.

77. Pasonen-Seppänen, S., Tammi, M., Törrönën, K., MacCallum, D., Hascall, V. C., Maytin, E., and Tammi, R. (2005). Retinoic acid upregulates hyaluronan production but retards keratinocyte differentiation. In *Hyaluronan: Structure, Metabolism, Biological Activities, Therapeutic Applications Volume II* (Eds. Balazs, E. A. , and Hascall, V. C.), Matrix Biology Institute, Edgewater, NJ (USA), 565-569.

78. Pienimäki, J. P., Kultti, A., Tammi, R., and Tammi, M. (2005). Fluctuation of hyaluronan synthesis during rat epidermal kerationcyte cell cycle. In *Hyaluronan: Structure, Metabolism, Biological Activities, Therapeutic Applications Volume II* (Eds. Balazs, E. A. , and Hascall, V. C.), Matrix Biology Institute, Edgewater, NJ (USA), 571-574.

79. Rilla, K., Hyttinen, J. M. T., Törrönen, K., Pasonen-Seppänen, S., Heldin, P., Spicer, A. P., Rieppo, J., Mättö, M., Tammi, M., and Tammi, R. (2005). Suppression of hyaluronan synthesis by 4-methylumbelliferone retards kerationcyte migration and proliferation. In *Hyaluronan: Structure, Metabolism, Biological Activities, Therapeutic Applications Volume II* (Eds. Balazs, E. A. , and Hascall, V. C.), Matrix Biology Institute, Edgewater, NJ (USA), 637-640.

80. Rilla, K., Siiskonen, H., Spicer, A. P., Hyttinen, J. M., Tammi, M. I., and Tammi, R. H. (2005). Plasma membrane residence of hyaluronan synthase is coupled to its enzymatic activity. J Biol Chem 280 (36), 31890-31897.

81. Rilla, K., and Tammi, R. (2005). Iho tavitsee hyaluornaania. Solubiologi 2, 10-15.

82. Saavalainen, K., Pasonen-Seppanen, S., Dunlop, T. W., Tammi, R., Tammi, M. I., and Carlberg, C. (2005). The human hyaluronan synthase 2 gene is a primary retinoic acid and epidermal growth factor responding gene. J Biol Chem 280 (15), 14636-14644.

83. Tammi, M., Törrönen, K., Pasonen-Seppänen, S., Karvinen, S., Rilla, K., Pienimäki, J.-P., and Tammi, R. (2005). Hyaluronan and CD44 in epidermal activation. In *Hyaluronan: Structure, Metabolism, Biological Activities, Therapeutic Applications Volume II* (Eds. Balazs, E. A. , and Hascall, V. C.), Matrix Biology Institute, Edgewater, NJ (USA), 641-647.

84. Tammi, R., Pasonen-Seppanen, S., Kolehmainen, E., and Tammi, M. (2005). Hyaluronan synthase induction and hyaluronan accumulation in mouse epidermis following skin injury. J Invest Dermatol 124 (5), 898-905.

85. Tammi, R. H., Pasonen-Seppanen, S., Kultti, A., Hyttinen, J. M., MacCallum, D., Hascall, V. C., and Tammi, M. I. (2005). Hyaluronan degradation in epidermis. In *Hyaluronan: Structure, Metabolism, Biological Activities, Therapeutic Applications Volume I* (Eds. Balazs, E. A. , and Hascall, V. C.), Matrix Biology Institute, Edgewater, NJ (USA), 241-245.

86. Törrönen, K., Rilla, K., Tammi, R., and Tammi, M. (2005). Hyaluronan size dependent migration and mitogen activated protein kinase signalling in human keratinocytes. In *Hyaluronan: Structure, Metabolism, Biological Activities, Therapeutic Applications Volume II* (Eds. Balazs, E. A., and Hascall, V.C.), Matrix Biology Institute, Edgewater, NJ (USA), 649-653.

87. Kaarniranta, K., Ihanamaki, T., Sahlman, J., Pulkkinen, H., Uusitalo, H., Arita, M., Tammi, R., Lammi, M. J., and Helminen, H. J. (2006). A mouse model for Stickler's syndrome: ocular phenotype of mice carrying a targeted heterozygous inactivation of type II (pro)collagen gene (Col2a1). Exp Eye Res 83 (2), 297-303.

88. Kultti, A., Rilla, K., Tiihonen, R., Spicer, A. P., Tammi, R. H., and Tammi, M. I. (2006). Hyaluronan synthesis induces microvillus-like cell surface protrusions. J Biol Chem 281 (23), 15821-15828.

89. Evanko, S. P., Tammi, M.I., Tammi, R. H., and Wight, T.N. (2007). Hyaluronan-dependent pericellular matrix. Adv Drug Deliv Rev 59 (13), 1351-1365.

90. Karihtala, P., Soini, Y., Auvinen, P., Tammi, R., Tammi, M., and Kosma, V. M. (2007). Hyaluronan in breast cancer: correlations with nitric oxide synthases and tyrosine nitrosylation. J Histochem Cytochem 55 (12), 1191-1198.

91. Bergamaschi, A., Tagliabue, E., Sorlie, T., Naume, B., Triulzi, T., Orlandi, R., Russnes, H. G., Nesland, J. M., Tammi, R., Auvinen, P., Kosma, V. M., Menard, S., and Borresen-Dale, A. L. (2008). Extracellular matrix signature identifies breast cancer subgroups with different clinical outcome. J Pathol 214 (3), 357-367.

92. Casalini, P., Carcangiu, M. L., Tammi, R., Auvinen, P., Kosma, V. M., Valagussa, P., Greco, M., Balsari, A., Menard, S., and Tagliabue, E. (2008). Two distinct local relapse subtypes in invasive breast cancer: effect on their prognostic impact. Clin Cancer Res 14 (1), 25-31.

93. Jokela, T. A., Jauhiainen, M., Auriola, S., Kauhanen, M., Tiihonen, R., Tammi, M. I., and Tammi, R. H. (2008). Mannose inhibits hyaluronan synthesis by down-regulation of the cellular pool of UDP-N-acetylhexosamines. J Biol Chem 283 (12), 7666-7673.

94. Pasonen-Seppanen, S. M., Maytin, E. V., Torronen, K. J., Hyttinen, J. M. T., Hascall, V. C., MacCallum, D. K., Kultti, A. H., Jokela, T. A., Tammi, M. I., and Tammi, R. H. (2008). All-trans Retinoic Acid-Induced Hyaluronan Production and Hyperplasia Are Partly Mediated by EGFR Signaling in Epidermal Keratinocytes. J Invest Dermatol 128 (4), 797-807.

95. Tammi, R. H., Kultti, A. H., Kosma, V. M., Pirinen, R., Auvinen, P., and Tammi, M. I. (2008). Hyaluronan in human tumors: importance of stromal and cancer cell-associated hyaluronan. Seminars Cancer Biology 18, 288-295.

96. Jokela, T., Lindgren, A., Rilla, K., Maytin, E., Hascall, V. C., Tammi, R. H., and Tammi, M. I. (2008). Induction of hyaluronan cables and monocyte adherence in epidermal keratinocytes. Connect Tissue Res 49(3), 115-119.

97. Nykopp, T. K., Sironen, R., Tammi, M. I., Tammi, R. H., Ropponen, K., Kosma, V.-M., and Anttila, M. Increased accumulation of hyaluronan in serious ovarian carcinoma correlates with decreased expression of HYAL1 hyaluronidase (Submitted for publication).

98. Rilla, K., Kultti, A., Tammi, M., and Tammi, R. (2008). Pericellular hyaluronan coat visualized in live cells with a fluorescent probe is scaffolded by plasma membrane protrusions. J. Histochem Cytochem June 23 (Epub ahead of print).

99. Hartmann-Petersen, S., Tammi, R.H., Tammi, M.I. and Kosma, V.M. Depletion of cell surface CD44 in non-melanoma skin tumors is associated with increased expression of MMP-7. Brit J Dermatol (in press).

100. Tammi, R.H., Kultti, A., Kosma, V. M., Pirinen, R., Auvinen, P., and tammi, M.I. (2008). Hyaluronan in human tumors: importance of stromal and cancer cell-associated hyaluronan. In *Hyaluronan and Cancer* (Ed. Stern, R.) Elsevier, Amsterdam, The Netherlands (in press).

Paul H. Weigel, 2003 (photograph by M. Hargittai)

Paul H. Weigel

Paul Henry Weigel (b. 1946, in New York City) received his B.A. degree in Chemistry at Cornell University (1968) and his M.A. (1969) and Ph.D. degrees (1975), both in Biochemistry, from the Johns Hopkins University School of Medicine. During that time, he was drafted into the U.S. Army (1969-71). He did his postdoctoral studies as a National Cancer Institute funded Fellow at Johns Hopkins University, Homewood campus (1975-78). He was Assistant Professor (1978-82), Associate Professor (1982-87), and Professor (1987-94) at the Department of Human Biological Chemistry and Genetics, The University of Texas Medical Branch in Galveston, Texas. He also served there as Vice Chairman (1990-93) and Acting Chairman (1992-93). In 1994 he moved to Oklahoma, where he has been Professor and Chair at the Department of Biochemistry & Molecular Biology, College of Medicine, University of Oklahoma Health Sciences Center. Dr. Weigel was appointed George Lynn Cross Research Professor in 2004. He has received numerous honors and distinctions and served on the editorial boards of scientific journals. He co-founded a biotech company, *Hyalose*, in 2000. He is also a founding member of the International Society for Hyaluronan Sciences (ISHAS).

Interview*

You were born in New York City – and now you live in Oklahoma. This is quite a change.

A little migration; I was born in New York, grew up in Queens; and then my parents moved to New Hyde Park, Long Island, when I was 8 years old; that's where I went to grammar and high school. I went to college at Cornell University in Ithaca New York. I was the first member of my family to go to college. My father is from Germany but his father took the family out in 1924, because he didn't like what was happening there. They were not Jewish, but they did not like the direction the country was moving and the political climate. My grandfather was in World War I, he was a pilot. He didn't talk very much about the reasons for leaving Germany, but I think he had a sense of where the country was going and even that early on, he didn't like it. So he brought his wife and his two little children to New York, where they had other family. That's where my father grew up. He started in college at Pratt Institute, but he didn't finish because of some family reasons. He was basically a self-taught mechanical and electrical engineer. One of the early things that made a difference in my career— which was not clear to me at that time—was choosing Cornell because it was an excellent place to be. I was a chemistry major and I had no clue how lucky I was to be studying chemistry there. I had several scholarships, which was how I could afford to send myself to college. I had a New York State Regents scholarship, a Pearsall scholarship from Cornell, and I also took out student loans.

Who do you remember from Cornell?

---

* This interview was recorded during the second meeting "Conversations on Hyaluronan" in St. Tropez, June 2003.

I remember several professors, Jerry Mindwald and Richard Caldwell, with whom I did research projects, and Simon Bauer, who taught physical chemistry. I was always interested in chemistry so I had played with chemistry sets in my basement, made lots of smoke and things like that, and got my mother a little nervous at times, but no explosions though. I guess the most influential person in the chemistry department for me, who is no longer there, was Richard Caldwell who was a photochemist. After my sophomore year, I got an NSF fellowship for a summer program to work in his lab and that was my first exposure to research. Even though I didn't accomplish anything very significant, I learned a lot and found that I enjoyed research, so then all the summers thereafter, I worked in different research labs. I think it was later in my sophomore year that I discovered biochemistry. I worked with Robert Holley, who was at Cornell in the Biochemistry Department, where he was working on deciphering the genetic code. He received the 1968 Nobel Prize in Physiology or Medicine together with Har Gobind Khorana and Marshall Nirenberg for discovering the code. That was my first exposure to biochemistry, doing chromatographic separations of proteins.

After I realized that I enjoyed research very much, I changed my direction from wanting to go to medical school to graduate school. But I only realized after I had been at Cornell for some time that I had ended up in a wonderful environment, just fortuitously, because neither of my parents could give me any perspective or inside information about choosing a college. I never lived at home or on Long Island again after I went to college. I decided that I really enjoyed research so I applied to a lot of graduate schools and I got into all of them except one. I went to Hopkins Medical School and thus I moved to Baltimore directly from Cornell. I got married early that summer and the first day we moved into our apartment in Baltimore, getting ready to go to graduate school, I had a notice from my Long Island draft board. That was in 1968. I was able to delay my induction for a year and during that year I got a Master's degree in biochemistry. It was not originally planned, but since I knew I was going to be drafted, I decided early that school year to do the extra work to get a Master's degree in one year. I took extra courses, passed a German proficiency test and wrote a thesis on a research project; the relevant publication came out some years later, after I had moved on. So the reason I have a Master's degree was to accomplish something academically before I got drafted—but as it turned out, that was an extremely important thing.

I got inducted shortly before my birthday in 1969, after a year of graduate school, went to boot camp at Fort Bragg, North Carolina, to do my basic training, and then I got orders to go to advanced training to be in the Military Police, probably because of my German authoritative background. You take a battery of tests when you go into the military, and they profile your strengths and weaknesses to determine what you might be good for.

Do you really think they took your German ancestry into consideration?

No, I think the traits the army wanted for Military Police turned up in my profiling test. But I like to joke about it, though perhaps I shouldn't. But before I left basic training camp, I received different overriding orders directly from the Department of Defense to Fort Detrick.

They took you from graduate school?

Yes, at that time there was no deferment for being married or for being in graduate school; they had just eliminated those. I was sent to Fort Detrick, Maryland, which was a military base at that time that was involved in the development of biological weapons. I was very unsure about that assignment, but shortly after I got there, while I was still waiting for a security clearance and I was waxing floors every day, President Nixon made his famous proclamation that the U.S. was going to get out of the production of biological weapons. So I ended up working in a laboratory where I was the only biochemist in a microbiology research group, which was mostly civilians working on *Pasteurella pestis*—the organism that causes bubonic plague. I had a lot of research and lab experience at that point. I was able to design my own research project and they accepted my research plan, so I was basically working on my own, doing mouse studies in a BioSafety Level 3 facility.

I didn't know what "secret" research they were doing at the time; obviously I didn't have access to that sort of information. The group that I worked in had 19 or so people, and besides me, there were only one or two other military people. They were mostly civilians headed up by a Ph.D. microbiologist. They might not have published everything they had done in terms of research, but they had a very steady publication rate in standard microbiology journals.

What happened after you left the military?

The next day after I got out of the military I went back to graduate school at Johns Hopkins School of Medicine, and went around to find a faculty mentor to work for my dissertation research. I did my Ph.D. research with Paul Englund, who was a new Assistant Professor just hired from a post-doctoral experience with Nobel laureate Arthur Kornberg studying DNA polymerase I. I made some life-long connections with other people there as well. Bill Lennarz was instrumental in recruiting me there in the first place; he's been the chair of the Biochemistry Department at Stony Brook for some time, he's member of the National Academy, a very charismatic person. I learned a lot from him even though I didn't work for him, just in terms of analytical thinking and his approach to science. The biggest thing I got out of Hopkins was the value of informal journal clubs. That meant just discussing papers in a really honest way, which is not something that occurs easily in every place, as I later found. So that was really valuable, I learned more in one year of sitting in on journal clubs and critiquing papers than I ever learned in any course I ever took.

Did you emulate this?

Ironically, I have tried to do this, but I'm so busy at this stage of my career that I can't attend. At the moment beside my university job I have a biotech company as well, so basically I have three jobs; running a scientific lab and a research group, being department chair, and being involved in a biotech company. Obviously, they take enough time that it's been difficult to actually go to the journal clubs. But I have managed to start up that tradition in my department at OUHSC; there are three or four different weekly journal clubs now, and we require all the students to participate in at least one journal club, and most of the faculty members participate as well. Another thing I learned at Hopkins was the work ethic; people were very interested in what they were doing and took their science very seriously. I was two floors below the future Nobel laureates Dan Nathans and Ham Smith. For my Ph.D. I ended up working on DNA replication with Paul Englund. He had just come to Hopkins when I first arrived there, and after I got back to school from the military, I wanted to work for someone relatively young because after 21 months in the army, with people constantly telling you what to do, I was very unwilling to have anyone else tell me what to do after I got discharged. So I let my hair grow long right away, grew a beard, and I was extremely independent; I know, I gave him (Paul) a very hard time but I was his first student and I was quite productive for him.

When did you enter hyaluronan research?

That's been an interesting evolution because I knew nothing about hyaluronan throughout my graduate studies. Indeed, I made a big shift in emphasis in my research when I moved from DNA replication as a graduate student to working with Saul Roseman and Yuan C. Lee to learn carbohydrate chemistry as a post-doctoral fellow on the Johns Hopkins University main campus. When I began my post doc there, I initially started doing carbohydrate chemistry for Y. C. Lee and made a variety of saccharide derivatives. I was one of the first people to immobilize sugars covalently on polyacrylimide gels, and make synthetic flat culture surfaces for cell adhesion studies—to put cells on and to determine how they responded to different sugar moieties on these substrates. I did the carbohydrate chemistry in Lee's lab and the cell adhesion studies in Roseman's lab, but they were both mentors and co-authors.

After my Ph.D., I stayed as a post–doctoral fellow at Hopkins, working on a cell adhesion problem, studying cell interactions with synthetically well defined carbohydrate surfaces. I discovered some very interesting things, including a sharp threshold phenomenon for cell adhesion, which is still today probably the best documented example of a threshold response, as a function of ligand concentration on a solid surface, to see a biological response. While I was a post-doc, reading more literature and going to journal clubs, I began to learn a little more about hyaluronan and was very impressed by the breadth of the literature and the biological processes that hyaluronan was involved in, in terms of cell behavior. And that was a seed of interest for me. I knew, I wanted to work on the molecule and I also knew I was interested in the problem of hyaluronan biosynthesis, but in Roseman's lab I had no opportunity to work on hyaluronan.

Interestingly, my research in hyaluronan and success in cloning the hyaluronan synthase comes back full circle to Karl Meyer, who first discovered and characterized hyaluronan in 1936. Al Dorfman was a contemporary of Meyer, and a famous hyaluronan researcher, and he was also the Ph.D. mentor for Saul Roseman, with whom I did a postdoctoral fellowship. So in a way, as the person who cloned the hyaluronan synthase gene, I feel related scientifically to the scientist who discovered hyaluronan—Karl Meyer; sort of my scientific hyaluronan grandfather.

After Johns Hopkins, I went to the University of Texas Medical Branch at Galveston as an Assistant Professor in 1978. I took with me a project that I could most easily work on and be productive with, and this project was related to cell adhesion. Then I had the good fortune to recognize that this cell adhesion process that I had characterized for hepatocytes interacting with galactosyl containing surfaces was likely mediated by the receptor that had been recently characterized by Gil Ashwell at the NIH – but he had purified it as a binding protein from liver. Janet, my first laboratory technician who is now my wife, and I characterized the activity of this molecule as a cell surface receptor for proteins that had been desialylated—that contained terminal galactose when the sialic acids were removed from the oligosaccharides. One of my first NIH-funded projects (1982) was on that asialoglycoprotein receptor, so I moved to that research area quickly because I was able to be productive on it. I had funding for that initial research project up until 2002, when I decided to give it up because of other projects and commitments. But even after I had started working on the asialoglycoprotein receptor project, I was still interested in hyaluronic acid, so I was always looking to move my lab in that direction.

I also made a fundamental decision early on after starting my own research lab, which, I think, turned out to be excellent. I recognized that investigators, who were studying hyaluronan binding proteins and interactions of hyaluronan with receptors, were very limited technically in their ability to measure those interactions because they were using metabolically labeled hyaluronan. They would let cell cultures grow with radioactive glucose or acetate that would radiolabel the sugars in the hyaluronan and then they would isolate the hyaluronan, which would be ^{3}H-labeled or ^{14}C-labeled but of very low specific radioactivity. In order to make progress in that field, and to actually characterize and be able to identify and purify binding proteins, I knew I needed a better way to radio-label hyaluronan. So my first hyaluronan paper was actually a methods paper, in which I described the generation of smaller hyaluronan fragments and used my carbohydrate chemistry knowledge to modify uniquely just one end of the fragment. Already at that time I was concerned that if you just took hyaluronan and modified it covalently at too high a frequency, you might perturb structural aspects of the molecule that could be involved in specific interactions with matrix proteins or cells. So by modifying the hyaluronan only at one end, the reducing end, in a way so that the molecule could then be iodinated using ^{125}I of high-specific radioactivity, I could make fragments of ~100 kDa—not full-sized native hyaluronan but still very large—with a high specific radioactivity that anybody could use to detect and monitor molecules that bind hyaluronan.

After creating the first iodinated hyaluronan, we started working on the receptor that Laurent's group had discovered, and which was an endocytic receptor that removed hyaluronan from the circulation. They had found this in the sinusoids of spleen, lymph nodes and in liver, so we used our new ^{125}I-labeled hyaluronan probe in the mid to late 1980s to characterize that receptor on isolated cells in parallel with what researchers in his group were doing.

I had obtained NIH funding for a hyaluronan project 4 or 5 years after starting my lab up, and we had two major research areas going on in the group: A grant for hyaluronan-related work, including the endothelial cell receptor, and then a separate grant on the asialoglycoprotein receptor. But my real, though secret, interest in the hyaluronan field was to find the enzyme that was involved in biosynthesis. A lot of very excellent biochemists, including Al Dorfman's group and Nancy Schwartz's group had tried to purify a hyaluronan synthase, and had made some progress; they had been able to solubilize it and characterize it in terms of magnesium ion and sugar nucleotide requirements, but nobody had been able to purify the enzyme and nobody had been able to clone any synthase gene. I had learned molecular biology techniques and theory earlier than most others, because I was just a few floors away from Ham Smith and Dan Nathans at Hopkins—a few years before they were awarded the Nobel Prize for their pioneering work using newly discovered restriction enzymes to analyze the SV40 genome. The microbiology faculty and students would have tea every day at 4 o'clock in the microbiology library, and I would go up with other students, and we would just chat about current papers and experiments we were doing. So I had done restriction enzyme digests before those enzymes were commercially available. Therefore, I decided that in order to clone the hyaluronan synthase, it was not likely that anyone was going to be successful doing it from a eukaryotic source or by first purifying the protein, so we focused on Group A *Streptococcus pyogenes,* which is a human pathogen. It had been known for many years that these bacteria make a capsule of hyaluronic acid, and it had been shown by Dorfman's group that membranes from streptococcal cells make hyaluronic acid if you give them the UDP-sugar substrates. Over three decades later, we were successful in identifying and then cloning the key gene for hyaluronan biosynthesis. We were the first group to report and clone an active hyaluronan synthase gene and express it functionally, and that discovery then led to the cloning of the eukaryotic genes.

Group of attendants at the Hyaluronan Meeting in St. Tropez, 2003.
From left to right: Jennifer Mayser, Vanya Jordan, Vince Hascall, Tony Day, Cheryl
Knudson, Tom Wight, Jenti Denlinger, Bandi Balazs, Istvan and Magdi Hargittai,
Ulla and Torvard Laurent, Paul and Janet Weigel, Bob Stern, Bryan and Anna Toole
(photograph courtesy of P. Weigel)

Paul and Janet Weigel in St. Tropez, 2003 (photograph by M. Hargittai)

Dinner tables during the St. Tropez Hyaluronan Meeting, 2003. From left to right, upper picture: Ulla Laurent, Vince Hascall, Tom Wight, Janet Weigel, Jennifer Mayser, Paul Weigel, Vanya Jordan, Bandi Balazs. Bottom picture: Cheryl Knudson, Bob Stern, Jenti Denlinger, Istvan Hargittai, Anna Toole, Torvard Laurent, Magdi Hargittai, Tony Day. (photographs courtesy of P. Weigel)

It turned out that there are three human genes that encode hyaluronan synthases; they are structurally similar, but they are distinct isozymes and so that's a major question in the field right now: why do we have three genes for the same enzyme? The answers to that are still developing. Perhaps there is a back-up capability in some cases for one synthase to substitute for another. Probably most of the people in the field now believe that at different times in development, or in different physiological situations such as wound healing or other specific physiological situations, one or another of the three hyaluronan synthases are important, or in some cases critical. But that is a big area, with many remaining questions. I think my lab has made a number of contributions in several different fields, but probably the most important was cloning the hyaluronan synthase. No one in the field even knew I was working on the hyaluronan synthase, so it was a big surprise when my first paper on the synthase was discovery of the gene, and my second paper was the cloning and sequence of the gene. My lab has continued to focus on the streptococcal enzymes, emphasizing the structure-function relationships of those enzymes, because nobody has been able to purify and characterize the human hyaluronan synthases. So we're trying to understand why. We found in the case of the streptococcal enzymes, for example, that there is a specific phospholipid requirement for activity. We believe that the membrane-bound human hyaluronan synthases are inactivated by detergent solubilization because key lipids needed for activity are stripped away by the detergent.

You did your Ph.D. on nucleic acids. Why did you move to carbohydrates? Nucleic acids and proteins are generally considered a more glamorous field than carbohydrates.

I understood at the time that the potential to encode complex biological information was so much greater for carbohydrates than for proteins or nucleic acids. The major difference between carbohydrate molecules and any of the other biomolecules that had been focused on for so long, like nucleic acids and proteins, is that the carbohydrate molecules can be branched. There are also multiple ways to link sugar monomer units, unlike for nucleic acids and proteins. This means that the complexity of structures that can be generated from a fairly small number of monomeric units is great. A few people recognized that complexity quite a few years ago, but now everybody in the field of glycobiology understands this. In fact, the degree of complexity is in some respects overwhelming because of the chemistry that's allowed by different linkages of monosaccharides, different ring conformations, different size of the sugar ring, etc so you get astronomical numbers of possible structures from just half a dozen monomers, compared to many orders of magnitude smaller numbers for a protein and even smaller for a nucleic acid. Saul Roseman had been a champion of the idea of "glyco-codes"—the glycol-based language that cells use for their complex higher order activities. The complexity of carbohydrates is greater than that of any other class of molecules. What kinds of molecules do you find on cell surfaces, in the extracellular—or as Bandi [Endre A. Balazs] would like to say, the intercellular spaces? You find molecules that almost exclusively contain carbohydrate. So why are all these carbohydrate-containing molecules there on cell surfaces, and not so much inside cells? Now we realize that there are some carbohydrate modified molecules inside cells, but based on mass they are almost exclusively outside and between cells. So you have the correlation between the presence of these molecules that can encode enormous amounts of biological information because of structural diversity and the fact that cells participate in complicated processes that we certainly don't understand yet – they know where to go, they talk to one another, they organize. I used to joke with other post docs in Roseman's lab that ultimately some day we would become cell psychologists, as we understood more about cell behavior. That's starting to happen a little bit already. But the idea was that the higher order of complex cellular functions must somehow be facilitated by or be made possible by these other complex carbohydrate molecules. Yes, proteins are obviously important, nucleic acids are important to give us the proteins and RNAs, but the structural diversity of complex carbohydrates may allow higher order functions that we haven't begun to even think about yet. So I don't know how far back and to whom that idea traces back, but certainly it was articulated at the time when I was making the transition to being a post-doctoral fellow in 1975.

You and others have recognized the importance of this field yet people complain about the field being under-funded and the researchers under-appreciated.

I agree. I think there are a couple of reasons for that. One is because of the very nature of this class of molecules being important in so many different areas. If you're a nucleic acid biochemist, you may be studying DNA repair, replication, chromosomal organization—all fields that are under the umbrella of knowledge for someone who works in the field of nucleic acids or transcription. The set of skills or tools or even the perspective of your thinking in that area is built, for the most part, on protein and nucleic acid interactions that evolved over the years.

Even though complex carbohydrates may be very similar in structure, they can have very different functions in different cellular locations – that is hard for many people to recognize or appreciate. Many fewer people have experience in graduate school with courses in carbohydrate chemistry and glycobiology than in proteins or nucleic acids. Even the structural diversity issue, for example, which has been out there for a long time is probably only very recently being more widely appreciated; that there's the potential for much more biological information in glyco-molecules. Take as an example the hyaluronan field. There was great excitement for a period of time after discovery of hyaluronan; then came the perception that hyaluronan was just a structural component of tissues and not very important, so there was not much interest in it—until suddenly the possibility that it is a biologically relevant signaling molecule, might be involved in cancer, and might alter cell behavior, came up. The hyaluroan field was rejuvenated by three mini-revolutions that occurred in the 1980-1990s: discovery and cloning of the hyaluronan synthases, the finding that CD44 is associated with cancer and metastasis and can bind to hyaluronan, and the finding that small hyaluronan oligosaccharides have special biological activities.

Do you anticipate more activity and more funding in this field?

One of the difficulties concerning funding is that the reviewer pool—the pool of peer reviewers who are competent to review things in the glycobiology area—is very small. I can review projects in protein or receptor biochemistry, and many other people can do that as well, but there are many fewer people with enough experience and understanding in the glycobiology area to serve as competent reviewers, or who appreciate and understand the discussions that occur in review panels before everyone votes a priority score. That's one of the long-standing difficulties, although it is getting slightly better now.

Will this current collective effort of sorting out the hyaluronan literature facilitate better recognition for this field?

The encyclopedia project? Yes, I think it will, it is a terrific idea, but it will involve a huge amount of work. The reason it might work well is because it would be in a web format. It might be useful for specialists as a hard-copy, but the real value is for people new to the field, or for people who are on the periphery of interest in an area related to hyaluronan, and who want to learn about it. To have one source of information that someone can go to could be of great value. But the ability to do that in a web-based format, where you can bring people to other related websites and links based on someone's interests—I think that would be very powerful. There is already an excellent website devoted to hyaluronan, it is the Hyaluronan Today – Glycoforum website, supported by the Japanese company Seikagaku. Seikagaku started this website, with Vince Hascall as a co-editor, in 1998. I wrote the 5th article in the original series, on bacterial hyaluronan synthases, and now many hyaluronan scientists from many different fields have contributed chapters. It is a terrific resource and a great way to introduce new students to this exciting field.

Is your biotech company related to glycobiology?

Yes. When I started the hyaluronan synthase project, trying to clone the enzyme responsible for the synthesis of hyaluronan, I was interested in it foremost from a scientific perspective. But I also realized—because of the work that Bandi had done in the development of rooster comb hyaluronan for viscoelastic supplementation and uses in eye surgery—that the potential economic impact of cloning the hyaluronan synthase genes could be enormous. Once you had the genes, you could put them into whatever organism or microorganism, you want, in order to produce it by fermentation, and you could choose an easier organism to grow than *Streptococcus*. This was in 1986-1987, and I also anticipated that the ability to modify and mutate the hyaluronan synthase gene might allow one to control some aspects of the hyaluronan product, such as its size or yield, or maybe even change the enzyme's UDP-sugar substrate specificity. A modified synthase might make novel and unusual copolymers that were hyaluronan-like, but that might have interesting, maybe even important, properties. I was able to develop that project slowly, initially with some grant support from a University of Texas Advanced Technology Program that supported biotechnology development. I believe I was awarded the first grant for that project in 1988, and it took another 5 years before we succeeded in cloning the hyaluronan synthase gene from *Streptococcus pyogenes*. When I moved to the University of Oklahoma Health Sciences Center in 1994, I continued my interest in the hyaluronan synthase project and continued working on it. In a few years we generated more intellectual property, so we had patents that had been generated in Texas, and we had patents that had been generated in Oklahoma. I wasn't very interested in forming a company myself, because I had mixed feeling about that, having seen other faculty be consumed by that effort. But another company (Emergent Technologies, Inc, in Austin, Texas) approached us in 1999, to license the technology from the University of Oklahoma and to form a company. So eventually I did that with a partner, Paul DeAngelis, who had been a post-doctoral fellow in my research group at the University of Texas involved in the cloning of the hyaluronan synthase. I recruited him as an Assistant Professor to the University of Oklahoma, where he has done very well. Before we could form a company, however, the

University of Oklahoma had to reach an agreement with the University of Texas regarding the intellectual property that I had created at the University in Galveston.   We were told that this was the first time Texas had ever released any of its intellectual property. So we formed a company in 2000, and I suggested the name Hyalose, LLC. Novozymes is now our collaborative partner for our bulk hyaluronan production technology.   We have three other technologies for producing unique hyaluronan preparations of defined mass with extremely low polydispersity: NanoHA™ SelectHA™ and PrimeHA™.   Our collaborative partner Novozymes now produces hyaluronan, initially for the cosmetic market, by fermentation using *Bacillus subtilis* with an engineered *Streptococcus* hyaluronan synthase gene and other genes to enhance UDP-sugar precursor production. It has been exciting and a great challenge to learn about business and patents; it's basically like having another big project in the lab.

Bibliography*

Hyaluronan-Related Publications

1. Raja, R. H., LeBoeuf, D., Stone, G. W., and Weigel, P. H. (1984). Preparation of alkylamine and [125]l-radiolabeled derivatives of hyaluronic acid uniquely modified at the reducing end. Anal Biochem 139, 168-177.

2. LeBoeuf, R., Raja, R., Fuller, G., and Weigel, P. (1986). Human fibrinogen specifically binds hyaluronic acid. J Biol Chem 261 (27), 12586-12592.

3. Weigel, P., Fuller, G., and LeBoeuf, R. (1986). A model for the role of hyaluronic acid and fibrin in the early events during the inflammatory response and wound healing. J Theor Biol 119, 219-234.

4. LeBoeuf, R. D., Gregg, R. R., Weigel, P. H., and Fuller, G. M. (1987). Effects of hyaluronic acid and other glycosaminoglycans on fibrin polymer formation. Biochem 26, 6052-6057.

5. Frost, S., McGary, C., Raja, R., and Weigel, P. (1988). Specific intracellular hyaluronic acid binding to isolated rat hepatocytes is membrane-associated. Biochim Biophys Acta 946, 66-74.

6. Raja, R. H., McGary, C. T., and Weigel, P. H. (1988). Affinity and distribution of surface an dintracellular hyaluronic acid receptors in isolated rat liver endothelial cells. J Biol Chem 263 (32), 16661-16668.

7. Weigel, P. H., Frost, S. J., McGary, C. T., and LeBoeuf, R. D. (1988). The role of hyaluronic acid in inflammation and wound healing. Int J Tiss Reac 10 (6), 355-365.

8. McGary, C. T., Raja, R. H., and Weigel, P. H. (1989). Endocytosis of hyaluronic acid by rat liver endothelial cells. Evidence for receptor recycling. Biochim Biophys Acta 257 (3), 875-884.

9. Weigel, P. H., Frost, S. J., LeBoeuf, R. D., and McGary, C. T. (1989). The specific interaction between fibrin(ogen) and hyaluronan: possible consequences in haemostasis, inflammation and wound healing. In *The*

---

* Provided by the interviewee.

Biology of Hyaluronan (Ciba Foundation Symposium #143) (Eds. Evered, D. and Whelan, J.), John Wiley and Sons, Chichester and New York, 248-264.

10. Frost, S. J., Raja, R. H., and Weigel, P. H. (1990). Characterization of an intracellular hyaluronic acid binding site in isolated rat hepatocytes. Biochemistry 29 (45), 10425-10432.

11. Frost, S. J., and Weigel, P. H. (1990). Binding of hyaluronic acid to mammalian fibrinogens. Biochim Biophys Acta 1034 (1), 39-45.

12. Frost, S. J., Kindberg, G. M., Oka, J. A., and Weigel, P. H. (1992). Rat hepatocyte hyaluronan -glycosaminoglycan binding proteins evidence for distinct divalent cation independent and divalent cation-dependent activities. Biochem Biophys Res Commun 189 (3), 1591-1597.

13. Yannariello-Brown, J., Frost, S. J., and Weigel, P. H. (1992). Identification of the Ca(2+)-independent endocytic hyaluronan receptor in rat liver sinusoidal endothelial cells using a photoaffinity cross-linking reagent. J Biol Chem 267 (28), 20451-20456.

14. Yannariello-Brown, J., McGary, C. T., and Weigel, P. H. (1992). The endocytic hyaluronan receptor in rat liver sinusoidal endothelial cells is Ca(+2)-independent and distinct from a Ca(+2)-dependent hyaluronan binding activity. J Cell Biochem 48 (1), 73-80.

15. Yannariello-Brown, J., and Weigel, P. H. (1992). Detergent solubilization of the endocytic Ca(2+)-independent hyaluronan recpetor from rat liver endothelial cells and separation from a Ca(2+)-dependent hyaluronan-binding activity. Biochemistry 31 (2), 576-584.

16. DeAngelis, P. L., Papaconstantinou, J., and Weigel, P. H. (1993). Molecular cloning, identification, and sequence of the hyaluronan synthase gene from Group A streptococcus-pyogenes. J Biol Chem 268 (26), 19181-19184.

17. DeAngelis, P. L., Papaconstantinou, J., and Weigel, P. H. (1993). Isolation of a streptococcus-pyogenes gene locus that directs hyaluronan biosynthesis in acapsular mutants and in heterologous bacteria. J Biol Chem 268 (20), 14568-14571.

18. McGary, C. T., Yannariello-Brown, J., Kim, D. W., Stinson, T. C., and Weigel, P. H. (1993). Degradation and intracellular accumulation of a residualizing hyaluronan derivative by liver endothelial cells. Hepatology 18 (6), 1465-1476.

19. DeAngelis, P. L., and Weigel, P. H. (1994). Immunochemical confirmation of the primary structure of streptococcal hyaluronan synthase and synthesis of high molecular weight product by the recombinant enzyme. Biochemistry 33 (31), 9033-9039.

20. DeAngelis, P. L., and Weigel, P. H. (1994). Rapid detection of hyaluronic acid capsules on group A streptococci by buoyant density centrifugation. Diagn Microbiol Infect Dis 20 (2), 77-80.

21. DeAngelis, P. L., Yang, N., and Weigel, P. H. (1994). The *Streptococcus pyogenes* hyaluronan synthase: sequence comparison and conservation among various group A strains. Biochem Biophys Res Commun 199 (1), 1-10.

22. DeAngelis, P. L., and Weigel, P. H. (1995). Characterization of the recombinant hyaluronic acid synthase from *Streptococcus pyogenes*. Dev Biol Stand 85, 225-229.

23. Yannariello-Brown, J., Chapman, S. H., Ward, W. F., Pappas, T. C., and Weigel, P. H. (1995). Circulating hyaluronan levels in the rodent: effects of age and diet. Amer J Physiol 268, C952-C957.

24. Yannariello-Brown, J., Zhou, B., Ritchie, D., Oka, J. A., and Weigel, P. H. (1996). A novel ligand blot assay detects different hyaluronan-binding proteins in rat liver hepatocytes and sinusoidal endothelial cells. Biochem Biophys Res Commun 218 (1), 314-319.

25. Kumari, K., and Weigel, P. H. (1997). Molecular cloning, expression, and characterization of the authentic hyaluronan synthase from group C Streptococcus equisimilis. J Biol Chem 272 (51), 32539-32546.

26. Weigel, P., Hascall, V., and Tammi, M. (1997). Hyaluronan synthases. J Biol Chem 272 (22), 13997-14000.

27. Yannariello-Brown, J., Zhou, B., and Weigel, P. H. (1997). Identification of a 175 kDa protein as the ligand-binding subunit of the rat liver sinusoidal endothelial cell hyaluronan receptor. Glycobiology 7 (1), 15-21.

28. Tlapak-Simmons, V. L., Kempner, E. S., Baggenstoss, B. A., and Weigel, P. H. (1998). The active streptococcal hyaluronan synthases (HASs) contain a single HAS monomer and multiple cardiolipin molecules. J Biol Chem 273 (40), 26100-26109.

29. Weigel, P. H. (1998). Bacterial hyaluronan synthases. In *Glycoforum. Hyaluronan Today* (Eds. Hascall, V. and Yanagishita, M.), Seikagaku Corporation   Glycoforum   (Accessed   at http://www.glycoforum.gr.jp/science/hyaluronan/HA06/HA06E.html).

30. Tlapak-Simmons, V. L., Baggenstoss, B. A., Clyne, T., and Weigel, P. H. (1999). Purification and lipid dependence of the recombinant hyaluronan synthases from Streptococcus pyogenes and Streptococcus equisimilis. J Biol Chem 274 (7), 4239-4245.

31. Tlapak-Simmons, V. L., Baggenstoss, B. A., Kumari, K., Heldermon, C., and Weigel, P. H. (1999). Kinetic characterization of the recombinant

hyaluronan synthases from Streptococcus pyogenes and Streptococcus equisimilis. J Biol Chem 274 (7), 4246-4253.

32. Tlapak-Simmons, V. L., Heldermon, C., Kempner, E. S., and Weigel, P. H. (1999). Properties of the hyaluronan synthase from group A streptococcus pyogenes. Biochem Soc Trans 27, 105-109.

33. Zhou, B., Oka, J. A., Singh, A., and Weigel, P. H. (1999). Purification and subunit characterization of the rat liver endocytic hyaluronan receptor. J Biol Chem 274 (48), 33831-33834.

34. Heldermon, C., Kumari, K., Tlapak-Simmons, V., and Weigel, P. (2000). Streptococcal hyaluronan synthases and the sunthesis of "designer" hyaluronan. In *New Frontiers in Medical Sciences: Redefining Hyaluronan (Proceedings of the Symposium held in Padua, Italy, 17-19 June 1999)* (Eds. Abatangelo, G. and Weigel, P.), Elsevier, Amsterdam, 41-50.

35. Weigel, P. H., Tlapak-Simmons, V., and Kempner, E. S. (2000). Lipid requirements of hyaluronan synthases enzymes revealed by radiation inactivation analysis. In *Lipases and Lipids: Structure, Function and Biotechnological Applications* (Eds. Kokotos, G. and Constantinou-Kototou, V.), Crete University Press, Athens, Greece, 89-96.

36. Zhou, B., Weigel, J. A., Fauss, L., and Weigel, P. H. (2000). Identification of the hyaluronan receptor for endocytosis (HARE). J Biol Chem 275 (48), 37733-37741.

37. Heldermon, C., DeAngelis, P. L., and Weigel, P. H. (2001). Topological organization of the hyaluronan synthase from *Streptococcus pyogenes**. J Biol Chem 276 (3), 2037-2046.

38. Heldermon, C. D., Tlapak-Simmons, V. L., Baggenstoss, B. A., and Weigel, P. H. (2001). Site-directed mutation of conserved cysteine residues does not inactivate the Streptococcus pyogenes hyaluronan synthase. Glycobiology 11 (12), 1017-1024.

39. Duff, B., Weigel, J. A., Bourne, P., Weigel, P. H., and McGary, C. T. (2002). Endothelium in hepatic cavernous hemangiomas does not express the hyaluronan receptor for endocytosis. Hum Pathol 33 (3), 265-269.

40. Kakizaki, I., Takagaki, K., Endo, Y., Kudo, D., Ikeya, H., Miyoshi, T., Baggenstoss, B. A., Tlapak-Simmons, V. L., Kumari, K., Nakane, A., Weigel, P. H., and Endo, M. (2002). Inhibition of hyaluronan synthesis in Streptococcus equi FM100 by 4-methylumbelliferone. Eur J Biochem 269 (20), 5066-5075.

41. Kumari, K., Tlapak-Simmons, V. O., Baggenstoss, B. A., and Weigel, P. H. (2002). The Streptococcal hyaluronan synthases are inhibited by sulfphydryl-

modifying reagents, but conserved cysteine residues are not essential for enzyme function. J Biol Chem 277 (16), 13943-13951.

42. Weigel, J. A., Raymond, R. C., and Weigel, P. (2002). The hyaluronan receptor for endocytosis (HARE) is not CD44 or CD54 (ICAM-1). Biochem Biophys Res Commun 294, 918-922.

43. Weigel, P. H. (2002). Functional characteristics and catalytic mechanisms of the bacterial hyaluronan synthases. Int Union Biochem Mol Biol Life 54 (4), 201-211.

44. Weigel, P. H. (2002). Hyaluronan synthase. In *Encyclopedia of Molecular Medicine* (Ed. Creighton, T.), John Wiley & Sons, New York, NY (USA), 1686-1688.

45. Weigel, P. H., McGulary, C., Zhou, B., and Weigel, J. A. (2002). Purification and characterization of the hyaluronan receptor for endocytosis (HARE). In *Hyaluronan Volume 1 Chemical, Biochemical and Biological Aspects* (Eds. Kennedy, J. F., Phillips, G. O., Williams, P. A., and Hascall, V.C.), Woodhead, Cambridge, UK, 401-410.

46. Weigel, P. H., and Yik, J. H. (2002). Glycans as endocytosis signals: the cases of the asialoglycoprotien and hyaluronan/chodroitin sulfate receptors. Biochim Biophys Acta 1572 (2-3), 341-363.

47. Zhou, B., Weigel, J. A., Saxena, A., and Weigel, P. H. (2002). Molecular cloning and functional expression of the rat 175-kDa hyaluronan receptor for endocytosis. Mol Biol Cell 13 (8), 2853-2868.

48. McGary, C. T., Weigel, J. A., and Weigel, P. H. (2003). Study of hyaluronan-binding proteins and receptors using iodinated hyaluronan derivatives. Methods Enzymol 363, 354-365.

49. Weigel, J. A., Raymond, R. C., McGary, C., Singh, A., and Weigel, P. H. (2003). A blocking antibody to the hyaluronan receptor for endocytosis (HARE) inhibits hyaluronan clearance by perfused liver. J Biol Chem 278 (11), 9808-9812.

50. Weigel, J. A., and Weigel, P. H. (2003). Characterization of the recombinant rat 175-kDa hyaluronan receptor for endocytosis (HARE). J Biol Chem 278 (44), 42802-42811.

51. Weigel, P. H. (2003). HARE raising. (Letter to the Glycoforum). Glycobiology 13, 12G-13G.

52. Weigel, P. H., McGary, C. T., and Weigel, J. A. (2003). Use of iodinated hyaluronan derivatives to study hyaluronan binding, endocytosis, and metabolism by cultured cells. Methods Enzymol 363, 382-391.

53. Zhou, B., McGary, C. T., Weigel, J. A., Saxena, A., and Weigel, P. H. (2003). Purification and molecular identification of the human hyaluronan receptor for endocytosis. Glycobiology 13 (5), 339-349.

54. Harris, E. N., Weigel, J. A., and Weigel, P. H. (2004). Endocytic function, glycosaminoglycan specificity, and antibody sensitivity of the recombinant human 190-kDa hyaluronan receptor for endocytosis (HARE). J Biol Chem 279 (35), 36201-36209.

55. Tlapak-Simmons, V. L., Baron, C. A., and Weigel, P. H. (2004). Characterization of the purified hyaluronan synthase from Streptococcus equisimilis. Biochemistry 43 (28), 9234-9242.

56. Weigel, P. (2004). Bacterial hyaluronan synthases---An update. In *Glycoforum. Hyaluronan Today* (Eds. Hascall, V. C. and Yanagishita, M.) Seikagaku Corporation   Glycoforum   *(Accessed   at* http://www.glycoforum.gr.jp/science/hyaluronan/HA06a/HA06aE.html*)*.

57. Weigel, P. H. (2004). The hyaluronan synthases. In *Chemistry and Biology of Hyaluronan* (Eds. Garg, H. G. and Hales, C. A.), Elsevier, Ltd., Amsterdam, 553-567.

58. Baggenstoss, B. A., and Weigel, P. H. (2005). Some problems associated with the use of GPG-Malls to analyze hyaluronan distributions made by hyaluronan synthases. In *Hyaluronan: Structure, Metabolism, Biological Activities, Therapeutic Applications Volume I* (Eds. Balazs, E. A. and Hascall, V.C.), Matrix Biology Institute, Edgewater, NJ 07020 (USA), 143-146.

59. Kakizaki, I., Baggenstoss, B. A., Tlapak-Simmons, V. L., Nakane, A., Weigel, P. H., Endo, M., and Takagaki, K. (2005). A possible cardiolipin-dependent inhibition mechanism of hyaluronan synthesis by 4-methylumbelliferone in *Streptococcus Equi* Fm100. In *Hyaluronan   Structure, Metabolism, Biological Activities, Therapeutic Applications   Volume I* (Eds. Balazs, E. A. and Hascall, V.C.), Matrix Biology Institute, Edgewater, NJ (USA), 159-163.

60. Kumari, K., and Weigel, P. H. (2005). Identification of a membrane-localized cysteine cluster near the substrate-binding sites of the Streptococcus equisimilis hyaluronan synthase. Glycobiology 15 (5), 529-539.

61. Tlapak-Simmons, V. L., Baron, C. A., Gotschall, R., Haque, D., Canfield, W. M., and Weigel, P. H. (2005). Mechanism of hyaluornan biosynthesis by the Class I Streptococcal hyaluronan synthases. In *Hyaluronan: Structure, Metabolism, Biological Activities, Therapeutic Applications Volume I* (Eds. Balazs, E. A. and Hascall, V.C.), Matrix Biology Institute, Edgewwater, NJ 07020 (USA), 121-127.

62. Tlapak-Simmons, V. L., Baron, C. A., Gotschall, R., Haque, D., Canfield, W. M., and Weigel, P. H. (2005). Hyaluronan biosynthesis by class I streptococcal hyaluronan synthases occurs at the reducing end. J Biol Chem 280 (13), 13012-13018.

63. Weigel, P. H. (2005). Current progress and limitations in understanding the molecular and cellular functions of hyaluronan synthases. In *Hyaluronan: Structure, Metabolism, Biological Activities, Therapeutic Applications Volume I* (Eds. Balazs, E.A. and Hascall, V.C.), Matrix Biology Institute, Edgewater, NJ (USA), 173-179.

64. Widner, B., Behr, R., Von Dollen, S., Tang, M., Heu, T., Sloma, A., Sternberg, D., Deangelis, P. L., Weigel, P. H., and Brown, S. (2005). Hyaluronic acid production in Bacillus subtilis. Appl Environ Microbiol 71 (7), 3747-3752.

65. Baggenstoss, B. A., and Weigel, P. H. (2006). Size exclusion chromatography-multiangle laser light scattering analysis of hyaluronan size distributions made by membrane-bound hyaluronan synthase. Anal Biochem 352 (2), 243-251.

66. Goentzel, B. J., Weigel, P. H., and Steinberg, R. A. (2006). Recombinant human hyaluronan synthase 3 is phosphorylated in mammalian cells. Biochem J 396 (2), 347-354.

67. Kumari, K., Baggenstoss, B. A., Parker, A. L., and Weigel, P. H. (2006). Mutation of two intramembrane polar residues conserved within the hyaluronan synthase family alters hyaluronan product size. J Biol Chem 281 (17), 11755-11760.

68. Weigel, P. H., Kyossev, Z., and Torres, L. C. (2006). Phospholipid dependence and liposome reconstitution of purified hyaluronan synthase. J Biol Chem 281 (48), 36542-36551.

69. Wein, R. O., McGary, C. T., Doerr, T. D., Popat, S. R., Howard, J. L., Weigel, J. A., and Weigel, P. H. (2006). Hyaluronan and its receptors in mucoepidermoid carcinoma. Head Neck 28 (2), 176-181.

70. Harris, E. N., Kyosseva, S. V., Weigel, J. A., and Weigel, P. H. (2007). Expression, processing, and glycosaminoglycan binding activity of the recombinant human 315-kDa hyaluronic acid receptor for endocytosis (HARE). J Biol Chem 282 (5), 2785-2797.

71. Kyossev, Z., and Weigel, P. H. (2007). An enzyme capture assay for analysis of active hyaluronan synthases. Anal Biochem 371 (1), 62-70.

72. Weigel, P. H., and Deangelis, P. L. (2007). Hyaluronan synthases: A decade-plus of novel glycosyltransferases. J Biol Chem 282 (51), 36777-36781.

73. Harris, E. N., Pandey, M. S., and Weigel, P. H. (2008). Endocytosis of glycosaminoglycans and other biomolecules mediated by human HARE--the hyaluronan receptor for endocytosis. In *Hepatic Endocytosis* (Eds. Berg, T., Sporstol, M., and Mousavi, S. A.), Biochem Biophys Res Comm (in press).

74. Harris, E. N., and Weigel, P. (2008). Functional aspects of the hyaluronan and chondroitin sulfate receptors. In *Animal Lectins: A Functional View* (Eds. Vasta, G. R. and Ahmed, H.), CRC Press, Taylor & Francis, London (UK).

75. Harris, E. N., and Weigel, P. H. (2008). The hyaluronan binding proteoglycans. In *Animal Lectins: A Functional View* (Eds. Vasta, G. R. and Ahmed, H.), CRC Press, Taylor & Francis, London (UK).

76. Kyosseva, S. V., Harris, E. N., and Weigel, P. H. (2008). The hyaluronan receptor for endocytosis (HARE) mediates hyaluronan-dependent signal transduction via extracellular signal-regulated kinases (ERK). J Biol Chem 283, 15047-15055.

77. Harris, E. N., Weigel, J. A., and Weigel, P. H. (2008). The human hyaluronan receptor for endocytosis (HARE/Stab2) is a systemic clearance receptor for heparin. J Biol Chem 283, 17341-17350.

78. Pandey, M. S., Harris, E. N., and Weigel, P. H. (2008). The cytoplasmic domain of the hyaluronan receptor for endocytosis (HARE) contains multiple endocytic motifs targeting coated pit mediated internalization. J Biol Chem 283 (31), 21453-21461.

79. Harris, E. N., and Weigel, P.H. (2008). The ligand-binding profile of HARE: hyaluronan and chondroitin sulfates A, C, and D bind to overlapping sites distinct from the sites for heparin, acetylated low-density lipoprotein, dermatan sulfate and CS-E. Glycobiology (May 22, Epub ahead of print).

80. Gupta, V., Barzilla, J. E., Mendez, J. S., Stephens, E. H., Lee, E. L., Collard, C. D., Laucirica, R., Weigel, P. H., and Grande-Allen, K. J. (2008). Abundance and location of proteoglycans and hyaluronan within normal and myxomatous mitral valves. Cardiovascular Pathology (in press).

Edited Book

1. Abatangelo, G., and Weigel, P. H., eds. (2000). *New Frontiers in Medical Sciences: Redefining Hyaluronan (Proceedings of the Symposium held in Padua, Italy, 17-19 June 1999).* Elsevier, Amsterdam (The Netherlands), 372 pgs.

Thomas N. Wight, 2003 (photograph by I. Hargittai)

Thomas N. Wight

Thomas N. Wight (b. 1943, Portland, Maine) received his B.A. degree at the University of Maine (1966), and his M.Sc. (1968) and Ph.D. (1972) degrees at the University of New Hampshire, Durham. He did his postdoctoral studies as an NIH Postdoctoral Fellow at the University of Washington in Seattle working in the laboratory of Dr. Russell Ross (1972−74). He then moved back to New Hampshire as an Assistant Professor of Animal Science and Director of Electron Microscopy at the University of New Hampshire (1974−78). He moved back to Seattle in 1978 as Assistant Professor of Pathology (1978−83); became Associate Professor of Pathology (1983-88) and Professor of Pathology (1988−2000) at the University of Washington School of Medicine. In 2000, he moved to The Hope Heart Institute, a small non-profit research institute in Seattle. He served as Chair of Vascular Biology there until 2004 when the Hope Heart Institute merged with The Benaroya Research Institute in Seattle. Presently, he is Director of the Hope Heart Program at the Benaroya Research Institute at Virginia Mason in Seattle and an Affiliate Professor of Pathology at the University of Washington School of Medicine. Dr. Wight is member of several scientific societies and has received many awards and fellowships. He has served on the editorial boards of many scientific journals, and is a founding member of the International Society for Hyaluronan Sciences (ISHAS).

Interview*

How did you become interested in science?

It really started in college. I went to college because all my friends were going to college, not because I had any particular interest in a specific field or discipline. I grew up and went to high school in Portland, Maine. I was a pretty good student in high school but probably more interested in sports than school at that time! I went to the University of Maine in Portland, a satellite campus of the main campus located in Orono, Maine. I started with a liberal arts course because I had no idea what I wanted to study. How I got interested in science is a funny story. I remember standing in the hallway outside a zoology lab when I was a freshman, looking in and telling a friend that I'd never be caught dead in there! I believe they were doing dissections on "dead" sharks. It is funny how things change! To fulfill a requirement in the liberal arts curriculum, I had to take a science and I chose botany! I had one of those experiences that changes one's life. The professor of that course, Dr. Abraham Kern, (he sort of looked like Peter Lorie!) was absolutely terrific. He opened up a new "world" to me and did it in such a kind and effective way. He genuinely took an interest in his students and I remember being so excited just to go to class! He also instilled in me a confidence and helped me recognize an aptitude that I didn't realize I had. After two years at the University of Maine in Portland (UMP for short!), I moved to the main campus in Orono, Maine, where my major was zoology. My senior year I did a special research project on the migration of the single cell fresh water organism *Euglena*. I was hooked. I knew I wanted to do research! I remember a schoolmate friend of mine, Richard Cook, also had a similar passion and we used to talk for hours about where to take our

---

*This interview was recorded during the second meeting "Conversations on Hyaluronan" in St. Tropez, June 2003.

interests. I have lost track of him and I would be interested in what he is doing today. We applied to different graduate programs and I ended up going to the University of New Hampshire in zoology! This was during the Kennedy administration years and there was a lot of funding available for graduate scholarships. My parents were of modest means and weren't able to pay for my going on to graduate school. Luckily I was able to get National Defense Education Fellowship, sponsored by the U.S. government to complete a Ph.D. program. At that time, my interests were in endocrinology and physiology and I went to work in the laboratory of Dr. Paul Wright, a reproductive endocrinologist at the University of New Hampshire.

Did you stay with the same advisor?

No, I didn't. My interests began to change. I became more interested in cell biology and biochemistry and I moved to the laboratory of Dr. Sam Smith who was a popular professor working on cellular mechanisms of vascular disease. My project was to follow the differentiation process of smooth muscle cells after they had been removed from atherosclerosis susceptible White Carneau pigeon embryos and grown in cell culture. Hard to believe but smooth muscle cell culture was just beginning about that time!

I got interested in the morphological aspects of the re-differentiation process, particularly following the process with electron microscopy. My advisor was a biochemist and not an electron microscopist but he gave me the "green light" to follow my interests, which meant I had to learn it on my own! At that time a fellow graduate student in the lab, Peter Cooke, was going to Boston to do electron microscopy at the Retina Foundation and so I tagged along with him—he essentially trained me in electron microscopy. I remember several times driving down to Boston and working with Peter. Just to show you what a small world it is, Dr. Balazs was at the Retina Foundation, I think as director at the time. I never met him but it is a bit ironic that 30 plus years later I am sitting here at his lovely home in St Tropez!! That's more or less how I started. It took me six years to do my Ph.D. at the University of New Hampshire. I remember that in my thesis, five or six chapters dealt with the events that took place inside smooth muscle cells as they developed a contractile apparatus. The last chapter was focused on the possibility that the cell, in addition to synthesizing and organizing components within the cell, was also synthesizing components and secreting them to the outside of the cell. Collagen and elastic fibers could be identified in the cultures using electron microscopy. However, there was an abundance of amorphous material also present throughout the space between cells. By histochemistry, this material turned out to be acid mucopolysaccharides, as they were called back then. This suggested that the smooth muscle cell was not only a contractile cell but also a connective tissue synthetic cell. This interested me at the time and continues to interest me today!

In 1972, I was finishing up my Ph.D., and I saw a notice for a seminar to be given at Harvard Medical School by Russell Ross, a well-known cell biologist who was at the University of Washington in Seattle. The title of his seminar was "The synthesis of elastic fibers by arterial smooth muscle cells in culture" and I thought to myself, my goodness, that's part of the last chapter of my thesis! So I jumped into my yellow VW beetle and drove to Boston to hear his seminar. Indeed, he was finding the same things that I was finding. I approached him after his talk and we had a marvelous time talking about our mutual findings! This was very special for me. His taking the time to talk with me after that seminar was another career changing event! We just hit it off real well; he was interested in what I had to say, and obviously I was interested in what he had to say, so we finished the conversation and he asked: "would you like to come to Seattle?" I said, "certainly!" I drove back home and I remember telling my wife, "I think we're going to be moving to Seattle." So I wrote a fellowship application to the NIH, a post doctoral fellowship application, and it got funded, and in 1972, we moved to Seattle. During those post doctoral years, I worked on showing that arterial smooth muscle cells made proteoglycans and hyaluronan!

At the end of 1973, a faculty position opened up at the University of New Hampshire and even though I was having a good experience in Seattle and it is a wonderful place to do science, I knew at the time that I wanted to go back to my "roots" in New England.

In retrospect, it wasn't the right decision for me professionally. I learned after five years of a heavy teaching load and modest funds for research that I was more ambitious with regards to research than I thought I was. I missed the research environment!

When I left the University of Washington, I kept in contact with everyone and they always kidded me that I would be back some day! Then one day I got a phone call and the Chairman of Pathology, Dr. Earl Benditt, asked if I would be interested in a faculty position in the Department of Pathology. Shortly after that phone call, I was in a very serious automobile accident that put me in the hospital for about seven months. So my career was put on hold! My family was also injured and it was a very tough time for us. But it did give me some time to think about whether I should leave the New England area and move west and develop a professional career or stay. In some ways, the car accident gave me time to make this difficult decision and I like to think that some good came from this very difficult situation. I decided to follow my passion for investigative research and again with the full support of my family! None of this would have happened without their full support! So that following year we moved to Seattle and the rest is 'history".

You moved to the Department of Pathology as a Ph.D. rather than an MD; how could one function as an Assistant Professor of Pathology with your background?

It is because the Department of Pathology at the University of Washington is a very unique department. It has a very strong basic science focus and it also has a fairly progressive attitude towards their faculty. Usually, in a medical school in the U.S., each faculty member has to have a service obligation, a teaching role and a successful research program. My service obligation was to direct the electron microscope operation in the department. Electron microscopy was used not only for research purposes but also for diagnostic purposes, especially in renal pathology. This filled my service roll. For teaching, I taught and continue to teach in the first year medical and dental introductory pathology course giving a series of lectures on cell injury and cell death. I also co-directed the graduate program in the Department of Pathology for eight years. It is a very strong department and a wonderful environment to work. I have been proud to be a member of this department throughout the years. It is at this time I met Vince Hascall, which was also a turning point in my life. Just after I joined the Department of Pathology, I had a grant turned down and my chairman asked me who would be the best person to help me develop a program in the biochemistry and cell biology of vascular proteoglycans. I immediately suggested Vince Hascall! He said, "Call him up and see if you can spend some time in his lab!" I was very nervous about all of this, but I did. He was terrific! He invited me to NIH where he was at the time and I spent about a month working in his lab. This is another turning point in my career. Not only did I acquire some skills working with these complex molecules, (I did get that grant funded eventually!) I developed a wonderful friendship that still exists today! We have lots of stories to tell, but better save that for another volume!

Eventually you left the University of Washington.

I did that in 2000. I was a full professor and I was well funded but I reached the point in my career when I realized that if I was going to do anything different in my professional career I needed to consider a change, age you know! I also was looking for something a little bit different and perhaps an experience to have some impact on shaping a "training ground" for students interested in the cell biology of the extracellular matrix. I feel fairly comfortable directing a research group, so I knew that is what I wanted to continue to do but perhaps outside of a university setting. There are essentially two possibilities; industry is one and research institutes are another. As fate would have it, just about that time I was thinking of a change, an opportunity opened up at one of the non-profit research institutes in Seattle. A colleague friend of mine, Helene Sage, a well respected and outstanding scientist,

Vince Hascall (center) and Tom Wight (to the left) in China in 1985, where they were invited to give a lecture series. They are standing in front of Fuwai Hospital in Bejing. To Wight's right is Kuofen Chen and to Hascall's left is Yingshan Chang, two Chinese physician scientists. (photograph courtesy of T. Wight)

From left to right, Tom Wight, Mark Bartold, and Harold Pearson at a Ciba Symposium on Proteoglycans held at the Ciba Foundation in London in 1986. (photograph courtesy of T. Wight)

Tom Wight at the Department of Pathology at the University of Washington School of Medicine preparing to give a "Science in Medicine" lecture on the "Role of Proteoglycans and Hyaluronan in Human Disease." (photograph courtesy of the University of Washington)

Two of Tom Wight's former post docs, Renato Iozzo, (left) and David Hajjar, (right), showing him their vote (kiddingly) on his acceptance into one of the pathology societies. Iozzo is now Professor of Pathology, Anatomy and Cell Biology at Jefferson Medical College in Philadelphia and Hajjar is the Dean of the Cornell University Graduate School of Medical Sciences and Professor of Pathology and Laboratory Medicine at Weill Medical College of Cornell University in New York City. (photograph courtesy of T. Wight)

moved from the University of Washington to become the Director of Research at the Hope Heart Institute. She and I were quite good friends and her research interests were in matrix biology as well. The best thing also was that the institute was in Seattle so it meant that a family move was not needed—probably the most difficult aspect of any re-location. With my interest in matrix biology and Helene's interest in matrix biology, we thought that it would be a wonderful challenge to develop an institute in extracellular matrix biology and cardiovascular disease. So that is what I have been doing these last eight years. Obviously it has not gone as quickly as one would hope due mainly to the need for fund raising to help support the activity of the institute. However, it is moving in the right direction! We recently merged with the Benaroya Research Institute at Virginia Mason in Seattle. We are a division within this larger institute (Hope Heart Program) and our goal is to focus and continue to build the field of extracellular matrix biology. We have developed a well-funded program in extracellular matrix biology and it is growing! It has been gratifying to me to watch the increased interest in this exciting field.

One final thing that I would like to say and I truly mean this; what little success I have had in science over the years I owe to the wonderful people that have worked with me. Many of the people have been with me for several years and have demonstrated a loyalty that is beyond belief! I have been very fortunate. Also, I have enjoyed and benefited enormously from all the students that have come through the lab from all over the world. There are a lot of aspects of being a "scientist" that just "can't be beat"!

The last question is about this project of creating a system of retrievable information of hyaluronan science. How do you view it?

Two things come to mind. One is that it is an exciting endeavor, a worthwhile constructive endeavor and it's been interesting to be involved with these discussions. We are really going after the "big picture" and discussing how hyaluronan fits into the world of science and technology. This is a worthwhile exercise because it puts the importance of this molecule into perspective. However, attempting to list every piece of work that involves hyaluronan is an enormous amount of work—not to say that it can't be done but it will need a lot of support in terms of resources and man–woman hours! As with any new plan, follow up after initial discussions will be critical. I trust this will be an ongoing process—a work in progress!

Bibliography*

Hyaluronan-Related Publications

1. Wight, T. N., and Ross, R. (1975). Proteoglycans in primate arteries. I. Ultrastructural localization and distribution in the intima. J Cell Biol 67 (3), 660-674.

2. Wight, T. N., and Ross, R. (1975). Proteoglycans in primate arteries. II. Synthesis and secretion of glycosaminoglycans by arterial smooth muscle cells in culture. J Cell Biol 67 (3), 675-686.

3. Wight, T. N. (1980). Differences in the synthesis and secretion of sulfated glycosaminoglycans by aorta explant monolayers cultured from atherosclerosis-susceptible and -resistant pigeons. Am J Pathol 101 (1), 127-142.

4. Iozzo, R. V., Goldes, J. A., Chen, W. J., and Wight, T. N. (1981). Glycosaminoglycans of pleural mesothelioma: a possible biochemical variant containing chondroitin sulfate. Cancer 48 (1), 89-97.

5. Iozzo, R. V., and Wight, T. N. (1982). Isolation and characterization of proteoglycans synthesized by human colon and colon carcinoma. J Biol Chem 257 (18), 11135-11144.

6. Wight, T. N. (1985). Proteoglycans in pathological conditions: atherosclerosis. Fed Proc 44 (2), 381-385.

7. Kapoor, R., Phelps, C. F., and Wight, T. N. (1986). Physical properties of chondroitin sulphate/dermatan sulphate proteoglycans from bovine aorta. Biochem J 240 (2), 575-583.

8. Wight, T. N., Kinsella, M. G., Keating, A., and Singer, J. W. (1986). Proteoglycans in human long-term bone marrow cultures: biochemical and ultrastructural analyses. Blood 67 (5), 1333-1343.

9. Kinsella, M. G., and Wight, T. N. (1988). Isolation and characterization of dermatan sulfate proteoglycans synthesized by cultured bovine aortic endothelial cells. J Biol Chem 263 (35), 19222-19231.

---

* Provided by the interviewee.

10. Iwata, M., Wight, T. N., and Carlson, S. S. (1992). Pgt1 a large chondroitin sulfate proteoglycan from adult rat brain binds to hyaluronic acid. 22nd Annual Meeting of The Society For Neuroscience, Anaheim, California, USA, October 18 (1-2), 1326.

11. Yeo, T. K., Yeo, K. T., and Wight, T. N. (1992). Differential transport kinetics of chondroitin sulfate and dermatan sulfate proteoglycan by monkey aorta smooth muscle cells. Arch Biochem Biophys 294 (1), 9-16.

12. Iwata, M., Wight, T. N., and Carlson, S. S. (1993). A brain extracellular matrix proteoglycan forms aggregates with hyaluronan. J Biol Chem 268 (20), 15061-15069.

13. Juul, S. E., Kinsella, M. G., Wight, T. N., and Hodson, W. A. (1993). Alterations in nonhuman primate (M. nemestrina) lung proteoglycans during normal development and acute hyaline membrane disease. Am J Respir Cell Mol Biol 8 (3), 299-310.

14. Savani, R. C., Wang, C., Yang, B., Kinsella, M., Wight, T. N., Stern, R., and Turley, E. A. (1993). Mechanism of smooth muscle cell migration the role of hyaluronan HA and the HA receptor RHAMM. Keystone Symposium on Extracellular Matrix In Development And Disease, Breckenridge, Colorado, USA, March 0 (17 PART E), 163.

15. Yao, L. Y., Moody, C., Schonherr, E., Wight, T. N., and Sandell, L. J. (1994). Identification of the proteoglycan versican in aorta and smooth muscle cells by DNA sequence analysis, in situ hybridization and immunohistochemistry. Matrix Biol 14 (3), 213-225.

16. Savani, R. C., Wang, C., Yang, B., Zhang, S., Kinsella, M. G., Wight, T. N., Stern, R., Nance, D. M., and Turley, E. A. (1995). Migration of bovine aortic smooth muscle cells after wounding injury. The role of hyaluronan and RHAMM. J Clin Invest 95 (3), 1158-1168.

17. Riessen, R., Wight, T. N., Pastore, C., Henley, C., and Isner, J. M. (1996). Distribution of hyaluronan during extracellular matrix remodeling in human restenotic arteries and balloon-injured rat carotid arteries. Circulation 93 (6), 1141-1147.

18. Wight, T. N. (1996). The vascular extracellular matrix. In Atherosclerosis and Coronary Artery Disease (Eds. Fuster, V., Ross, R., and Topol, E. J.), Lippincott-Raven Publishers, Philadelphia, PA (USA), 421-440.

19. Evanko, S. P., Raines, E. W., Ross, R., Gold, L. I., and Wight, T. N. (1998). Proteoglycan distribution in lesions of atherosclerosis depends on lesion severity, structural characteristics, and the proximity of platelet-derived growth factor and transforming growth factor-beta. Am J Pathol 152 (2), 533-546.

20. Evanko, S. P., Angello, J. C., and Wight, T. N. (1999). Formation of hyaluronan- and versican-rich pericellular matrix is required for proliferation and migration of vascular smooth muscle cells. Arterioscler Thromb Vasc Biol 19 (4), 1004-1013.

21. Evanko, S. P., and Wight, T. N. (1999). Intracellular localization of hyaluronan in proliferating cells. J Histochem Cytochem 47 (10), 1331-1341.

22. Lemire, J. M., Braun, K. R., Maurel, P., Kaplan, E. D., Schwartz, S. M., and Wight, T. N. (1999). Versican/PG-M isoforms in vascular smooth muscle cells. Arterioscler Thromb Vasc Biol 19 (7), 1630-1639.

23. Wight, T. N. (1999). Hyaluronan in atherosclerosis and restenosis. In *Glycoforum Hyaluronan Today*. (Eds. Hascall, V.C. and Yanagishita, M.) (Seikagaku Corporation Glycoforum) (Accessed at http://www.glycoforum.gr.jp/science/hyaluronan/HA09/HA09E.html) (Tokyo, Japan) (Feb. 15, 1999).

24. Wight, T. N. (2000). Proteoglycans and hyaluronan in vascular disease. In *Oligosaccharides in Chemistry and Biology* (Ed. B. Ernst, G. H., and P. Sinay), Wiley VCH., New York, 743-754.

25. Evanko, S. and Wight, T. N. (2001). Intracellular hyaluronan. In *Glycoforum. Hyaluronan Today*. (Eds. Hascall, V.C. and Yanagishita, M.) (Seikagaku Corporation Glycoforum) (Accessed at http://www.glycoforum.gr.jp/science/hyaluronan/HA20/HA20E.html) (Tokyo, Japan) (July 25, 2001).

26. Evanko, S. P., Johnson, P. Y., Braun, K. R., Underhill, C. B., Dudhia, J., and Wight, T. N. (2001). Platelet-derived growth factor stimulates the formation of versican-hyaluronan aggregates and pericellular matrix expansion in arterial smooth muscle cells. Arch Biochem Biophys 394 (1), 29-38.

27. Lara, S. L., Evanko, S. P., and Wight, T. N. (2001). Morphological evaluation of proteoglycans in cells and tissues. Methods Mol Biol 171, 271-290.

28. Lee, R. T., Yamamoto, C., Feng, Y., Potter-Perigo, S., Briggs, W. H., Landschulz, K. T., Turi, T. G., Thompson, J. F., Libby, P., and Wight, T. N. (2001). Mechanical strain induces specific changes in the synthesis and organization of proteoglycans by vascular smooth muscle cells. J Biol Chem 276 (17), 13847-13851.

29. Lundmark, K., Tran, P. K., Kinsella, M. G., Clowes, A. W., Wight, T. N., and Hedin, U. (2001). Perlecan inhibits smooth muscle cell adhesion to fibronectin: role of heparan sulfate. J Cell Physiol 188 (1), 67-74.

30. Chung, I. M., Gold, H. K., Schwartz, S. M., Ikari, Y., Reidy, M. A., and Wight, T. N. (2002). Enhanced extracellular matrix accumulation in

restenosis of coronary arteries after stent deployment. J Am Coll Cardiol 40 (12), 2072-2081.

31. Evanko, S. P., and Wight, T. N. (2002). The presence and processing of intercellular hyaluronan in proliferating cells. In *Hyaluronan Volume 1* (Eds. Kennedy, J. F., Phillips, G. O., Williams, P. A., and Hascall, V. C.), Woodhead, Cambridge, UK, 451-456.

32. Finn, A. V., Gold, H. K., Tang, A., Weber, D. K., Wight, T. N., Clermont, A., Virmani, R., and Kolodgie, F. D. (2002). A novel rat model of carotid artery stenting for the understanding of restenosis in metabolic diseases. J Vasc Res 39 (5), 414-425.

33. Kolodgie, F. D., Burke, A. P., Farb, A., Weber, D. K., Kutys, R., Wight, T. N., and Virmani, R. (2002). Differential accumulation of proteoglycans and hyaluronan in culprit lesions: insights into plaque erosion. Arterioscler Thromb Vasc Biol 22 (10), 1642-1648.

34. Lemire, J. M., Merrilees, M. J., Braun, K. R., and Wight, T. N. (2002). Overexpression of the V3 variant of versican alters arterial smooth muscle cell adhesion, migration, and proliferation in vitro. J Cell Physiol 190 (1), 38-45.

35. Toole, B. P., Wight, T. N., and Tammi, M. I. (2002). Hyaluronan -cell interactions in cancer and vascular disease. J Biol Chem 277 (7), 4593-4596.

36. Wight, T. N., and Evanko, S. P. (2002). Hyaluronan is a critical component in atherosclerosis and restenosis and in determining arterial smooth muscle cell phenotype. In *Hyaluronan Volume 2 Biomedical, Medical and Clinical Aspects* (Eds. Kennedy, J. F., Phillips, G. O., Williams, P. A. , and Hascall, V. C.), Woodhead, Cambridge, UK, 173-176.

37. Evanko, S. P., Parks, W. T., and Wight, T. N. (2004). Intracellular hyaluronan in arterial smooth muscle cells: association with microtubules, RHAMM, and the mitotic spindle. J Histochem Cytochem 52 (12), 1525-1535.

38. Farb, A., Kolodgie, F. D., Hwang, J. Y., Burke, A. P., Tefera, K., Weber, D. K., Wight, T. N., and Virmani, R. (2004). Extracellular matrix changes in stented human coronary arteries. Circulation 110 (8), 940-947.

39. Grande-Allen, K. J., Calabro, A., Gupta, V., Wight, T. N., Hascall, V. C., and Vesely, I. (2004). Glycosaminoglycans and proteoglycans in normal mitral valve leaflets and chordae: association with regions of tensile and compressive loading. Glycobiology 14 (7), 621-633.

40. Hascall, V. C., Majors, A. K., De La Motte, C. A., Evanko, S. P., Wang, A., Drazba, J. A., Strong, S. A., and Wight, T. N. (2004). Intracellular

hyaluronan: a new frontier for inflammation? Biochim Biophys Acta 1673 (1-2), 3-12.

41. Kolodgie, F. D., Burke, A. P., Wight, T. N., and Virmani, R. (2004). The accumulation of specific types of proteoglycans in eroded plaques: a role in coronary thrombosis in the absence of rupture. Curr Opin Lipidol 15 (5), 575-582.

42. Wight, T. N., Evanko, S. P., Kolodgie, F., Farb, A., and Virmani, R. (2004). Hyaluronan in atherosclerosis and restenosis. In *Chemistry and Biology of Hyaluronan* (Eds. Garg, H. G., and Hales, C. A.), Elsevier Ltd. 307-321.

43. Wight, T. N., and Merrilees, M. J. (2004). Proteoglycans in atherosclerosis and restenosis: key roles for versican. Circ Res 94 (9), 1158-1167.

44. Wilkinson, T. S., Potter-Perigo, S., Tsoi, C., Altman, L. C., and Wight, T. N. (2004). Pro- and anti-inflammatory factors cooperate to control hyaluronan synthesis in lung fibroblasts. Am J Respir Cell Mol Biol 31 (1), 92-99.

45. Kenagy, R. D., Fischer, J. W., Lara, S., Sandy, J. D., Clowes, A. W., and Wight, T. N. (2005). Accumulation and loss of extracellular matrix during shear stress-mediated intimal growth and regression in baboon vascular grafts. J Histochem Cytochem 53 (1), 131-140.

46. Serra, M., Miquel, L., Domenzain, C., Docampo, M. J., Fabra, A., Wight, T. N., and Bassols, A. (2005). V3 versican isoform expression alters the phenotype of melanoma cells and their tumorigenic potential. Int J Cancer 114 (6), 879-886.

47. Wight, T. N., Evanko, S. P., Sakr, S., Wilkinson, T., and Goueffic, Y. (2005). Hyaluronan in the cardiovascular system. In *Hyaluronan: Structure, Metabolism, Biological Activities, Therapeutic Applications Volume II* (Eds. Balazs, E. A., and Hascall, V.C.), Matrix Biology Institute, Edgewater, NJ (USA), 655-661.

48. Kuznetsova, S. A., Issa, P., Perruccio, E. M., Zeng, B., Sipes, J. M., Ward, Y., Seyfried, N. T., Fielder, H. L., Day, A. J., Wight, T. N., and Roberts, D. D. (2006). Versican-thrombospondin-1 binding in vitro and colocalization in microfibrils induced by inflammation on vascular smooth muscle cells. J Cell Sci 119 (Pt 21), 4499-4509.

49. Miquel-Serra, L., Serra, M., Hernandez, D., Domenzain, C., Docampo, M. J., Rabanal, R. M., de Torres, I., Wight, T. N., Fabra, A., and Bassols, A. (2006). V3 versican isoform expression has a dual role in human melanoma tumor growth and metastasis. Lab Invest 86 (9), 889-901.

50. Wilkinson, T. S., Bressler, S. L., Evanko, S. P., Braun, K. R., and Wight, T. N. (2006). Overexpression of hyaluronan synthases alters vascular smooth muscle cell phenotype and promotes monocyte adhesion. J Cell Physiol 206 (2), 378-385.

51. Allison, D. D., Vasco, N., Braun, K. R., Wight, T. N., and Grande-Allen, K. J. (2007). The effect of endogenous overexpression of hyaluronan synthases on material, morphological, and biochemical properties of uncrosslinked collagen biomaterials. Biomaterials 28 (36), 5509-5517.

52. Bollyky, P. L., Lord, J. D., Masewicz, S. A., Evanko, S. P., Buckner, J. H., Wight, T. N., and Nepom, G. T. (2007). Cutting edge: high molecular weight hyaluronan promotes the suppressive effects of CD4+CD25+ regulatory T cells. J Immunol 179 (2), 744-747.

53. Evanko, S. P., Tammi, M. I., Tammi, R. H., and Wight, T. N. (2007). Hyaluronan-dependent pericellular matrix. Adv Drug Deliv Rev 59 (13), 1351-1365.

54. Goueffic, Y., Potter-Perigo, S., Chan, C. K., Johnson, P. Y., Braun, K., Evanko, S. P., and Wight, T. N. (2007). Sirolimus blocks the accumulation of hyaluronan (HA) by arterial smooth muscle cells and reduces monocyte adhesion to the ECM. Atherosclerosis 195 (1), 23-30.

55. Han, C.Y., Subramanian, S., Chan, C.K., Omer, M., Chiba, T., Wight, T.N., and Chait, A. (2007). Adipocyte-derived serum amyloid A3 and hyaluronan play a role in monocyte recruitment and adhesion. Diabetes 56 (9), 2260-2273.

56. McDonald, T.O., Gerrity, R.G., Jen, C., Chen, H.J., Wark, K., Wight, T.N. Chait, A., and O'Brien, K.D. (2007). Diabetes and arterial extracellular matrix changes in a porcine model of atherosclerosis. J Histochem Cytochem 55 (11), 1149-1157.